MIXING the Hits of COUNTRY

Dave Martin

HAL•LEONARD®
Hal Leonard Books
An Imprint of Hal Leonard Corporation
New York

Published in 2009 by Hal Leonard Books
An Imprint of Hal Leonard Corporation
7777 West Bluemound Road
Milwaukee, WI 53213

Trade Book Division Editorial Offices
19 West 21st Street, New York, NY 10010

Cover photography: John Williams (www.soundartmanagement.com)

Printed in the United States of America

Book design by Stephen Ramirez

Library of Congress Cataloging-in-Publication Data is available upon request.

ISBN 978-1-4234-3850-2

www.halleonard.com

Contents

Introduction

This book is designed to give you some insight into the methods used to create a contemporary country mix. While it is specifically about mixing "in the box"—that is, doing the entire mix inside a digital audio workstation—the concepts discussed may well be applied to other digital or analog mixing methods.

Mixing the Hits of Country is structured to help you dive right into analyzing audio tracks and the processes that make a hit record sound the way it does. By loading the WAV files for each song (included on the accompanying DVDs) into your multitrack digital audio application and following along with the text, you can create a final mix using your own program and plug-ins and compare your mix to the stereo mix provided. Appendix A supplies general technical information about processing, effects, subgroups, aux sends and returns, bussing, plug-ins, and other terms and methods that apply to the mixes discussed in the main part of the book. Appendix B provides specific information about the way the tracks on the DVDs were recorded.

Some software programs, including Pro Tools, shorten the display name for certain tracks. Therefore, the labels you see in some of the screenshots may be abbreviated; for example: TrVr, TruVrb, and Trvrb. However, the proper term represented by the abbreviations will be spelled out ("true verb") in the text for consistency and to make reading easier. (Please note that the name TrueVerb indicates the trademarked Waves plug-in).

The meat of the book is, of course, the ten songs chosen as examples; each of the ten songs is covered in its own chapter. These songs were chosen for particular reasons: they represent a fairly wide range of styles; each song can be used to illustrate a different facet of mixing; and each will be familiar to most purchasers of this book. While these multitrack sessions are *not* the original recordings, they faithfully represent the sounds, instruments, and effects used in the originals.

Acknowledgments

Special thanks must go not only to Mike Lawson for coming to me with the idea of writing this book, but also to the musicians and singers who worked on these recordings; to my beautiful bride, Carolyn Martin (the best swing singer on the planet); to Lynn Fuston for his help; and to the guy who got me involved with recording in the first place, Michael Henry Martin, whose Castle Sound Recording was (and in many ways still is) an inspiration.

Dave Martin
Java Jive Studio
Nashville, TN

CHAPTER 1

"Anyway"

(As Recorded by Martina McBride)

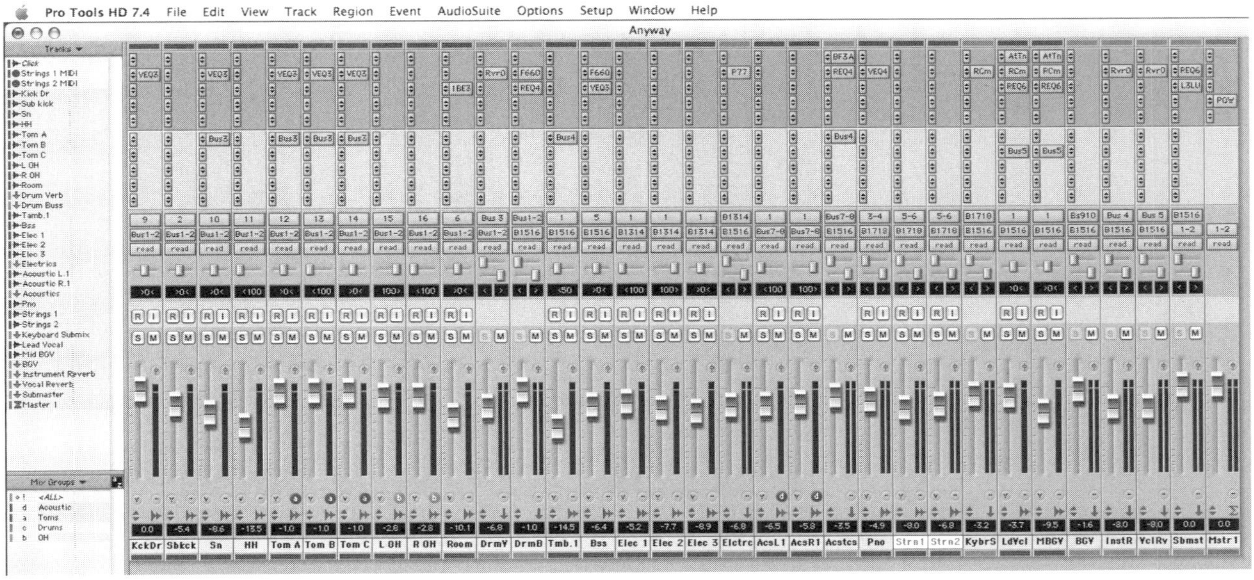

Fig. 1.1. Mix Window

"Anyway," like many of Martina McBride's releases, features dramatic changes in volume and intensity—the intro and verse are fairly sparse, and the full band enters at the chorus. Mixing such a record requires a certain amount of finesse and the willingness to allow the final mix to be dynamic—that is, allowing the piano and strings in the introduction to be quiet enough to give the mix somewhere to go as it builds.

DRUMS

Like the others in this book, the drum tracks on "Anyway" are recorded in a way that allows for a fairly wide range of manipulation in the mixing process. You may notice that there are two kick drum tracks—one track, labeled "kick" (KckDr in the screenshot below, and Kick_1 in the accompanying audio file) was recorded with a Shure Beta 52 placed inside the drum about three inches from the batter head, while the "subkick"(Sbkck) track was recorded with a Yamaha Subkick placed directly in front of the drum. These two signals sound quite different from each other. Most mixing engineers will combine the two sounds while processing each as needed to create the final kick drum sound.

Fig. 1.2. Drum Mix.

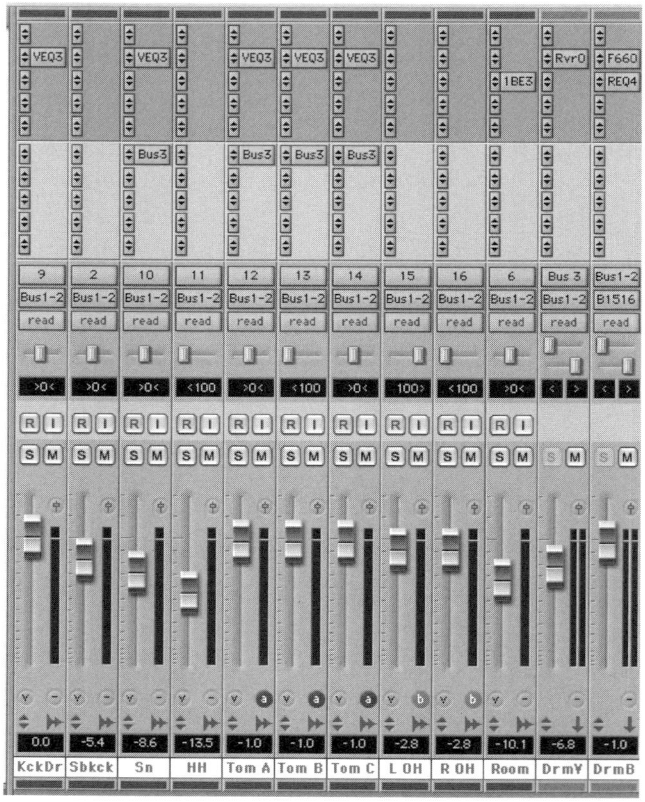

The snare track was recorded with a Shure SM57 microphone above the snare. There's also a track labeled "room mic." The room microphone was a Telefunken U 47 placed around 20 feet from the drum set. The usual purpose of room mics is to capture the ambient and reflected sound generated by the drums rather than a direct sound.

Note: Throughout the book I'll describe the levels of audio tracks in decibels (dB) above or below *unity gain*—that is, how much a track is turned up or down from *the default levels* in the computer software.

Kick Drum

When building a track from the drums up (as opposed to building one from the vocals down) and setting the level of the kick (in this case, setting the levels of both kick tracks), I will work to keep the kick—after adding EQ, compression, and any other processing—at somewhere between –4 dBFS and –8 dBFS, or between 4 and 8 dB below full scale. That usually leaves room for all of the other instruments and sources to be added to the kick without overloading the output bus and requiring that all the tracks be turned down. Because it's generally a good idea to mix (and check mixes) at several different levels—from the lower threshold of audibility to the highest threshold of tolerance—keeping the kick drum at a fairly consistent level (–6 dB at the output of the DAW) helps keep all the mixes in a project uniform.

Before adding EQ to the kick drum, it's best to spend some time working with the two tracks; adjust the tracks until the two sound best before any processing. For this song, the kick track felt most solid with the subkick track (which is providing the low thump of the kick sound) set 5.4 dB lower than the main kick track, so that the kick level is at unity, or 0 dB of gain, and the subkick level is at –5.4 dB.

I chose to use the Waves V Series EQs for the drums on "Anyway." The V-EQ3 is modeled on the classic Neve 1066 and 1073 equalizers. Because those vintage EQs had fixed EQ points (rather than the sweepable frequencies on most modern EQs), the frequencies I've chosen to boost or cut are, to some extent, determined by the design of the plug-in. In other words, with the V-EQ3, it's not possible to cut 500 Hz; with this particular plug-in, the closest available frequencies are 360 Hz and 700 Hz. (This isn't necessarily a problem; some of the greatest records of the rock era were mixed before sweepable EQs were available to recording engineers.)

To clear up a bit of the muddiness in the kick drum and add definition, I've added a V series 3-band EQ with a high-pass filter to the main kick drum track. The high-pass is set to 45 Hz and is used to remove low frequencies that can't be reproduced by most stereo speakers yet eat up available headroom. The low-EQ band is a shelving filter that adds quite a bit of boost (at 60 Hz and below), down to where the high-pass filter takes over and removes anything below about 40 Hz. The mid-EQ band is a bell-shaped EQ centered at 360 Hz; if the kick drum sounds boxy, cutting frequencies somewhere in the 350–600 Hz area will usually mitigate that boxiness. To add a bit of a point to the kick drum sound, I've added a 9 dB boost at 10 kHz. Though there may seem to be quite a lot of boost on the kick drum sound (with 10 dB at 60 Hz and 9 dB at 10 kHz), the adjustment certainly works with this power ballad—especially in combination with the Yamaha Subkick. The output of the plug-in has been reduced by 5 dB to help make up for the gain added by boosting the high and low frequencies.

Fig. 1.3. Kick V-EQ3

Waves V-EQ3 Kick Drum Settings					
control	high-pass	LF	MF	HF	output
frequency	45 Hz	60 Hz	0.36 kHz	10 kHz	
adjustment	in	+10.7 dB	–3.1 dB	+9.0 dB	–5.0 dB

Whenever there are multiple tracks from one source, such as these two kick drum tracks, it's very important to check the phase relationship between the tracks. There are a couple of ways to do this, ranging from low tech to high tech.

The old-school way is simply to turn both tracks up to the same relative level and then mute (and un-mute) one of the two while listening to see if the sound changes for the better. Do this with both of the tracks, and see if you hear anything problematic (for example, if the volume drops when the second kick drum track is added, or if there are dramatic tonal differences when both kick drum tracks are turned up). If you hear that there are phase issues between the two tracks, then one of two things is likely to be the culprit: either one track was recorded with its polarity set opposite to the other track's polarity, or (more likely) the difference between the two times that it took for the sound wave to reach the two microphones created a phase problem.

If you hear something funny happening when the two kick drum tracks are soloed, then you need to determine whether one of the tracks is out of phase with the other. The easiest approach is to magnify the two tracks onscreen to ascertain what's going on. If you zoom in to the point that one kick drum hit fills up the screen, then you should be able to see two things. The first is whether the initial impacts of the two tracks match. (In this case, the beginning of the curve that shows the signal should be positive, or up on both tracks.) The second is whether the kick drums line up exactly; if they don't, it sometimes helps the sound if you move one of the two tracks so that they *do* line up exactly. When I do this, it's usually the subkick track that I move.

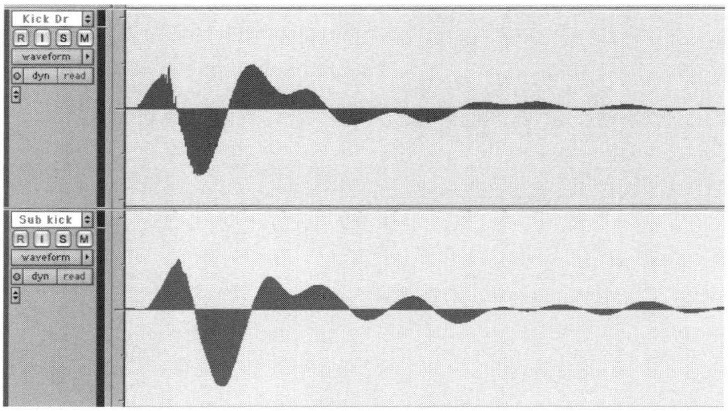

Fig.1.4. Kick Drums In Phase

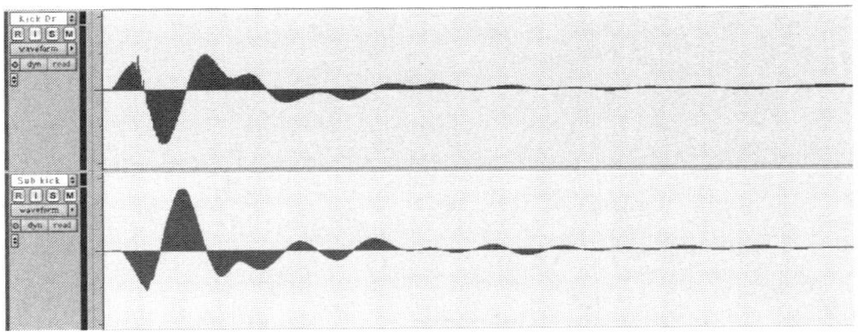

Fig. 1.5. Kick Drums Out of Phase

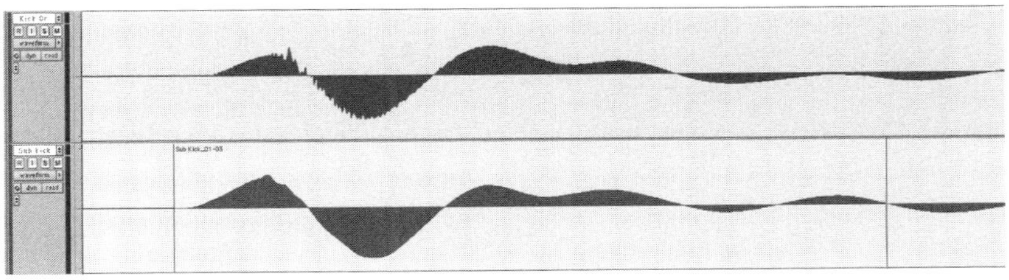

Fig. 1.6. Kicks Aligned

The high-tech method of checking the phase of two tracks generated from the same source is with a phase meter: solo the two tracks, pan them hard left and right, and put a phase meter on the main stereo output; the meter will show the phase difference between the two. But because the phase meter is more suited for (actually, it's designed for) stereo tracks, I'll examine it in detail at a later time.

In the early days of digital recording and mixing, the amount of processing power available in a workstation was limited. Trying to add plug-ins to every track in a session could bog down or even crash the computer. While that's less of an issue in this day of quad-core (and even 8-core) processors (and even less with systems like a Pro Tools HD setup or those DAWs that use processing cards like those made by Universal Audio), running too many plug-ins still can cause problems for some users. But even with powerful computers, it isn't necessary (or even a good thing) to add processing like an EQ or a compressor to every track. There are two kick drum sources in this mix: a Yamaha Subkick and the Shure Beta 52. While the Shure microphone signal has quite a bit of EQ added to it, the Subkick track has neither equalization nor compression plug-ins added—in other words, the track used in the final mix sounds exactly like it was recorded. Adding additional low-end EQ to the Subkick would change the sound from "warm and deep" to "muddy," and so it's best (actually, best in a surprising number of instances) to leave the recorded track alone. There are no rules or requirements that mixing engineers *have* to alter every single track on a project. Naturally, if the mix *does* require an engineer's intervention, then by all means, intervene.

Snare

The level of the snare track is generally determined by the level of the kick drum; with the kick averaging around –6 dBFS, the snare drum seemed to fit with the rest of the track a tiny bit lower—at around –7 dB. Naturally, that's song specific, but with this particular song, the kick and snare work well together at those levels. Though the snare volume is set to –8.6 dB, the EQ (another Waves V-EQ3) is boosting a number of frequencies.

Because "Anyway" is a fairly dense track, the snare track is high-passed at 160 Hz. The high-pass filter does a couple of things that are good for the mix. First, the high-pass filter minimizes the amount of kick drum in the snare mic, which means that EQ added to the snare will have a minimal effect on the sound of the kick drum in the mix. Second, keeping the amount of kick drum in the snare track to a minimum helps to keep reverb on the kick drum to a minimum. To add a bit of meat to the snare, a shelving EQ was added, starting at 320 Hz, with a 5.6 dB boost. Another EQ band centered at 2.4 kHz boosted that range by 6.5 dB, and a high-frequency shelving EQ added 5 dB from 10 kHz up. The output of the EQ is reduced to –7.9 dB.

Fig. 1.7. Snare V-EQ3

Waves V-EQ3 Snare Settings

control	high-pass	LF	MF	HF	output
frequency	160 Hz	220 Hz	2.4 kHz	10 kHz	
adjustment	in	+5.6 dB	+6.5 dB	+5.0 dB	–7.9 dB

Snare Compression and Limiting

While compressing and/or limiting the snare drum track(s) has become a standard (if not necessary) way of working, it's important to keep the reason for using a compressor in mind. As stated with the kick drum, compressors can even out inconsistent playing or they can be used to change the tonal characteristics of a track. If neither of these things needs to be done, there's no reason to put the plug-in on the track. I chose to not use a compressor or limiter on either the kick or the snare on this particular song because the tracks (in my view) needed neither the tone added by a compressor nor any adjustments to even out the levels.

Hi-hat

Much like a bottom snare mic, a hi-hat mic's use is optional and depends on the engineer, the drummer, and the song being mixed. Some engineers—especially those who tend to build their drum sound primarily from the overhead microphones—often will not set up a mic for the hi-hat; others regularly record the hat mic and just as regularly may mute that track and not use it at all. Other engineers will use and even emphasize the hi-hat track within the larger context of the overall drum sound and the song. If the hi-hat track is used, it should be panned to reflect the drum set as a whole. If the drums are mixed from the drummer's perspective, pan the hat to the left. If mixing drums from the audience's perspective, pan the hat to the right. I used the hi-hat track on "Anyway" because it added needed definition—especially during the second verse. The output level of the hi-hat track is fairly low but nevertheless is quite useful. The hat on "Anyway" is fairly low at –13.5 dB; the hi-hat track can be heard, but it doesn't overwhelm the hi-hat sound coming from the overhead mics, the room mic, and the snare drum.

Toms

The "correct" method of positioning individual drums in a stereo mix is a matter of some dispute in certain circles; the two main options are "audience perspective" and "drummer perspective." Those who feel that the audience perspective is correct will position the toms (in order of pitch and size from the smallest mounted tom to the floor tom) from right to left, as though the listener was sitting in front of the drum set; others will position the toms as though they were sitting behind the drums playing them, with the toms panned from left to right. And at least some folks pan the high tom to the right, the middle tom to the left, and the floor tom in the center. Whichever perspective you choose, there's one more option: you may pan the high and low toms hard left and right (or right and left), or you may pan them soft left and right (or right and left). Soft panning the toms seems, to some engineers, to sound more "natural" than hard panning. In this mix, the drums are panned from the drummer's perspective. They are panned with the first tom hard left, the middle tom to the center and the floor tom panned hard right. Make sure that, whichever way you choose to pan the toms, the overheads are panned in the same direction.

The same plug-in (Waves V-EQ3) that was used on the kick and snare was also used on the tom tracks on "Anyway." On Tom A, a high-pass filter is set at 70 Hz, 320 Hz is boosted 7.1 dB, and 4.8 kHz is boosted by 7 dB. For the high frequencies, 10 kHz is boosted 2.5 dB. Tom B is set the same way: a high-pass filter set at 70 Hz, 320 Hz is boosted 7.1 dB, 4.8 kHz is boosted by 7 dB, and for the high frequencies, 10 kHz is boosted 2.5 dB. Only the floor tom is different: the high-pass filter is off, 60 Hz is boosted 8.5 dB, 360 Hz is dropped by 1.2 dB, and 10 kHz is boosted 6 dB. The output of the plug-ins on the first two toms is reduced by 2.5 dB, while the output of the plug-in on the floor tom is boosted 2 dB. You may notice that the frequencies in the 500 Hz range are not boosted; this is a similar effect to cutting the midrange frequencies, which helps to reduce muddiness in the toms.

Fig. 1.8. Tom EQ

Waves V-EQ3 Tom A Settings					
control	high-pass	LF	MF	HF	output
frequency	70 Hz	220 Hz	4.8 kHz	10 kHz	
adjustment	in	+7.2 dB	+7.0 dB	+2.5 dB	–2.0 dB

Waves V-EQ3 Tom B Settings					
control	high-pass	LF	MF	HF	output
frequency	70 Hz	220 Hz	4.8 kHz	10 kHz	
adjustment	in	+7.2 dB	+7.0 dB	+2.4 dB	–2.0 dB

Waves V-EQ3 Tom C Settings					
control	high-pass	LF	MF	HF	output
frequency	off	60 Hz	0.36 kHz	10 kHz	
adjustment	off	+8.5 dB	–1.2 dB	+6.0 dB	–2.0 dB

One other point should be made concerning the tom tracks: if you solo the toms during the sections when the drums are playing, you'll hear that they are vibrating sympathetically with the kick drum and the snare. Some folks refer to this as humming. You'll also notice that the rest of the drum kit (kick, snare, cymbals) are bleeding into the tom mics; this isn't necessarily a bad thing—remember that a drum set is a single instrument, not a bunch of individual noise makers. In some of the other chapters, we'll look at different approaches to minimizing (or eliminating) tom hum. On this track, I didn't think that tom hum was a detriment to the sound of the mix, so it was left alone.

Overheads

Overhead microphones present another range of options for the mixing engineer. Some folks like to use the overheads as the primary element of the drum sound, with the snare, tom, and hi-hat mics used to help fill out the sound of the overheads, while others will use the overhead microphones more as cymbal mics, with the main sound of the drum set delivered by the close-miked snare, toms, and hi-hat. In any case, make sure that the overhead tracks and the tom tracks are panned in similar directions. The overheads are typically panned hard left and right. No EQ was used on the overhead mics, which were Telefunken M16s processed through a Phoenix Audio DRS-2 mic pre. The sound of the mics worked well with the track with no further manipulation. Both of the overhead tracks were set at –2.8 dB.

Room Mics

Room mics have become popular again. There was a time when engineers and producers worked very hard to isolate the various elements that make up a drum kit—some even went to the extreme of recording part of the kit separately. On one pass, the drummer might play only the hi-hat; on the next pass, he would play the kick drum only. On the third, the snare, and so on. But that approach to recording drums has (fortunately) passed into history along with 8-track players. These days, room ambience is again popular. This version of "Anyway" includes a stereo room-mic track, which can be used to add an ambient quality to the drum sound that can't be duplicated by a reverb. For "Anyway," the room mic is at –10 dB, with a high-pass filter (a Digidesign DigiRack 1-band EQ) set at 600 Hz with a 12 dB-per-octave slope. This means that the sound of the kick drum in the room mic is minimized (though not eliminated), and the snare and cymbals receive a nice bit of ambience from the track.

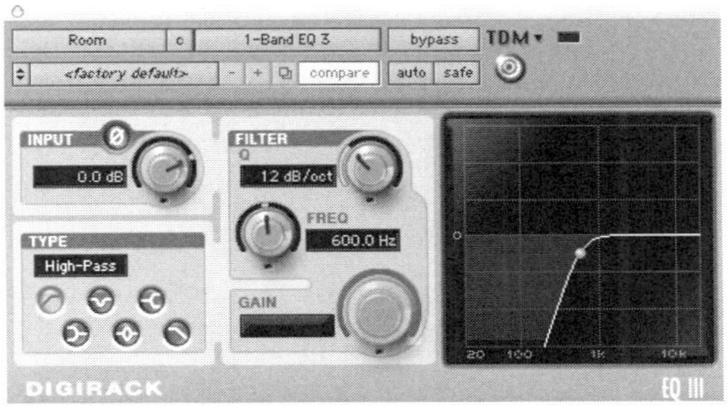

Fig. 1.9. Room EQ

DigiRack 1-band EQ III Room Mic Settings	
parameter	**value**
input	0 dB
type	high-pass
Q (slope)	12 dB/octave
frequency	600.0 Hz

Drum Routing, Grouping, and Effects

The tracks that make up the drum kit are routed to a stereo buss so that EQ and a stereo buss compressor can be inserted across the whole kit. Remember that ultimately a drum set is a single instrument; each drum in the set is part of the whole. By bussing all of the drum tracks together, you have control over not only the overall level of the kit, but also over any sonic changes that need to affect the whole kit sound.

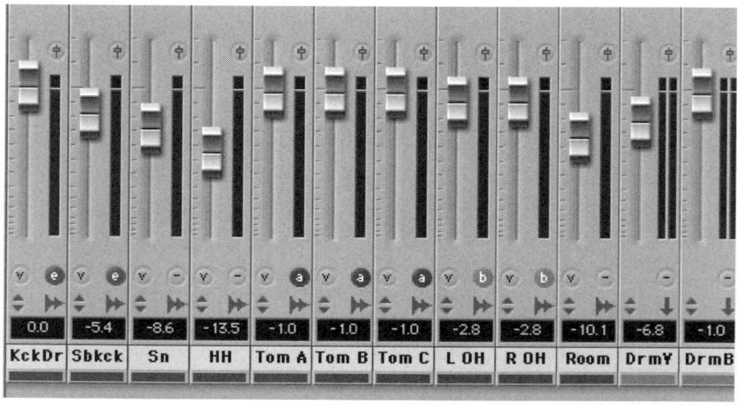

Fig. 1.10. Drum Groups

For ease of mixing, I typically create several groups among the drum tracks. I set up three groups for the drums. The first group is the three toms, because once the levels of the toms are set (relative to each other), it's more common to adjust the volumes of all three to adjust their relation to the rest of the kit rather than adjusting each tom individually. The second group is the overhead mics; I put the overheads on two mono tracks rather than one stereo track, because it's not uncommon to adjust one of the two overhead tracks in order to create the best stereo image. Once the relative levels between the two overhead mics are set, grouping them (so that the relative levels of the two tracks remain the same when turning the overheads up or down) makes further adjustments easier and more accurate. The third group is all the tracks that make up the drum kit; though the drum group is usually inactive, it's sometimes convenient to turn all of the tracks up or down to optimize the levels going to the drum buss.

It's usually a good idea to set up an effects buss with some sort of reverb for the drums only. While they might occasionally use the same type of reverb sound as other instruments, it's more common on contemporary records for drums to sound as though they were in their own acoustic space. Setting up an effects send for just the drums is quite easy to do. In the sessions on the DVD, I use a mono auxiliary send that is dedicated to the drums—specifically, to the snare and toms (the overheads and room mics aren't usually sending anything to the drum reverb, though from time to time, the room mics will be used as part of the reverb send). A mono aux input track is created, and a stereo reverb is inserted on that track, becoming a stereo effects return. The output is sent to the drum buss, so that adjusting the volume of the drum buss also adjusts the volume of the drum reverb. By routing the drum reverb return to the drum buss, you ensure that turning down the drums (using the buss output rather than either adjusting each track individually or grouping the drums and turning down all the tracks at once) also turns down the ambience created by the reverb.

The drums on "Anyway" are run through a Digidesign Reverb One set to the Fat Plate preset. The aux send on the snare track is set to –4 dB, while the aux sends on the toms are set at –1.2 dB. The output of the reverb return is at –6.8 dB.

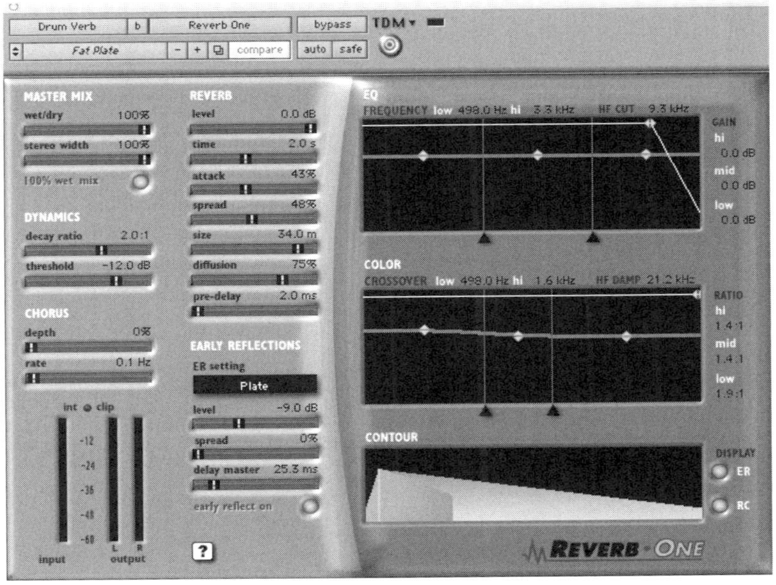

Fig. 1.11. Drum Reverb

Reverb One Drums Settings	
parameter	**value**
wet/dry	100%
stereo width	100%
decay ratio	2.0:1
threshold	–12 db

Reverb One Drums Settings continued	
parameter	**value**
reverb level	0 db
reverb time	2.0 seconds
attack	43%
spread	48%
size	34.0 meters
diffusion	75%
pre-delay	2.0 ms
early reflection (ER) setting	plate
ER level	–9.0 db
ER spread	0%
ER delay master	23.5 ms

The drum buss—that is, the stereo buss where all the drum tracks and their reverb assignments go before being combined with the other instrument and vocal tracks—is where any processing that applies to the entire drum track is added. On "Anyway," a compressor/limiter and an EQ have been added. The compressor, a Fairchild 660 emulation, is only adding mild compression—less than 2 dB—with a fairly slow attack and release time. The EQ, a Waves Renaissance EQ, has a shelving EQ set at 75 Hz and boosted by 1.5 dB, and a high-frequency shelving EQ set at 9 kHz and boosted 1.4 dB.

Fig. 1.12. Drum Buss Compressor

Fairchild 660 Drum Buss Settings			
control	**input gain**	**threshold**	**time constant**
setting	23	4.75	2

Fig. 1.13. Drum Buss EQ

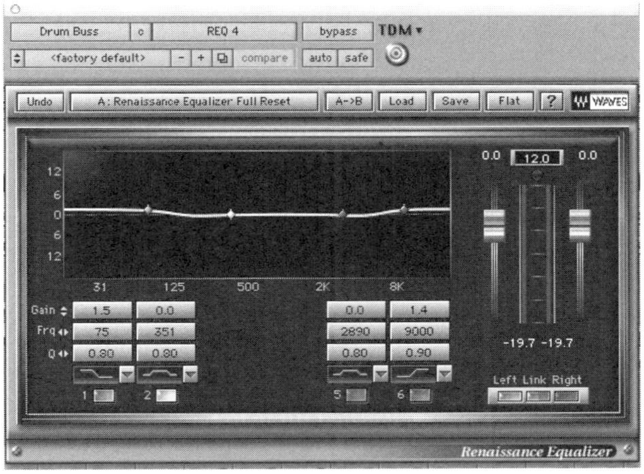

Waves Renaissance REQ-4 Drum Buss Settings				
parameter	band 1	band 2	band 3	band 4
gain	+1.5 dB	0 dB	0 dB	+1.4 dB
frequency	75 Hz	351 Hz	2890 Hz	9000 Hz
Q	0.80	1.02	0.80	0.90
shape	shelf	bell	bell	shelf

PERCUSSION

The only percussion on "Anyway" is a tambourine, which in this case is not routed through the drum buss (some of the other songs in this book will treat percussion as an extension of the drum set). Instead, it will be routed directly to the main output buss along with most of the other instruments (though several groups of instruments are routed to their own busses before being sent to the main output, the tambourine track isn't one of them). There is no EQ or compression used on the tambourine, though an auxiliary is used as an effects send to the instrument reverb (more on the instrument reverb later). The tambourine level is set at –14.5 dB, and it's panned to the left side of the sound field—not hard left, but midway between the center and the left side.

BASS

The Fender Precision bass used to record this track was routed through an Éclair Engineering Evil Twin DI and a Tube-Tech CL 1B. A bit of compression—more to add a slightly "compressed" tone than to actually control the level—was added to this track. With most instrument tracks, when a gain reduction of less than 3 dB is used—especially when the attack and release times on the compressor are fairly mild—the result is a compressor plug-in that doesn't make a track sound "squashed." As with most of the other tracks in this particular session, the Waves V series 3-band EQ was used. The 100 Hz band was boosted 8.4 dB, 360 Hz was cut 2.5 dB, and 10 kHz was cut 3.5 dB (not much of a cut, because there's very little sonic information from an electric bass at 10 kHz). In addition, the output of the plug-in was 1 dB. The overall level of the bass track was 6.4 dB below unity gain.

Fig. 1.14. Bass Compressor

Fairchild 660 Bass Settings			
control	**input gain**	**threshold**	**time constant**
value	29	5.5	2

Fig. 1.15. Bass EQ

Waves V-EQ3 Bass Settings					
control	**high-pass**	**LF**	**MF**	**HF**	**output**
frequency	off	100 Hz	0.36 kHz	10 kHz	
adjustment	off	+8.4 dB	–2.5 dB	–3.5 dB	–1.0 dB

GUITARS

Though a number of guitar types (not to mention guitar styles) are played in contemporary country music, I tend to separate them into two main groups for mixing purposes—electric guitars and acoustic guitars. Under the general heading of electric guitar, I'll include 12-string electric guitars, baritone guitars, tic-tac basses, and even the electric sitar (an instrument that seems to experience short bursts of popularity followed by long periods when it isn't heard on country radio).

Acoustic guitars, including nylon-string classical guitars, high-strung acoustics, small guitars like the Baby Taylor, and resonator guitars show up from time to time on acoustic-based material or ballads, where they add a lovely high-end sheen to the recording. The Baby Taylor is a guitar that sounds pretty terrible in a standard tuning but develops a wonderful tone when tuned a 4th high. These guitars (not including dobros, which are played with a bar and usually have square necks in place of the round necks used on guitars) are usually bussed together and processed in a similar way. While individual tracks may be equalized differently, all of the acoustic guitars tend to be bussed to a stereo aux and processed along with the other acoustic guitars.

At first listen, it may seem that a classic country guitar sound (like the relatively clean Telecaster sound that session ace Brent Mason is known for) and a distorted rock guitar tone (the type of sound that started showing up on country records somewhere in the late 1980s) would be treated differently in the mix, but that's not generally the case. The sound of the guitar—the tone, the texture, and usually the effects—on country records is generally in the hands of the guitarist (and the producer) at the time of recording. When the time comes to mix, the engineer is left to find the correct balance and placement. Of course, there are exceptions to this, which I'll explore in a later chapter.

ELECTRIC GUITARS

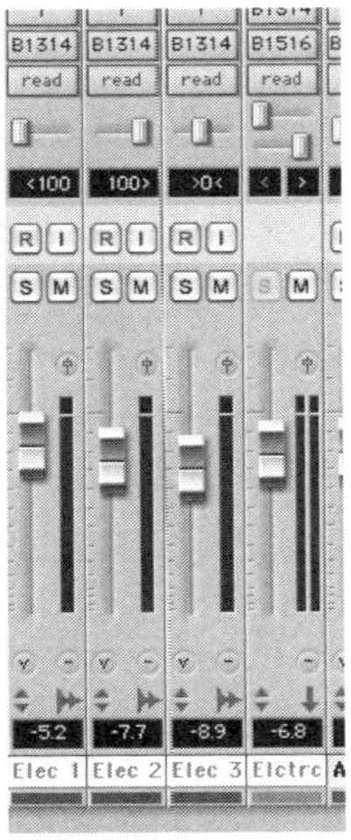

Fig. 1.16. Electric Guitar Buss

"Anyway" has three electric guitar tracks. Because the guitar sounds on the original recording of "Anyway" were available when the tracks accompanying this book were recorded, it was a relatively simple matter to match the sounds. Because of that, very little needs to be done in the way of processing or effects. The guitars are panned left, right, and center, and are routed through a stereo buss. This buss has a plug-in that emulates the classic UREI 1176—a compressor known for its tone. In this situation, the threshold of the 1176 is set high enough that no gain reduction is taking place. The output of the plug-in is slightly boosted to add a bit of the 1176 sound—a task it performs quite well, by the way. The levels of the left and right guitars were set at –5.2 and –7.7 respectively. Even when these two instruments are soloed, the difference of 2.5 dB between the two tracks reflects the volume settings when the guitars were recorded. It wasn't my desire to make one louder than the other in the mix. The center guitar's level was set to –8.9 dB.

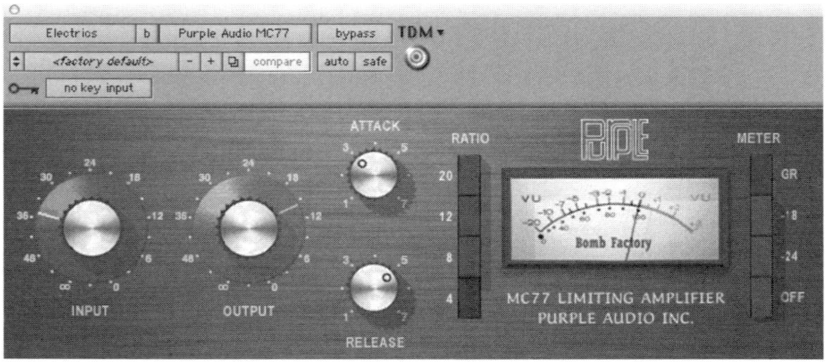

Fig. 1.17. Electric Guitar Buss Compressor

Bomb Factory BF76 Electric Guitar Buss Settings				
input	output	attack	release	ratio
35	14.5	3	5	4:1

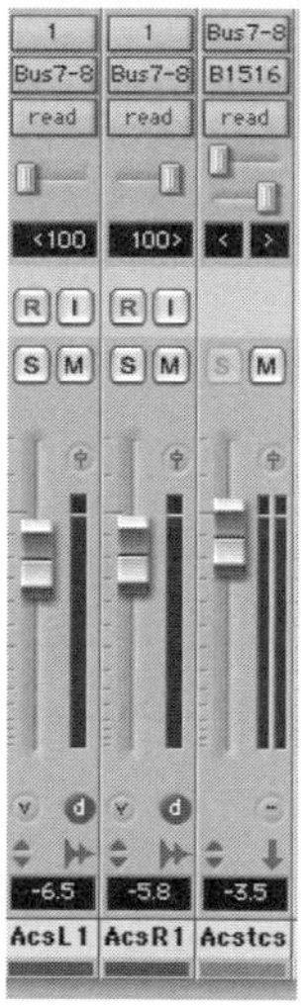

Fig. 1.18. Acoustic Guitar Buss

ACOUSTIC GUITARS

The acoustic guitar on this song isn't actually a "stereo" track; the two microphones used to record the acoustic were placed with one mic between the sound hole and the neck of the instrument about four inches from the face of the guitar while the other mic was placed approximately even with the guitarist's shoulder and pointing at the lower bout from approximately twelve inches away. These two tracks are generally treated and processed as a stereo pair, but because purists would argue that "stereo" has a specific meaning in audio, it might be better to refer to it as a "two-microphone" technique. In any case, the two tracks have a pretty different tone—Acoustic A is a bit more direct sounding and has more presence than Acoustic B. Nevertheless, these two tracks can be panned hard left and right, and provide a full acoustic guitar sound.

Fig. 1.19. Acoustic Buss Compressor

The level of the left acoustic track (recorded from the microphone near the guitar's neck) was set at –6.5 dB, while the right acoustic track was a bit higher at –5.8 dB to more closely match the levels. As with the drums, I grouped the acoustic guitar tracks once the relative levels were set correctly. This allows for changes in volume without losing the relationship between the two tracks. These tracks were grouped to their own stereo buss so that both tracks could be processed simultaneously. First, a Bomb Factory BF-3A, a software emulation of the classic UREI LA-3A, was inserted to add a bit of compression. Rather mild settings were used; even at the loudest part of the song, the compressor was only reducing gain by about 2 dB.

To EQ the acoustics I used a 4–band Waves Renaissance EQ. The low band was set as a high-pass filter, rolling off frequencies below 90 Hz. An open E string (which wasn't used on this song) has a frequency of 80 Hz, so the use of the high-pass was, as much as anything else, intended to minimize the low end of the drums bleeding into the acoustic guitar microphones (the entire rhythm section was recording together on this song). A bell-shaped EQ was set at a center frequency of 3,500 Hz and boosted by 4 dB, while a high-frequency shelving filter at 4,500 Hz boosted the high end of the guitar tracks by 4.2 dB. The Renaissance EQ is a parametric EQ, which means that not only can the center frequency be chosen, but also the width (or Q) of the boost can be adjusted from a wide "tone shaping" curve to a very narrow notch that can remove a problem frequency without messing too much with adjacent frequencies. The band centered at 3,500 Hz was fairly wide, being more of a tone-shaping tool than a problem-solving tool.

Fig. 1.20 Acoustic Guitar Buss EQ

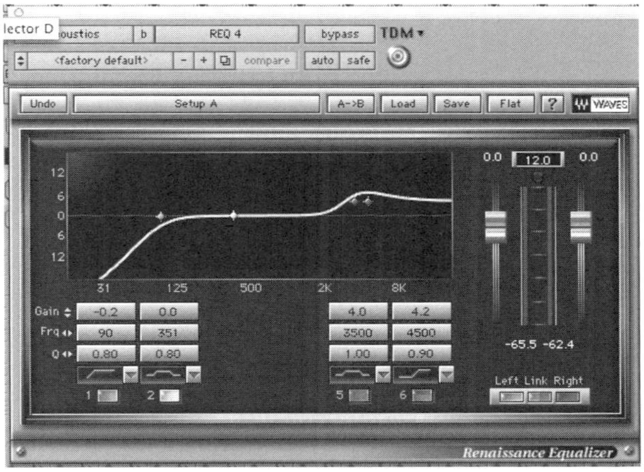

Waves Renaissance REQ-4 Acoustic Guitar Buss Settings				
parameter	**band 1**	**band 2**	**band 3**	**band 4**
gain	–0.2 dB	0 dB	+4.0 dB	+4.2 dB
frequency	90 Hz	351 Hz	3,500 Hz	4,500 Hz
Q	0.80	0.80	1.00	0.90
shape	high-pass	bell	bell	shelf

KEYBOARD INSTRUMENTS

"Anyway" has three stereo keyboard tracks: piano, high strings, and low strings. A Yamaha C7 grand piano was recorded with a pair of AKG 480 microphones set up as a spaced pair. The two string passes were recorded using the "warm strings" patch on a Roland JV-880 synth module; there are two tracks because the keyboard player found it easier to separate the string parts into two passes to duplicate the notes that are on the original version.

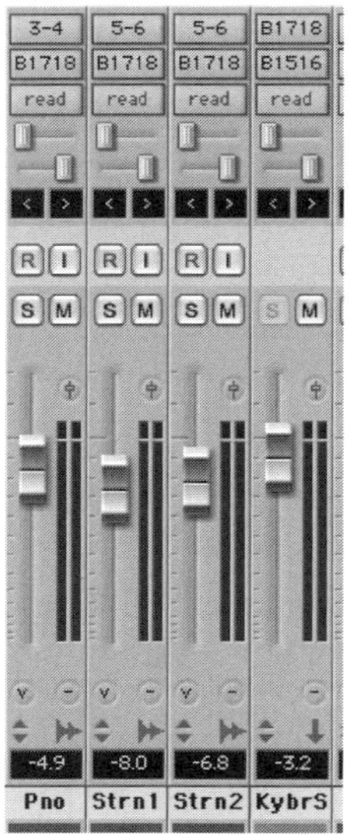

Fig. 1.21. Keyboard Buss

Piano

From a mixing perspective, the piano on "Anyway" shouldn't require much processing—a minimal amount of equalization to brighten it up a bit. Many of the studio pianos in Nashville are quite bright, although the piano used on this project is intentionally voiced a bit darker. The pianist's attack is pretty consistent, so the mild compression on the keyboard buss will suffice. However, to match the sound of the original recording, some EQ needs to be added. The level of the piano track was set at –6 dB, but of course, that is after the EQ (and before the keyboard buss, which was set to –3.2 dB). The plug-in chosen for the piano was the Waves V-EQ4, which was modeled after the highly regarded Neve 1081 console EQ. A high-pass filter removed frequencies below 62 Hz; the low-frequency band boosted 160 Hz by 7 dB, while the low-mid band cut 1 kHz by 4 dB with a broadband cut. The high-mid band cut 4.7 dB by 6.7 dB with a fairly narrow Q (not as narrow as is possible with a parametric, but narrower than the low-mid band). The high-frequency band boosted 6.8 kHz by 1.3 dB.

Fig. 1.22. Piano EQ

Waves REQ-4 Piano Settings

parameter	high-pass	LF	LMF	HMF	HF	output
frequency	52 Hz	180 Hz	1,000 Hz	4.7 kHz	6.8 kHz	
adjustment	in	+7.0 dB	–4.0 dB	+6.7 dB	+1.3 dB	–3.0
shape		shelf	broad Q	narrow Q	shelf	

Strings

The synthesized strings sound heavily processed when they're generated by the JV-880, so the biggest issue in mixing will be to automate the volume of the strings so that they're out of the way of the vocals and other instruments when used more as a pad, yet loud enough to cut through in the instrumental section.

No EQ was used on the strings for the reason mentioned above. Although the keyboard player made most of the necessary volume changes (for making the strings lie well in the track), I boosted the Strings 1 track (the high strings) by 3 dB at the solo section.

The piano and string tracks were routed to a stereo keyboard buss with a Renaissance Compressor inserted; this was set to a 3:1 compression ratio with a medium attack and release. The threshold of the keyboard buss compressor was set so that the maximum gain reduction was around 3 dB, and the output of the compressor was set to add 1.6 dB of gain makeup.

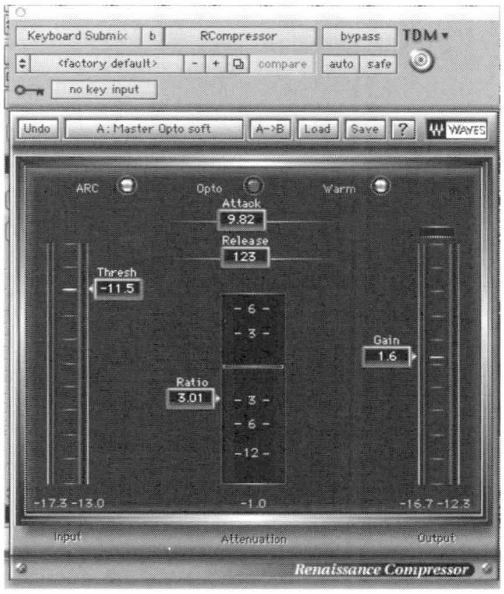

Fig. 1.23. Keyboard Buss Compressor

Waves Renaissance Compressor Keyboard Buss Settings

threshold	attack	release	ratio	gain
–11.5 dB	9.82	123	3.01:1	+1.6 dB

Thoughts on Strings and Synths

Few of us have the option of having real strings in our mixes—and it's a darned shame, because real string sections are truly lovely. What most of us get to work with instead are either sample libraries (when time and money are available) or synthesized string patches (when they're not). But all is not lost—many of the string parts heard these days, even on major label releases, are either samples or synth strings. There is a vast array of choices available, too. Not only are the sample libraries and virtual instrument string sounds much better than they once were, but even string patches in the latest versions of hardware synth modules work very well. An elderly Roland module—the JV-880—generated all of the strings sounds used in this volume. While a number of the synthesizers these days have "better" string sounds (two synths that are currently quite popular among the session players are Korg's Triton and Yamaha's Motif keyboards), the 880's "warm strings" patch has served us admirably for many years. A number of Nashville session keyboard players use laptop computers that generate the sounds with large sample libraries. The general rule here is that "whatever works" works.

In the last ten or twelve years a number of engineers and producers in town have begun recording the MIDI data that the keyboard player generates in addition to recording the sounds from his keyboard. Engineers can do a number of cool things with this data, from either changing the sound completely or layering other sounds (textures) on top of what was recorded, to moving individual notes or quantizing tracks that weren't played precisely in time. One caveat: because of the slow attack time that many string patches have, the musicians playing them learn to anticipate the attack and play the notes ahead of the time they need to be heard. This practice (which works quite well when recording synth parts) can make strings impossible to quantize later.

Though it wasn't done on this track, it can be very nice to have a fiddle player play a part along with the string patch; this can add a realistic texture to synthesized strings.

LEAD VOCAL

Despite the existence of Felix Mendelssohn's "Lieder ohne Worte" (Songs Without Words), a song without words is not a song; it's a "tune." Therefore, it behooves the mixing engineer to make sure that the words of the song can be clearly heard and understood in the context of the mix.

The lead vocal on this song was recorded with a Telefunken U 47 into a Vintech X73 and a Tube Tech CL 1B. Because the singer's tone worked well with the combination of the microphone and the rest of the signal chain, not a lot of processing is necessary to make it sit on top of the track. The lead vocal on "Anyway" has three different processors on it, as well as an effects send that assigns the lead (and background) vocals to the vocal reverb.

The first processor is the Antares Auto-Tune 4 plug-in. This wasn't done necessarily because I felt that the singer needed to be tuned; it was simply because the Auto-Tune plug-in isn't particularly transparent; everything that passes through it, tuned or not, develops a bit of that "Auto-Tune sound." And like it or not, that's a big part of the sound of country records these days. Fortunately, the over-tuned machine-like voices that ended up on a couple of big artists' records seem to have been a fad that has run its course (at least, if there's any justice or fairness in the world, it has run its course). In any event, the Auto-Tune 4 plug-in was set to very mild levels; the re-tuning speed was set to be quite slow and the tracking speed was set to a relaxed setting.

Fig. 1.24. Lead Vocal Auto-Tune

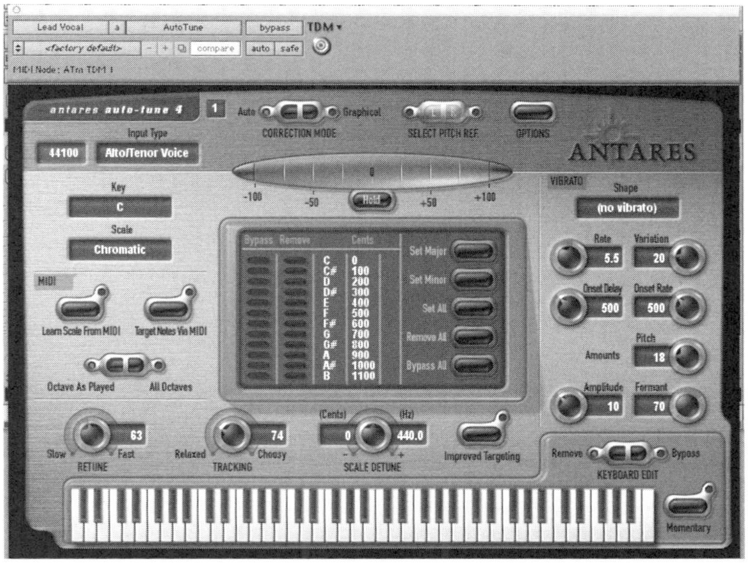

Antares Auto-Tune 4 Settings:

Input Type: Alto/Tenor Voice

Retune: 63

Tracking: 74

Fig. 1.25. Lead Vocal Compressor

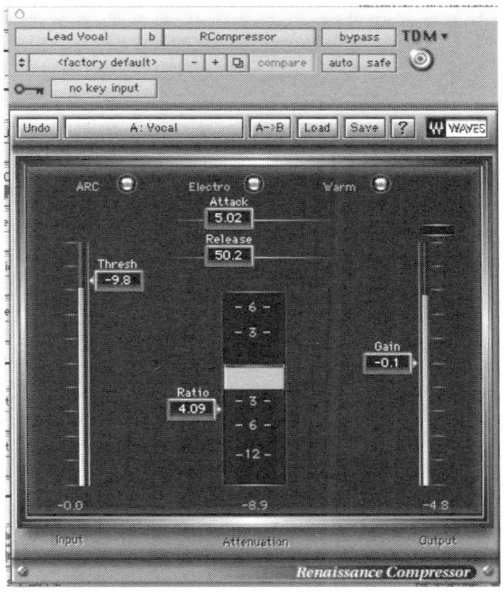

Waves Renaissance Compressor Lead Vocal Settings				
threshold	attack	release	ratio	gain
–9.8 dB	5.02	50.2	4.09:1	– 0.1 dB

A Waves Renaissance EQ-6 is also on the lead vocal track, not doing any major surgery, but simply touching up those frequencies that need it. The table on the following page shows the settings of the lead vocal EQ.

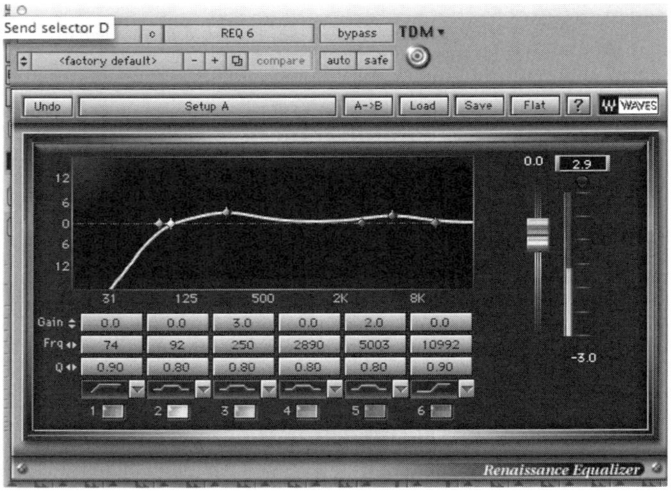

Fig. 1.26. Lead Vocal EQ

Waves Renaissance REQ-6 Lead Vocal Settings

parameter	band 1	band 2	band 3	band 4	band 5	band 6
gain	0 dB	0 dB	+3.0 dB	0 dB	+2 dB	0 dB
frequency	74 Hz	92 Hz	250 Hz	2,890 Hz	5,003Hz	10,992 Hz
Q	0.90	0.80	0.80	0.80	0.80	0.90
shape	high-pass	bell	bell	bell	bell	shelving

Both lead and background vocals were compressed with the Renaissance Compressor with a 4:1 ratio and a fairly fast attack and release. The threshold (the level at which compression begins) was set at –9.8 dB, but because the peaks on the vocal track come perilously close to full scale, that allows for quite a bit of gain reduction—somewhere in excess of 9 dB of gain reduction. Does this make the vocals sound compressed? Sure. But that's part of the sound of records these days. The use of compression on country vocals has evolved over the last fifteen or twenty years; as late as the 1980s, the compressor of choice for vocals in Nashville was a Teletronix LA-2A; a legendary optical processor with a tube amplifier as part of the gain makeup stage. LA-2As were ubiquitous in Nashville's studios—and most of them hadn't been adjusted in years. At the time, it was quite common for the LA-2A used for vocals to have marks next to the controls that indicated where the unit was *supposed* to be used. Nevertheless, the use of compression has changed more than the practice of simply using a "standard" compressor; contemporary country vocals have a lot more compression than was common a few years ago.

BACKGROUND VOCALS

There's only one background vocal part on "Anyway," so instead of bussing the BGV to a stereo pair (the typical method for many of the other songs on this project), the processing used on the lead vocal (Antares Auto-Tune 4, a Waves Renaissance Compressor, and Waves Renaissance EQ-6) was also used for the background vocal, which was then sent to the output buss. (Astute readers may note the presence of the unused BGV buss.) The background vocal track volume was set at –9.5 dB.

Fig. 1.27. BGV Auto Tune

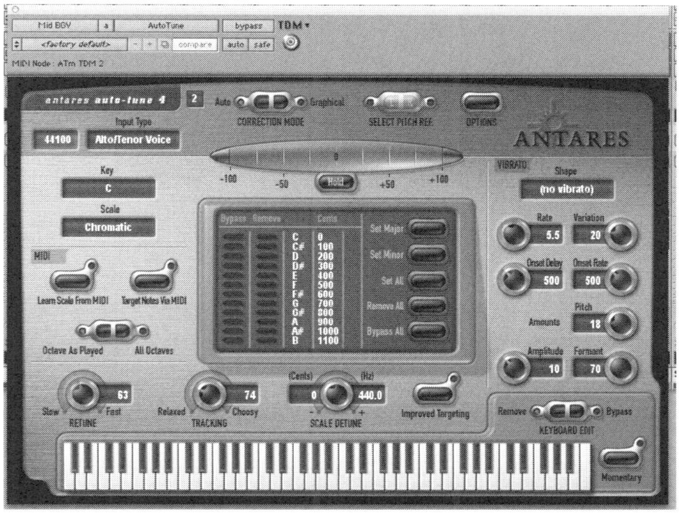

Antares Auto-Tune 4 Settings

Input Type: Alto/Tenor Voice
Retune: 63
Tracking: 74

Fig. 1.28. BGV Compressor

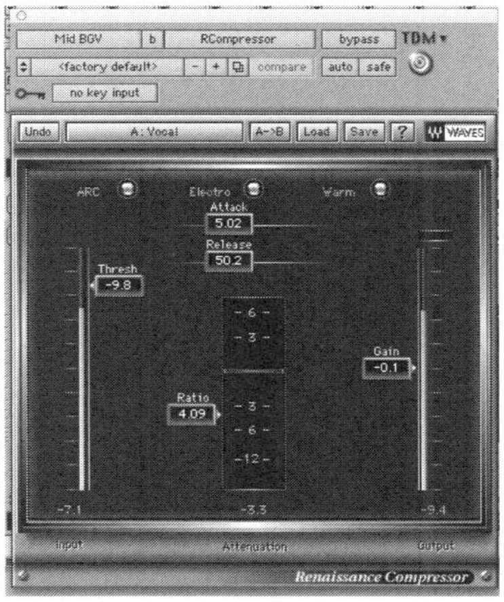

Waves Renaissance Compressor Background Vocal Settings				
threshold	attack	release	ratio	gain
–9.8 dB	5.02	50.2	4.09:1	–0.1 dB

A Waves Renaissance EQ-6 is also on the background vocal track, touching up those frequencies that need it. Here are the settings on the background vocal EQ:

Fig. 1.29. BGV EQ

Waves Renaissance REQ-6 Background Vocal Settings

parameter	band 1	band 2	band 3	band 4	band 5	band 6
gain	0 dB	0 dB	+2.8 dB	0 dB	–1.9 dB	0 dB
frequency	50 Hz	92 Hz	327 Hz	2,890 Hz	5,781 Hz	10,992 Hz
Q	0.90	0.80	0.80	0.80	0.80	0.90
shape	high-pass	bell	bell	bell	bell	shelving

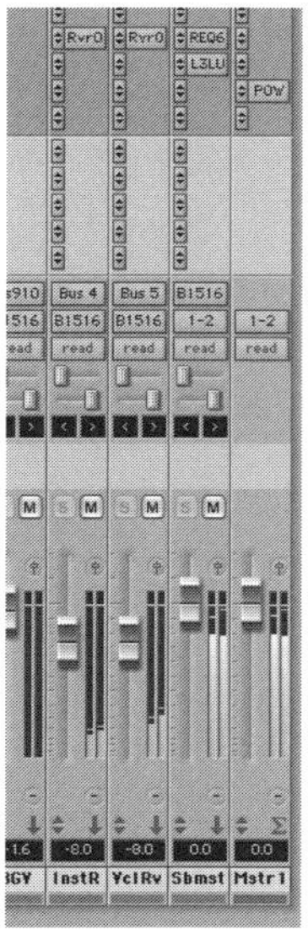

Fig. 1.30. Buss Effects and Processing

AUX SENDS AND BUSS PROCESSING

As mentioned previously, the drums have their own reverb buss; a second aux send is dedicated to the instrument reverb and is set to emulate a medium plate. This reverb is primarily used to add ambience to the acoustic instruments: acoustic guitars, fiddle, mandolin, and anything else that would benefit from it. On this track, the tambourine is also using the instrument reverb. A third aux send is the vocal reverb. For "Anyway," the reverb used is a Digidesign Reverb One set to a Small Plate preset. Should there be a need for different amounts of reverb between the lead and background vocals, that is controlled through the auxiliary sends.

INSTRUMENT REVERB

For the instrumental reverb send, a reverb one set to a "medium plate" was used, and the output level was at –8.0 dB.

Fig. 1.31. Instrument Reverb

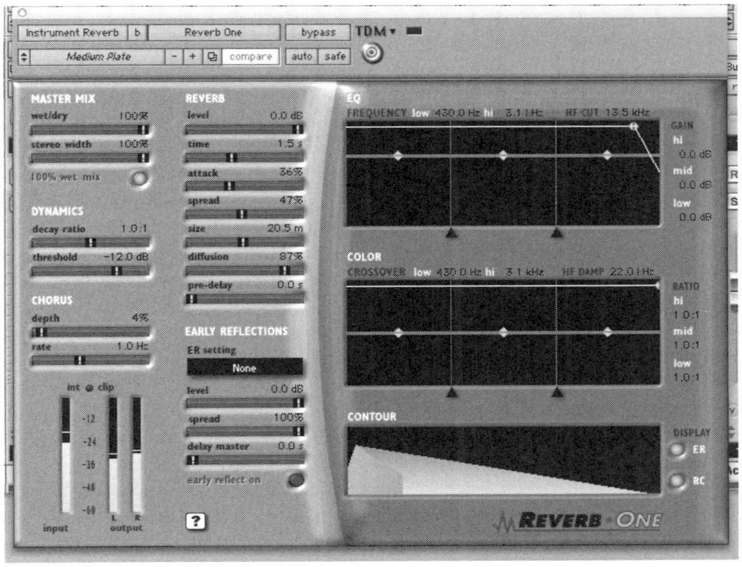

Reverb One Instrument Reverb Settings

parameter	value
wet/dry	100%
stereo width	100%
decay ratio	1.0:1
threshold	–12 dB
chorus depth	4%
chorus rate	1.0 Hz
reverb level	0 dB
reverb time	1.5 seconds
attack	36%
spread	47%
size	20.5 meters
diffusion	87%
pre-delay	0 ms
early reflection (ER) setting	None
ER level	0 dB
ER spread	100%
ER delay master	0 ms

Fig. 1. 32. Vocal Reverb

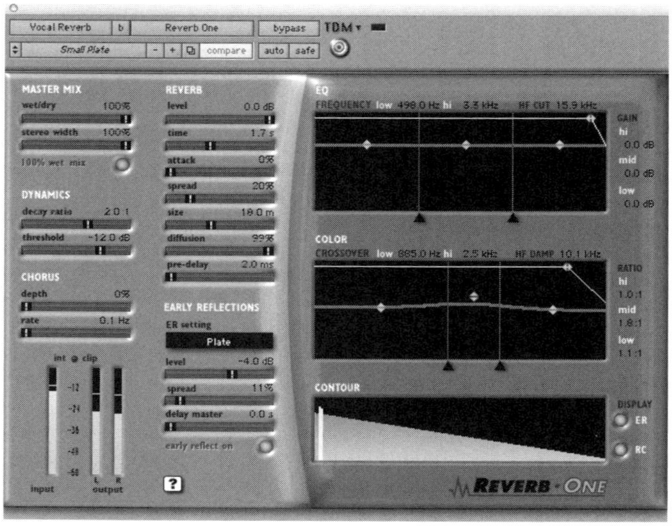

Here are the settings used for the vocal reverb, a Small Plate preset on a Reverb One.

Reverb One Vocal Reverb Settings

parameter	setting
wet/dry	100%
stereo width	100%
decay ratio	2.0:1
threshold	–12 dB
reverb level	0 dB
reverb time	1.5 seconds
attack	0%
spread	20%
size	18.0 meters
diffusion	99%
pre-delay	2.0 ms
early reflection (ER) setting	Plate
ER level	–4.0 dB
ER spread	11%
ER delay master	0 ms

All of the tracks and effects returns end up at the submaster buss; this buss has an EQ plug-in (which can be used as needed to tweak the overall tone of the mix) and a stereo limiter. The limiter is used to bring up the average volume of the mix to contemporary levels. The EQ is the Waves Renaissance EQ-6; here are the settings on that plug-in:

Fig. 1.33. Buss EQ

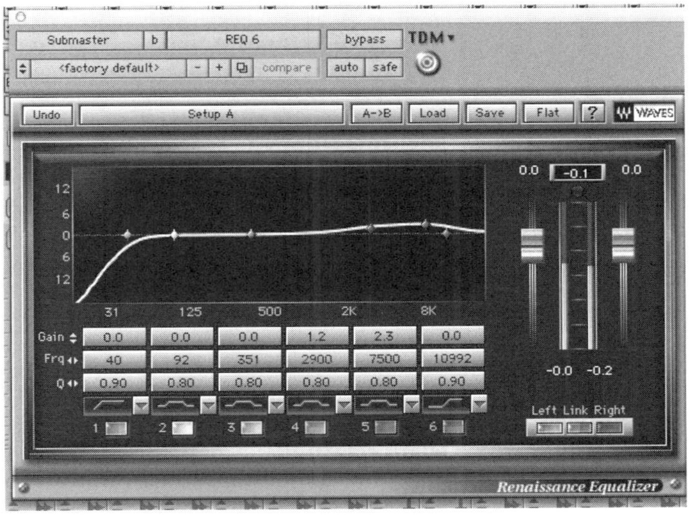

Waves Renaissance REQ-6 on the Submaster Buss						
parameter	**band 1**	**band 2**	**band 3**	**band 4**	**band 5**	**band 6**
gain	0 dB	0 dB	0 dB	+1.2 dB	+2.3 dB	0 dB
frequency	40 Hz	92 Hz	351 Hz	2,900 Hz	7,500 Hz	10,992 Hz
Q	0.90	0.80	0.80	0.80	0.80	0.90
shape	high-pass	bell	bell	bell	bell	shelving

As you can see, three of the six bands of EQ are unused, although I use the EQ-6 on the output buss of the mixes as a general rule in case the other bands are needed on a given mix. In an ideal world, the output limiter (here, a Waves L3) should be used sparingly. Although different limiters have different strengths and weaknesses, the L1 was the original "look-ahead" limiter used (and overused) as Pro Tools became more popular for mixing in the box. When overused, the L1 doesn't necessarily get any "louder" (remember that digital audio has an absolute upper limit of 0 dB), but it does add distortion. When using an L1, I prefer to have no more than 2.5 dB of gain reduction at the maximum for the whole song; with the Waves L3, a bit more limiting is acceptable, but is nevertheless capable of doing quite a bit of damage to the mix.

Fig. 1.34. Buss Limiter

The main output buss contains only a Pow-R Dither plug-in. Here's a short explanation of the concept of dither—why it's necessary, what it does, and what options are available.

Fig. 1.35. Dither

SAMPLING RATE AND BIT DEPTH

Audio CDs contain digital audio files in the AIFF format, at a sampling rate of 44.1 kHz and a bit depth of 16 bits. Sampling rate and bit depth are related to the frequency response and the dynamic range possible with the file, respectively. The science behind sample rates goes back to the 1940s, with the development of the Nyquist-Shannon theorem. This theorem states that perfect reconstruction of a signal is possible when the sampling frequency is greater than twice the maximum frequency of the signal being sampled. Another way to put it is that if the Nyquist frequency (half the sample rate) exceeds the highest frequency of the signal being sampled, the original analog signal can be reconstructed. If lower sampling rates are used, the original signal's information may not be completely recoverable from the sampled signal.

With a sampling frequency of 44.1 kHz, the highest frequencies that can be captured and stored are a bit less than half of the sampling frequency, or around 22 kHz. Remember that the accepted standard for the human hearing range is from 20 Hz to 20,000 Hz or 20 kHz, though in practice, most of the readers of this book do *not* hear frequencies that high.

Raising the sampling rate to 48 kHz raises the cut-off frequency to a bit less that 24 kHz, and recording at 96 kHz moves the cutoff frequency to a bit less that 48 kHz—far beyond range of audibility.

So why should engineers even consider recording at these higher sampling rates? Well, for two—no, three—reasons. The first is that the filters used to cut off frequencies above the Nyquist frequency, even though that frequency is above the audible frequency band, can create artifacts that can be heard. The second reason is that some analog-to-digital converters, for one reason or another, sound better at higher sampling rates. The third, sadly, is a reflection of the various converter manufacturers' advertising claims. The first converter builders to claim 96 kHz (and a bit later, 192 kHz converters) gained market share by these claims—even when no major software developer was able to support the higher sampling rates.

Bit depth is a different issue. The theoretical dynamic range of a 16-bit signal is 96 dB—and a 24-bit signal has a theoretical dynamic range of around 144 dB—far more than is actually usable (or practical). With 0 dB being the softest sound that an average human can hear, normal conversation being from 60 to 70 dB, and sustained exposure to 95 dB being capable of causing permanent hearing damage, it's easy to see that the average recording will need nowhere near 96 dB of dynamic range. But there's more to it than that, and here's why: every time a mathematical function is performed on a digital audio signal, the bit depth of that track increases. Everything you do with a digital audio track is a mathematical function—from changing the level to adding a compressor plug-in. A number of different approaches to dealing with this increased bit depth have been implemented by software manufacturers. Some will use floating-point processing, some use fixed-point processing with intermediate bit depths up to 56 bits. In any case, at the end of the process, the file needs to be reduced back to the original 16- or 24-bit depth. The three options for this are truncating, rounding, and dithering. Truncating simply chops off those bits that that are longer than needed. This can add undesirable artifacts in the form of distortion to the signal. Rounding effectively performs a mathematical function to the last usable bit. For example, when converting a 24-bit file to a 16-bit file, the sixteenth bit will be rounded up or down in a consistent manner. While this is generally less obtrusive than truncating, it can also add artifacts, because of the consistent manner of the rounding. Dither, at its most basic, simply adds a small amount of noise to make the processing more random, and therefore, less noticeable. The Pow-R Dither used on the output buss of this track is a type 1 dither (the Pow-R Dither plug-in offers different dithering shapes and types); experimenting with the different varieties can be an instructive (or frustrating) experience, but is well worth the effort. With Digidesign's Pro Tools, there's a difference in the way auxiliary busses and master outputs process audio. Any plug-ins on an auxiliary buss are processed pre-fader—that is, the signal level that goes into the plug-in is not affected by the volume control. It's different with the master fader; the plug-ins are post-fader. This means that the level of the fader affects the levels going into plug-ins inserted on the master fader. This may not be an issue in many applications, but if, for example, the master output fader is used to create a fade out at the end of a song, that would have an impact on any plug-ins—especially a limiter like the L3—that would change the way the fade sounds. In that application, the first part of the fade (those signals that are above the threshold of the limiter) would be minimally affected by the fade, and only after the signal strength goes below the threshold of limiting would the fade proceed as intended. For this reason, I'll usually make it a practice to route all of the tracks in a project through an auxiliary buss that contains an EQ (if desired) and the limiter. With some mixes it's not an issue, but with others, it is.

AUTOMATION

"Anyway" required little in the way of automation; only the Strings 1 track used it with a 3 dB rise in volume level during the solo section as the only automation written on an individual track. Besides that, the master fader (with only the dither plug-in inserted) was used to create the fade at the end of the song.

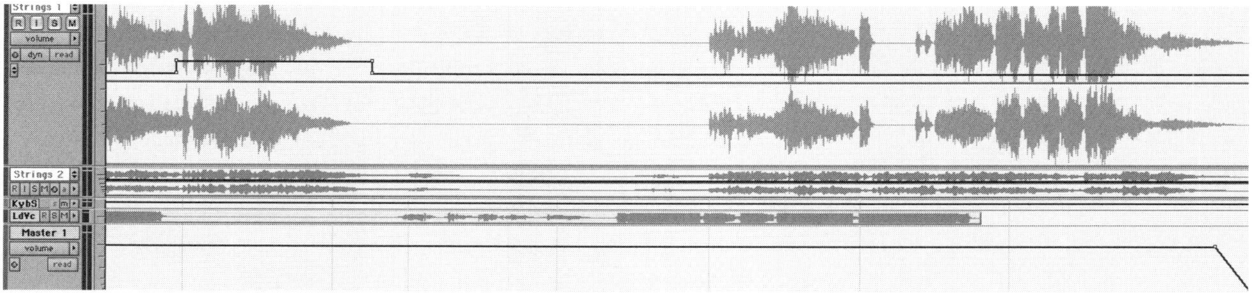

Fig. 1.36. Automation

PRINTING MIXES

When printing the mixes of each song in this volume, my approach was consistent: I use a track that plays continuously for the full length of the song (typically an acoustic guitar track or the piano track) to set the length of the mix. I'll trim the chosen track to just before the first note. By "just before," I mean that I'll trim that track to within a single frame, or one-thirtieth of a second before the start. Then, at whatever point the fade at the end of the track is completed, I'll trim the back of that same track about a frame after the fade. In Pro Tools, selecting this trimmed track will cause the program to play from the beginning to the end of that track (and thereby from the beginning to the end of the mix) now having excess audio or time at the beginning or end. In those situations where multiple mixes of a song must be done—for example, if a producer wants vocal up or vocal down versions, TV mixes, instrumental mixes, and so on—all of the versions are the same length, and can be easily lined up for editing.

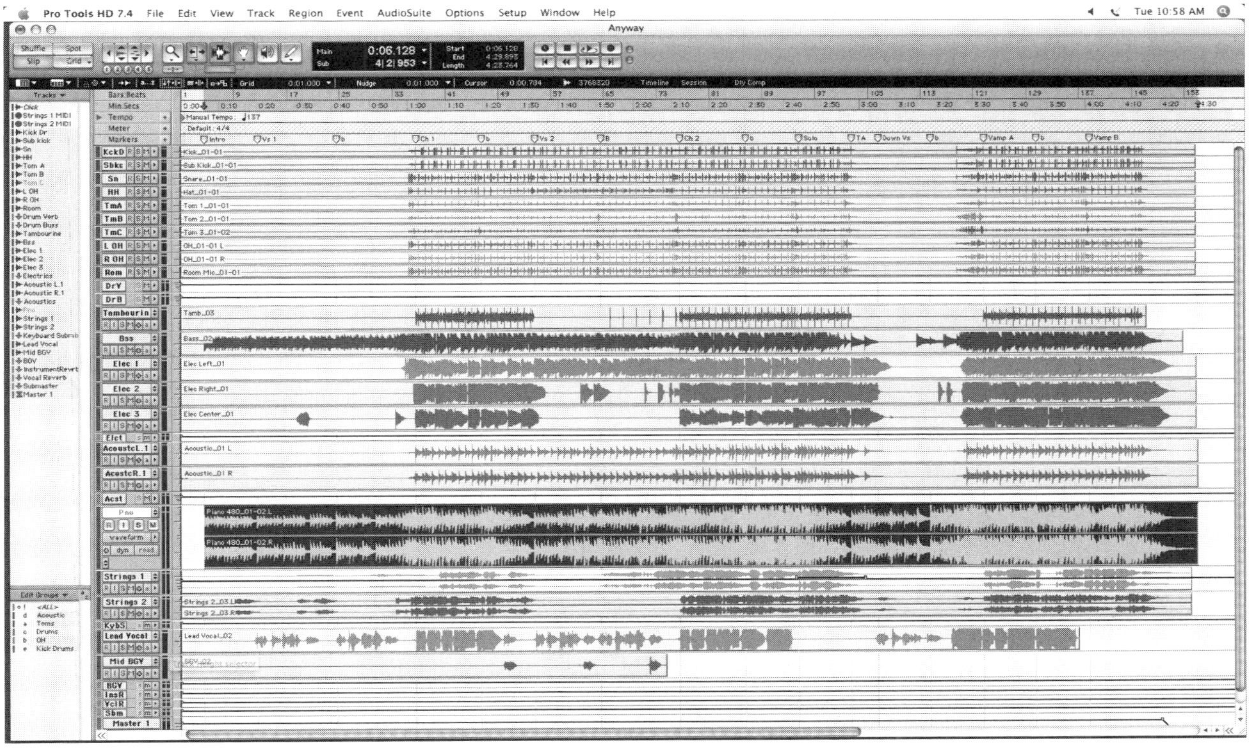

Fig. 1.37. Print Mix

MASTERING

"Anyway," like the other tracks in this project, was not mixed with the intention of mastering. Because of this, EQ was inserted on the master aux buss, along with the limiter. If this song had been going to a mastering house (a process I strongly suggest for projects intended for commercial release), the processing on this buss would have been removed or at least used in a minimal fashion—especially the L1 and L3—so that the mastering engineer would not be hampered or constricted because the mix had already been limited.

CHAPTER 2

"Before He Cheats"

(As Recorded by Carrie Underwood)

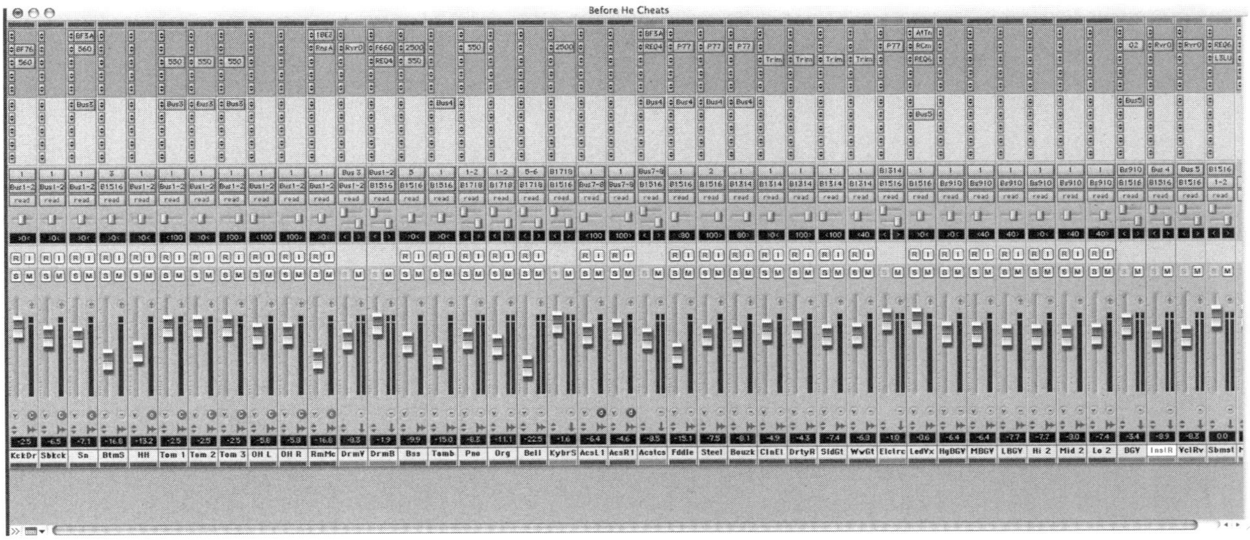

Fig. 2.1. Mix Window

"Before He Cheats" falls squarely into the "pop country" category; there's more than a passing similarity between the guitar and drum sounds on this song and the guitar and drum sounds of '80s rock. The processing of the various instruments and their relative balances reflect these similarities, though the sound (and the placement) of the lead vocal is quite different. The background vocals are also fairly involved, and will take some special handling.

DRUMS

The drum tracks on "Before He Cheats" were recorded without EQ and with little compression, so that the mixing process would be a bit more informative; if I made all the necessary EQ adjustments in the tracking stage, then little or no EQ would be needed on the drums. By recording without processing, the raw tracks can be manipulated in a manner that's a bit more creative. You may notice that there are two kick drum tracks—one track, labeled "kick," is from a Shure Beta 52 placed inside the drum about three inches from the batter head and routed through a Daking preamp, while the "subkick" track was recorded with a Yamaha Subkick placed directly in front of the drum and recorded through a Great River NV preamp. These two signals sound quite different from each other; most mixing engineers will combine the two sounds while processing each as needed to create the final kick drum sound.

Fig. 2.2. Drum Mix

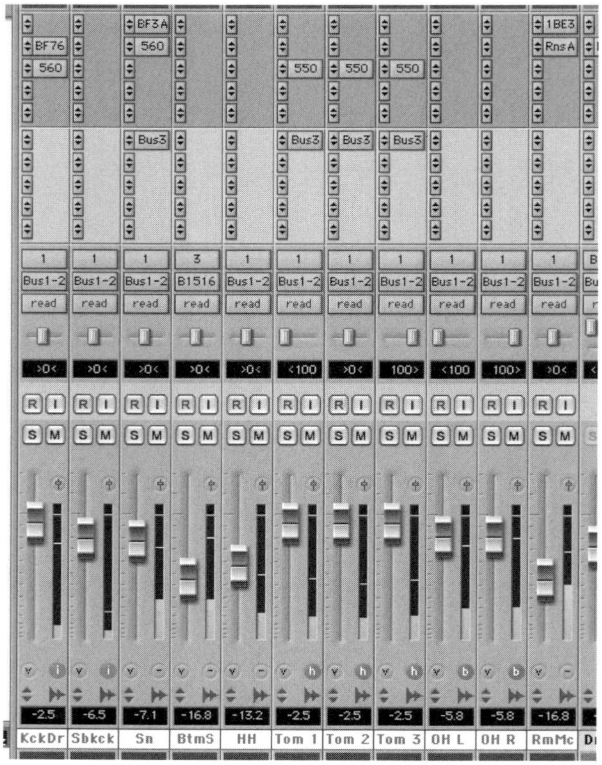

When building a track from the drums up, I've found that when setting the level of the kick (in this case, setting the levels of both kick tracks), it's a mistake to try and make the drums as loud and as full as possible before turning up the other instruments. This will usually cause problems when the other tracks are turned up. Keeping the kick drum level (at the output stage of the mixer) somewhere between –4 dBFS and –8 dBFS leaves the necessary room for all of the other instruments and sources to be added without overloading the output buss and requiring that all the tracks be turned down. Since it's generally a good idea to mix (and check mixes) at several different levels—from the lower threshold of audibility to the highest threshold of tolerance—keeping the kick drum at a fairly consistent –6 dB at the output of the DAW allows a certain amount of consistency when mixing an entire project and makes the job of mastering the final product much easier.

Experimenting with the levels of the two kick drum tracks before adding EQ or compression to find the best balance is usually a good practice, even though the processing (in this case, both EQ and compression) will change the levels of the track quite a bit. The reason for that experimentation is to get a feel for how the raw tracks sound, which in turn will give you an idea of what processing should be done. On "Before He Cheats," the kick track felt most solid with the subkick track (which is providing the lowest thump of the kick sound) 4 dB lower than the main kick track, so that the subkick level is at –6.5 dB and the kick level is at –2.5 dB. Of course, that all changed with the processing, but that's how things sometimes work out.

Before adding any EQ to the kick drum track, Bomb Factory's 1176 emulation, the BF76, was added to the kick drum track. The numbers on the BF76 don't translate to definite levels in decibels. By the way, the BF76, like the classic black-faced 1176, uses 0 as full up and the infinity sign (∞) for fully off. The attack time was fairly slow and the release time was pretty fast, and the unit was set to operate at a 4:1 compression ratio. Because of the slow attack and fast release times, the BF76 wasn't doing that much in the way of gain reduction, though it did add the characteristic 1176 texture to the kick drum.

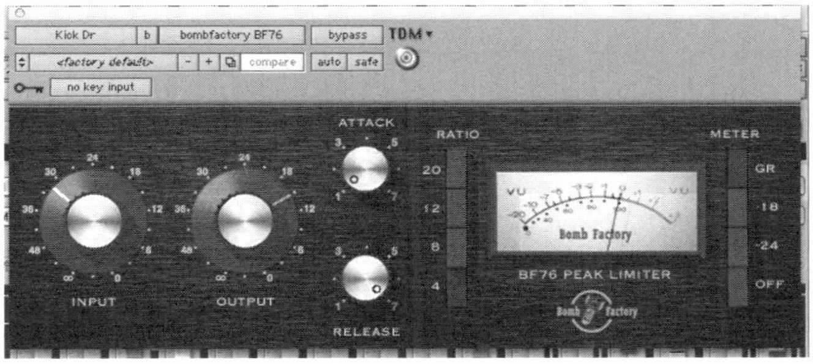

Fig. 2.3. Kick Compression

Bomb Factory BF76 Kick Drum Settings				
input	**output**	**attack**	**release**	**ratio**
32	15	1	7	4:1

I chose to use the Waves API EQ plug-ins for the drums on "Before He Cheats." These plug-ins are pretty faithful emulations of not only the famed API 10-band equalizer, but also the later 3-band 550A and 4-band 550B equalizers. Since the 560 EQs have fixed EQ points (rather than sweepable frequencies like most modern EQs), the frequencies chosen to boost or cut are determined by the design of the plug-in. In other words, with the API 560, it's not possible to cut 750 Hz (should that need to be done); the closest available frequency bands on the 560 are 500 Hz and 1 kHz. This, by the way, isn't necessarily a problem; some of the greatest records of the rock era were mixed before sweepable EQs for every track were available to recording engineers.

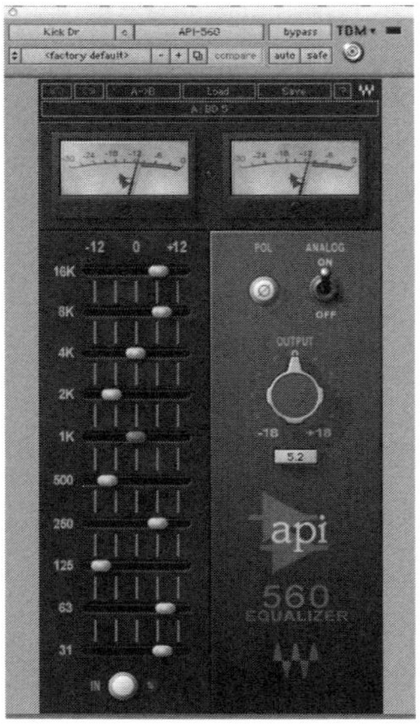

Fig. 2.4. Kick EQ

But to continue, the ten octaves on the 560 do offer a broad range of EQ possibilities. Here's a table showing each band and how they were set:

Waves API 560 Equalizer Kick Drum Settings	
center frequency	**change**
31 Hz	+7.3 dB
63 Hz	+8.3 dB
125 Hz	–9.6 dB
250 Hz	+6.1 dB
500 Hz	–7.6 dB
1 kHz	0 dB
2 kHz	–6.6 dB
4 kHz	0 dB
8 kHz	+7.3 dB
16 kHz	+6.5 dB

The output level of the 560 added 1.1 dB of gain going to the kick drum fader.

Snare

The main snare track was recorded with a Shure SM57 microphone above the snare. But on "Before He Cheats," there's a second microphone;

a Neumann KM 84 placed under the snare drum is referred to as the "bottom snare" mic.

Whenever there are multiple tracks from one source, such as these two snare drum tracks, it's very important to check the phase relationship between the two tracks. The mechanics of miking the top and the bottom of a drum mean that the two tracks will naturally be phase reversed; hitting the snare causes the top drum head to move away from the microphone, while the bottom drum head will move towards the microphone. The absolute phase of one of the tracks must be reversed so that the top and bottom snare tracks are in phase with each other. There are a couple of ways to do this; the best method is to do it at the tracking stage. The other method is to deal with it at the mix stage (not really an issue, since most DAWs have a way to invert the phase of individual tracks). In Pro Tools, that's an audio suite function called "invert." Invert does nothing more than invert the phase of a chosen track. The old-school way to figure out whether the tracks are phase reversed is to simply turn both tracks up to the same relative level and then mute (and un-mute) one of the two while listening to see if the sound changes for the better when one of them is muted. Do this with both of the tracks, and see if you hear anything problematic (for example, if there are dramatic subtractive tonal differences when both snare drum tracks are turned up).

The high-tech method is to simply look at the tracks to see if they're in phase (I'm referring to this as "high-tech" simply because it wasn't easy to do in the days when drums were recorded to tape). To determine whether one of the tracks is 180 degrees out of phase with the other, the easiest approach is to magnify the two tracks to visually ascertain what's going on. If you zoom in to the point that one hit on the snare drum fills up the screen, you should be able to see two things. The first is whether the initial impact for each of the two tracks goes in the same direction (in this case, the beginning of the curve that shows the signal should be positive, or up on both tracks). The second item to see is whether the drum tracks line up exactly; if they don't, it sometimes helps the sound to move one of the two tracks so that they *do* line up exactly. When I'm dealing with two snare tracks (and not two kick drum tracks), it seems to be less of an issue.

Fig. 2.5. Phase Reversed Snare Tracks

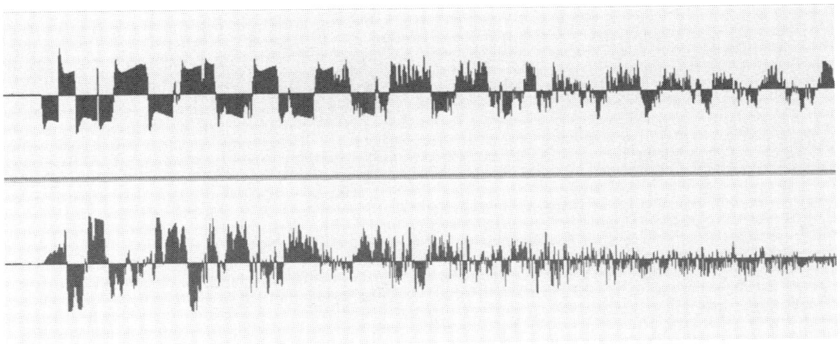

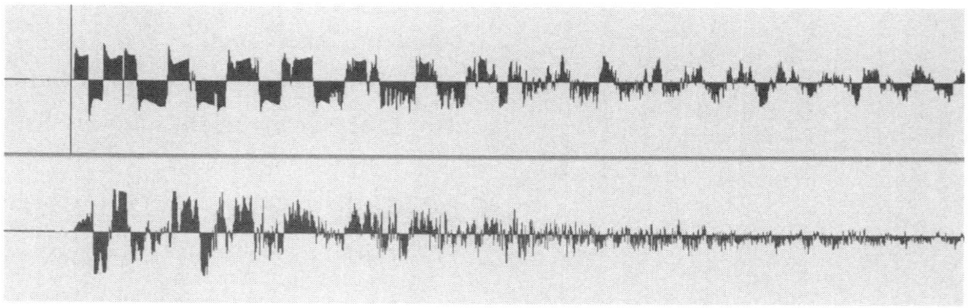

Fig. 2.6. Phase Corrected Snare Tracks

The level of the snare track is generally determined by the level of the kick drum; with the kick averaging around –6 dBFS, the snare drum seemed to fit with the rest of the track at about the same level—at around –6 dB. Naturally, that's song specific, but with this particular song, the kick and snare work well together at those levels. Though the snare fader volume is at –7.1 dB, there's a Bomb Factory compressor plug-in (a BF-3A, a software emulation of the UREI LA-3A), and an EQ (another API 560 plug-in) is boosting a number of frequencies. The bottom snare track will be discussed in a bit.

Compression/Limiting

The Bomb Factory BF-3A, like its analog counterpart, is a simple compressor. Essentially, there are input and output level controls and a switch that changes the ratio from compression to limiting. I'm going for a bit of mild compression with this plug-in, with a maximum of only 2 or 3 dB of gain reduction. The input level is set to 4 and the output level is set to a bit less than 4 (like the BF76, the numbers don't correlate to decibels). The switch is at the lower ratio "com" position. When the amount of gain reduction is this minimal, the box is acting more as a tone changer than as a full-on compressor. But that's not unusual; engineers have been doing exactly that in the analog domain for many years.

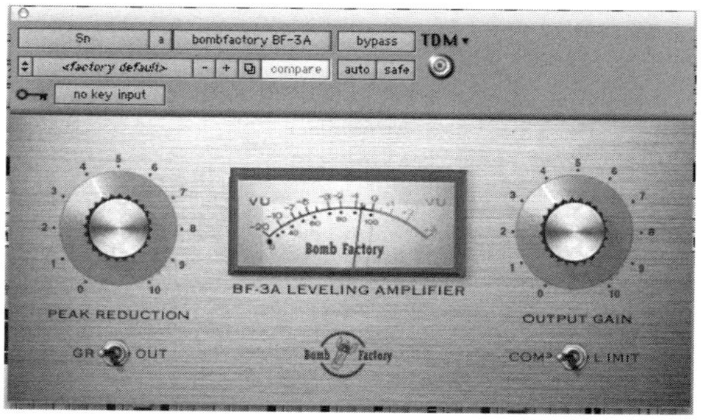

Fig. 2.7. Snare Compression

Snare EQ

The snare sound on "Before He Cheats" was also processed with an API 560 graphic EQ set in the following manner:

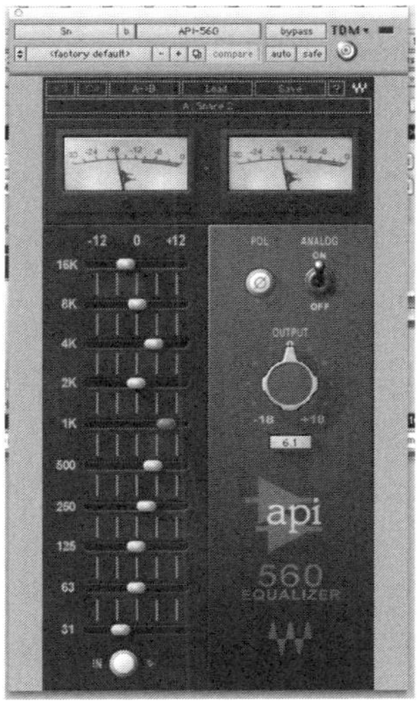

Fig. 2.8. Snare EQ

Snare Track EQ

center frequency	change
31 Hz	–4.3 dB
63 Hz	0 dB
125 Hz	0 dB
250 Hz	+3.1 dB
500 Hz	+4.9 dB
1 kHz	+8.5 dB
2 kHz	0 dB
4 kHz	+5.1 dB
8 kHz	+0.3 dB
16 kHz	–3.0 dB

You may notice the 4.9 dB boost at 500 Hz. Sure, 500 Hz can be obnoxious, but snare drums are obnoxious; it works out. The output level of the 560 was flat going to the snare drum fader. But in the case of "Before He Cheats," the snare track isn't the only source of the snare sound; there's also a bottom snare track.

Bottom Snare Drum

Any number of reasons, good and otherwise, can be given for miking the bottom of a snare drum. Certainly the sound of the resulting signal is different than that resulting from snare drums miked on top of the snare, but I've heard other reasons for this practice. One engineer said that he started doing it when 2-inch 24-track machines became available, simply because he couldn't think of anything else to do with all those extra tracks. Those who started recording music within the last five or ten years and who are used to the essentially unlimited tracks available in DAWs might not understand the quantum leap for engineers when 8-track machines (and later 16- and 24-track recorders) became available—not only were that many tracks intimidating on some level, they required a different recording paradigm from the engineers who were used to recording multiple instruments to one or two tracks, so that the other two tracks could be used for overdubs. In any case, once the bottom snare was recorded, the next question for those engineers was "What do we do with it now?" A bit earlier, we discussed the need to invert the phase on bottom snare tracks, either when tracking (using the phase switch on the mic pre) or at the mixing stage (some programs have a plug-in that does that, while others, including Digidesign's Pro Tools, have an offline process for inverting the track). Once the top snare and bottom snare tracks have the same phase relationship, some amount of experimentation can take place.

Simply bringing up the bottom snare track in volume changes the overall snare drum sound considerably. To begin with, the bottom snare track is brighter than the top snare track. This is partly because of the microphone's proximity to the metal snares (not only are the snares farther away from the top snare mic, they're also muffled by the thicknesses of the two drum heads between them), and partly due, at least with the tracks in this volume, to the use of a condenser microphone (Neumann KM 84) on the bottom snare, while a dynamic mic, (Shure SM57) was used on the top of the snare. But in addition to the brightness, the bottom snare sound is typically shorter as well, since the top snare head is likely to resonate more than the bottom head. All things being equal, external influences—from the toms causing a sympathetic resonance with the bottom snare to a bass amp sitting next to the drummer—can cause the snares to continue to vibrate.

There's also a third difference between the top and bottom snare tracks: the bottom snare track typically has less bleed from the other drums than the top mic. This is simple mechanics; while the bottom snare mic typically points directly at the snares from a couple inches distance, the top snare mic must point at an angle across the top head. And while there is likely to be a bit of bleed from the kick drum into the bottom snare mic (easily minimized with a high-pass filter), the top mic will be picking up sound from the toms, the hi-hat, and even the cymbals. Because of this isolation, the bottom snare is sometimes an excellent source for an effects send. For example, a mix may require a snare sound that is quite reverberant—the classic "power-balled" sound—while the hi-hat needs to be quite dry. If the top snare track is the only one used as an effects send, the bleed from the hi-hat into the snare may well make the hi-hat sound too reverberant. In this case, using the bottom snare track as an effects send for the reverb will minimize (or eliminate) the hi-hat bleed into the snare mic.

The bottom snare mic can also be used in a simpler way—to add a bit of brightness or cut to the snare sound. This is a more typical use for the bottom snare track, even though the track can sound quite obnoxious when heard in isolation. The top snare mic sounds very different from the bottom snare mic; often a combination of the two sounds better than either one alone. But don't be afraid to not use the bottom mic at all—many engineers never put a mic under the snare, and many others who record a bottom snare track never end up using it in the final mix. In this mix, the bottom snare is used simply to add a bit of snap, to help the snare sound cut through the mix. No EQ or compression was used on the bottom snare mic, and its level was set to –16.8 dB. Though it was mentioned as a possibility, the reverb send for this song came from the main snare track rather than the bottom snare track; an aux send on the main snare track was set to unity gain.

Hi-hat

Much like a bottom snare mic, the hi-hat mic can be used or not used, depending on the engineer, the drummer, and the song being mixed. Some engineers—especially those who tend to build their drums sound primarily from the overhead microphones—will often not even set up a mic for the hi-hat. Others regularly record the hat mic and just as regularly, mute that track and not use it at all. Other engineers will use and even emphasize the hi-hat track within the larger context of the overall drum sound and the song. When (if) the hi-hat track is used in the mix, it should be panned to reflect the drum set as a whole. If the drums are mixed from the drummer's perspective, pan the hat to the left; if mixing drums from the audience's perspective, pan the hat to the right.

Toms

For "Before He Cheats," the toms need to sound big and full, so they are both louder and more heavily equalized than the toms on "Anyway." They're panned from the drummer's perspective (with the high tom to the left and the floor tom to the right), with the high tom and the floor tom panned hard, 100 percent left and right rather than 60 to 80 percent, which would be more of a soft pan. Though there's no real reason to pan them in this manner rather than from the audience's perspective (with the high tom to the right and the floor tom to the left) other than the taste of the mixing engineer. That's a good enough reason to do so.

Fig. 2.9. Tom EQ

With a well-tuned drum set, the toms will vibrate sympathetically with the other drums; this is nothing to be concerned about. If you solo the drums during the sections that the drums are playing, you'll hear why some folks refer to this as tom hum. You'll also notice that the rest of the drum kit (kick, snare, cymbals) are bleeding into the tom mics; this isn't necessarily a bad thing—remember that a drum set is a single instrument, not a bunch of individual noise makers. In other chapters in this book, some different approaches to minimizing (or eliminating) tom hum will be discussed. On this track, I don't think that tom hum is a detriment to the sound of the mix. API 550B EQs were used for the toms on this track: the 550B is a 4-band EQ that offers 12 dB of boost or cut, and each of the three bands offers a choice of a number of fixed frequencies.

API 550B EQ Center Frequencies

low band	low mid band	high mid band	high band
30 Hz	75 Hz	800 Hz	2.5 kHz
40 Hz	150 Hz	1.5 kHz	5 kHz
50 Hz	180 Hz	3 kHz	7 kHz
100 Hz	240 Hz	4 kHz	10 kHz
200 Hz	500 Hz	8 kHz	12 kHz
300 Hz	700 Hz	10 kHz	15 kHz
400 Hz	1 kHz	12.5 kHz	20 kHz

The low and high band EQs can be switched between shelving and bell-shaped filters. As you can see, even though a maximum of four bands of EQ can be used at once, a large amount of control is available with the PA550B plug-in (and, naturally, the original API 550B module).

API 550B EQ Tom 1 Settings

frequency	100 Hz	500 Hz	800 Hz	5 kHz
change	+4 dB	–2 dB	–6 dB	+6 dB

API 550B EQ Tom 2 Settings

frequency	100 Hz	500 Hz	800 Hz	5 kHz
change	+4 dB (shelf)	–2 dB	–6 dB	+6 dB

API 550B EQ Tom 3 Settings

frequency	200 Hz	500 Hz	800 Hz	5 kHz
change	+6 dB (shelf)	–2 dB	–6 dB	+6 dB

The effects send (going to the drum reverb) on all three toms were set to –4 dB (less than the snare, which was at unity gain).

Overheads

Other than reminding the reader to pan the overheads in the same direction as the toms, there's little to add to the last chapter's discussion of overhead microphones. They can be used either to augment the primary drum sound that comes from the close mics, or they can *be* the primary sound, with the close mics used to augment them. Though the end result is quite different, both approaches are viable. The overheads are typically panned hard left and right. No EQ was used on the overhead mics (Telefunken M16s through a Phoenix Audio DRS-2 mic pre); the sound of the mics worked well with the track with no further manipulation. Both of the overhead tracks were set at –5.8 dB.

Room Mic

Because "Before He Cheats" has a rocking drum track, the room mic track will see a bit more use in this mix. The ambience that is on the room mic track (recorded with a Telefunken U 47 in an omni-directional pattern) can be used to add a texture to the drum tracks that can't be precisely duplicated in any other manner. In general, the idea of the room mic is to use the reflected ambience of the room rather than the direct sound from the drums themselves. To help achieve that goal, a high-pass filter is used to minimize or eliminate those frequencies below 400 Hz. A 12 dB-per-octave slope on the high-pass filter means that below the cutoff frequency, the signal is decreased by a substantial 12 dB per octave. This means that 200 Hz is 12 dB lower in level than 400, and that 100 Hz is 24 dB lower in level than those frequencies above the cutoff point.

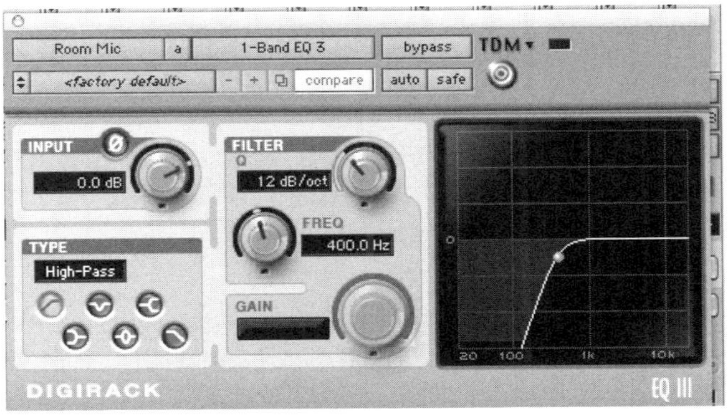

Fig. 2.10. Room Mic EQ

But after that is done, a hard limiter plug-in was inserted to the room-mic track; the fast attack on the limiter (especially with the high threshold setting used) helped to minimize, but not eliminate, the attack of the drums while the fast release time brought up the reflections (because of the room's design, mid and high frequencies are more present). The limiter used was Waves Renaissance Axx, a plug-in designed for guitar, but eminently workable for this application. The threshold of the plug-in was set at –23 dB, and the output of the compressor was set at –6 dB. The low threshold means that up to 20 dB of gain reduction was taking place, giving the soloed room mic a pretty gnarly sound. But brought up under the rest of the drums, it worked well at adding ambience.

Digirack 1-band EQ III Room Mic Settings	
parameter	low
slope	12 dB/Octave
frequency	400 Hz
input	0 dB
filter	high-pass

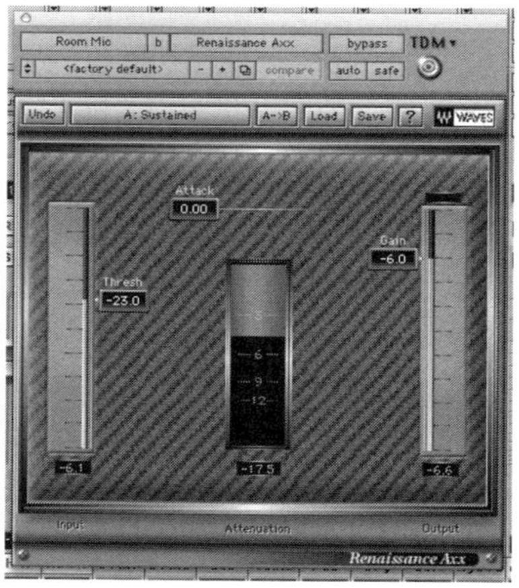

Fig. 2.11. Room Limiter

Waves Renaissance Axx Room Mic Settings

Threshold: –23.0 dB
Attack: .00 ms
Gain: –6.0 dB

Drum Routing, Grouping, and Effects

The tracks that make up the drum kit do not go directly to the submaster output; instead, they are routed to a stereo buss so that EQ and a stereo buss compressor can be inserted across the whole kit. Remember that ultimately, a drum set is a single instrument; each drum in the set is part of the whole. By bussing all of the drum tracks together, you have control over not only the overall level of the kit, but to any processing that needs to affect the entire kit.

Several groups were created within the drum tracks as a whole. One group consists of the three tom tracks, another group had only the two overhead cymbal tracks, while the third was for the two kick drum tracks. The last group included all of the drum tracks, but not the reverb return or the drum buss fader. With the toms, once the relative levels are set, it's more common to adjust the volumes of all three to adjust their relation to the rest of the kit rather than to adjust each tom individually. The overhead tracks and the kick drums tracks were grouped for the same reason; once the relative levels of the tracks in each group are set, their levels (in relation to the rest of the track) is likely going to remain constant. Though the drum group is usually inactive, it's sometimes convenient to turn all of the tracks up or down to optimize the levels going to the drum buss.

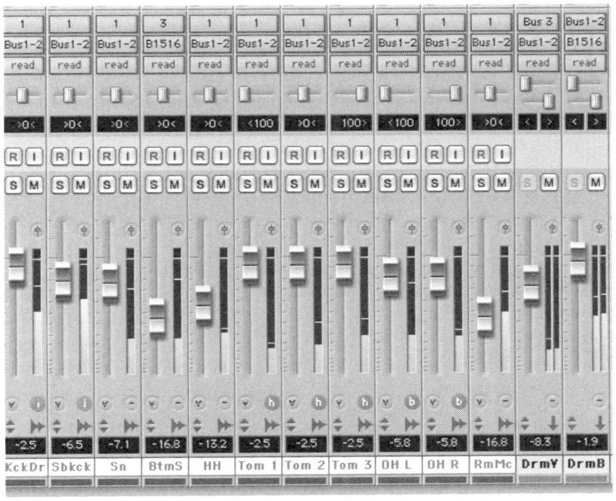

Fig. 2.12. Drum Routing and Grouping

It's common practice to instantiate a reverb that's used only for the drums (and sometimes the percussion). Though the reverb setting for the drums might use the same type of reverb sound as other instruments, it's more common on contemporary records to give them their own acoustic space. Setting up an effects send just for the drums is quite easy to do. In the sessions on the DVD, I use a mono auxiliary send that is dedicated to the drums—specifically, to the snare and toms. The overheads and room mics aren't usually sending anything to the drum reverb. From time to time, the room mics will be used as part of the reverb send. A mono aux input track is created, and a stereo reverb is inserted on that track, becoming a stereo effects return. The output of the drum reverb is often sent to the drum buss rather than to the submaster, so that adjusting the volume of the drum buss also adjusts the volume of the drum reverb.

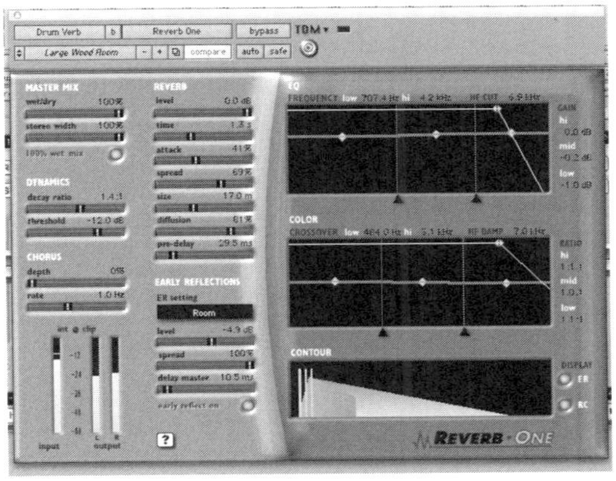

Fig. 2.13. Drum Reverb

The drum reverb on "Before He Cheats" is a Digidesign Reverb One set to a slightly altered Large Wood Room preset. Digi's Reverb One has many parameters that can be altered to suit the needs of a given track, in addition to a whole bunch of presets. Here's a table that shows these settings a bit more clearly:

Reverb One Drum Reverb Settings	
parameter	**setting**
wet/dry	100%
stereo width	100%
decay ratio	1.4:1
threshold	–12 dB
reverb level	0 dB
reverb time	1.3 seconds
attack	41%
spread	69%
size	17.0 meters
diffusion	81%
pre-delay	29.5 ms
early reflection (ER) setting	room
ER level	–4.9 dB
ER spread	100%
ER delay master	10.5 ms

The Reverb One has a number of other settings available—a 3-band EQ, a high-frequency cut, high-frequency damping and even a "color" window that has more adjustments. But since these were not altered from the preset Large Wood Room, I won't bring them into the discussion—there are more than enough parameters for tweaking already mentioned. On the reverb return fader, the output of the drum reverb is set to –8.3 dB.

The stereo buss where all the drum tracks and the drum reverb end up (before being combined with the other instrument and vocal tracks) are where any processing that applies to the entire drum track are added. "Before He Cheats" has a compressor/limiter and an EQ on the drum buss. The compressor, a Fairchild 660 emulation, is only adding mild compression—less than 2 dB—with a fairly slow attack and release time. (The numbers on the input and threshold settings don't correspond to specific levels; rather they're graphic representations of the original Fairchild limiters.)

Fig. 2.14. Drum Buss Compressor

Fairchild 660 Drum Buss Settings			
control	input gain	threshold	time constant
setting	23	4.75	2

The EQ, a Waves Renaissance REQ-4, has a high-pass filter at 40 Hz and bell-shaped filters boosting 1.9 dB at 2.5 kHz and 3 dB at 7 kHz.

Fig. 2.15. Drum Buss EQ

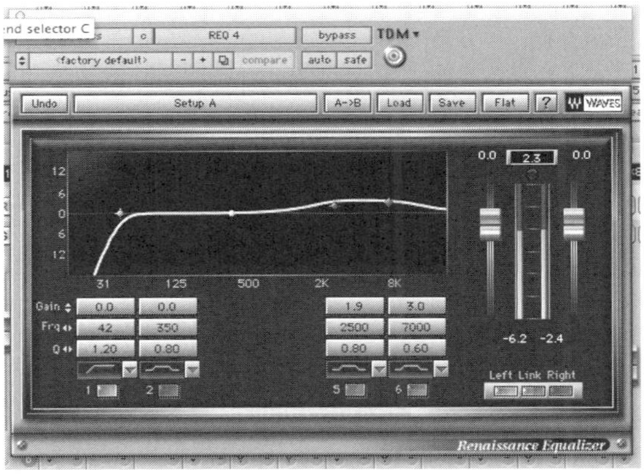

Waves Renaissance REQ-4 Drum Buss Settings				
parameter	band 1	band 2	band 3	band 4
gain	0 dB	0 dB	+1.9 dB	+3 dB
frequency	42 Hz	350 Hz	2500 Hz	7 kHz
Q	1.20	0.80	0.80	0.60
shape	low-pass	bell	bell	bell

BASS GUITAR

The bass track on "Before He Cheats" was recorded using a Music Man 5-string StingRay bass; since it was recorded without any equalization, what you hear on the track is pretty much an honest representation of the sound of that instrument. Continuing with the API-dominant mix on "Before He Cheats," an API 2500 Compressor and an API 550B EQ were used on the bass track. The compressor is the first plug-in in the signal path, so that will be discussed first.

Fig. 2.16. Bass Compressor

The settings were intended to produce only a mild amount of compression (though, like its analog counterpart, the 2500 is capable of doing much more interesting things). The threshold of the compressor was set to +8.75, with a fast attack (0.03 ms) and slow (1 second) release. A compression ratio of 4:1 was chosen, along with a medium setting on the threshold knee.

SOFT KNEE VERSUS HARD KNEE

Some (though not all) compressors offer a choice of either a soft knee or hard knee threshold. A hard knee compressor (the most common) doesn't compress at all until the threshold is passed; at that point, its compression ratio matches the settings on the unit. A soft knee compressor actually begins compressing somewhere a little above the threshold at a very small compression ratio—a ratio that increases as the threshold is passed until at a point a little below the threshold, the compression ratio matches the settings on the plug-in. In many cases, this can make the onset of compression more transparent.

The API 2500 compressor (and the plug-in version) has settings not only for hard knee and soft knee, but also a medium knee that falls somewhere in the middle of the other two. It also has a couple of other settings that are rather unique; its "detector" setting, called "thrust," essentially places a filter into the detection circuitry, which means that the compressor can be set to ignore low frequency information. Thrust inserts any of three different filters before the compressor's RMS detector. Normal position is flat; "med" decreases the energy in the low frequencies and slightly boosts the high frequencies; and "loud" decreases even more lows and adds more highs to the detector's input. This has the effect of making the low end of signals with a lot of low frequency content like electric bass or drums appear louder, since the compressor doesn't see those low frequencies as crossing the threshold to compression. While this can be (and has been done for years) by using an EQ in the sidechain of the compressor with a high-pass filter setting, the API 2500 does it without an external sidechain EQ.

The "type" function allows the user to choose between two types of circuit topology—in truth, the choice is between emulations of two types of circuit topology, but the principle is the same. The old-style feedback detector is when the output of the compressor is fed back to the filter (and the RMS detector). Feed forward simply connects the thrust filter to the input of the compressor. This means that the 2500 can be made to act more like an old-style compressor such as the Fairchild 660 (feedback) or newer and more aggressive, like a UREI 7110 limiter/compressor (feed forward).

API 2500 Compressor Bass Compression Settings

parameter	threshold	attack	ratio	release
setting	+8.75 dB	0.03 ms	4:1	1 second

API 2500 Compressor Bass Tone Settings

parameter	knee	thrust	type
setting	medium	loud	new (feed forward)

Fig. 2.17. Bass EQ

Bass EQ				
frequency	50 Hz	150 Hz	1.5 kHz	2.5 kHz
change	+4 dB (shelf)	–2 dB	–4 dB	–2 dB (shelf)

The bass track was EQ'd with the help of an API 550B plug-in. The low frequencies were boosted by 4 dB, while the mid and high frequencies were reduced in level. The output level of the bass was –9.9 dB

PERCUSSION

The only percussion used on "Before He Cheats" is a tambourine, which plays on beats two and four during the intro and the choruses. No EQ or compression was used on the tambourine track. An effects send was added to the track (with the level set at unity gain) and sent to the instrument reverb track (discussed below). The tambourine track was bussed to the submaster, and the fader was set to –15 dB.

KEYBOARDS

"Before He Cheats" has three keyboard tracks—piano, organ, and bells (which only appear for a few measures).

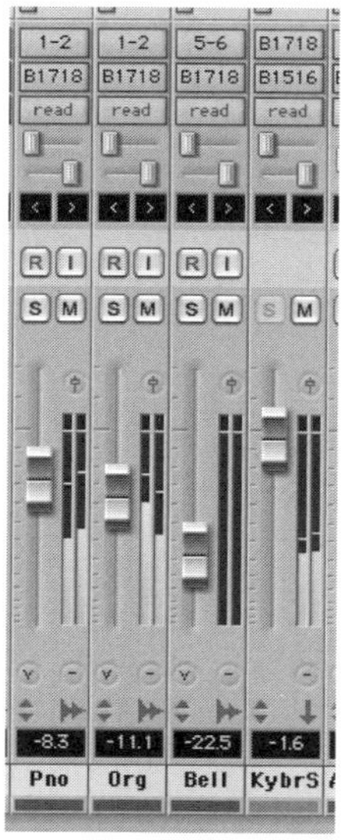

Fig. 2.18. Keyboard Buss

Fig. 2.19. Piano EQ

Piano

Since the piano on the original recording is a bit brighter than the one used for this volume, the EQ was used to bring the track sound a bit closer to the original. Another API 550B EQ was used for the piano track, with the following settings:

API 550 Piano EQ				
frequency	**50 Hz**	**700 Hz**	**5 kHz**	**10 kHz**
change	–4 dB (shelf)	–4 dB	+5 dB	+9 dB

The output level of the piano track (which is sent to the keyboard buss), is –8.3 dB.

Organ

The organ track was neither equalized nor compressed on this track other than the buss compression used on the keyboard buss. The organ fader was set at: –11.1 dB.

Bells

A Korg 05R/W module provided the bell sound used in the down section that follows the bridge (a module that proves its usefulness on a regular basis for the quality of its sounds). No EQ was used, and the buss compressor took care of that function.

Keyboard Buss

The three keyboard tracks were bussed to a stereo buss with an API 2500 compressor inserted. The compressor was set with a threshold of 1 dB above unity. An attack time of 3 ms and a long release time, coupled with a 3:1 compression ratio allow the buss compressor to control the immediate transients while not sounding over-compressed. In addition to the above settings, the 2500 plug-in had a medium knee and a loud setting on the thrust control (as discussed above, the thrust control works by inserting a high-pass filter on the compressor's side-chain). The output level of the keyboard buss is –1.6 dB below unity gain.

Fig. 2.20. Keyboard Compressor

API 2500 Compressor Keyboard Buss Compression Settings				
parameter	**threshold**	**attack**	**ratio**	**release**
setting	+1.0 dB	3.0 ms	3:1	0.52 seconds

API 2500 Compressor Keyboard Buss Tone Settings			
parameter	knee	thrust	type
setting	medium	loud	old (feed back)

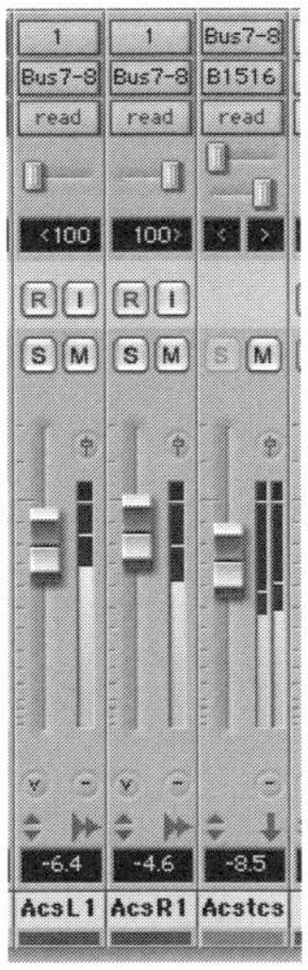

Fig. 2.21. Acoustic Buss

ACOUSTIC GUITAR

The two tracks of acoustic guitar are panned hard left and right, with output levels of –6.4 dB and –4.6 dB respectively. These tracks are bussed to the acoustic submaster, which has a Bomb Factory BF-3A compressor and a Waves Renaissance EQ-4 inserted.

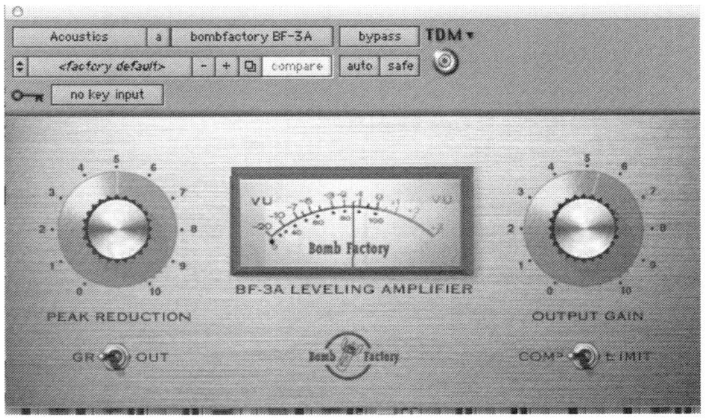

Fig. 2.22. Acoustic Compressor

The BF-3A has the input at 5, the output at 5.5 and the compress/limit switch set to compress (a lower ratio than limiting).

Fig. 2.23. Acoustic EQ

Waves Renaissance EQ4 Acoustic Buss Settings				
parameter	band 1	band 2	band 3	band 4
gain	0	0	+4 dB	+6 dB
frequency	120 Hz	350 Hz	3,400 Hz	5.5 kHz
Q	0.80	0.80	0.80	0.60
shape	high-pass	bell	bell	shelving

The level of the acoustic guitar buss was automated. Automation will be discussed in a bit more detail below.

FIDDLE

The fiddle track was panned 80 percent to the left, and the output level was set to –10.8 dB. The only processing used on the track was a Purple Audio MC77 plug-in, which is an emulation of a UREI 1176. The input was set to 34 and the output was set to 15, with the attack at 3, the release set to 5, and a compression ratio of 4:1. The effects send on the fiddle (which is sent to the instrument reverb) is set at –3.4 dB.

Fig. 2.24. Fiddle Compressor

Bomb Factory BF76 Fiddle Settings				
input	**output**	**attack**	**release**	**ratio**
34	15	3	5	4:1

STEEL

The steel track was panned 100 percent to the right, and the output level was set to –7.5 dB. The same processing was used on this track as the fiddle track—a Purple Audio MC77 plug-in, which is an emulation of a UREI 1176. The input was set to 32 and the output was set to 14, with the attack at 3, the release set to 5, and a compression ratio of 4:1 The steel's effect send was set at –4 (and is also sent to the instrument reverb).

Fig. 2.25. Steel Compressor

Bomb Factory BF76 Steel Settings				
input	**output**	**attack**	**release**	**ratio**
32	14	3	5	4:1

BOUZOUKI

The bouzouki track was panned 100 percent to the right, and the output level was set to –7.5 dB. The same processing was used on this track as the fiddle track—the Purple Audio MC77. The bouzouki's effects send, which goes to the instrument reverb, was set to –4.9 dB.

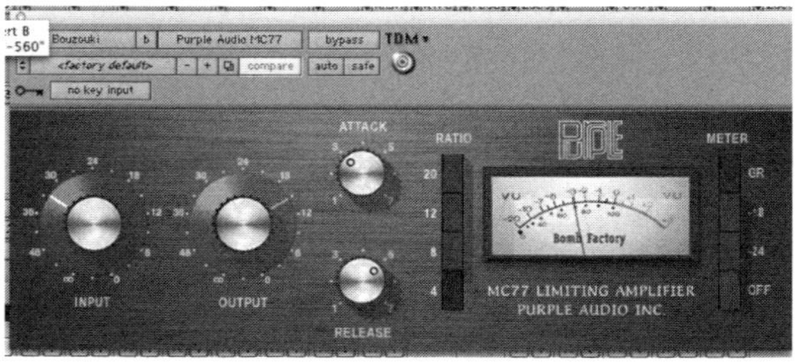

Fig. 2.26. Bouzouki Compressor

Bomb Factory BF76 Bouzouki Settings				
input	output	attack	release	ratio
32	14	3	5	4:1

You may notice, if you listen to country radio with a critical ear, that a number of rather odd instruments can show up in the latest country singles. For example, both "Before He Cheats" and Jo Dee Messina's "My Give a Damn's Busted," have a bouzouki as one of the rhythm instruments. Some instruments—electric sitar, electric 12-string, guitjo (essentially a guitar with a banjo body) and even the venerable Danelectro "tic-tac" basses and baritone guitars—will go unheard for decades but will then show up on a number of country records at essentially the same time. Some instruments appear because a single session musician decides to buy one, or happens to bring it out during a session. I've also heard mandolas and mandocellos used on contemporary country releases, along with such oddities as a Baby Taylor acoustic guitar. Tuned a 4th above standard tuning, this imparts an autoharp flavor to a track.

Another rather obscure instrument that appeared on a number of publisher's demos, though not (as yet) on a great number of records, is a tiple, a small member of the guitar family that has ten or twelve strings arranged in groups of three unisons, and tuned like the high strings of a guitar. The tiple started showing up on demos when one of Nashville's session players bought one and started bringing it along. I suspect that the only reason it didn't show up on a lot of records is because none of the demos that featured it were recorded and released by an artist. It seems to take just one big song with a unique sound before a half dozen other songs emulate that sound.

ELECTRIC GUITARS

There are four electric guitar tracks on "Before He Cheats": a clean guitar (panned center with an output of –4.9 dB), a dirty guitar (panned 100 percent right at –4.3 dB below unity), a slide guitar (panned 100 percent left at –7.4 dB), and a wah-wah guitar that's panned left at 40 percent with an output level of –6.8 dB. But each of these instruments has a trim plug-in inserted. All the trims do is reduce the level of the signal. The electric guitar trims are all set at –8 dB.

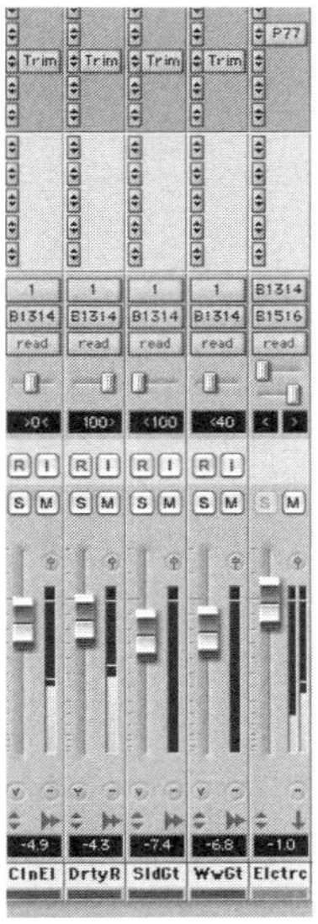

Fig. 2.27. Electric Guitar Buss

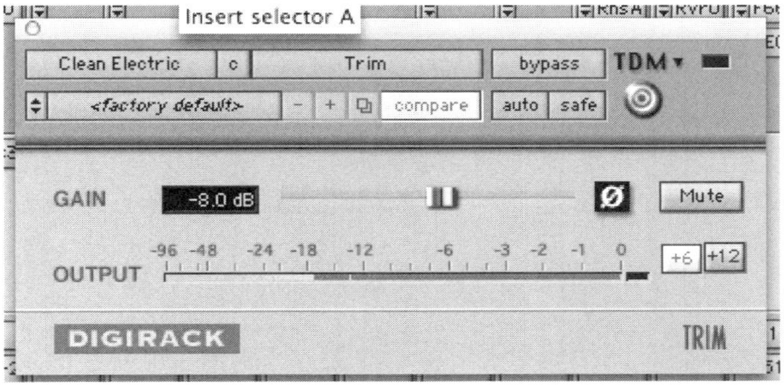

Fig. 2.28. Electric Trim

The reason for adding a trim plug-in to the guitar is two-fold (though one of the two reasons doesn't come into play in this song). The first is that some plug-ins don't handle extremely hot signals gracefully; a trim can reduce the input level to a point that even finicky plug-ins can deal with it. That doesn't apply here, since there are no other plug-ins on these tracks. Therefore, the second reason that these trims were inserted was simply so that the faders for each track can be closer to unity gain. This is a holdover from the analog mixing days, when many engineers wanted to keep all the faders near the "sweet spot" of their travel, where they offered the finest resolution. In those days, the input was trimmed via a pot at the top of the console. In essence, you might say that the trims were added to these tracks to remind readers that it's okay to avoid running levels at the very top of the faders.

The electric guitars are bussed together to the aptly named "electric guitar buss," where another Purple Audio MC77 was inserted into the signal path.

Fig. 2.29. Electric Buss Compressor

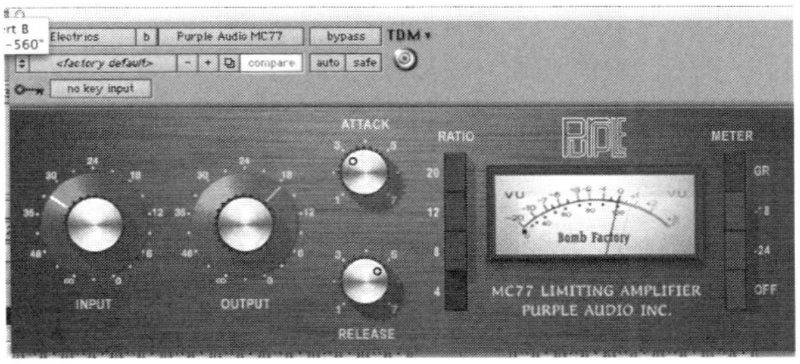

Bomb Factory BF76 Electric Guitar Buss Settings				
input	output	attack	release	ratio
33	18	3	5	4:1

LEAD VOCAL

The lead vocal on "Before He Cheats" has three different processors on it, as well as an effects send that send the lead (and background) vocals the vocal reverb. The first is the Antares Auto-Tune 4 plug-in. This wasn't done necessarily because I feel that the singer needs to be tuned (the tracks on the DVD are not tuned; you can form your own opinions); it's simply that the Auto-Tune plug-in isn't particularly transparent; everything that passes through it, tuned or not, develops a bit of that "Auto-Tune sound." And like it or not, that's a big part of the sound of country records these days. Fortunately, the over-tuned, machine-like voices that ended up on a couple of big artists' records seem to have been a fad that has run its course.

In any event, the Auto-Tune plug-in was set to very mild levels. (A number of major artists' vocals are adjusted with Auto-Tune. Some vocal-tuning engineers use the Melodyne program, while others have adopted the newer Waves Tune. But Auto-Tune is still the biggie.) The way that Auto-Tune is used depends greatly on the budget; those sessions with little to no budget do what you see here—Auto-Tune set on automatic, where it's a "set and forget" process. Those who have a bit more time/money to spend on tuning would involve setting the retuning speed much higher than I've set it for "Before He Cheats" and the tracking to a lot tighter setting. Then, while playing the song, only those words or phrases which cause the plug-in to wobble, move the vocal to the wrong note, or otherwise sound funny are tuned manually in the graphic tuning mode. With major label releases (with major label budgets), the entire lead vocal track may be tuned in the graphical mode.

Fig. 2.30. Lead Vocal Auto-Tune

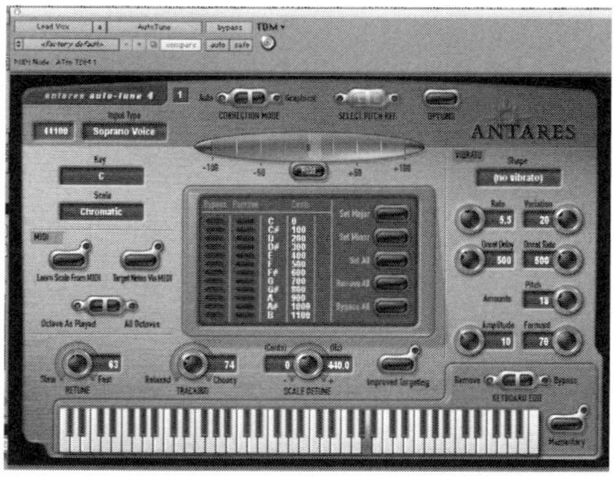

Antares Auto-Tune 4 Settings:

Input Type: Alto/Tenor Voice
Retune: 63
Tracking: 74

The lead vocals were compressed with the Renaissance compressor. The threshold (the level at which compression begins) was set at –10.6 dB, but since the peaks on the vocal track come perilously close to full scale, that allows for quite a bit of gainreduction—around 9 dB.. Does this make the vocals sound compressed? Sure. But that's part of the sound of records these days.

Fig. 2.31. Lead Vocal Compressor

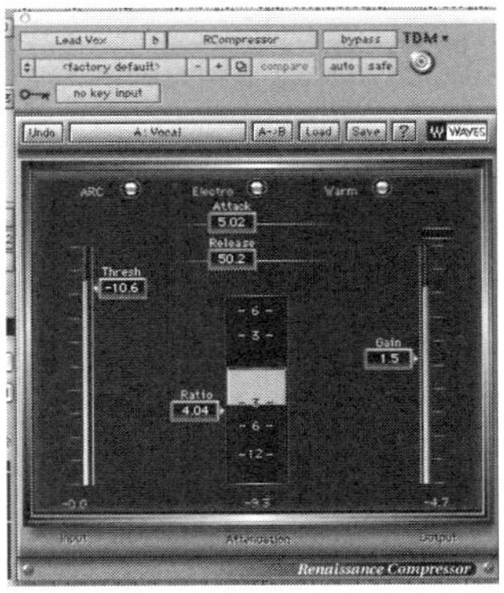

Waves Renaissance Compressor Lead Vocal Settings				
threshold	**attack**	**release**	**ratio**	**gain**
–1.6 dB	5.02	50.2	4.04:1	+1.5 dB

A Waves Renaissance EQ-6 is also on the lead vocal track, not doing anything major, but simply touching up frequencies as needed. Here are the settings on the vocal EQ:

Fig. 2.32. Lead Vocal EQ

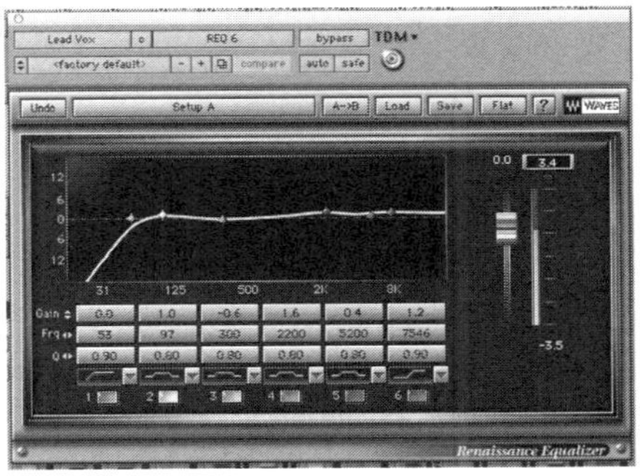

Waves Renaissance REQ-6 Lead Vocal Settings						
parameter	**band 1**	**band 2**	**band 3**	**band 4**	**band 5**	**band 6**
gain	0	+ 1 dB	–0.6 dB	+1.6 dB	+0.4 dB	+1.2 dB
frequency	53 Hz	97 Hz	300 Hz	2.2 kHz	5.2 kHz	7.5 kHz
Q	0.80	0.80	0.80	0.80	0.80	0.90
shape	high-pass	bell	bell	bell	bell	shelving

BACKGROUND VOCALS

There are basically three background vocal parts on "Before He Cheats"—a high, a mid, and a low BGV. Since there's also a part in the song where the background vocals overlap, three more tracks were necessary for the overlapped vocals, making a total of six tracks of BGVs. All six of the background vocal tracks were bussed to the stereo BGV track. A consistent panning scheme for the background vocals is to leave the high voice in the center, the middle voice panned 40 percent to the left, and the low voice panned 40 percent to the right. By doing this, the voices are slightly separated, but still sound as though they're part of the same group in the same part of the soundfield. Keeping all of the voices panned to the center would have been fine, but I like the slight panning better. The overlapping vocals were panned in the same manner. A Waves Q2 Paragraphic EQ was inserted on the BGV buss.

Fig. 2.33. BGV Buss

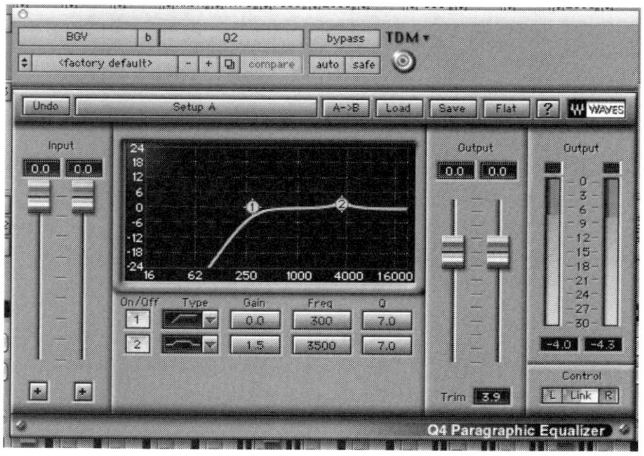

Fig. 2.34. BGV EQ

Settings for Waves Q2 on the BGV Buss		
parameter	**band 1**	**band 2**
gain	0	+1.5 dB
frequency	300 Hz	3,500 Hz
Q	7.0	7.0
shape	high-pass	bell

This plug-in is a simple two-band EQ that allows each band to be used as either a shelving filter, a bell filter, a high- or low-pass filter. High-passing at 300 Hz removes unneeded frequencies, while the slight boost at 3.5 kHz adds a bit of cut to the BGVs.

Thoughts on Background Vocals

Background vocals can be really fun to work with or they can be a giant pain that sucks up hours of mixing time. One of the things that can really save time in the mix is to make sure that when recording the background vocal, all of the parts are put consistently onto specific tracks. For example, if the background vocal has a high, a mid, and a low track, make sure that each of these parts is on the same track all the way through. This isn't always as easy as it sounds; it's not uncommon for the verses to a song to have fewer background vocal parts than the choruses. And when the background vocal parts are doubled, things can get even messier. If a project comes in to be mixed that has different vocal parts scattered through a number of different tracks, it's often worth taking a few minutes to sort through them and re-organize all of the vocals so that they make sense to you.

When vocals are doubled (that is, each of the parts is sung twice), each of the two tracks of each part is typically panned hard left and right. Another option when three parts are doubled, is to pan one part 100 percent to the outsides with the middle parts at about 80 percent, and the third part to about 60 percent; this keeps a wide stereo spread while giving each track its own space in the stereo field.

There are also times when, at the mix stage, you realize that the parts *should* have been doubled, but weren't. Though the result isn't quite the same as it would be with actual sung vocals (and works better when the vocalists are singing oohs and aahs rather than words), here's a quick artificial doubling method: Duplicate the parts, and then nudge the duplicated tracks one frame (a thirtieth of a second) later than the original, and then pan the duplicates hard left and the original parts hard right. Though it sounds a bit artificial (and if the mix is summed to mono, can create major phase cancellation), this kind of duplication can be very useful when trying to make vocal tracks sound wider. If the original background vocal parts were sung all the way through the song rather than being sung once and then copied and pasted in the other sections of the song, it's sometimes possible to copy the first chorus (for instance), and paste it to three new tracks in the second chorus, and then paste the original second chorus into three new tracks of the first chorus. This, of course, can only work in specific situations—but when it does work, it's a lovely result.

When a mix consists of a lot of different elements, it's often hard to find the sonic space for every part to be heard. High-passing the background vocals to clear out room for other low frequency information can work quite well. The key is to set the high-pass filter so that essential information isn't missing. For example (again, this is song specific), the background vocal group can be high-passed somewhere between 500 and 600 Hz, which may have the added benefit of making them audible in the track at a bit lower level. By adding compression to the background vocal buss after they are high-passed, transients can be controlled without low frequencies making the backgrounds pump.

When the levels of the background vocals need to be automated—for instance, if in some parts of the song the vocalists are doing quiet, breathy oohs and in other parts of the song, they're singing in full voice—try writing the automation to the BGV master rather than on each part. This will not only keep the relative levels of the different parts the same, it may also ease a bit of the CPU load on DAWs that use the computer for all processing.

AUX SENDS AND BUSS PROCESSING

As mentioned earlier, the drums have their own reverb buss; a second aux send is dedicated to the instrument reverb, and is set to emulate a medium plate. This reverb is primarily used to add ambience to the acoustic instruments: acoustic guitars, fiddle, mandolin, and anything else that would benefit from it. On this track, the tambourine is also using the instrument reverb.

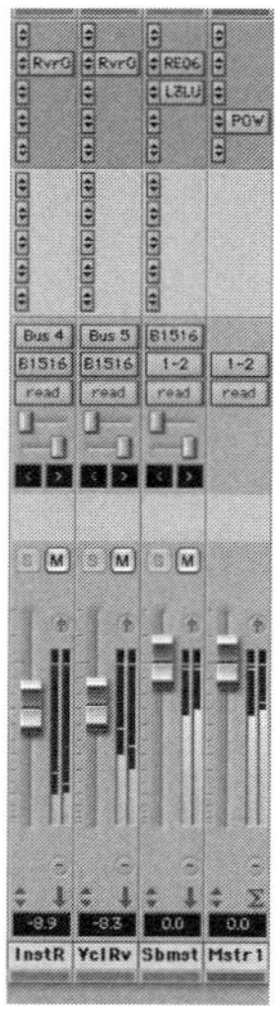

Fig. 2.35. Effects Sends and Buss Processing

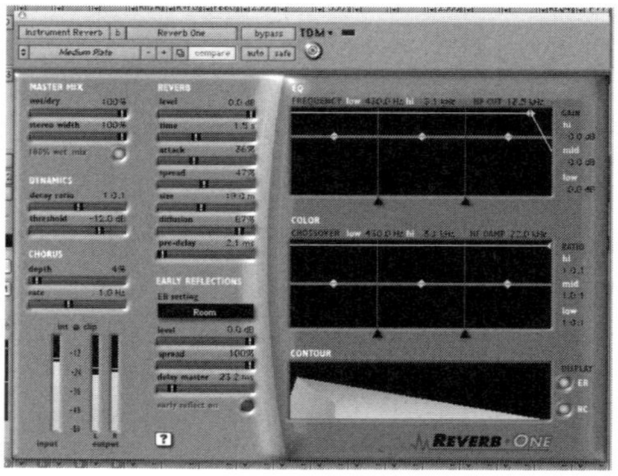

Fig. 2.36. Instrument Reverb

Digidesign Reverb One Instruments Settings	
parameter	**setting**
wet/dry	100%
stereo width	100%
decay ratio	1.0:1
threshold	–12 dB
reverb level	0 dB
reverb time	1.5 seconds
attack	36%
spread	47%
size	19.0 meters
diffusion	87%
pre-delay	2.1ms
early reflection (ER) setting	room
ER level	0 dB
ER spread	100%
ER delay master	23.2 ms

A third aux send is the vocal reverb. For "Before He Cheats," the reverb used is a Digidesign Reverb One with a modified early reflection preset named In the Studio. Should there be a need for different amounts of reverb between the lead and background vocals, that is controlled through the auxiliary sends. In this case, the lead vocal needed to be fairly dry, so the effect send was set to –6.2 dB, while the effects send from the BGV buss was at unity gain. This allowed the background vocals to be much more ambient than the lead vocal, which is the desired result.

Fig. 2.37. Vocal Reverb

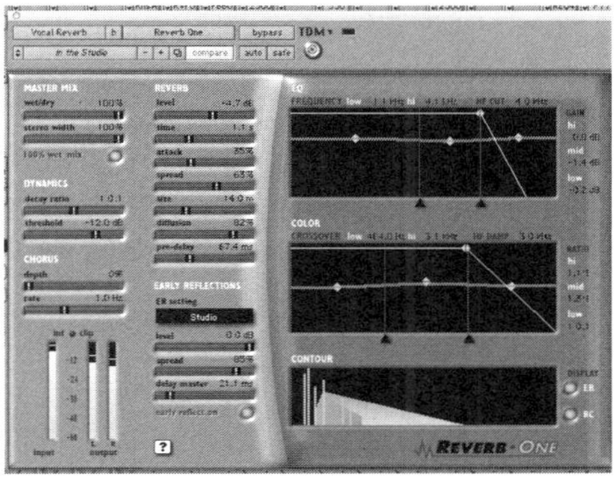

Reverb One Vocal Reverb Settings	
parameter	**setting**
wet/dry	100% wet
stereo width	100%
decay ratio	1.0:1
threshold	–12 dB
reverb level	–4.7 dB
reverb time	1.1 seconds
attack	35%
spread	63%
size	14.0 meters
diffusion	82%
pre-delay	67.4 ms
early reflection (ER) setting	studio
ER level	0
ER spread	85%
ER delay Master	21.1 ms

All of the tracks and effects returns end up at the submaster buss. This buss has an EQ plug-in, which can be used at need to tweak the overall tone of the mix, and a stereo limiter, which is used to bring up the average volume of the mix to contemporary levels. The EQ is the Waves Renaissance EQ-6; here are the settings on that plug-in:

Fig. 2.38. Buss EQ

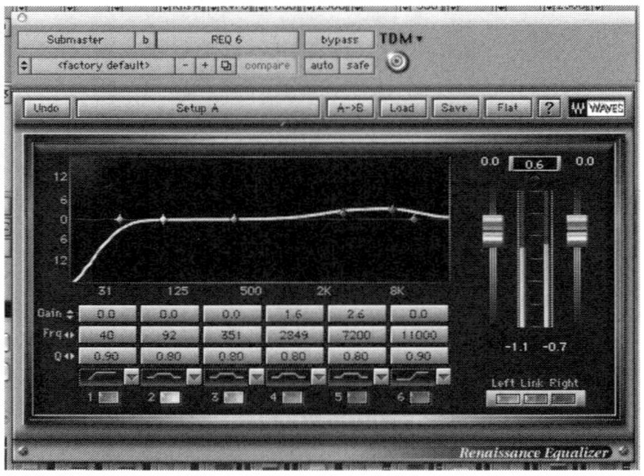

Waves Renaissance REQ-6 on the Submaster Buss						
parameter	**band 1**	**band 2**	**band 3**	**band 4**	**band 5**	**band 6**
gain	0 dB	0 dB	0 dB	+1.6 dB	+2.6 dB	0 dB
frequency	40 Hz	92 Hz	351 Hz	2.85 kHz	7.2 kHz	11 kHz
Q	0.90	0.80	0.80	0.80	0.80	0.90
shape	high-pass	bell	bell	bell	bell	shelving

As you can see, three of the six bands of EQ are unused, though I use the REQ-6 on the output buss of my mixes as a general rule in case the other bands are needed on given mix.

Fig. 2.39. Buss Limiter

Fig. 2.40. Dither

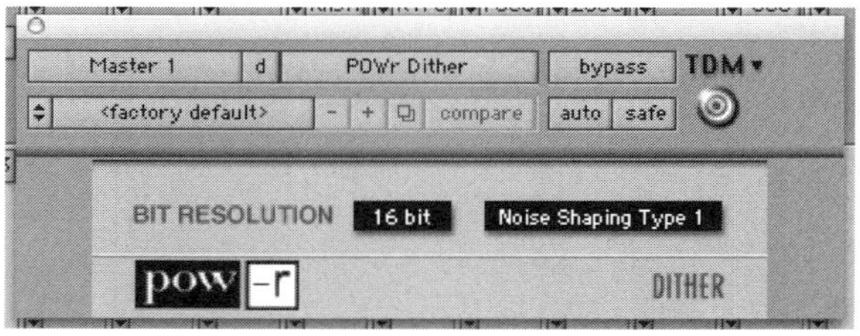

The output limiter (here, a Waves L3) should be used sparingly. Although different limiters have different strengths and weaknesses, the L1 was the original "look-ahead" limiter used (and over-used) as Pro Tools became more popular for mixing in the box. When overused, the L1 doesn't necessarily get any "louder" (remember that digital audio has an absolute upper limit of 0 dB), but it does add distortion. Using the Waves L3 on this mix, the threshold is set to –4.1 dB and the output ceiling is at –0.3 dB. The main output buss contains only a Pow-R Dither plug-in.

With Digidesign's Pro Tools, there's a difference in the way auxiliary busses and master outputs process audio. Any plug-ins on an auxiliary buss are processed pre-fader—that is, the signal level that goes into the plug-in is not affected by the volume control. It's different with the master fader; the plug-ins are post-fader. This means that the level of the fader affects the levels going into plug-ins inserted on the master fader. This may not be an issue in many applications. But if, for example, the master output fader is used to create a fade out at the end of a song, that would have an impact on any plug-ins—especially a limiter like the L3 because that would change the way the fade sounds. In that application, the first part of the fade (those signals that are above the threshold of the limiter) would be minimally affected by the fade, and only after the signal strength goes below the threshold of limiting, would the fade proceed as intended. For this reason, I'll usually make it a practice to route all of the tracks in a project through an auxiliary buss that contains an EQ (if desired) and the limiter. With some mixes, it's not an issue, but with others, it is.

AUTOMATION

Unlike "Anyway," a bit more automation was necessary on "Before He Cheats." To make the mix work at its best, automation was written on four tracks: the buss master for the acoustic guitar, the buss master for the background vocals, the fiddle, and the lead vocal.

In the quiet section following the bridge and all the way to the end of the song, the acoustic guitar changes from a full strum to a melodic motif. To make that section stand out as it should, the acoustic buss master was raised by 5.2 dB (from –8.5 dB in the rest of the song to –2.3 dB during the down section). The BGV buss was automated in the same manner; at those points in the song where the vocals are singing oohs, the level of the master was raised by 1 dB to keep them from disappearing into the mix. Also, during the bridge of the song, BGVs went from three parts to two parts; raising the level of the BGV buss at that point also seemed to be an improvement.

The fiddle track was automated to bring out those places where it was playing unison licks with the guitar, to minimize the places where it was simply playing long held notes, and to generally make it sit well as part of the instrumentation. And finally, the lead vocal track was automated so that the verses (which were sung more softly) matched the choruses a bit better, as well as a few lines that simply needed to be tweaked a bit to sit correctly in the track.

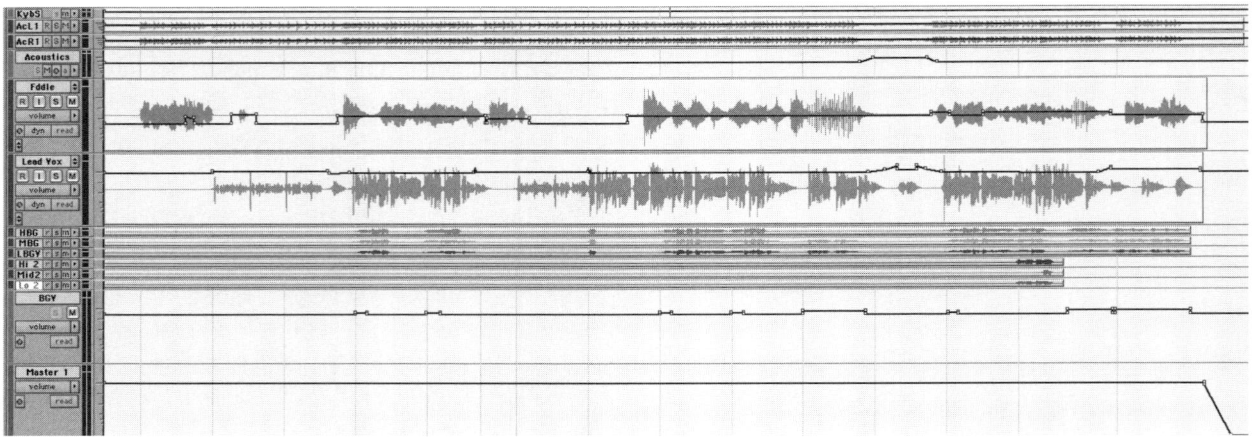

Fig. 2.41. Automation

After all processing and other automation is done, the master fader (with only the dither plug-in inserted) was used for the fade at the end of the song.

PRINTING MIXES

When printing the mix of each of the songs in this volume, I used a consistent approach: a track that plays continuously for the full length of the song ("Before He Cheats" used the piano track) is used to set the final length of the song. I'll trim the chosen track to just before the first note. Then, at whatever point the fade at the end of the track is completed, I'll trim the back of that same track to about a frame after the fade. In Pro Tools, selecting this trimmed track will cause the program to play from the beginning to the end of that track with no excess audio or time at the beginning or end. In those situations where multiple mixes of a song must be done—for example, if a producer wants vocal up or vocal down versions, TV mixes, instrumental mixes, and so on—all of the versions are the same length, and can be easily lined up for editing.

MASTERING

For this book "Before He Cheats" was mixed with the knowledge that it would not be mastered. Because of this, the 6-band EQ and a limiter were inserted on the submaster buss. If this mix had been going to a mastering house (a process I strongly suggest for projects intended for commercial release), the processing—especially the L1 and L3— on this buss would have been removed or at least used in a minimal fashion so that the mastering engineer's work would not be hampered or constricted by something that was done in the mixing process.

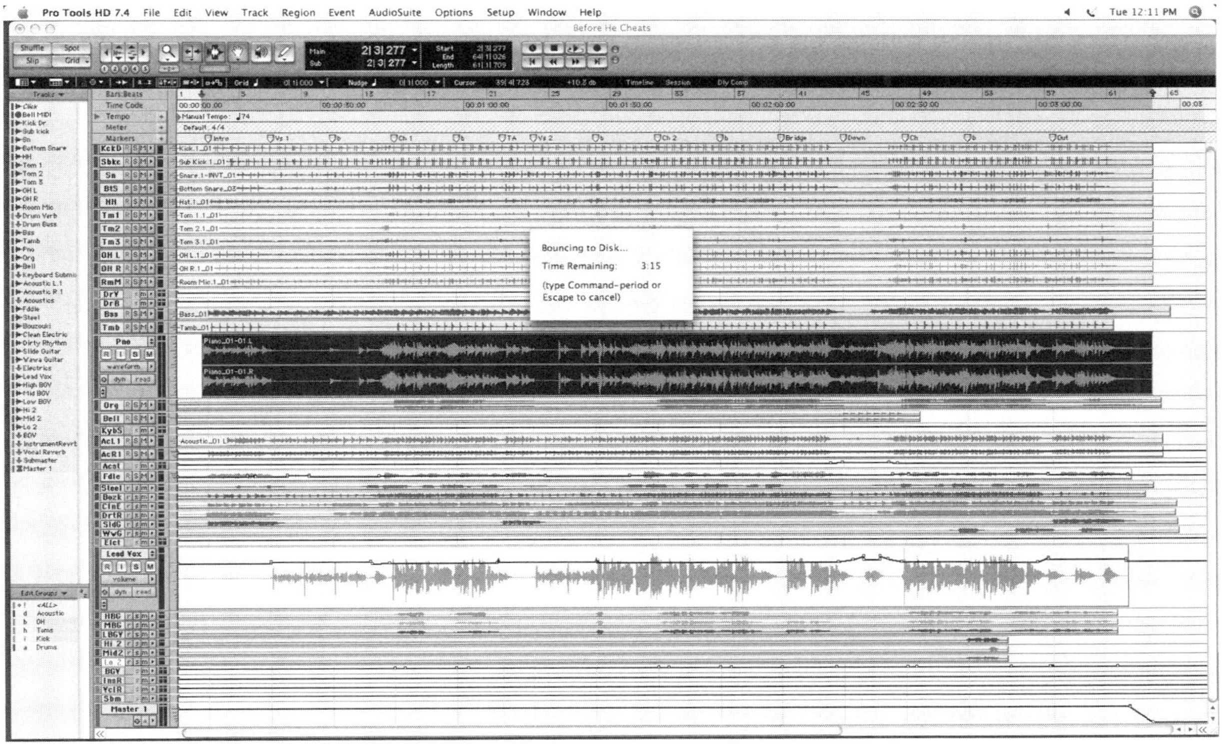

Fig. 2.42. Print Mixes

CHAPTER 3

"Bless the Broken Road"

(As Recorded by Rascal Flatts)

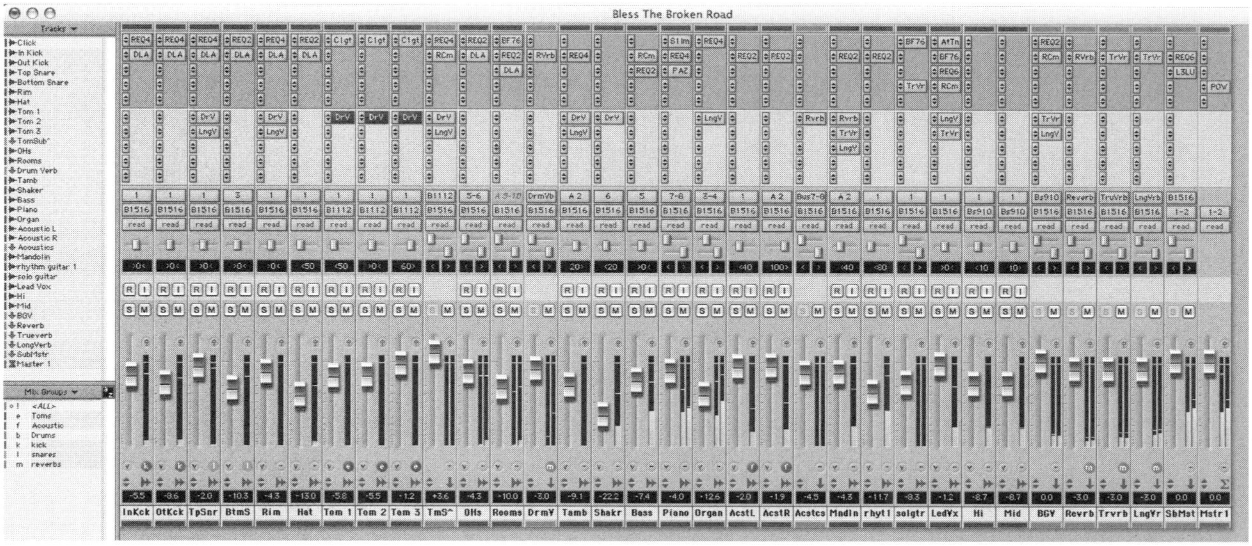

Fig. 3.1. Mix Window

There are some interesting aspects to the production and mixing of "Bless the Broken Road." In addition to having mandolin as one of the dominant instruments, the song also has a pretty wide dynamic range. The use of a shaker as a big part of the drum sound along with a tambourine gives the mix a sound that accentuates the acoustic side of the recording. Like Martina McBride's "Anyway," the mix has to have room to build without losing energy in the quieter parts of the song.

DRUMS

The drum tracks on "Bless the Broken Road" were recorded without EQ and with little compression so that the mixing process would be a bit more informative; if all the necessary EQ was done in the tracking stage, then little or no EQ would be needed on the drums. By recording without processing, the raw tracks can be manipulated in a bit more creative manner. You may notice that there are two kick drum tracks—one track, labeled "in-kick" is from an Electro-Voice RE20 placed inside the drum about three inches from the batter head. The RE20 was, for many years, a standard kick drum microphone in studios around the country, though in the last decade it appears to have been supplanted by microphones that were designed and voiced to get a bit closer to a contemporary kick drum sound. So while the RE20 is certainly a workable microphone for a kick drum, it takes quite a bit more in the way of EQ to get close to the current "standard" sound. The other kick drum track, labeled "out-kick" was recorded with a CAD Trion mic. The Trion was placed a couple of inches out from the front head, in a similar position to where some engineers will place a venerable Neumann U 47 FET. These two signals sound quite different from each other; most mixing engineers will combine the two sounds while processing each as needed to create the final kick drum sound.

Fig. 3.2. Drum Mix

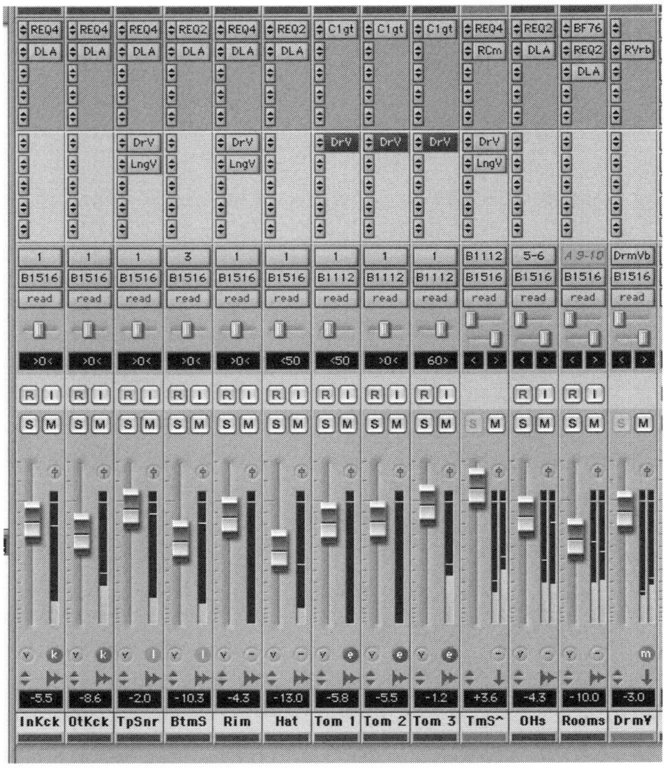

Delay Compensation

While automatic delay compensation has become a standard for most recording software, there are still some audio programs that don't have it, including Digidesign's Pro Tools LE. For this reason, on certain songs I'll discuss the delays that would need to be added to the drum tracks to make them line up correctly on those DAWs without delay compensation built in.

It usually takes a finite length of time for audio to be passed into a plug-in, be processed, and sent on its way. The amount of processing delay depends in large part on the plug-in; some take just a few microseconds, while others can take a few milliseconds. In addition, some common practices like bussing audio tracks to a submaster, also take a certain amount of time. And though it's beyond the scope of the current discussion, outboard processing—like sending audio through the converters to a piece of outboard equipment and then back into the DAW—also are delayed by some amount of time due to the latency of the A/D and D/A converters. But back to the subject at hand; if automatic delay compensation isn't available with a given DAW, then the processing delays should be calculated and compensated for. It works like this: the audio track with the highest amount of delay (for instance, a track that has plug-ins inserted, and is then sent to an aux buss, where more plug-ins are used) is the starting point; all of the other relevant tracks have delay plug-ins added to them, so that all of the other tracks match the one with the most delay. In the case of the drum tracks on "Bless the Broken Road," 65 samples or (1.48 ms) added to most of the tracks allows them to be lined up perfectly to the longest delay—the tom tracks which have Waves C1 gates and are also bussed to the tom buss, where a couple of more plug-ins were used.

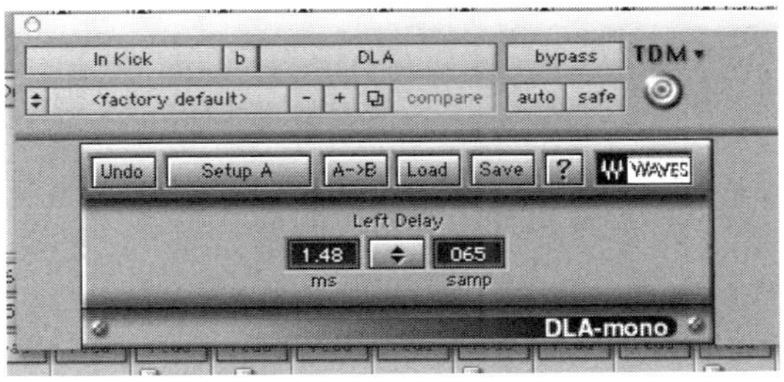

Fig. 3.3. Mono Delay

Kick Drum

While experimenting with the levels of the two kick drum tracks before adding EQ or compression to find the best balance is usually a good practice, it's not always worth the time and effort; there are times when you hear the raw tracks and try to find a way to make them useable.

In-Kick

The in-kick track (the audio track is called "alt kick"), recorded with the RE20, has a quite different sound than the Shure Beta 52 used on some of the other songs; while it isn't the sound that is commonly used on records today, this particular track is amenable to even radical amounts of EQ. In this instance, the EQ isn't particularly radical, though a mild boost in the low end and an upper-midrange boost to add clarity pretty much sum up the needs of the moment. The fader level of the in-kick track was set at –5.5 dB. Here are the settings for the 4-band Waves Renaissance EQ used on the in-kick.

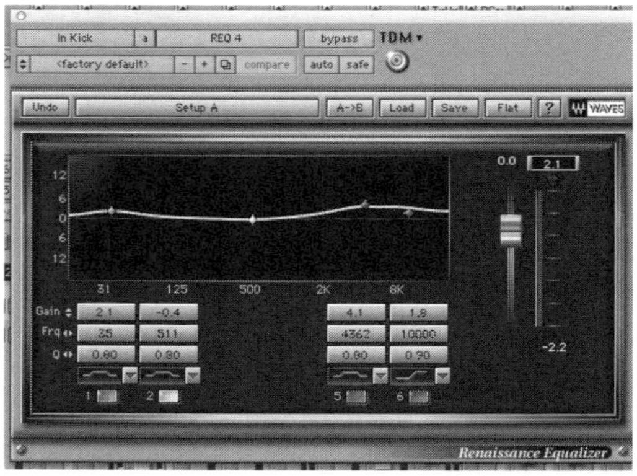

Fig. 3.4. In-Kick EQ

Waves Renaissance REQ-4 In-Kick Settings				
parameter	**band 1**	**band 2**	**band 3**	**band 4**
gain	+2.1 dB	–0.4 dB	+4.1 dB	+1.8 dB
frequency	35 Hz	511 Hz	4,362 Hz	10 kHz
Q	0.80	0.80	0.80	0.90
shape	bell	bell	bell	shelf

Out-Kick

"Bless the Broken Road" is the first appearance in this volume of the Cad Trion microphone. The Trion is a large diaphragm condenser mic that—well, it happened to be in the mic closet and not otherwise in use when the drum mics were being set up for this project. (Yeah, I know you thought that there was some arcane or deeply meaningful approach to choosing microphones. Nah, most of the time, availability is the deciding factor.)

The out-kick track is used to add both low end thump and upper-midrange intelligibility to the overall kick drum sound; to this end, a low frequency boost coupled with a mid range scoop and another boost in the upper midrange seemed to be the best choice. The fader level of the out-kick as set at –8.6 dB.

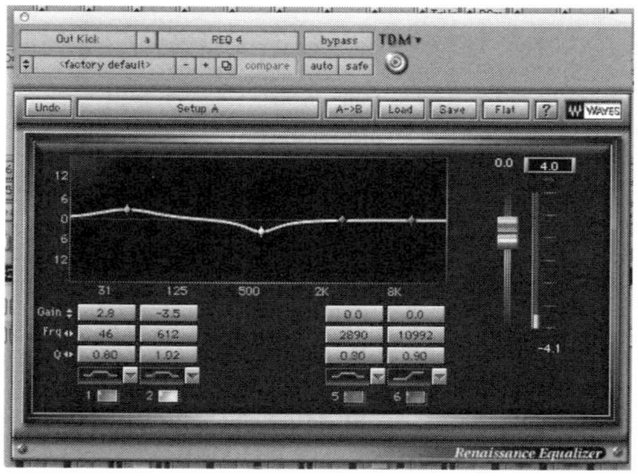

Fig. 3.5. Out-Kick EQ

Waves Renaissance REQ-4 Out-Kick Settings				
parameter	band 1	band 2	band 3	band 4
gain	+2.8 dB	–3.5 dB	+4.1 dB	0 dB
frequency	46 Hz	612 Hz	2,890 Hz	11 kHz
Q	0.80	1.02	0.80	0.90
shape	bell	bell	bell	shelf

Snare

A somewhat different approach was used to mix the snare drum tracks on "Bless the Broken Road." The verses of the song were played with a side-stick (or "rim") rather than with the full snare, and the sidestick required a different EQ and reverb send than the full snare sound. This could have been done in a number of different ways—the effects sends and EQ could have been automated (along with the volume levels of the snare), or multiple effects sends and EQs could have been used on the track—muted and un-muted as needed.

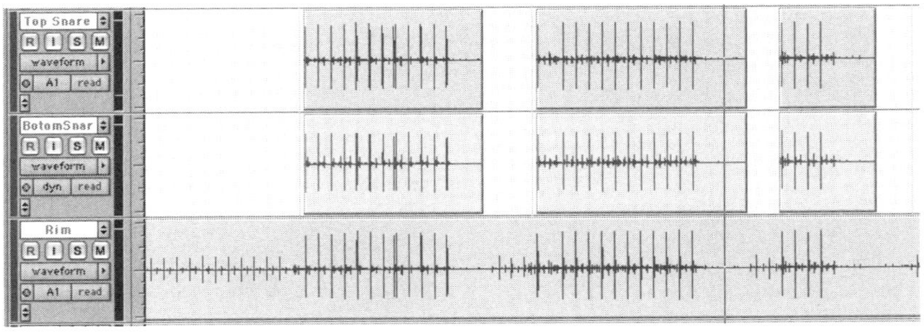

Fig. 3.6. Rim Edit

But the simplest approach (in the workstation environment, at least) was to create another track for the rim, and copy the top snare track to it. Those parts of the top snare track where the full snare was played remained on the top snare track, but the audio in all of the other areas of the top snare track were cleared, so that no audio was present. In this manner, the appropriate processing and effects could be added to the full snare where it was being played, and a different set of processors and effects could be added to the rim where the rim was playing. Though the rim parts were copied rather than dragged (the difference being that during those parts where the snare is being played, the audio is still present on the rim track). The reason that both tracks (the original snare track as well as the newly created rim track) don't play at the same time is because they are assigned the same voice. Here's how that works:

Audio Voices

With Digital Audio Workstations (DAW), there are a finite number of voices available (think of a "voice" as one complete audio track); the number of voices doesn't necessarily correspond to the number of tracks that a workstation can have. For example, a workstation with 32 voices could play back a 40-track session, as long as no more than 32 tracks need to play at any one time. Many programs have dynamic voices, where any available voice can play any track. But it's also possible to assign a specific voice to specific tracks; when this is done and the tracks overlap, only one of the tracks will play. With Digidesign's Pro Tools, the voice that's closest to the top of the screen in the edit window, or the leftmost voice in the mix window has priority. That's what's used in this track; the rim track and the top snare track are sharing a voice; when audio is present on the top snare track, no sound will come from the rim track. As mentioned earlier, there are other approaches that will do the same thing, but the voice-sharing method is a nice way of finding a solution with what, under other circumstances, could have been seen as a shortcoming.

Top Snare

The top snare track was recorded using a Neumann KM 84, which certainly gives the raw track a different sound and texture than the Shure SM57 used elsewhere. The Waves Renaissance EQ is primarily used to add a bit of bite and air to the snare track. The output of the top snare track is at –2.8 dB; the send to the drum reverb is –5.5 dB, while the send to another reverb, the "long verb," is set at –7.4 dB.

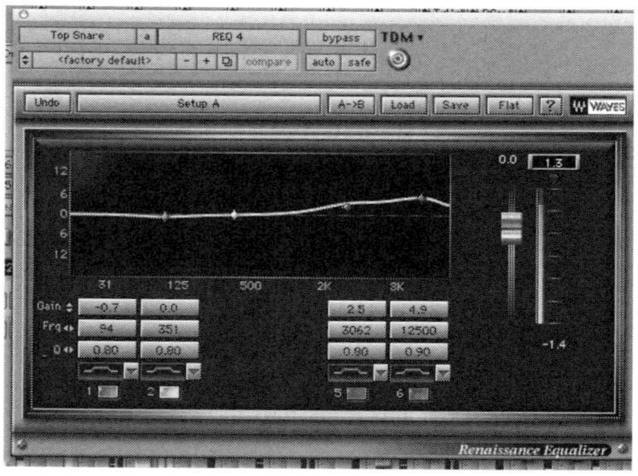

Fig. 3.7. Top Snare EQ

Waves Renaissance REQ-4 Top Snare Settings

parameter	band 1	band 2	band 3	band 4
gain	–0.7 dB	0 dB	+2.5 dB	+4.9 dB
frequency	94 Hz	612 Hz	3,062 Hz	12.5 kHz
Q	0.80	1.02	0.80	0.90
shape	bell	bell	bell	bell

Bottom Snare

The bottom snare track has no EQ; while a 2-band Renaissance EQ was inserted on the track, it's set flat. The reason that it's on the track is because of the delay compensation; a Renaissance EQ inserted on a drum track will cause a consistent amount of processing delay. Making that delay consistent across all of the drum tracks makes it easier to compensate for those plug-ins that are needed on some tracks, like the sidestick track (below).

Rim

The output level of the rim track is at –5.2 dB. The rim track also sends to two different reverbs, the drum reverb and the long verb. The send level to the drum reverb is –10.7 dB, while the send to the long verb is at –1.9 dB. As can be seen below, the EQ settings for the rim track are quite a bit different than those for the snare track.

Fig. 3.8. Rim EQ

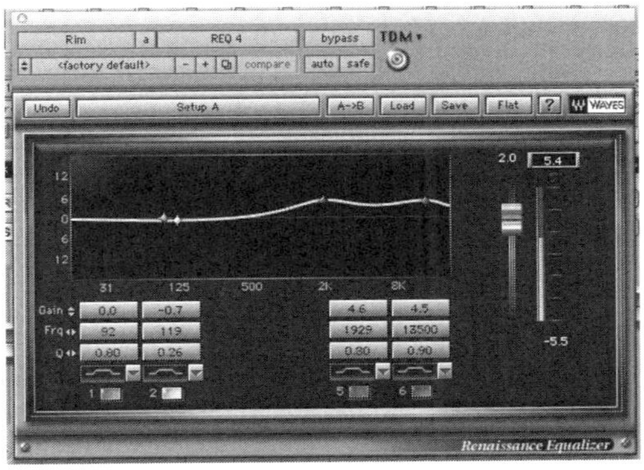

Waves Renaissance REQ-4 Rim Settings

parameter	band 1	band 2	band 3	band 4
gain	0 dB	–0.7 dB	+4.6 dB	+4.5 dB
frequency	92 Hz	119 Hz	1,929 Hz	13.5 kHz
Q	0.80	0.26	0.80	0.90
shape	bell	bell	bell	bell

Hi-hat

There's little to add to what's been discussed previously; the hi-hat's fader level at –13.0 dB helps to add a bit of definition to the overall drum track while not being obtrusive on its own. A 2-band EQ and a delay plug-in were added to the hi-hat track, but like the bottom snare track, the EQ was set flat; it was only added to the track to make calculating delays easier.

Toms

On "Bless the Broken Road," the toms are gated to eliminate the tom hum that has been discussed earlier. A gate has a threshold that opens when that threshold is exceeded, and that shuts again when the signal strength drops below the threshold. This is one way to eliminate unwanted noise from a track. When using gates on an drum track, the primary goal is to keep the threshold high enough to exclude extraneous peaks from opening the gate, while keeping it low enough that it opens whenever the gated drum is struck. The toms on this track are bussed to a stereo tom buss, where the EQ and compression for the toms is added. There's no compelling reason, by the way, to put compression and equalization on the buss inserts rather than on the individual toms other than the savings in processor power when using one plug-in instead of three. Nevertheless, it's done fairly often—possibly as a holdover from the early days of mixing in the DAW.

Fig. 3.9. Tom Gates

Astute readers may notice that the three tom tracks have a reverb send; the brighter color means that those sends are bypassed. These sends are a remnant of a mixing template that was used for the first two tracks, where the toms (and the rest of the drum tracks) were bussed together. Since this mix has the tom reverb sent from the tom buss rather than from the tom tracks themselves, these sends are unused. They were left in the session to serve as a reminder that most mixes (at least, by experienced engineers) are based, at least in part, on mixing templates that save time and make those routing options that the engineer is used to working with available for every mix. The output level of the first tom is –5.8 dB, the second tom is –5.5 dB, and the third tom is –1.2 dB. The settings for the Waves C1 gates used on the toms are detailed below.

Waves C1 Gate for Tom 1					
floor	**gate open**	**gate close**	**attack**	**release**	**hold**
infinite	–9.8	–9.8	1.78	545	0.01

Waves C1 Gate for Tom 2					
floor	**gate open**	**gate close**	**attack**	**release**	**hold**
infinite	–12.1	–12.1	1.78	545	0.01

Waves C1 Gate for Tom 3					
floor	**gate open**	**gate close**	**attack**	**release**	**hold**
infinite	–15.4	–15.4	1.78	545	0.01

Tom Buss

Though not necessarily compelling, another reason to put effects processing on an auxiliary stereo buss rather than on individual tracks is so that the processing affects all of the tracks sent through the buss in the same way. Like many things related to audio, this is application specific; choosing whether to send multiple tracks through a single buss depends on the situation. A 4-band Waves Renaissance EQ and a Renaissance Compressor were used on the tom buss. The output level is +3.6 dB.

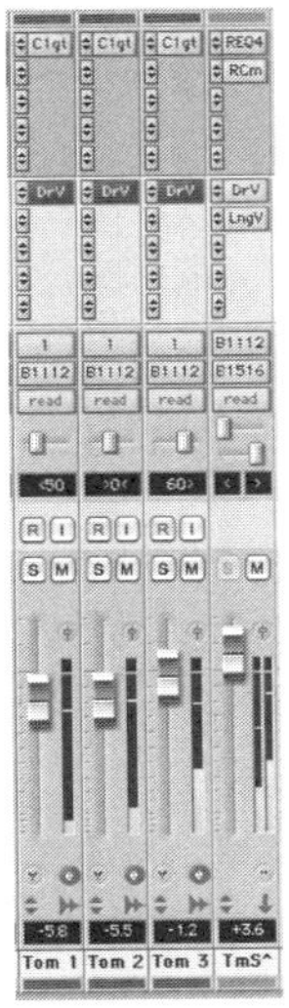

Fig. 3.10. Tom Buss

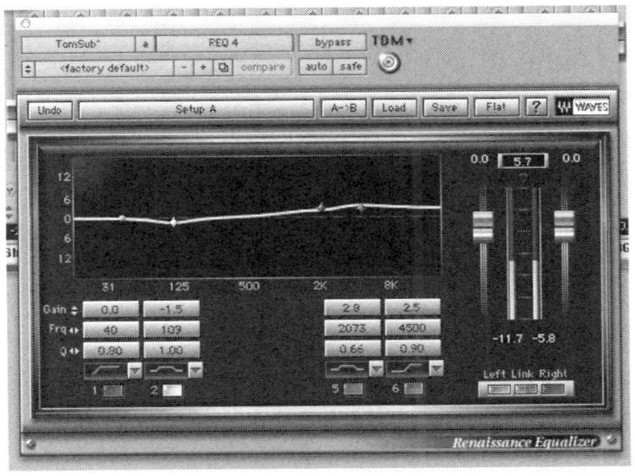

Fig. 3.11. Tom Buss EQ

Two different reverbs are used on the tom buss—the drum verb send is at –8.9 dB while the long verb send is at –17.1 dB.

Waves Renaissance REQ-4 Tom Buss Settings				
parameter	band 1	band 2	band 3	band 4
gain	0 dB	–1.5 dB	+2.8 dB	+2.5 dB
frequency	40 Hz	109 Hz	2,073 Hz	4.5 kHz
Q	0.80	1.00	0.66	0.90
shape	bell (inactive)	bell	bell	shelf

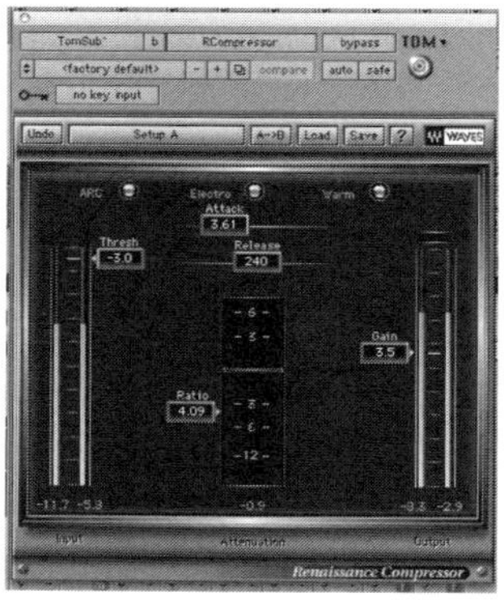

Fig. 3.12. Tom Buss Compressor

Waves Renaissance Compressor Tom Buss Settings				
threshold	attack	release	ratio	gain
–3.0	3.61	240	4.09:1	+3.5 dB

Overheads

The overhead drum tracks on "Bless the Broken Road" were recorded in the same manner as the other overhead drum tracks in this volume—as two mono tracks. However, the tracks were dragged from their original tracks to a single stereo track, which some engineers feel is easier to work with. No processing was used on the overhead tracks on this mix; however, moving the mono audio tracks to a stereo track in the session is simply another possible way to work with the audio. If it makes more sense to see the overheads as a stereo track, then by all means, move the two mono tracks to a single stereo track. The fader level on the overheads was set to –4.3 dB. A 2-band EQ (set flat) and a stereo DLA plug-in were added to the track.

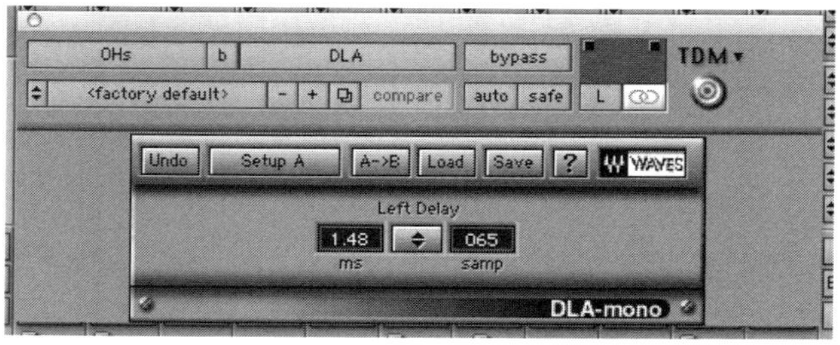

Fig. 3.13. Stereo DLA

Stereo Room Mic

Unlike the two prior tracks, "Bless the Broken Road" uses a pair of microphones to capture room sounds. These microphones, Neumann TLM 103s, were placed in the corners of the tracking room and pointed upwards to capture the ambient and reflected sounds of the room.

Room mics are typically not used at anywhere near their full levels; not only would doing so usually make the sounds of the drums far more ambient then necessary, the delay between the close microphones and the room microphones would smear the attack of the drums in what would usually be an unacceptable manner. That's not to say that using the room mics as the primary source of drums sounds would never work, but it certainly doesn't work well in this situation. The output of the two room mics were panned hard left and right, and set at –7.0 dB below unity gain. To emphasize the ambient nature of the room mics, a Bomb Factory BF76 was added to the room track as well as a 2-band Waves Renaissance EQ.

Fig. 3.14. Room Mic Compressor

Bomb Factory BF76 Room Mic Settings				
input	**output**	**attack**	**release**	**ratio**
28	18	2.5	3.6	4:1

Fig. 3.15. Room Mic EQ

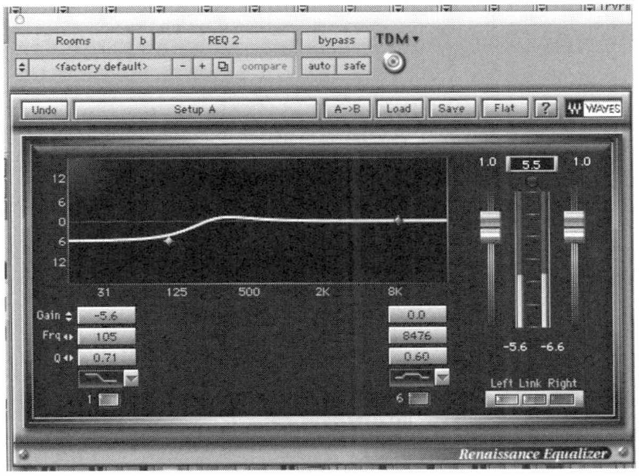

Waves Renaissance REQ-2 Room Mic settings		
parameter	band 1	band 2
gain	–5.6 dB	0 dB
frequency	105 Hz	8,476 Hz
Q	0.71	0.60
shape	shelf	bell

Drum Reverb

The reverb plug-in used for the drum reverb is a Waves Renaissance Reverberator set to a Drum Plate preset. The output level of the reverb return is set at –3.0 dB.

Fig. 3.16. Drum Reverb

Waves Renaissance Reverberator Drum Reverb Settings	
parameter	setting
REVERB DAMPING	
frequency 1	258
ratio 1	0.90
frequency 2	4,312
ratio 2	0.39
reverb type	hall 1
decorrelation	var: 4
REVERB EQ	
frequency 1	215
gain 1	–2.5 dB
frequency 2	7,619
gain 2	–5.9 dB
predelay	0.0

time	1.14 sec.
size	34.4
diffusion	24.5
decay	linear
early reflection level	–22.3 dB
reverb	0.0 dB
wet/dry	100%
gain	0

Drum Routing, Grouping, and Effects

The first two tracks in this volume had all of the drum tracks on their own stereo buss, so that EQ and a stereo buss compressor can be inserted across the whole kit. That, of course, is not the only way to mix drums—it's simply *one* way to mix them. Remember that ultimately, a drum set is a single instrument; each drum in the set is part of the whole. As long as the sound of the drums fits what the mixer (or the producer) has in mind for the track, any approach that works is a good approach.

For ease of mixing, I typically create several groups among the drum tracks. I set up three groups for the drums. The first group is the three toms, since once the levels of the toms are set (relative to each other), it's more common to adjust the volumes of all three to adjust their relation to the rest of the kit rather than adjusting each tom individually. The second group is the two kick drum tracks. Once the relative balance between the two is set, grouping these two tracks allows the kick drum to be adjusted as a single entity rather than as two individual audio tracks. The third group is the top and bottom snare tracks, which are grouped for the same reason as the two kick drum tracks. Notice that I didn't group the rim track with the other two snare tracks; since it was being adjusted separately from the snare, it made more sense (to me, at least) to leave it ungrouped. I typically also group all of the tracks that make up the drum kit (on this song, that would be a fourth group). Though the drum group is usually inactive, it's sometimes convenient to turn all of the drum tracks up or down to optimize the levels going to the main output.

Fig. 3.17. Drum Groups

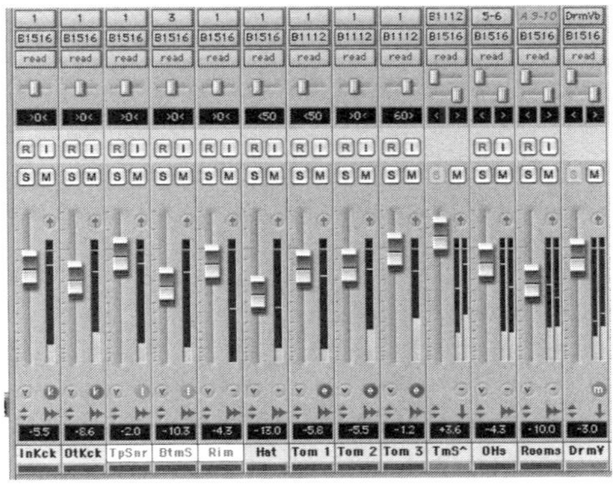

PERCUSSION

"Bless the Broken Road" has two tracks of percussion: tambourine and shaker. The percussion tracks were created with real percussion instruments (a Rhythm Tech tambourine and a simple egg shaker) rather than with either triggered samples or a programmed loop. While both sampled percussion sounds and programmed (or recorded) loops certainly have a place in contemporary country, there was no compelling reason to do so for this track—and in this engineer's opinion, live percussion generally feels better than programmed percussion. Others may well have different opinions.

Tambourine

Because the tambourine on "Bless the Broken Road" is pretty well buried in the track, the fader level was set to –9.1 dB. Two reverbs were used on the tambourine—the drum reverb and the long verb. The send to the drum verb was –4.1 dB, while the send to the long verb was set at –6.8 dB. A 4-band Waves Renaissance EQ was used on the tambourine track to add a bit of meat to the sound and to minimize unneeded high frequencies.

Fig. 3.18. Tambourine EQ

Waves Renaissance REQ-4 Tambourine Settings				
parameter	**band 1**	**band 2**	**band 3**	**band 4**
gain	0 dB	+1.9 dB	+1.1 dB	–9.3 dB
frequency	92 Hz	221 Hz	1,424 Hz	4.5 kHz
Q	0.80	0.80	0.80	0.55
shape	bell	bell	bell	bell

Shaker

The egg shaker, used to add a soft sixteenth-note pulse to the track, needed no processing to make it sit well with the other instruments. The fader level was set at –22.2 dB, and the drum verb send was at –8.3 dB.

BASS GUITAR

The bass tracks on "Bless the Broken Road" used a Waves Renaissance Compressor and a 2-band Waves Renaissance EQ as plug-ins. The output fader of the bass was set at –7.4 dB. Not a whole lot of gain reduction was used on the bass track; it was added primarily to even out any inequities in the track. The EQ was primarily used to add bottom end to the bass track. The Q setting for each band of equalization determines the width of the band; the lower the number, the wider the frequency range affected by any changes to the level of that band. A high number means that a much narrower range is affected by any adjustment to that frequency band. You may notice that the center frequency is quite low—below the cut-off point for most speakers—but because the Q setting is quite wide, a fairly wide range of frequencies that *can* be reproduced are also affected by the first EQ band. In addition to that, keep in mind that a lot of what is perceived as bass is not necessarily the fundamental note (the low E note on a bass is at 41 Hz, and notes played on the B string are lower than that), but are harmonics an octave (and more) higher than the fundamental. Boosting the fundamental frequency will also raise the level of the harmonic notes associated with that frequency.

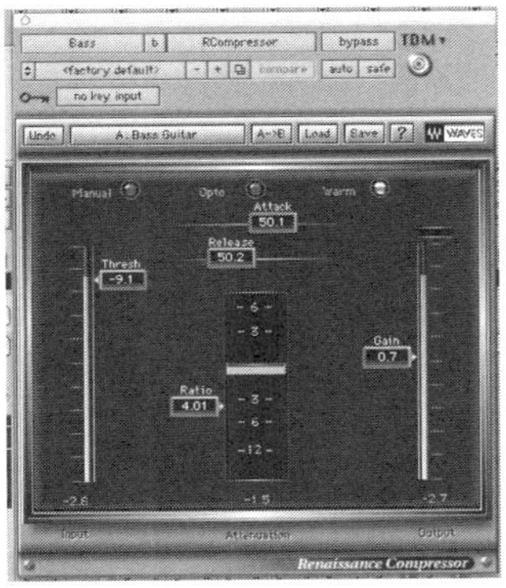

Fig. 3.19. Bass Compressor

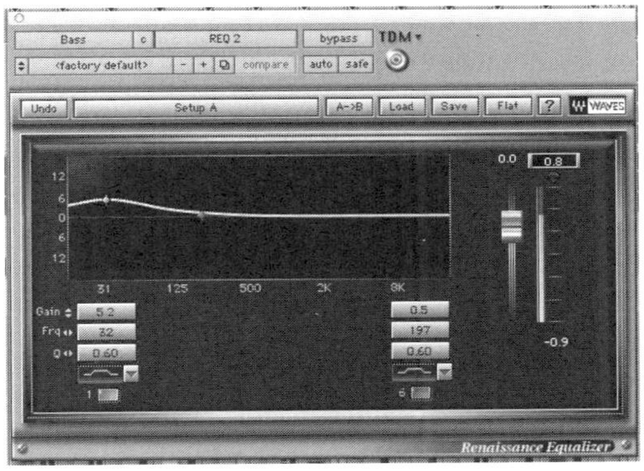

Fig. 3.20. Bass EQ

Waves Renaissance Compressor Bass Settings				
threshold	**attack**	**release**	**ratio**	**gain**
–9.1	50.1	50.2	4.01:1	+0.7 dB

Waves Renaissance REQ-2 Bass Settings		
parameter	**band 1**	**band 2**
gain	+5.2 dB	+0.5 dB
frequency	32 Hz	197 Hz
Q	0.60	0.60
shape	bell	bell

PIANO

The piano on "Bless the Broken Road" was recorded with a pair of Telefunken 251 microphones placed over the low and high strings, respectively. For the tracks included in this volume, the piano, a Yamaha C7 grand piano was recorded with multiple miking configurations: a pair of Telefunken 251s, one pair of AKG 480 small diaphragm condensers in an XY pattern, and a pair of 480s as a spaced pair. In addition, a couple of the tracks were done using a Kurzweil K2500 RM with an external controller so that a wider range of processing would be needed on different songs. If I'd used only my usual piano miking setup, then whatever processing I did for the first song in this book would be duplicated for the other nine songs. Different miking setups allow for more opportunities to show different processing approaches. The output level of the piano was –4.0 dB. For a number of reasons, including the need to fit three different pairs of microphones into the piano at one time, the placement of these particular microphones gave a narrower image than some of the other mic placements.

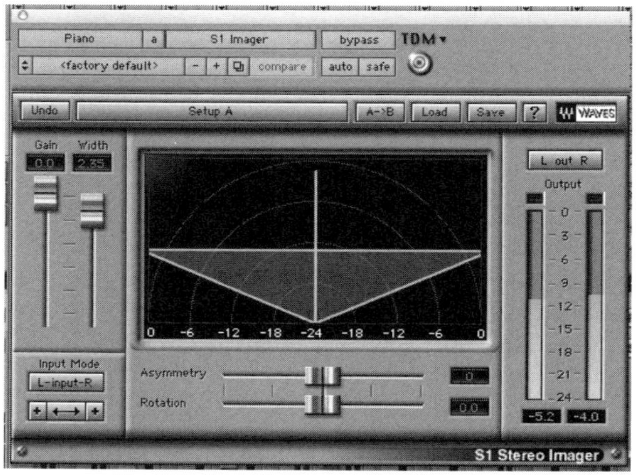

Fig. 3.21. Piano S1 Imager

The first plug-in used on this piano track was a Waves S1 Imager. The S1 widens the image of the piano by adding out-of-phase information to the track, though this can affect the mono compatibility of the mix, which generally doesn't become a problem unless extreme settings are used. The S1 can also be used to change the balance of stereo tracks that lean either to the left or the right, but that function wasn't needed in this particular case.

Mono Compatibility

Mono compatibility was at one point a very important issue for recording engineers for two reasons. The first reason was that most broadcasts were mono—that is, on AM radio. When stereo recordings were widely introduced in the 1960s, radio stations would simply sum the left and right channels for the monaural broadcast. When sonic information (for instance, a stereo guitar) on the left channel was out of phase with sonic information on the right channel, the frequencies would cancel out, and effectively disappear. At the minimum, stereo instruments that were out of phase would get a strange, hollow sound as though the instruments had a phase shifter on them.

Mono compatibility was also important because if too much out-of-phase information is present in the stereo mix, it becomes difficult (and sometimes impossible) to create a vinyl disc that can reproduce the mix correctly; in extreme cases (when low-frequency information is out of phase, for example), the needle would jump out of the groove.

These days, very little music is released on vinyl, but phase issues between the two channels can still become an issue. It seems that every playback device—from car stereos to iPods are stereo, but many monophonic playback devices are still in use. Ring tones, for instance, are played back on one cell phone speaker so the two channels are summed to mono. And many music playback systems in public places, from airports to fine restaurants, also sum the two channels to one mono channel.

In any event, here are two screen shots of the Waves Paz Meter; in-phase information is depicted as being in the center of the graph, while out-of-phase information shows as spikes at the far left and far right of the graph. The first shot shows the piano track without the S1 Imager plug-in and the second picture is of the piano track with the S1 inserted. While this is certainly a high-tech way to check the phase of individual tracks (and there's no reason that something like the PAZ meter couldn't be inserted on the main outputs of the DAW), there's a much easier way to tell whether there are phase issues with a given mix: just play the mix in mono. Most DAWs have a main output that's panned hard left and right. Simply change the panning on both channels to the center (alternatively, pan the right channel all the way to the left so that both sides are playing out of one speaker) and listen. If you don't hear a problem, then there's not a problem. If you do, then consider taking steps to minimize that problem. With the screenshot (below), the S1 is bypassed so that the piano track is "normal."

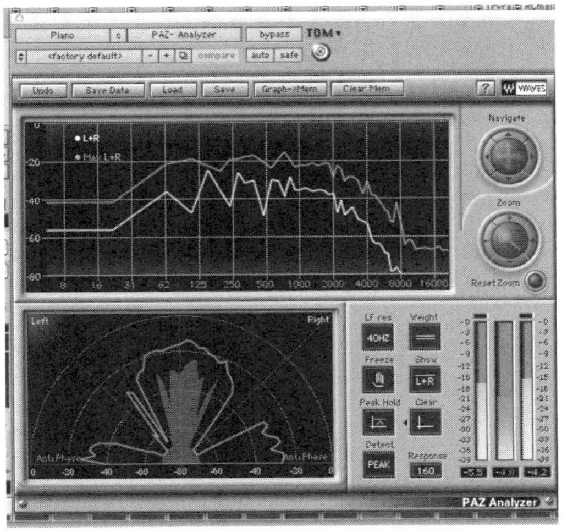

Fig. 3.22. Imager Bypassed

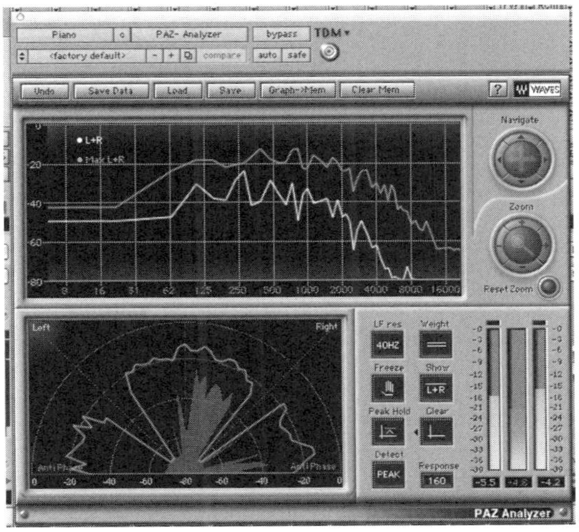

Fig. 3.23. Imager Active

The above screenshot shows the stereo signal with the S1 as active; notice that at the left and right of the phase meter, more information is present, a sign that out-of-phase information is present.

When dealing with samples and synth patches, the amount of out-of-phase information varies with both the sound used and the developer of the sound. In the early days of stereo synthesizers, there were some patches that were made to sound stereo by reversing the phase of one side. While this sounded quite "wide" in stereo, when summed to mono, the sound would disappear completely. The Kurzweil piano sound used on "Bless the Broken Road" is quite narrow, so the S1 Imager was inserted to add a bit of out-of-phase information to make it sound bigger.

Fig. 3.24. Piano EQ

Waves Renaissance REQ-4 Piano Settings

parameter	band 1	band 2	band 3	band 4
gain	–2.6 dB	–3.3 dB	+3.5 dB	+1.9 dB
frequency	25 Hz	189 Hz	4,147 Hz	13.7 kHz
Q	0.80	0.80	0.80	0.90
shape	bell	bell	bell	bell

ORGAN

The organ needed little processing other than a slight boost at 14 kHz. The natural sound of the Hammond C3 used on this track was left alone. The fader level was set at –13.9 dB, and the effects send to the long verb was at –10.1 dB. The Hammond organ is capable of so many different sounds that I find it much easier to get the sound from the instrument, and then see if any equalization is needed.

As an aside, it might seem logical that the Hammond organ, long associated with rhythm and blues music, would be a late-comer to the palette of sounds used on country recordings (like the electric sitar and drum loops), but in reality, that isn't so. Some of country artist Red Foley's songs from the 1950s featured the Hammond organ (played, as a matter of fact, by legendary producer and pianist Owen Bradley), and even the venerable Grand Ole Opry had a Hammond C3 on stage for many years.

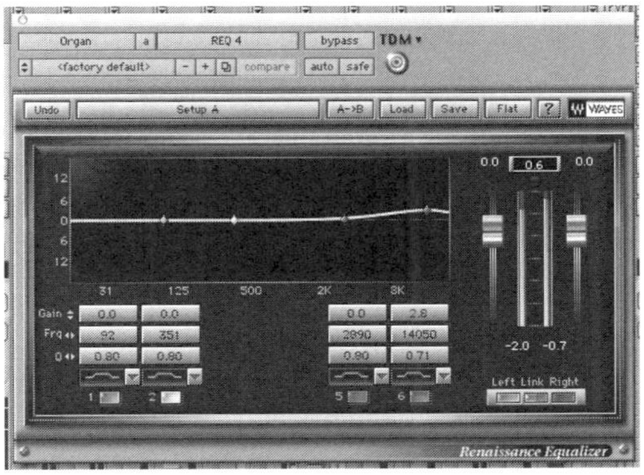

Fig. 3.25. Organ EQ

Waves Renaissance REQ-4 Organ Settings				
parameter	**band 1**	**band 2**	**band 3**	**band 4**
gain	0 dB	0 dB	0 dB	+2.8 dB
frequency	92 Hz	351 Hz	2,890 Hz	14 kHz
Q	0.80	0.80	0.80	0.71
shape	bell	bell	bell	bell

ACOUSTIC GUITARS

Instead of using a buss EQ on the acoustic guitar tracks, "Bless the Broken Road" has a simple 2-band EQ on each of the guitar tracks. For both of the guitar tracks, the first EQ band was used as a high-pass filter, clearing away unneeded low-frequency information while the second EQ band is used to add a presence peak that allows the acoustic to cut through the mix. The acoustic left track output is at –2.0 dB, while the acoustic right output is at –1.9 dB. The acoustics are bussed to an acoustic guitar buss. Not much is happening on this buss other than a reverb send to the instrument reverb; the level of that send is –10.7 dB, and the output of the acoustic guitar buss is set at –4.5 dB.

Notice that the acoustic guitar buss is still present, though it's not being used. This is (like the bypassed reverb sends associated with the tom tracks) a simple remnant of the template that was used as a basis or this mix of "Bless the Broken Road."

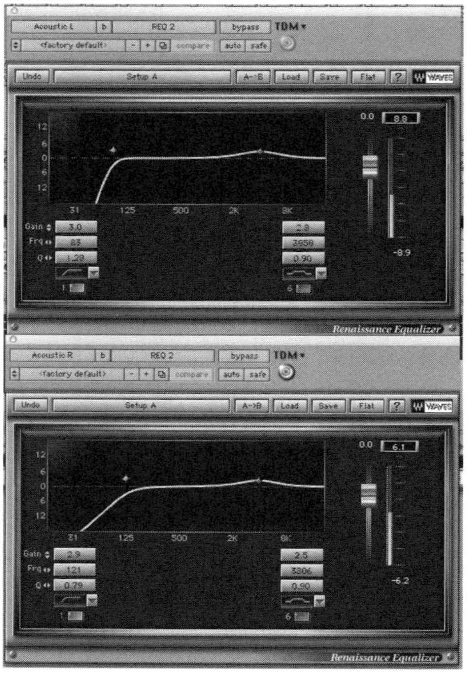

Fig. 3.26. Acoustic Guitar EQ

Waves Renaissance REQ-2 Acoustic L Settings		
parameter	**band 1**	**band 2**
gain	+3.0 dB	2.8 dB
frequency	80 Hz	3,858 Hz
1.28	0.80	0.90
shape	high-pass	bell

Waves Renaissance REQ-2 Acoustic R Settings		
parameter	**band 1**	**band 2**
gain	+2.9 dB	2.5 dB
frequency	80 Hz	3,886 Hz
1.28	0.79	0.90
shape	high-pass	bell

Hiding Tracks

You may be wondering, if no buss processing is used on the acoustic guitars, why the buss was used at all. That's a good question that has two answers: the first is that when mixing in the box, a mix with a lot of tracks, busses, effects returns, and so forth takes up a lot of screen space. Finding a specific track in a large mix can be problematic. One way to make it easier to work with large sessions is to simply hide some of the tracks in the session. In Pro Tools, this is done with a window called "show/hide tracks." By bussing the acoustic guitars to their stereo buss, the two acoustic tracks can be hidden from view in the mix window, though their relative levels can be adjusted by the acoustic guitar buss. The same is true for the tom tracks (mentioned earlier); the three tom tracks can easily be hidden from view and only the stereo tom buss will be visible. There are other methods to create fader moves on hidden tracks (in Pro Tools for example, by grouping tracks together so that changes made to any track in a group affect the hidden tracks that are part of the group). But bussing is another way to accomplish the same thing.

The other answer is much more prosaic; some of the things done in these mixing sessions are done because that's the way they're usually done. For example, I usually put the acoustic guitars (or electric guitars, or background vocals) on their own buss because it's common to want to do something that requires that they be routed to a buss. If I don't need to use the buss for a given song, it's not hurting anything. Nevertheless, from this song on, bussing will be used a bit less; the principles behind bussing have been discussed, and you know that if it's something that you need, you can do it.

MANDOLIN

Since the mandolin plays a major role in "Bless the Broken Road," playing along with the piano in the intro and turnaround, it needs to be heard over the piano track. Boosting its EQ in the upper midrange, around 2.5 kHz, allows it to live in a frequency range where the piano is not dominant. This boost gives the mandolin an airy quality that isn't necessarily what the instrument sounds like in the room, but is certainly part of the sounds that people associate with the mandolin in contemporary music.

For decades, mandolin recordings had more of a woody, lower midrange sound that helped to add—for want of a better word—"thrust" to the songs where it was used. This old-school mandolin sound goes back as far as Bill Monroe's classic recordings of 1946, and was still present in the New Grass Revival's hit records of the 1980s, and even on mandolin virtuoso Sam Bush's current CDs. When talking with other Nashville engineers about the light and airy mandolin sound that has become more common, some have opined that it started as far back as 1987 with Bruce Hornsby's "Mandolin Rain." Others suggest that engineer Gary Paczosa brought a lighter and more delicate mandolin sound to contemporary radio while working with the Dixie Chicks and Alison Krauss and Union Station.

In any event, three different reverbs were used on the mandolin on "Bless the Broken Road." The instrument reverb was at –19.5 dB, the TrueVerb was at –10.7 dB, and the long verb send was at –14.8 dB.

Fig. 3.27. Mandolin EQ

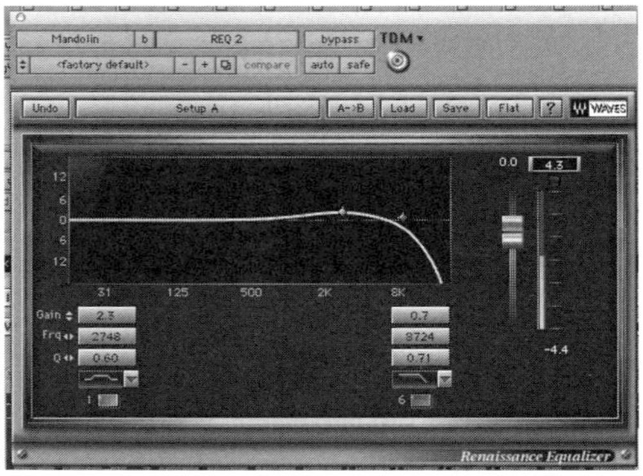

Waves Renaissance REQ-2 Mandolin Settings		
parameter	**band 1**	**band 2**
gain	+2.3 dB	0.7 dB
frequency	2,478 Hz	8,724 Hz
1.28	0.60	0.71
shape	bell	low pass

ELECTRIC GUITARS

There are two electric guitar tracks on "Bless the Broken Road"—a rhythm guitar and a lead guitar. The electric guitars are not bussed together to an electric guitar buss as was the case in a couple of the earlier chapters; instead, the two guitars are processed individually before being routed to the submaster buss.

Rhythm Electric

The rhythm guitar was high-passed at 92 Hz, and had a broad frequency boost around 5 kHz. Notice that on this particular mix, the electric guitar doesn't enter until the turnaround following the first chorus; there are no rules requiring that every instrument in a given song play the entire song from start to finish; when arranging and recording music, knowing when *not* to play is at least as important as knowing when to play. The rhythm guitar's output level was set at –12.6 dB.

Fig. 3.28. Rhythm Guitar EQ

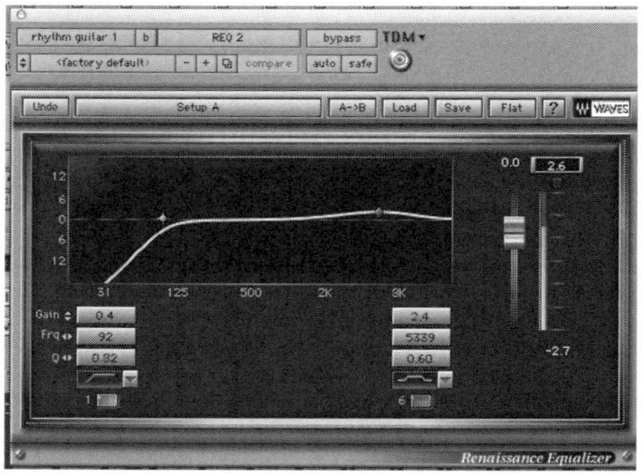

Waves Renaissance REQ-2 Rhythm Electric Settings		
parameter	band 1	band 2
gain	+0.4 dB	+2.4 dB
frequency	92 Hz	5,339 Hz
1.28	0.82	0.60
shape	high-pass	bell

Solo Electric

The solo electric guitar track doesn't enter until the first solo begins (with some songs, the solo guitar sound is used in other places, like intros and turnarounds), and only plays in a few specific spots. The output level of the solo guitar is –8.3 dB. There are two plug-ins used on the solo guitar—one is the Bomb Factory BF76, which is an emulation of the classic UREI 1176. The other is a Waves TrueVerb reverb plug-in. This is used as an insert on this track, not as an effects return. There are a couple of reasons for using the reverb as an insert in this particular application rather than as an effect. The first is that only the solo guitar will be using this reverb, which is set to a Rock Guitar Room preset. By using the reverb as an insert, it's easy to change parameters without inadvertently changing the reverb sound on some other instrument. The second reason is that adjusting the wet/dry level can, in some ways, sound a bit different than simply adjusting the sends and returns to a reverb which is set up as an aux send.

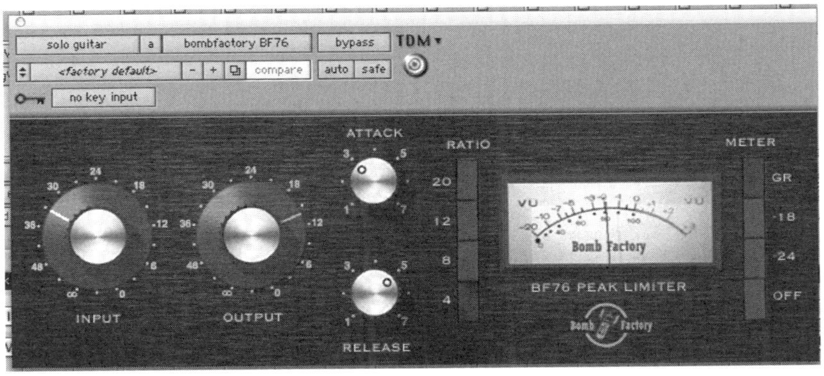

Fig. 3.29. Lead Guitar Compressor

Bomb Factory BF76 Solo Electric Settings				
input	output	attack	release	ratio
34	14	3	35	4:1

Fig. 3.30. Lead Guitar Reverb

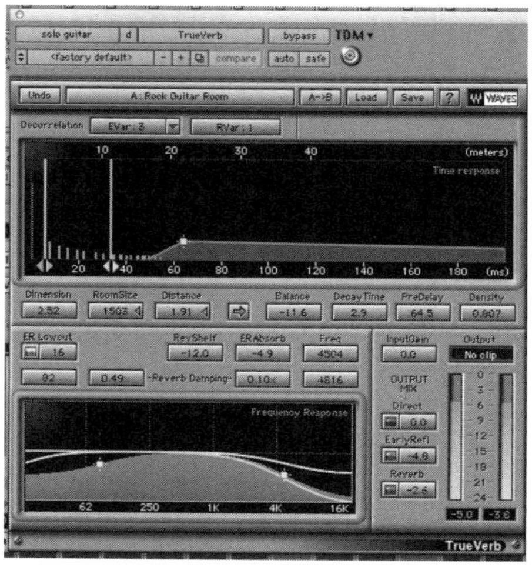

Waves TrueVerb Solo Electric Settings	
parameter	**setting**
dimension	2.52
room size	1,503
distance	1.91
balance	–11.6
decay time	2.9
predelay	64.5
density	0.807
EARLY REFLECTION (ER)	
low cut	16
reverb damping frequency low	82
damping	0.49¥
reverb damping frequency high	4,816
damping	0.10¥
reverb shelf	–12.0
ER absorb	–4.9
ER absorb freq	4,504
input gain	0.0
direct output	0.0
ER output	–4.8
reverb output	–2.6

LEAD VOCAL

The lead vocal on "Bless the Broken Road" has four different processors on it, as well as two effects sends that send the lead vocals to the vocal reverb (in this mix, a Waves TrueVerb) and to the long reverb. The lead vocal track was automated to a certain extent, but −1.9 was used as a general starting point. The aux sent to the long reverb was −18.2 dB while the TrueVerb send was at −16.1 dB.

The first is the Antares Auto-Tune 4 plug-in. This wasn't done necessarily because I feel that the singer needs to be tuned (the tracks on the DVD are not tuned; you can form your own opinions), it's simply that the Auto-Tune plug-in isn't particularly transparent. Everything that passes through it, tuned or not, develops a bit of that "Auto-tune sound." And like it or not, that's a big part of the sound of country records these days. The retune and tracking parameters are set to a medium-slow level, but this particular instance of Auto-Tune has a twist that won't be seen again in this book—the scale is de-tuned to −13 cents, which is the equivalent of changing from an A=440 Hz tuning to an A=436.7 Hz. The de-tuning would be a lot more noticeable if the tracking and retuning parameters were tighter; with the settings chosen for those parameters, the scale de-tune simply softens the notes a bit. It's also possible that it works in this application because of the way that the vocal and the microphone used to record it interact; the mic, a] (a modern version of the classic AKG C12) is a bright microphone that picks up harmonics from the vocal chords quite well. If some of those upper frequencies are a bit high when compared to the fundamental note, then detuning may help to minimize any edginess that results. Finally, the input type is set to low male voice (which the lead vocal on this song certainly is *not*); this would make a difference in the way that the signal is processed.

Fig. 3.31. Lead Vocal Auto-Tune

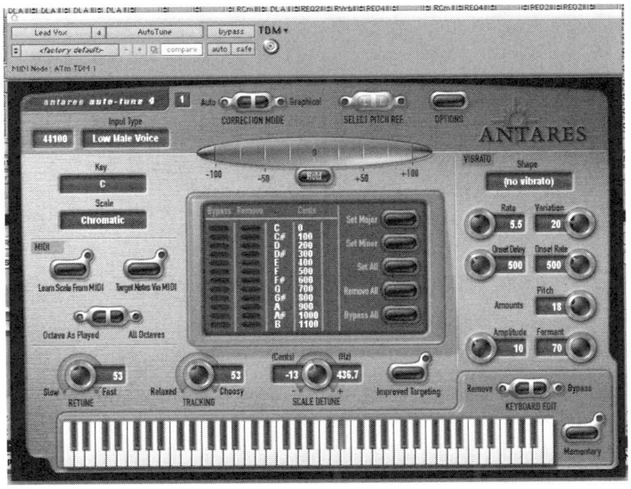

Auto-Tune

Retune: 53

Tracking: 53

Scale detune: −13 cents

Input Type: Low Male Voice

After the Auto-Tune 4 plug-in is another Bomb Factory BF76; the BF76's attack and release times are quite fast, and this helps to emulate the highly processed vocal sound of the original recording.

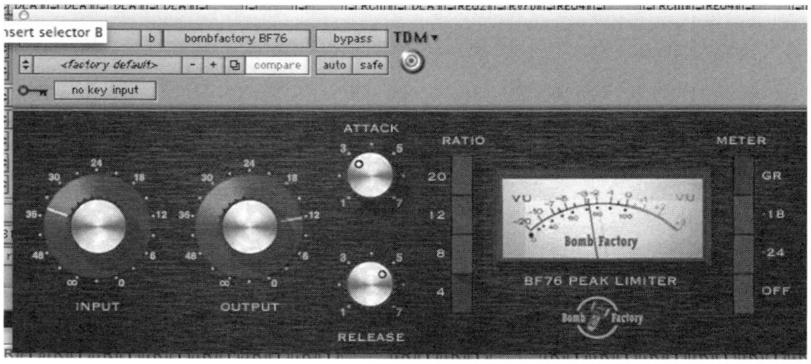

Fig. 3.32. Lead Vocal BF76

Bomb Factory BF76 Lead Vocal Settings				
input	**output**	**attack**	**release**	**ratio**
34	12	3	5	4:1

A 6-band Waves Renaissance EQ is next in the chain; this vocal track needed primarily some added warmth in the low end and a bit of presence in the high end. This was done with a boost at around 150 Hz and another near 9 kHz, while the 3 kHz band was cut a bit.

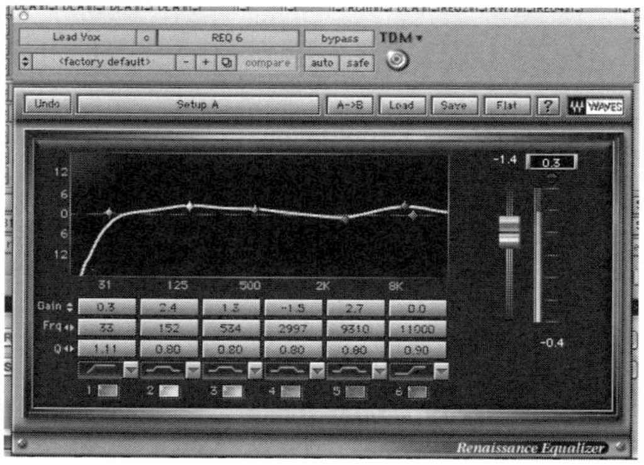

Fig. 3.33. Lead Vocal EQ

Waves Renaissance REQ-6 Lead Vocal Settings						
parameter	**band 1**	**band 2**	**band 3**	**band 4**	**band 5**	**band 6**
gain	+0.3 dB	+2.4 dB	+1.3 dB	–1.5 dB	+2.7 dB	0 dB
frequency	33 Hz	152 Hz	534 Hz	2,997 Hz	9,310 Hz	11 kHz
Q	1.11	0.80	0.80	0.80	0.80	0.90
shape	high-pass	bell	bell	bell	bell	shelving

Last in the chain is a Waves Renaissance Compressor. With a 3:1 compression ratio, a pretty fast attack and fairly slow release, the RennComp adds a bit of warmth to the signal chain, mitigating (though not minimizing) the aggression imparted by the BF76.

Fig. 3.34. Lead Vocal Compressor

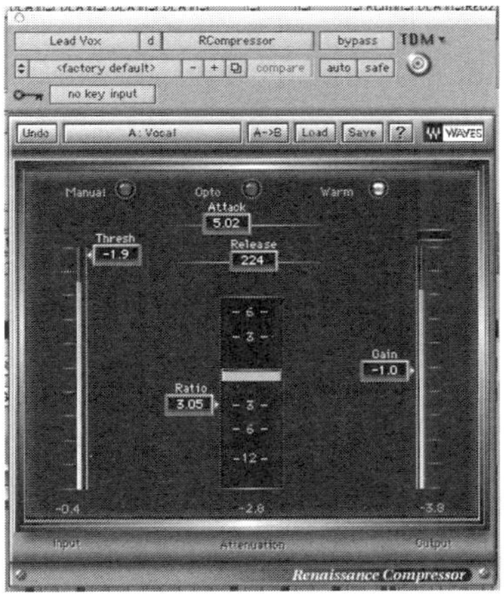

Waves Renaissance Compressor Lead Vocal Settings				
threshold	**attack**	**release**	**ratio**	**gain**
–1.9 dB	5.02	224	3.05:1	–1.0 dB

BACKGROUND VOCALS

There are two background vocals (BGV) on "Bless the Broken Road"; the high BGV is set to –9.5 dB while the mid BGV level is at –7.7 dB. The high BGV has no automation, and the mid BGV has some tweaks to it, to make the two BGV tracks blend with the lead vocal. These two tracks are bussed to the BGV buss (the BGV buss is set at unity gain), with the effects send to the TrueVerb at –8.0 dB and the Long Reverb at –12.0 dB. The BGV buss has a 2-band Waves Renaissance EQ inserted, though only one band is active, with a broad boost around 8 kHz to add clarity. It also has a Renaissance Compressor, which helps to smooth out the peaks in the BGV tracks.

Fig. 3.35. BGV EQ

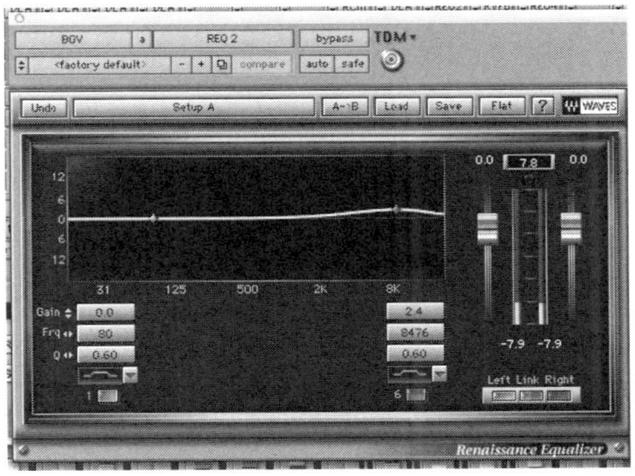

Waves Renaissance REQ-2 BGV Buss Settings		
parameter	band 1	band 2
gain	0 dB	+2.4 dB
frequency	80 Hz	8,746 Hz
1.28	0.60	0.60
shape	high-pass	bell

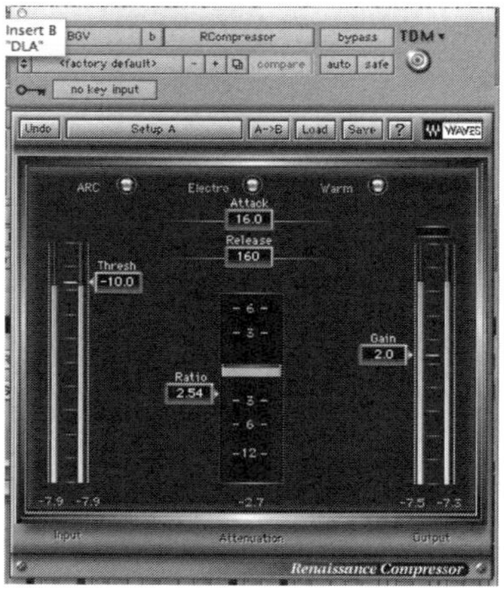

Fig. 3.36. BGV Compressor

Waves Renaissance Compressor BGV Buss Settings				
threshold	attack	release	ratio	gain
–10dB	16.0	160	2.54:1	+2.0 dB

Fig. 3.37. Aux Sends and Processing

AUX SENDS AND BUSS PROCESSING

As mentioned earlier, the drums have their own reverb buss. Three additional reverb returns have been set up for this mix. The first, called "reverb" is a Waves Renaissance Reverberator set to a Medium Room setting; the second, named "true verb" (TrVr, TruVrb, and Trvrb in the screenshot) has a Waves TrueVerb set to a Nice Plate setting; and the third, another Waves TrueVerb, is called a "long verb." Any combination of these three (well, four counting the drum reverb) can be used on any track, as the mandolin track shows. The practice of setting up multiple reverbs of different lengths and flavors is another holdover from the days of mixing on consoles. Well-equipped studios in the 1970s would likely have a plate reverb or two (set to different reverb times) and possibly a chamber as well; when mixing, any combination of these would be used to meet a given need. Though modern workstation technology allows an almost unlimited number of reverbs (subject to the processing power available), in reality, there's seldom a need to go to such lengths. The output of the three reverb returns is set to 3 dB below unity gain. Below are the settings for the reverbs used in "Bless the Broken Road."

REVERB

Fig. 3.38. Reverb

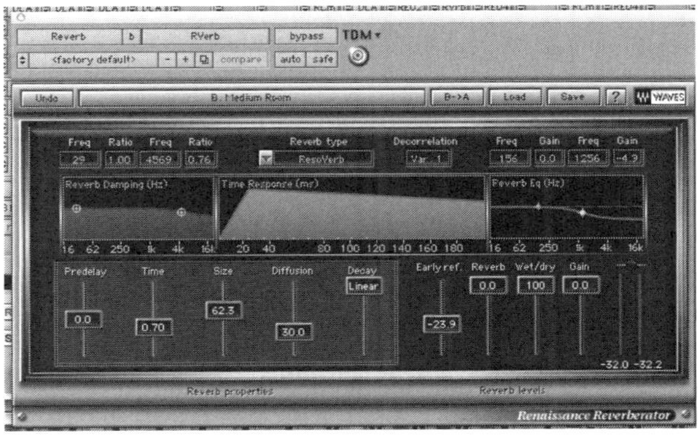

Waves Renaissance Reverberator Reverb Settings

parameter	setting
REVERB DAMPING	
frequency 1	29
ratio 1	1.00
frequency 2	4,569
ratio 2	0.76
reverb type	resoverb
decorrelation	var: 1
REVERB EQ	
frequency 1	156
gain 1	0
frequency 2	1,256
gain 2	–4.9 dB
predelay	0.0
time	0.7
size	62.3
diffusion	30
decay	linear
early reflection level	–23.9dB
reverb	0.0dB
wet/dry	100%
gain	0

Fig. 3.39. TrueVerb

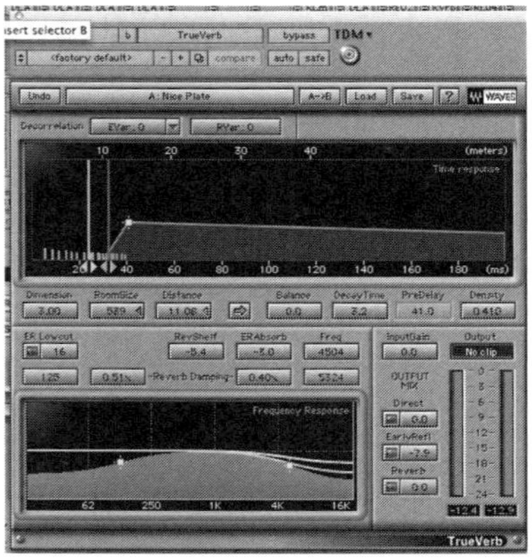

Waves TrueVerb Settings	
parameter	**setting**
dimension	3.00
room size	539
distance	11.08
balance	0.0
decay time	3.2
predelay	41.0
density	0.410
EARLY REFLECTION (ER)	
low cut	16
reverb damping frequency low	125
damping	0.51¥
reverb damping frequency high	5,324
damping	0.40¥
reverb shelf	–5.4
ER absorb	–3.0
ER absorb freq	4,504
input gain	0.0
direct output	0.0
early reflection output	–7.9
reverb output	0.0

Fig. 3.40. Long Verb

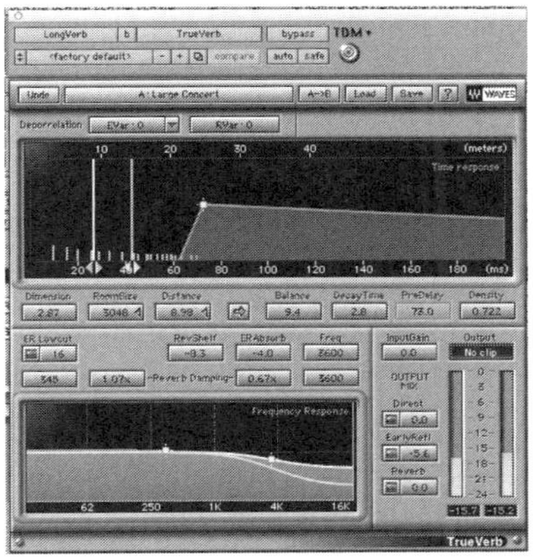

Waves TrueVerb Long Verb Settings	
parameter	**setting**
dimension	2.87
room size	3,048
distance	8.98
balance	9.4
decay time	2.8
predelay	73.0
density	0.722
EARLY REFLECTION (ER)	
low cut	16
reverb damping frequency low	345
damping	1.07¥
reverb damping frequency high	3,600
damping	0.67¥
reverb shelf	–8.3
ER absorb	–4.0
ER absorb freq	3,600
input gain	0.0
direct output	0.0
early reflection output	–5.6
reverb output	0

SUBMASTER BUSS

The submaster buss uses a 6-band Waves Renaissance EQ, which is used to tweak the overall tone of the mix, and a Waves L3-LL Ultramaximizer, a stereo limiter which is used to bring up the average volume of the mix to contemporary levels while protecting against the possibility of the signal level going over 0 dBFS. "FS" is an acronym for "full scale," the maximum level that a digital signal can reach. Any signal louder than full scale simply results in clipping with the resultant distortion.

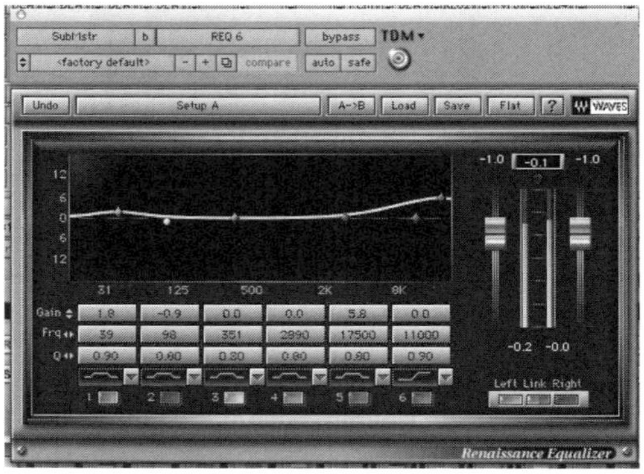

Fig. 3.41. Buss EQ

Waves Renaissance EQ-6 Submaster Settings						
parameter	**band 1**	**band 2**	**band 3**	**band 4**	**band 5**	**band 6**
gain	+1.8 dB	–0.9 dB	0 dB	0 dB	+5.8 dB	0 dB
frequency	39 Hz	98 Hz	351 Hz	2,890 Hz	17.5 Hz	11 kHz
Q	0.90	0.80	0.80	0.80	0.80	0.90
shape	bell	bell	bell	bell	bell	shelving

Fig. 3.42. Buss Limiter

Submaster Limiter
Waves L-3
Threshold: –4.2 dB
Out Ceiling: –0.2 dB

The master output buss contains only a Pow-R Dither plug-in, which reduces the bit depth of the output to 16 bits. The main output buss is used for the fade at the end of the song.

Fig. 3.43. Dither

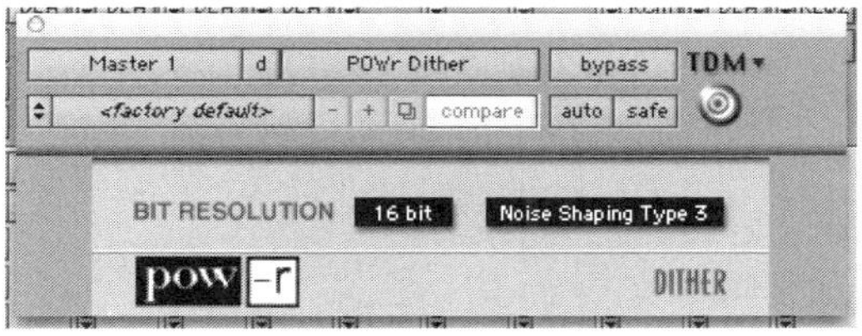

Automation

"Bless the Broken Road" has more automation than the songs discussed in the prior chapters: the organ track is smoothed in the introduction of the song as well as during the guitar solo, and the mandolin track was primarily raised for those sections where it plays the melody (the intro, turnaround and outro). The solo guitar track was also automated, with the primary moves made to reduce the levels of the track where it would conflict with the lead vocals.

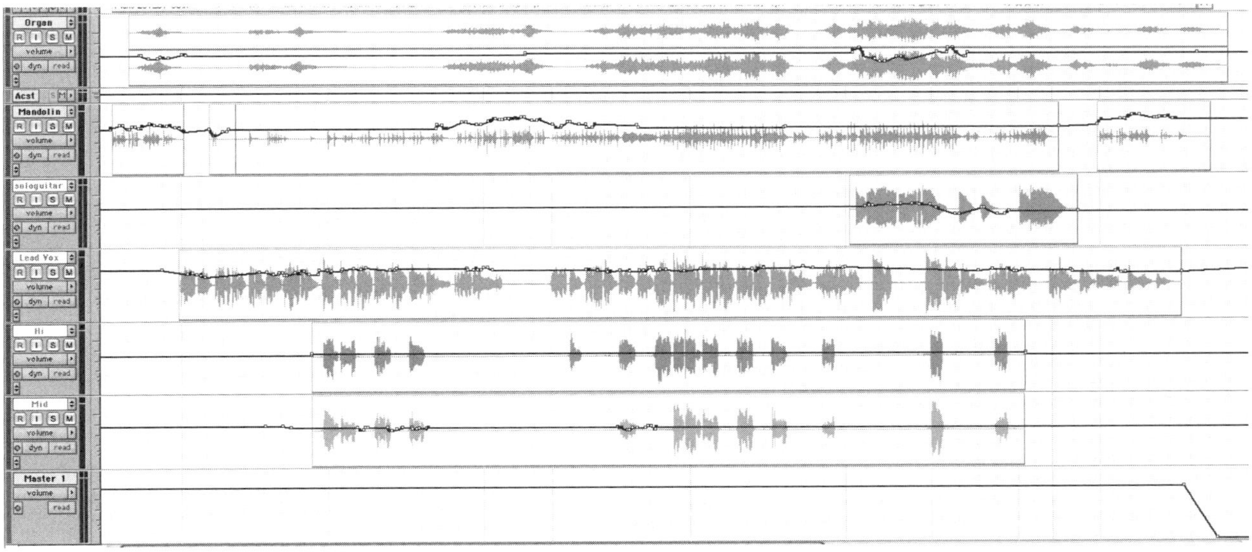

Fig. 3.44. Automation

The background vocals—specifically the mid BGV—were automated primarily in the first chorus and second verse. The greatest amount of automation was on the lead vocal track; through the course of the song, the fader levels were changed by a total of less than 6 dB. Notice that while a number of tracks have smoothly drawn automation, most of the automation in this session was done by hand, using a trackball.

EDITS

Few changes were made to the audio tracks at the mixing stage of "Bless the Broken Road." As with many of the other songs included in this volume, each of the tracks were trimmed up to the point that the audio started on that track. For example, the lead vocal was trimmed to the beginning of the first verse and then was cleared until the first chorus where it entered. Many of the tracks were also trimmed at the end of the song. But all of this is simply for visual clarity; only a couple of changes to the audio track were made for this mix.

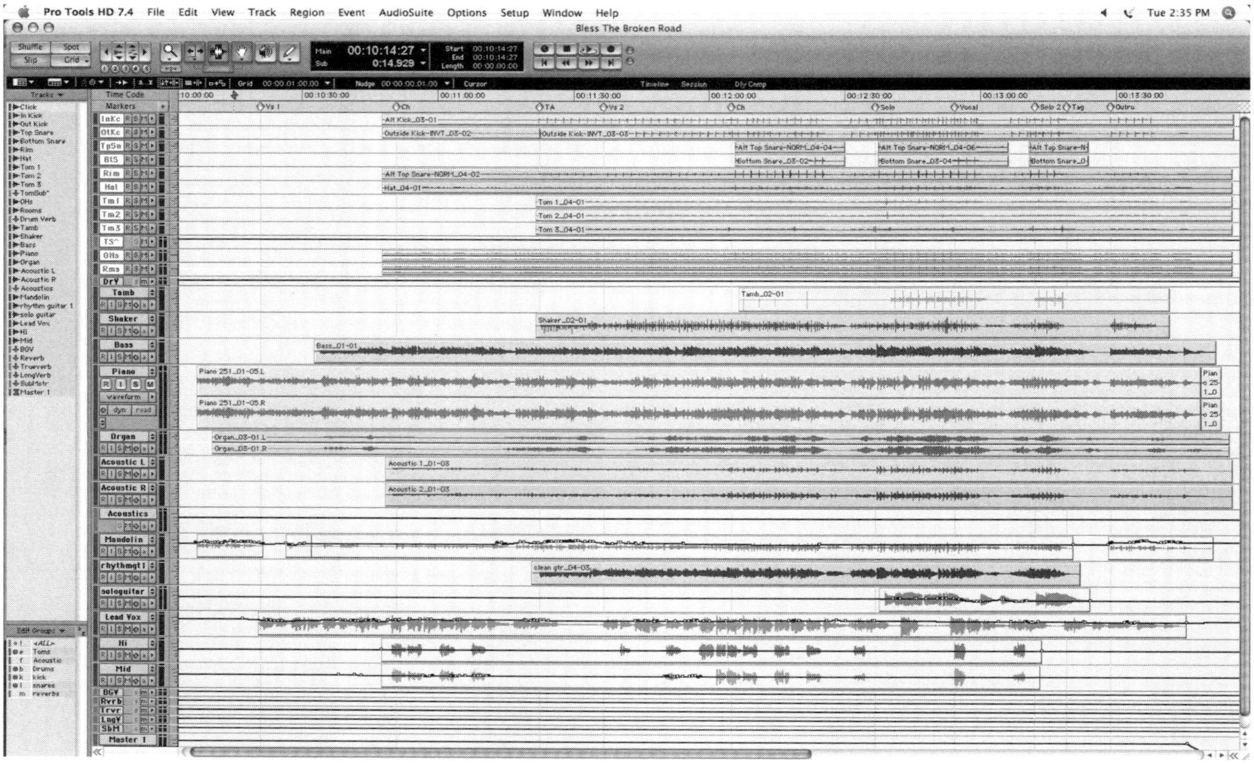

Fig. 3.45. Edit Window

In addition to the creation of tracks for the rim sound (discussed earlier), one region of the mandolin track (in the first verse) was made inactive because of a note that shouldn't have been there, and one region was cleared (at the end of the tag) for the same reason.

Fig. 3.46. Mandolin Edit

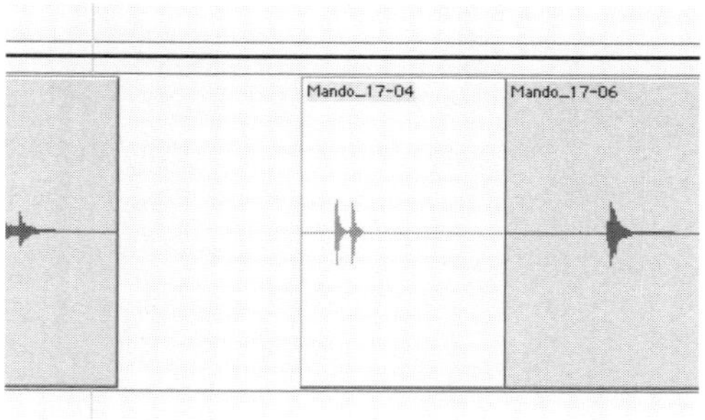

Also, on the last note of the piano track, a glitch appeared; I minimized (if not repaired) it by removing the glitch and sliding the rest of the piano over the cleared spot. I then created a fade to try to hide the edit.

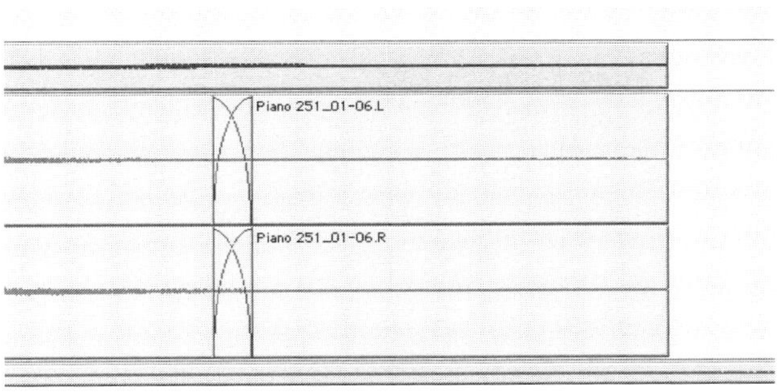

Fig. 3.47. Piano Edit

The first chapter discussed the issue of inverting the phase of a track as well as the possibility of lining up the two kick drum tracks; both of those things were done on "Bless the Broken Road." The line just before the hit on the outside kick track is the point at which the track was separated, and when using the Pro Tools Audio Suite function, the process used is appended to the name of the track—which is why the screen shot shows the track name as "Outside Kick-INVT."

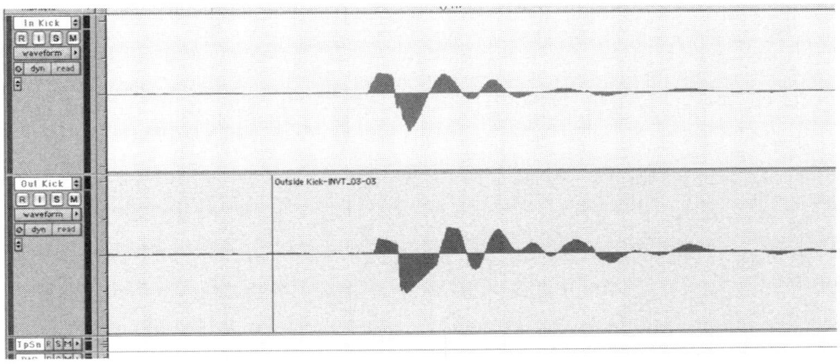

Fig. 3.48. Out-Kick Edit

PRINTING MIXES

When printing the mix of each of the songs in this volume, I used one of the continuous tracks (typically an acoustic guitar track or piano track) to set the final length of the song. The chosen track is trimmed at a point just before the beginning of the first note of the song and also at a point just after the end of the fade (written on the master output fader). In Pro Tools, selecting this trimmed track will cause the program to play from the beginning to the end of that track with no excess audio or time at the beginning or end. In those situations where multiple mixes of a song must be done—for example, if a producer wants vocal up or vocal down versions, TV mixes, instrumental mixes, and so on—all of the versions are the same length, and can be easily lined up for editing.

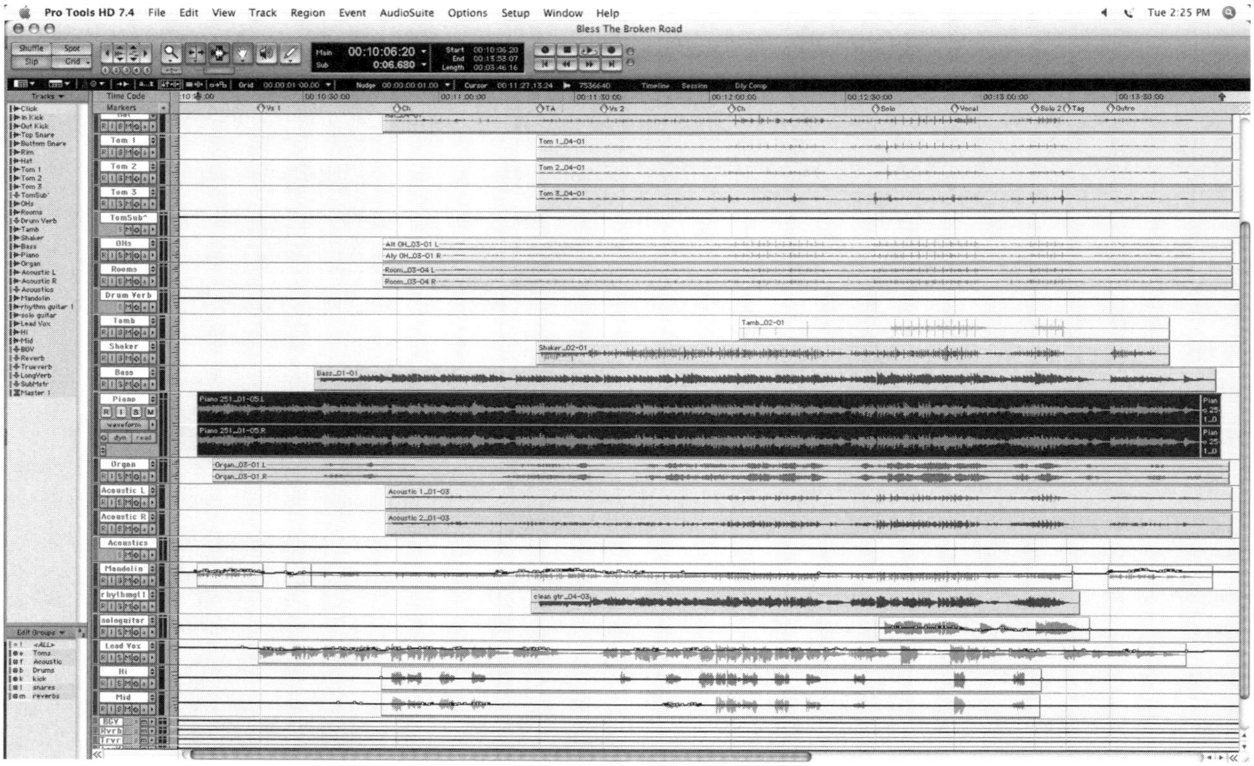

Fig. 3.49. Print Mix.

CHAPTER 4

"It Just Comes Natural"

(As Recorded by George Strait)

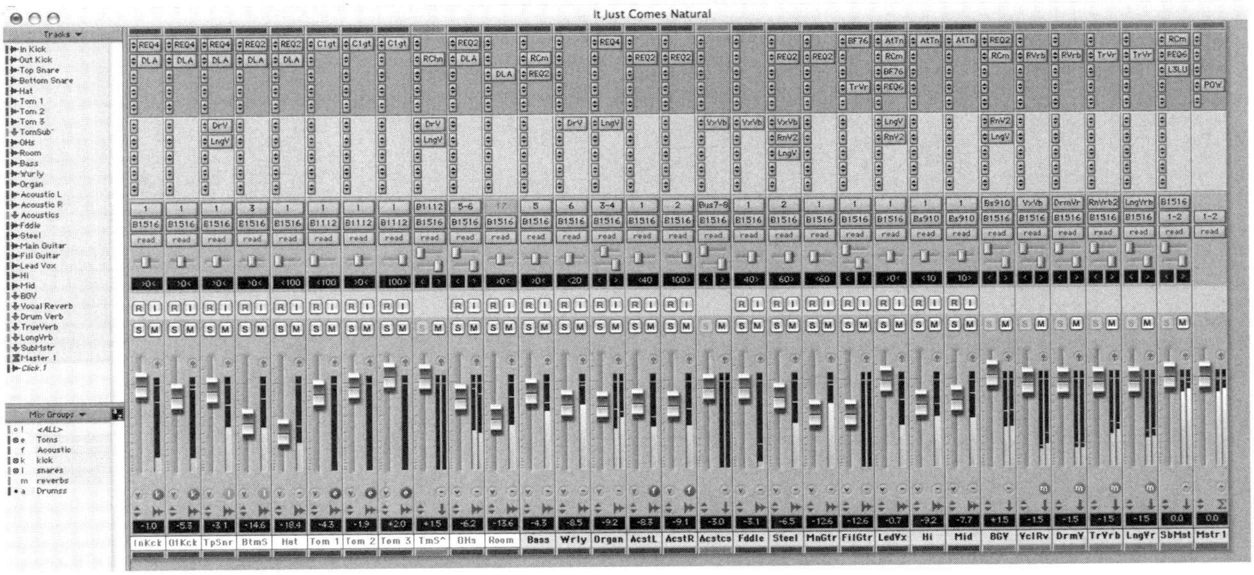

Fig. 4.1. Mix Window

George Strait's "It Just Comes Natural" takes a different approach to contemporary country, as the arrangement is a bit more traditional than most of the tracks in this project. Another change from earlier songs is the prominence that's given to the steel guitar as both a solo and fill instrument.

DRUMS

The drum tracks on "It Just Comes Natural" were recorded without EQ and with little compression so that the mixing process would be a bit more informative; if all the necessary EQ was done in the tracking stage, then little or no EQ would be needed on the drums. By recording without processing, the raw tracks can be manipulated in a bit more creative manner. You may notice that there are two kick drum tracks—one track, labeled "kick" is from a Shure Beta 52 placed inside the drum about three inches from the batter head (and recorded with a Daking preamp), while the subkick track was recorded with a Yamaha Subkick placed directly in front of the drum and recorded through a Great River NV preamp. These two signals sound quite different from each other; most mixing engineers will combine the two sounds while processing each as needed to create the final kick drum sound.

Fig. 4.2. Drum Mix

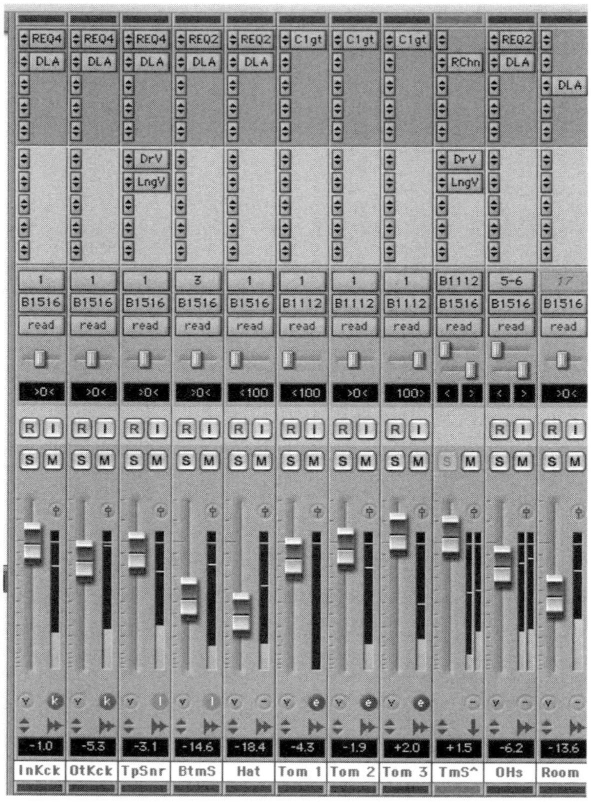

Delay Compensation

As mentioned in the last chapter, some recording and mixing software applications don't automatically compensate for the processing delays caused by inserting plug-ins onto a track. In those cases where plug-in delay interferes with the sound of a track or because the groove goes away, manual delay compensation must be used. When a plug-in algorithm induces enough latency to cause problems with musical timing, something needs to be done to compensate. Remember that it usually takes a finite length of time for audio to be passed into a plug-in, be processed, and sent on its way. The amount of processing delay depends in large part on the plug-in; some take just a few microseconds, while others can take a few milliseconds. While some plug-ins do not introduce any delay to a track when they're inserted. Others, like Digidesign's Maxim plug-in, induce over a thousand samples of delay; this equates to more than 22 ms, which is certainly more than enough to mess with a groove.

Latency can also become an issue when nearly identical sources are on separate tracks—for instance, the two kick drum tracks in this song, or the top and bottom snare tracks. Should a plug-in that induces latency be inserted on only one of the two nearly identical tracks, phase cancellation can cause some frequencies to be missing or barely audible. For these reasons, our look at "It Just Comes Natural" will also examine the delays that would need to be added to the drum tracks to make them line up correctly on those DAWs without delay compensation built in. Waves plug-ins were used for most (or all) of the processing on the drum tracks on "It Just Comes Natural." The tom tracks were processed with Waves C1 gate plug-ins, and also were assigned to their own buss where a couple of additional plug-ins were added. Sixty-five samples (1.48 ms) of delay were added to the other drum tracks; this allows them to be lined up with the toms.

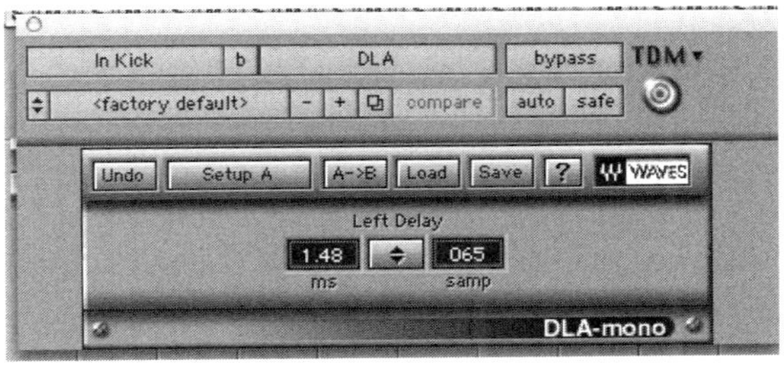

Fig. 4.3. Delay Plug-in

There was a movement in the early days of digital workstations to make all of the drum tracks match up with the tracks recorded by the overhead microphones, so that hits on the snare track, for example, lined up precisely with the snare hits picked up by the overhead mics. The tom tracks were also delayed so that they lined up exactly with the tom hits picked up by the overhead mics. The idea was to compensate for the time it took the sound of the snare to travel the three to five feet of distance between the drum and the overheads and therefore minimize phasing issues between the overhead mics and the snare mic. Fortunately, this practice has fallen into disuse—partly because it was a lot of trouble for little return, and partly because the sound of recorded drums that most of us know comes from years of listening to records that did not do this kind of compensation. In other words, any slight phasing issues are part of what most of us think of as "drums."

Kick Drum

When building a track from the drums up, I've found that when setting the level of the kick (in this case, setting the levels of both kick tracks), it's a mistake to try and make the drums as loud and as full as possible before turning up the other instruments. This will usually cause problems when the other tracks are turned up. Keeping the kick drum level (at the output stage of the mixer) somewhere between –4 dBFS and –8 dBFS leaves the necessary room for all of the other instruments and sources to be added without overloading the output buss and requiring that all the tracks be turned down. Since it's generally a good idea to mix (and check mixes) at several different levels—from the lower threshold of audibility to the highest threshold of tolerance— keeping the kick drum at a fairly consistent –6 dB at the output of the DAW allows a certain amount of consistency when mixing an entire project and makes the job of mastering the final product much easier.

Neither of the kick drum tracks on "It Just Comes Natural" used (or needed) a compressor; besides the delay compensation plug-in, only a 4-band Waves Renaissance EQ was inserted onto the track. The inside kick track has a 2 dB boost around 35 Hz. Keep in mind that 35 Hz is the center frequency for this EQ band. Since that band has a fairly wide Q, those frequencies higher than 35 Hz in the useable audio range are also boosted slightly. Two other bands, centered near 4 kHz and around 10 kHz, are also boosted, which enhances definition by adding a bit of a click to the kick drum sound. The inside kick fader level was –1.0 dB, while the outside kick level was set at –5.3 dB. The out-kick track also has a 4-band Renaissance EQ, with a boost centered at 46 Hz and a 3.5 dB cut around 600 Hz.

The out-kick was recorded with a Yamaha Subkick; this is a new version of a fairly old idea. The subkick is essentially a speaker that's wired with an XLR connection so that it can be used as a microphone. Conceptually, there's not much difference between a dynamic microphone and a speaker. A microphone converts vibrations into electrical impulses, while a speaker converts electrical impulses into vibrations. They are two sides of the same coin. Of course, a speaker is a really inefficient microphone, and one that doesn't handle high frequencies well—perfect for a kick drum, where high sound pressure levels are the norm, and where high frequencies aren't wanted.

In the 1960s, a resourceful recording engineer in California came up with this line of reasoning; and to test it, he simply rolled an Ampeg B-15 amp (a bass amp common in studios at the time) directly in front of a bass drum, and ran a guitar cord from the speaker jack to a convenient DI box. The result was essentially the same as you can hear on the out-kick track—a band-limited insensitive microphone. Later, smaller speakers (in the 6- to 8-inch range) were suspended in front of kick drums—more often on rock tracks than country songs—and the results blended in with the primary kick drum mic. Though the practice has been used in Nashville for many years, it became much more common a couple of years ago when Yamaha introduced their Subkick, a conveniently packed version of the original idea.

But back to "It Just Comes Natural"; both the in- and the out-kick tracks have the delay compensation plug-in inserted, with 65 samples or 1.48 ms of delay added to each of the tracks.

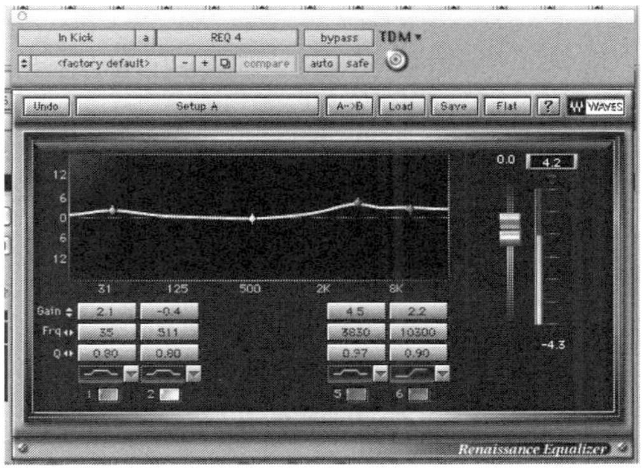

Fig. 4.4. In-Kick EQ

Waves Renaissance REQ-4 In-Kick Settings

parameter	band 1	band 2	band 3	band 4
gain	+2.1 dB	–0.4 dB	+4.5 dB	+2.2 dB
frequency	35 Hz	511 Hz	4,362 Hz	10,300 Hz
Q	0.80	0.80	0.97	0.90
shape	bell	bell	bell	shelf

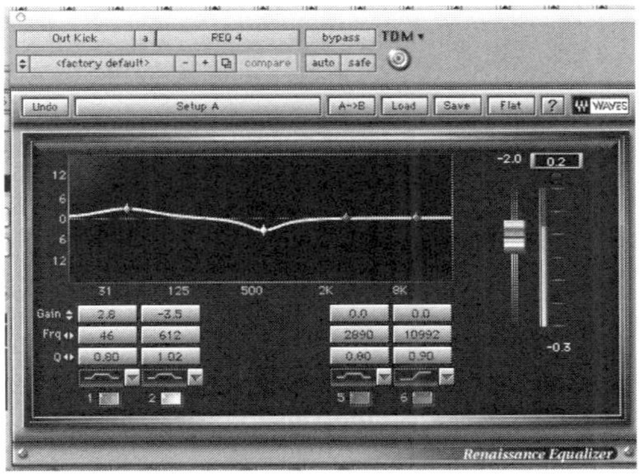

Fig. 4.5. Out-Kick EQ

Waves Renaissance REQ-4 Out-Kick Settings

parameter	band 1	band 2	band 3	band 4
gain	+2.8 dB	–3.5 dB	0 dB	0 dB
frequency	46 Hz	612 Hz	2,890 Hz	10,992 Hz
Q	0.80	1.02	0.80	0.90
shape	bell	bell	bell	shelf

Snare Drum

Top Snare

The top snare track also uses a 4-band Waves Renaissance EQ; a 2.2 dB boost at 109 Hz adds some meat to the snare track, and a 1.6 dB boost at 341 Hz helps with adding some body. A 1 dB rise at 3 kHz helps the snare track to cut through, and a shelving filter at 13 kHz with a 4.9 kHz boost emphasizes the high end.

Fig. 4.6. Top Snare EQ

Waves Renaissance REQ-4 Top Snare Settings				
parameter	**band 1**	**band 2**	**band 3**	**band 4**
gain	+2.2 dB	+1.6 dB	+1.0 dB	+4.9 dB
frequency	109 Hz	341 Hz	3,084 Hz	12,884 Hz
Q	0.80	1.02	0.80	0.90
shape	bell	bell	bell	bell

Bottom Snare

A Neumann KM 84 was used for the bottom snare track. There's a 2-band Renaissance EQ on the track, but no frequencies are altered by it. It's there more to make the math easy when working out the amount of delay needed by the various drum tracks; even though there's no equalization changes taking place, the Waves Renaissance EQ adds a specific amount of delay to the track. By inserting it onto the bottom snare track—even though it doesn't change any frequencies—the time delay is consistent with the top snare track. The fader level of the bottom snare track is set to −14.6 dB, and the delay is consistent with the other delays on the drums at 1.48 ms (or 65 samples).

Hi-hat

Much like the bottom snare mic, the hi-hat mic can be used or not used, depending on the engineer, the drummer, and the song being mixed. If the hi-hat track is used in the mix, it should be panned to reflect the drum set as a whole. If the drums are mixed from the drummer's perspective, pan the hat to the left; if mixing drums from the audience's perspective, pan the hat to the right. I used the hi-hat track on "It Just Comes Natural" because it added a bit of needed definition.

In the same manner as the bottom snare track, a 2-band Renaissance EQ was added to the hi-hat track, with no adjustments made to the EQ. like the other drum tracks on this song, 1.48 ms (or 65 samples) of delay was added. The level of the hi-hat track was set at –18.4 dB.

Toms

There are two ways to pan a drum set: audience perspective and drummer perspective. Those who feel that the audience perspective is correct will pan the toms from right to left, as though they were sitting in front of the drum set; others will pan the toms as though they were sitting behind the drums playing them, with the toms panned from left to right.

Whichever perspective you choose, there's one more option: you may pan the high and low toms hard left and right (or right and left) or you may pan them soft left and right (or right and left). Soft panning the toms seems, to some engineers, to sound more natural than hard panning. In this mix, the drums are panned from the drummer's perspective. They are panned with the first tom hard left, the middle tom to the center, and the floor tom panned hard right. Make sure that whichever way you choose to pan the toms, the overheads are panned in the same direction. The toms on "It Just Comes Natural" are gated to eliminate the tom hum that has been discussed earlier. A gate has a threshold that opens when that threshold is exceeded, and that shuts again when the signal strength drops below the threshold.

Fig. 4.7. Tom Gates

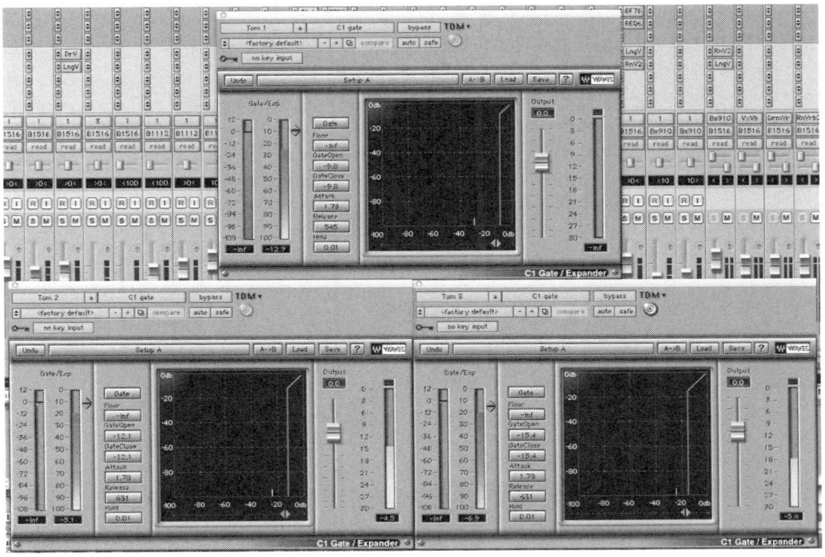

This is one way to eliminate unwanted noise from a track. When using gates on an drum track, the primary goal is to keep the threshold high enough to exclude extraneous peaks from opening the gate, while keeping it low enough that it opens whenever the gated drum is struck. The toms on this song are bussed to a stereo tom buss, where the EQ and compression for the toms is added. There's no compelling reason, by the way, to put compression and equalization on the buss inserts rather than on the individual toms other than the savings in processor power when using one plug-in instead of three. Nevertheless, it's done fairly often—possibly as a holdover from the early days of mixing in the DAW. The output level for the first tom is –4.3 dB; the second tom is at 1.9 dB, and the third tom is at +2.0 dB. The tom tracks are bussed to a tom buss, which has a Waves Renaissance Channel inserted.

Gates

Waves C1 Gate for Tom 1

floor	gate open	gate close	attack	release	hold
infinite	–9.8	–9.8	1.78	545	0.01

Waves C1 Gate for Tom 2

floor	gate open	gate close	attack	release	hold
infinite	–12.1	–12.1	1.78	545	0.01

Waves C1 Gate for Tom 3

floor	gate open	gate close	attack	release	hold
infinite	–15.4	–15.4	1.78	545	0.01

Tom Buss

Another reason to put effects processing on an auxiliary stereo buss rather than on individual tracks is so that the processing affects all of the tracks sent through the buss in the same way. Instead of using an EQ and a compressor on the tom buss, the Waves Renaissance Channel was inserted. The Renaissance Channel is a plug-in version of a console's channel strip, where a number of processors are available in a single plug-in. In the case of the Renaissance Channel, a 4-band EQ, a compressor, and an expander are available. Additionally, the Renaissance Channel offers parameters that aren't available with the single function versions. The Channel also offers a choice of either the compressor or the EQ being first in the signal path, sidechain filters on the compressor and on the gate, as well as a phase reverse switch that inverts the polarity of the signal passing through it. In this instance, the polarity switch is activated, which simply means the toms sounded better (especially in relation to the overheads) when the switch was engaged than when it wasn't.

Fig. 4.8. Tom Buss Processing

The output of the tom buss is +1.5 dB. Two reverb sends were used: the drum verb send was at –9.5 dB, and a send to the long verb was at –17.1 dB.

Waves Renaissance Channel Tom Buss Settings EQ				
parameter	**band 1**	**band 2**	**band 3**	**band 4**
gain	–0.3 dB	0 dB	+1.7 dB	+1.3 dB
frequency	115 Hz	110 Hz	2,074 Hz	4,621 Hz
Q	0.80	1.00	0.66	0.90
shape	bell	bell	bell	shelf

Phase Reverse On

Waves Renaissance Channel Tom Buss Settings Compressor				
threshold	**attack**	**release**	**ratio**	**gain**
–3.0 db	3.60	240	3.7:1	0.2 db

Overheads

Overhead microphones present another range of options for the mixing engineer—some folks like to use the overheads as the primary element of the drum sound, with the snare, tom, and hi-hat mics used to help fill out the sound of the overheads, while others will use the overhead microphones more as cymbal mics, with the main sound of the drum set delivered by the close-miked snare, toms, and hi-hat. In any case, make sure that the overhead tracks and the tom tracks are panned in similar directions. The overheads are panned hard left and right. While the overhead tracks (which were recorded with a pair of Telefunken 251 microphones set about a foot behind and two feet above the drummer's head, pointing over his shoulders at the drums set) were originally recorded to two mono tracks, they were moved to a stereo track for ease of viewing and processing. Another 2-band Renaissance EQ was inserted onto the overhead track, though like the hat and the bottom snare mic, it is used merely to help with the delay compensation computation. Like the other tracks, the overheads have a delay of 1.48 ms or 65 samples added to them, the output level of the overheads is -6.2 dB.

While most of the mixes included in this volume leave the overhead tracks unprocessed (other than the odd bit of buss compression and EQ added to the drum kit as a whole), it isn't uncommon to process the overheads. This processing can include compression or EQ. Compressing (or limiting) the overhead mics, especially when they are used as the main sound source for the drums, goes back at least to the time of Geoff Emerick's sessions with The Beatles. And it's still a viable approach—not a particularly natural sound, but certainly a sound that is once again becoming more common. There's a sound that happens when a track is highly compressed called "pumping." This happens when the compressor's release time allows the output volume of the track to rise dramatically (and audibly) as the compressor releases. While it would generally not be something to aim for, allowing the overhead tracks to pump can by a nice effect—when the release time is adjusted to allow the compressor to pump along with the track. It takes a bit of adjusting (and listening) to achieve this effect, but it's quite cool when it works. Of course, you can also compress the overhead tracks simply to control the level of the track rather than to create an effect.

If the overhead tracks sound boxy, a high-pass filter can do wonders at clearing up the issue; set the filter so it filters out everything below about 100 Hz, and then try raising the filter frequency to hear at what point this "thinning out" of the low end becomes objectionable—or desirable. If the cymbals have a clangy sound (well, an objectionable clangy sound), try cutting frequencies in the 400-to-800 Hz range to minimize the obnoxious qualities of the cymbals. And adding a broad bell shaped boost in the 12 to 15 kHz range can add a nice sheen to the overhead sound.

Room Mic

Room mics are typically not used at anywhere near their full levels, and the room mic on this song is no exception. The track level is at –13.6 dB and no processing was added to it other than a delay program that adds 1.55 ms (or 68 samples) of delay to the track.

Unlike some of the other songs in this volume, the drum tracks were not routed to a drum buss; instead, the are routed directly to the submaster buss. Ultimately, the choice of whether or not to use busses as part of the mixing process (other than as effects returns) depends more on the way the engineer prefers to work than on any sonic advantages inherent in the use of busses.

BASS

The bass tracks on "It Just Comes Natural" didn't require the use of a 5-string bass and the low notes available on the low B string, so a Fender Precision bass was used to record the track. A Waves Renaissance Compressor and a 2-band Waves Renaissance EQ were used on the track at the time of the mix.. The output fader of the bass was set at –7.4 dB. Not a whole lot of gain reduction was used on the bass track; the compressor was added primarily to even out any inequities in the bass, while the EQ was primarily used to add warmth to the low end of the track. You may notice that the low band of the Renaissance EQ is centered at 34 Hz. Remember that since the Q setting affects the width of an EQ band—that is, the lower the number, the wider the frequency range effect by any changes to the level of that band. Even though the center frequency of this EQ band is quite low—not only below the lowest frequency that the bass can create, but lower than the lowest frequency that most consumer speakers can reproduce—the Q setting is wide enough that a fairly wide range of frequencies that *can* be reproduced are affected by this EQ band.

Fig. 4.9. Bass Compressor

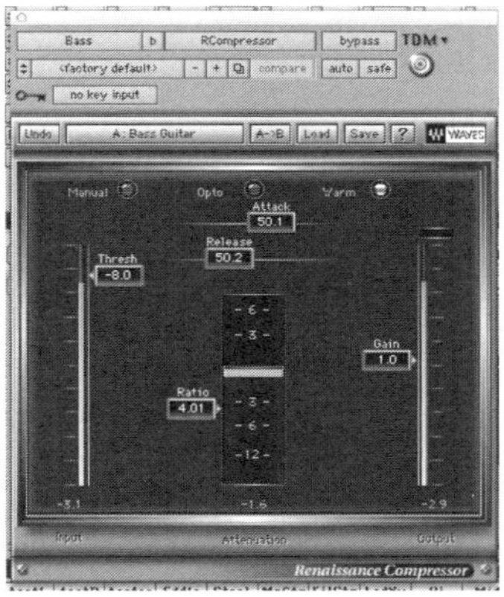

Waves Renaissance Compressor Bass Settings				
threshold	**attack**	**release**	**ratio**	**gain**
–8.0 dB	50.1	50.2	4.01:1	+1.0 dB

Fig. 4.10. Bass EQ

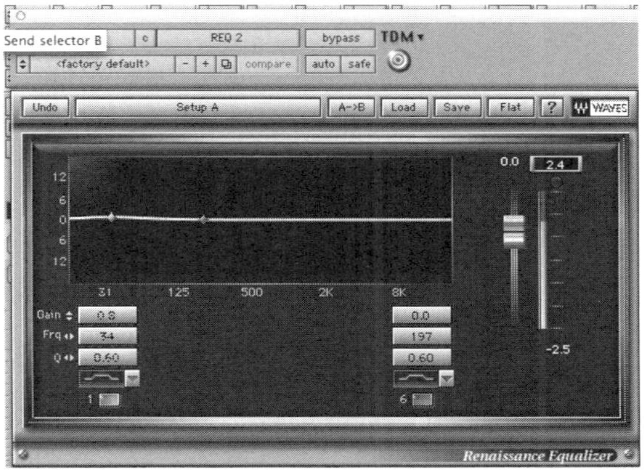

Waves Renaissance REQ-2 Bass Settings		
parameter	band 1	band 2
gain	+0.8 dB	+0.5 dB
frequency	34 Hz	197 Hz
Q	0.60	0.60
shape	bell	bell

WURLITZER ELECTRIC PIANO

There are many wonderful things about the sound of a Wurlitzer electric piano, but one of the most interesting is that it fits so well into a mix without the use of any processing—no EQ, no compression, nothing—except the sound of the instrument.

The Wurlitzer electric piano was first introduced in the 1950s, and the Rhodes electric piano was introduced in the middle 1960s; each immediately found adherents. While the Rhodes sound is known primarily for its bell-like qualities, the Wurly has a certain grungy quality when played hard that makes it blend well as a rhythm instrument with guitar dominated music—though when played softly, the instrument has a sweet vibraphone-like texture. The Wurly's distinctive tremolo is as much a part of its sound as the actual notes and shouldn't be overlooked. The Wurlitzer's action is usually much more comfortable for pianists, too. It's for these two reasons that the classic Motown tracks that used an electric piano always used the Wurly—the folks at Motown felt like it "played well with guitars."

Though there are a few of the early Model 100 Wurlys around Nashville (their owners usually brag about the fact that Model 100's amplifiers have tubes), most of the Wurlys in Nashville studios are the Model 200s, which were introduced in 1969. The Wurly is one of the few instruments that I don't recommend the use of either compression or EQ—the instrument doesn't have a particularly large dynamic range. It is limited on one end by the noise of the circuitry and on the other by a lack of headroom by the amplifier; it's also bandwidth limited, lacking both extremely low and extremely high frequencies. This isn't a problem, since I've found that if I need to record a Wurly, I want it to sound like a Wurly. It should be noted, though, that Wurlitzer EP sounds generated by synth modules and virtual instruments may not be either dynamically or frequency limited; when those tracks come in, I will EQ and compress the track to suit the needs of the song.

This particular Wurly, a Model 200, was recorded through an A Designs REDDI DI into a Vac Rac tube preamp. The fader output was set at –8.5 dB and the effect send (to the drum reverb) was at –10.7 dB.

Organ

The organ used on the tracks in this book, a 1957 Hammond C-3 with a Leslie 21H cabinet, was recorded in a consistent manner—with a pair of

AEA R84s at two corners of the cabinet to capture the upper rotor, and an Electro-Voice RE20 capturing the lower rotor. The three microphones were bussed to a stereo track with the R84s panned hard left and right and the RE20 panned in the middle. The relative levels between the upper rotor and the lower rotor were determined at the stereo buss. But that's not the only way to record an organ, just the way that it was recorded for this project. If the engineer wanted to have greater control over the volume of the low rotor, all three tracks could have been recorded. Some engineers will also record the upper rotor from each side of the cabinet; this not only makes the organ quite wide, it also makes it sound as though the upper rotor is going twice as fast as it actually is (though it appears that the upper rotor on a Leslie cabinet has two horns, one of those is strictly a counter-balance and has no sound). Another approach to recording the organ would have been to use two microphones—one on the upper rotor and one on the lower rotor. There have been successful recordings where the low rotor wasn't miked at all, but that misses a lot of the magic of the Leslie sound, since the two rotors speed up and slow down at different rates. The reader is welcome to experiment with the sound that results from a single mic on the upper rotor by the simple expedient of turning off one of the tracks.

Though the normal panning for a Leslie cabinet would be hard left and right, turning down one of the two organ channels will move the organ across the soundfield. Reducing the volume of the left channel will move the organ toward the right side of the soundfield, and vice versa. Simply panning both channels to one side will make the sound of the rotating upper rotor sound as though it's spinning at double speed.

Before leaving the discussion of panning the organ tracks, one interesting possibility should be mentioned. Some of the early Steppenwolf records panned the upper rotor to one side of the stereo field and the lower rotor to the other side of the stereo field. If you'd like to experiment with that sound (either on this song or one of the others that have an organ), you'll need to start by converting the stereo organ track into two mono tracks. Different programs will require different methods of doing this; with Pro Tools, the trick would be to create two new mono tracks and simply drag the stereo organ to the new tracks. Once you have two mono organ tracks, filter the two organ tracks. Try using a high-pass filter on one track with a 12 dB-per-octave slope and a cutoff frequency of 800 Hz; on the other track, use a low-pass filter that also cuts off at 800 Hz with a 12 dB-per-octave slope. Though the result is not quite the same as the sound that would come from a single mic on each rotor—mostly because of the differences in the way the upper and lower rotors speed up and slow down—these settings should remove most of the low rotor from one track and most of the high rotor from the other.

But to get back to the specifics of the organ on "It Just Comes Natural," the track needed little processing; other than a slight boost at 14 kHz, the natural sound of the Hammond C3 used on this track was left alone. The organ volume is at –9.2 dB, and the reverb send (to the long verb) is at –10.1 dB.

Fig. 4.11. Organ EQ

Waves Renaissance REQ-4 Organ Settings				
parameter	**band 1**	**band 2**	**band 3**	**band 4**
gain	0 dB	0 dB	0 dB	+2.8 dB
frequency	92 Hz	351 Hz	2,890 Hz	14,050 Hz
Q	0.80	0.80	0.80	0.71
shape	bell	bell	bell	bell

ACOUSTIC GUITARS

Instead of using a buss EQ on the acoustic guitar tracks, "It Just Comes Natural" has a simple 2-band EQ on each of the guitar tracks. For both of the guitar tracks, the first EQ band was used as a high-pass filter, clearing away unneeded low frequency information while the second EQ band is used to add a presence peak that allows the acoustic to cut through the mix. The acoustic left track output is at –8.3 dB, while the acoustic right output is at –9.1 dB. The acoustics are assigned to an acoustic guitar buss; not much is happening on this buss other than a reverb send to the instrument reverb. The level of that send is –10.7 dB, and the output of the acoustic guitar buss is set at –3.0 dB.

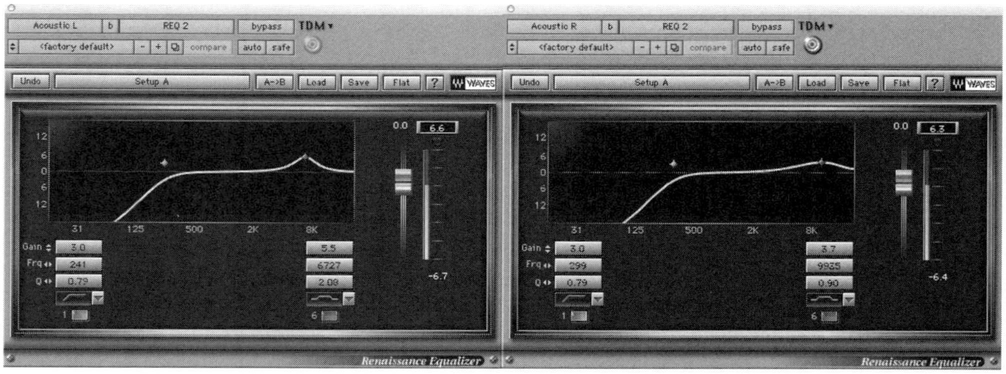

Fig. 4.12. Acoustic Guitar EQ

Waves Renaissance REQ-2 Acoustic L Settings		
parameter	band 1	band 2
gain	+3.0 dB	+5.5 dB
frequency	241 Hz	6,727 Hz
1.28	0.79	2.08
shape	high-pass	bell

Waves Renaissance REQ-2 Acoustic R Settings		
parameter	band 1	band 2
gain	+3.0 dB	+3.7 dB
frequency	299 Hz	9,935 Hz
1.28	0.79	0.90
shape	high-pass	bell

FIDDLE

As with many other acoustic instruments, the sound of the fiddle on a typical country record may or may not sound all that similar to the way that same fiddle sounded in the room as it was being played. The single biggest reason for this may well be that very few listeners (other than the folks who actually play the instrument) have ever listened to a fiddle from a foot or two above the instrument—the normal mic placement when recording them.

Nevertheless, the sound of a well-recorded fiddle has become what most people think of as the sound of a fiddle. On this track, the fiddle was recorded using a Neumann/Gefell M 582; this East German microphone was built in the 1960s, and is related to Neumann's KM 54, a small diaphragm tube mic with a cardioid capsule. The proximity effect of the cardioid pattern can be very useful when trying to capture a certain warmth from the top of the fiddle; moving the mic closer to the instrument can enhance the low end (and conversely, moving the mic farther away will decrease it). Since the proximity effect is greater with a figure 8 mic than with a cardioid, using a microphone that has a figure-8 pattern (like Neumann's KM 86) will allow the mic to be moved even farther from the instrument while using the proximity effect to its greatest effect.

It's not uncommon for fiddle tracks to need no EQ to fit into the overall mix, but when adjustments need to be made, they're typically either in the low range (somewhere in the 300–500 Hz) range to add warmth, or above 3 kHz, to minimize any edginess or scratchy sounds coming from the instrument. Be aware, though, that cutting high frequencies in an overly enthusiastic manner can bring unwanted results (like the producer asking why there's a harmonica on his track instead of a fiddle); be gentle when reducing the high frequencies on the fiddle track. As it happens, no equalization was required for the fiddle track on "It Just Comes Natural." The fader level on the fiddle track was set at –3.1 dB and the reverb send (to the Vox Verb) was at –3.0 dB.

STEEL GUITAR

The steel guitar was panned towards the right side of the soundfield—not 100 percent right, but more like 60 percent right. With Digidesign's Pro Tools, panning goes from 100 percent right to 100 percent left, with 0 percent being in the center. The level of the steel was –6.5 dB, and a 2-band Waves Renaissance EQ was used on the track. This EQ added a bit of presence with a 2.3 dB peak around 2.5 kHz and then removed unnecessary high frequencies with a low-pass filter beginning at 8.7 kHz.

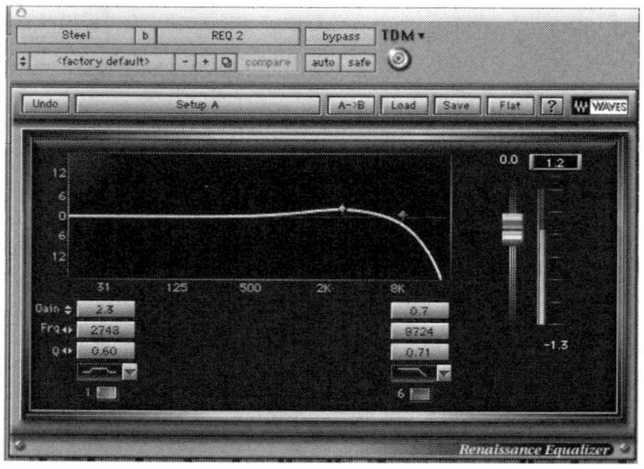

Fig.4.13. Steel EQ

Three different reverbs were used on the steel guitar track: the vocal reverb, the true verb, and the long reverb. The vocal reverb send was at –4.0 dB, the true verb send was at –10.7 dB, and the long reverb send was at –14.8 dB.

Waves Renaissance REQ-2 Steel Guitar Settings

parameter	band 1	band 2
gain	+2.3 dB	+0.7 dB
frequency	2,748 Hz	8,724 Hz
1.28	0.60	0.60
shape	bell	low-pass

ELECTRIC GUITARS

Though there are two electric guitar tracks on "It Just Comes Natural," it would be a bit of a misnomer to say that there are two guitars. It may well have been that on the George Strait session that produced the original version of this song, there was only one electric guitar pass. But since there is essentially an unlimited number of tracks available, anytime a guitar track needs to be processed in a different manner, or when the tone changes dramatically, or even when a panning or level change might need to be made, the changed guitar sound will be put on two tracks of its own. (You'll see more of this with some other songs in this book.) This practice simply makes it easier (and faster) to create a final mix, and here's why: instead of having to write a bunch of automation data to change the sound of the instrument, you simply create the sounds you need on a track for that one section. In this song, most of the guitar part goes on one track, with the guitar that plays the fills in one verse on a different track.

Main Guitar

The primary electric guitar pass has a 2-band Waves Renaissance EQ inserted; the low band is a high-pass filter at 92 Hz, while the second band is a bell-shaped filter boosting almost 2 dB at around 5 kHz. Other than a bit of automation written in the first chorus and second verse, the level of the guitar is –12.6 dB.

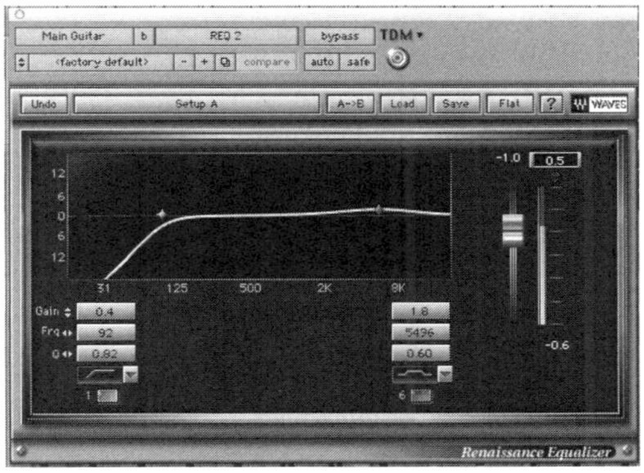

Fig. 4.14. Main Guitar EQ

Waves Renaissance REQ-2 Main Guitar Settings

parameter	band 1	band 2
gain	+0.4 dB	+1.8 dB
frequency	92 Hz	5,496 Hz
1.28	0.60	0.60
shape	high-pass	bell

Fill Guitar

The fill guitar is treated quite differently than the main guitar—there's no EQ, a Bomb Factory BF76 compressor is used, and (the biggest difference) a Waves TrueVerb is used as an insert rather than as an effects send. The TrueVerb, set to a "rock guitar room" setting, adds a welcome ambience to the fill guitar sound.

Fig.4.15. Fill Guitar EQ

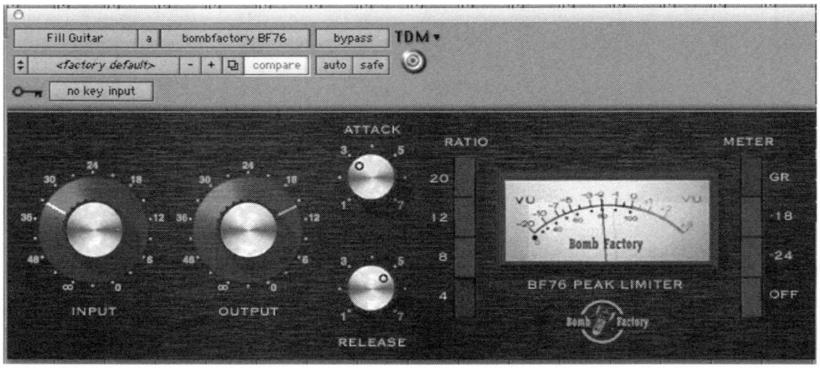

Bomb Factory BF76 Fill Guitar Settings				
input	**output**	**attack**	**release**	**ratio**
33	15	3	5	4:1

Fig. 4.16. Fill Guitar Reverb

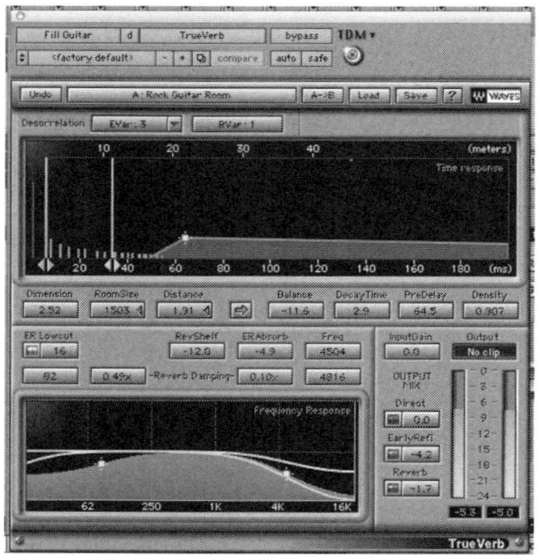

Waves TrueVerb Fill Guitar Settings	
Parameter	**Setting**
Dimension	2.52
Room Size	1,503
Distance	1.91
Balance	–11.6
Decay Time	2.9
Predelay	64.5
Density	0.807

EARLY REFLECTION (ER)	
Low Cut	16
Reverb Damping Frequency Low	82
Damping	0.49x
Reverb Damping Frequency High	4,816
Damping	0.10x
Reverb Shelf	–12.0
ER Absorb	–4.9
ER Absorb Freq	4,504
Input gain	0.0
Direct Output	0.0
Early Reflection Output	–4.8
Reverb Output	–2.6

LEAD VOCAL

The lead vocal on "It Just Comes Natural" has four different processors on it, as well as two effects sends that send the lead vocals to the vocal reverb (in this mix, a Waves TrueVerb) and to the long reverb. The aux send to the long reverb was –26.3 dB while the "true-verb" send was at –12.0 dB. The output level was set at –0.7 dB.

The first is the Antares Auto-Tune 4 plug-in. Like the other vocals in this volume, the Auto-Tune plug-in wasn't added necessarily because I feel that the singer needed to be tuned (the tracks on the DVD are not tuned; you can form your own opinion as you play with the tracks); it's simply that the Auto-Tune plug-in isn't particularly transparent; everything that passes through it develops a bit of that Auto-Tune sound. So the Auto-Tune plug-in is set to unobtrusive levels.

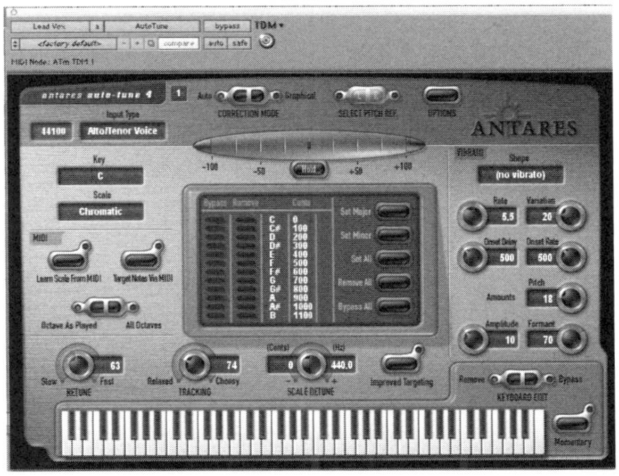

Fig. 4.17. Lead Vocal Auto-Tune.0

Auto-Tune

Retune: 63

Tracking: 74

Input Type: Alto/Tenor Voice

Following the Auto-Tune plug-in is a Waves Renaissance compressor, which adds a bit of warmth while compressing in a fairly mild manner. Next in line is a Bomb Factory BF76 compressor, which is a much more aggressive sounding plug-in than the Renaissance Compressor. The aggressive nature of the BF76 is due in large part to its attack time, which is quite fast. The numbers on the BF76, like the classic UREI upon which it has been modeled, don't reflect a measured time—instead, they reflect the faceplate of the original unit.

Fig. 4.18. Lead Vocal Compressor

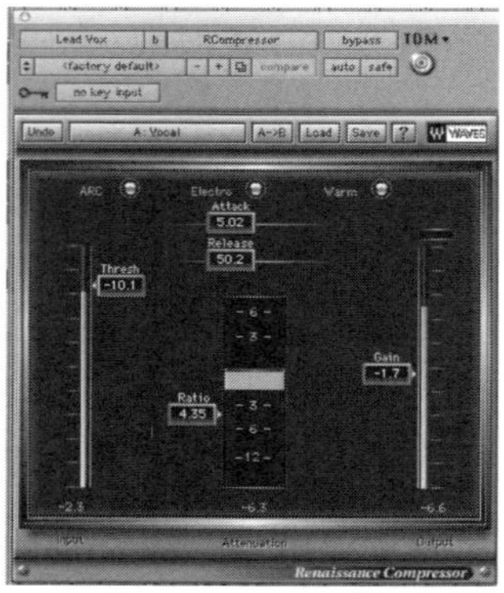

Waves Renaissance Compressor Lead Vocal Settings				
threshold	**attack**	**release**	**ratio**	**gain**
–10.1 db	5.02	50.2	4.35:1	–1.07 db

Fig. 4.19. Lead Vocal BF 76

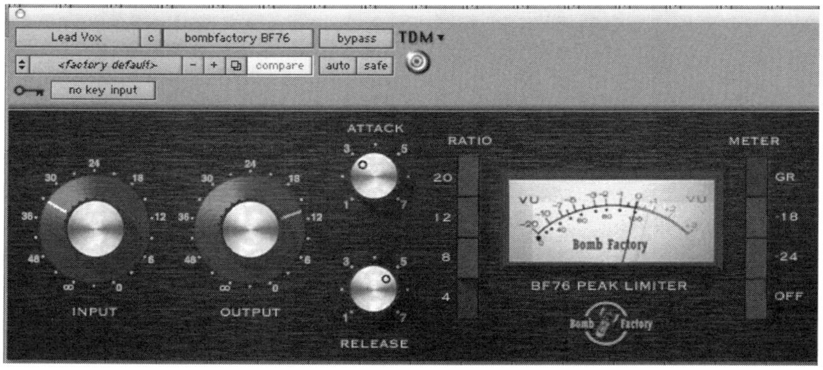

Bomb Factory BF76 Lead Vocal Settings				
input	**output**	**attack**	**release**	**ratio**
33	13.5	3	5	4:1

The final plug-in in the lead vocal chain is a 6-band Waves Renaissance EQ that primarily brightens the track by tilting the frequency response above 5 kHz, as well as high-passing the frequencies below 75 Hz.

Fig. 4.20. Lead Vocal EQ

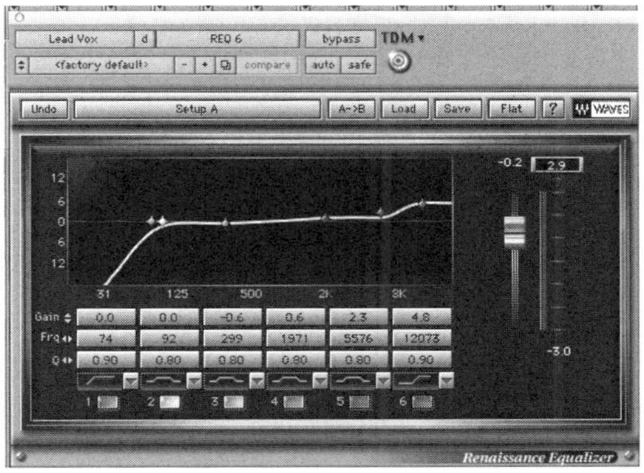

Waves Renaissance REQ-6 Lead Vocal Settings						
parameter	**band 1**	**band 2**	**band 3**	**band 4**	**band 5**	**band 6**
gain	0 dB	0 dB	–0.6 dB	+0.6 dB	+2.3 dB	+4.8 dB
frequency	74 Hz	92 Hz	299 Hz	1,971 Hz	5,576 Hz	12,073 Hz
Q	0.90	0.80	0.80	0.80	0.80	0.90
shape	high-pass	bell	bell	bell	bell	shelving

Parallel Compression on Vocal

The lead vocal on "It Just Comes Natural" was recorded with two different compressors in the vocal chain, and there's another trick that should be mentioned. By multing the lead vocals—that is, bringing the lead vocal track up on two different channels of the workstation—you can transparently raise the average levels of a vocal track without it sounding like the vocals are compressed too heavily.

Here's how it works: set up two vocal channels, either by duplicating (or copying) the one in the session—even duplicating the plug-ins. Then, on the second channel, add a limiter or a compressor with a 20:1 ratio with a fast attack and release, and a threshold that will essentially remove all of the dynamics from the performance. Now, bring the second channel (the one with the limiter up to between 60 to 70 percent of the first channel's level, so that on the louder vocals, the first (mildly compressed) vocal dominates. On the quieter sections, the second (hard-limited) channel will become more audible. Parallel compression can be used to brings up the average level of the vocal in the quiet parts without making the louder sections sound as though the life were sucked out of them by the limiter. There are a couple of things that need to be watched out for when doing parallel compression inside the DAW. The biggest is that with DAWs that don't have delay compensation built in, you can have phasing issues that must be eliminated by advancing or delaying individual tracks.

Background Vocals

There are two background vocals (BGV) on "It Just Comes Natural." The high BGV is set to –9.2 dB while the mid BGV level is at –7.7 dB. The background vocals have no automation, but an Auto-Tune plug-in has been inserted on each of the tracks. In much the same manner as the Auto-Tune on the lead vocal, these are used more as a matter of principle than due to any need. These two tracks are bussed to the BGV buss (the BGV buss is set at +1.5), with the effects send to the TrueVerb at –5.5 dB and the long reverb at –12.9 dB. The BGV buss has a 2-band Waves Renaissance EQ inserted though only one band is active with a broad boost around 8 kHz to add clarity. It also has a Renaissance Compressor, which helps to smooth out the peaks in the BGV tracks.

The two BGV tracks have mild settings, as follows:

Fig. 4.21. High Vocal Auto Tune

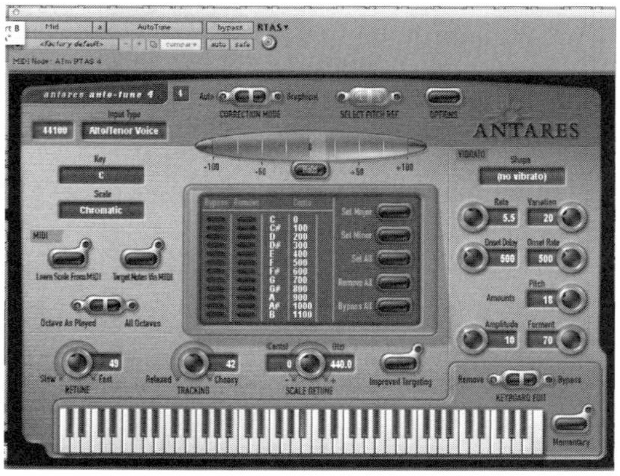

High BGV Auto-Tune

Retune: 49
Tracking: 42
Scale detune: 0 cents
Input Type: Alto/Tenor Voice

Fig. 4.22. Mid Vocal Auto Tune

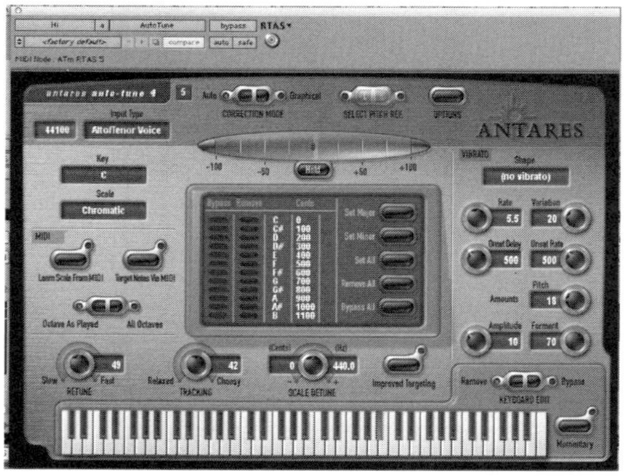

Low BGV Auto-Tune

Retune: 49
Tracking: 42
Scale detune: 0 cents
Input Type: Alto/Tenor Voice

Fig. 4.23. BGV Buss EQ

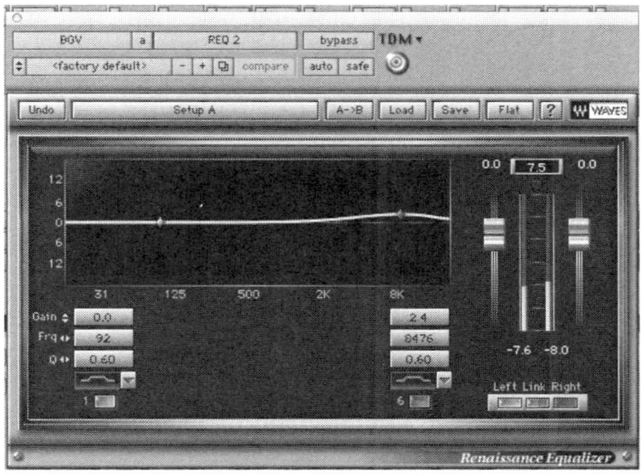

Waves Renaissance EQ 2 BGV Buss Settings		
parameter	**band 1**	**band 2**
gain	0 dB	+2.4 dB
frequency	92 Hz	8,476 Hz
1.28	0.60	0.60
shape	bell	bell

Fig. 4.24. BGV Buss Compressor

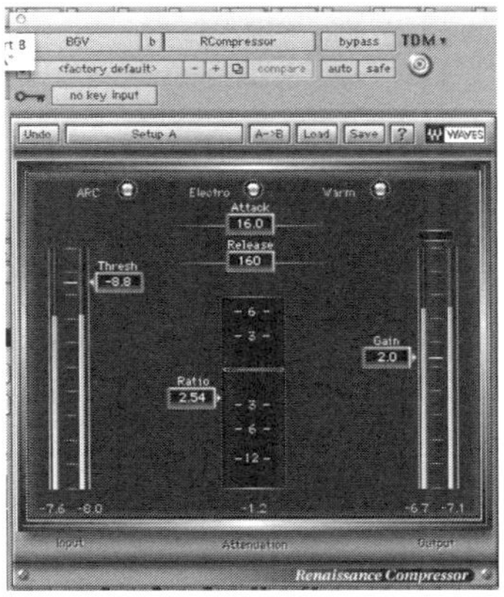

Waves Renaissance Compressor BGV Buss Settings				
threshold	**attack**	**release**	**ratio**	**gain**
–8.8 db	16.0	160	2.54:1	–12.0 db

AUX SENDS AND BUSS PROCESSING

Four reverb returns are used on "It Just Comes Natural" in addition to the reverb used as an insert on the fill-guitar track. The first of these reverbs is the "vocal reverb," a Waves Renaissance Reverberator set to a medium room setting. The drum reverb is another Renaissance Reverb with a Drum Plate

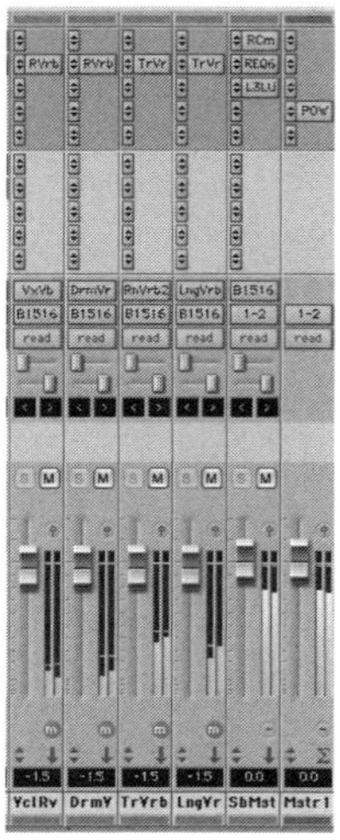

Fig. 4.25. Aux Sends

setting. The third, named "true verb," has a Waves TrueVerb set to a Nice Plate setting, and the last, another Waves TrueVerb, is called a "long verb" and is set to a Large Concert setting. Any combination of these four can be used on any track. The practice of setting up multiple reverbs of different lengths and flavors is another holdover from the days of mixing on consoles. Well-equipped studios in the 1970s would likely have a plate reverb or two (set to different reverb times) and possibly a chamber as well; when mixing, any combination of these would be used to meet a given need. Though modern workstation technology allows an almost unlimited number of reverbs (subject to the processing power available), in reality, there's seldom a need to go to such lengths. The output of the four reverb returns is set to 1.5 dB below unity gain. Below are the settings for the reverbs used in "It Just Comes Natural."

Fig, 4.26. Vocal Reverb

Waves Renaissance Reverberator Vocal Reverb Settings	
parameter	**setting**
REVERB DAMPING	
frequency 1	29
ratio 1	1.00
frequency 2	4,569
ratio 2	0.76
reverb type	Resoverb
decorrelation	Var: 1
REVERB EQ	
frequency 1	156
gain 1	0
frequency 2	1,256
gain 2	–4.9 dB
predelay	0.0
time	0.70
size	62.3

diffusion	30
decay	linear
early reflection level	–23.9 dB
reverb	0.0 dB
wet/dry	100%
gain	0

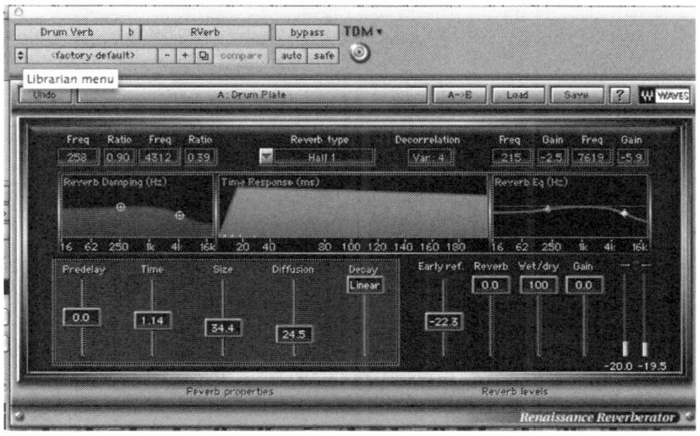

Fig. 4.27. Drum Reverb

Waves Renaissance Reverberator Drum Reverb Settings	
parameter	**setting**
REVERB DAMPING	
frequency 1	258
ratio 1	0.90
frequency 2	4,312
ratio 2	0.39
reverb type	Hall 1
decorrelation	Var: 4
REVERB EQ	
frequency 1	215
gain 1	–2.5 dB
frequency 2	7,619
gain 2	–5.9 dB
predelay	0.0
time	1.14 sec.
size	34.4
diffusion	24.5
decay	linear
early reflection level	–22.3 dB
reverb	0.0 dB
wet/dry	100%
gain	0

Fig. 4.28. TrueVerb

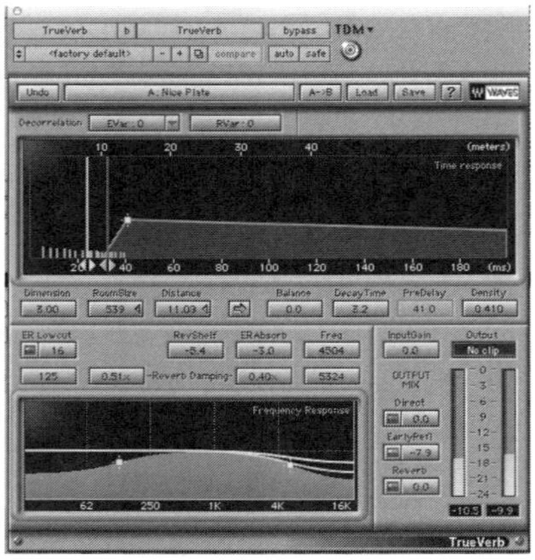

Waves TrueVerb "True Verb" Settings	
parameter	**setting**
dimension	3.00
room size	539
distance	11.08
balance	0.0
decay time	3.2
predelay	41.0
density	0.410
EARLY REFLECTION (ER)	
low cut	16
reverb damping frequency low	125
damping	0.51¥
reverb damping frequency high	5,324
damping	0.40¥
reverb shelf	–5.4
ER absorb	–3.0
ER absorb freq	4,504
input gain	0.0
direct output	0.0
early reflection output	–7.9
reverb output	0.0

Fig. 4.29. Long Verb

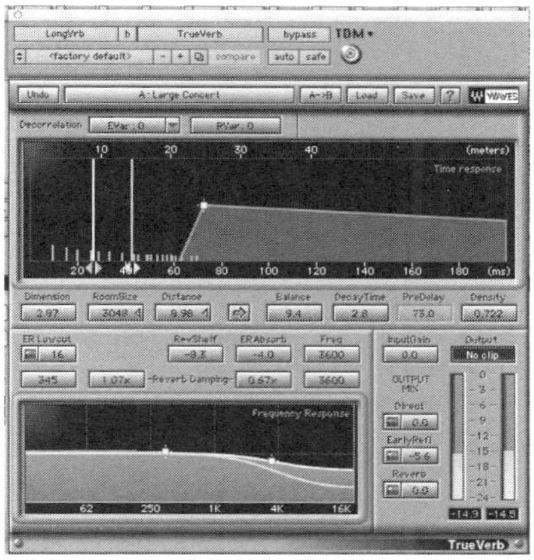

Waves TrueVerb Long Verb Settings	
parameter	**setting**
dimension	2.87
room size	3,048
distance	8.98
balance	9.4
decay time	2.8
predelay	73.0
density	0.722
EARLY REFLECTION (ER)	
low cut	16
reverb damping frequency low	345
damping	1.07¥
reverb damping frequency high	3,600
damping	0.67¥
reverb shelf	–8.3
ER absorb	–4.0
ER absorb freq	3,600
input gain	0.0
direct output	0.0
early reflection output	–5.6
reverb output	0

SUBMASTER BUSS

The submaster buss has a Renaissance Compressor, a 6-band Waves Renaissance EQ (used to tweak the overall tone of the mix) and a Waves L3 Ultramaximizer as plug-ins. As mentioned in other chapters, the L3 is a stereo limiter that is used to bring up the average volume of the mix to contemporary levels while protecting against the possibility of clipping with the inevitable distortion that's the result of clipping a digital signal.

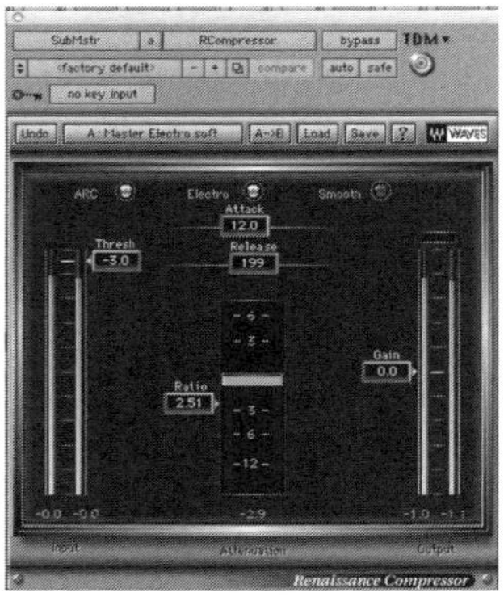

Fig. 4.30. Submaster Compressor

Waves Renaissance Compressor Submaster Settings				
threshold	**attack**	**release**	**ratio**	**gain**
–3.0 dB	12.0	199	2.51:1	0 dB

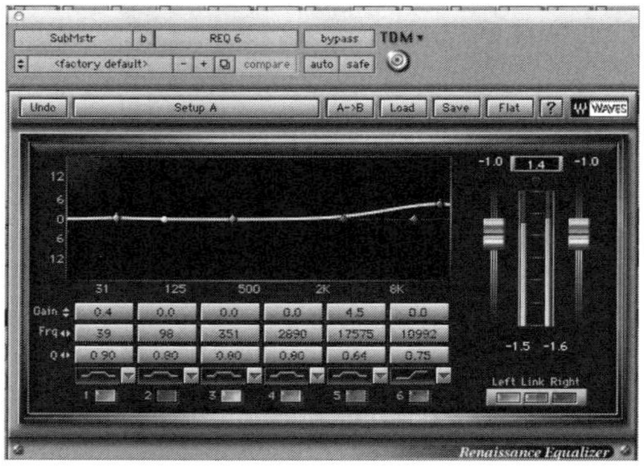

Fig. 4.31. Submaster EQ

Waves Renaissance REQ-6 Submaster Settings						
parameter	**band 1**	**band 2**	**band 3**	**band 4**	**band 5**	**band 6**
gain	+0.4 dB	0 dB	0 dB	0 dB	+4.5 dB	0 dB
frequency	39 Hz	98 Hz	351 Hz	2,890	17,575 Hz	10,992 Hz
Q	0.90	0.80	0.80	0.80	0.80	0.90
shape	bell	bell	bell	bell	bell	shelving

Fig. 4.32. Submaster Buss Limiter

Submaster Limiter

Waves L-3

Threshold: –4.0 dB

Out Ceiling: –0.2 dB

Master Output

The master output buss contains only a Pow-R Dither plug-in, which reduces the bit depth of the output to 16 bits. For a change, the submaster buss is used to create the fade at the end of "It Just Comes Natural" rather than the master output.

Fig. 4.33. Dither

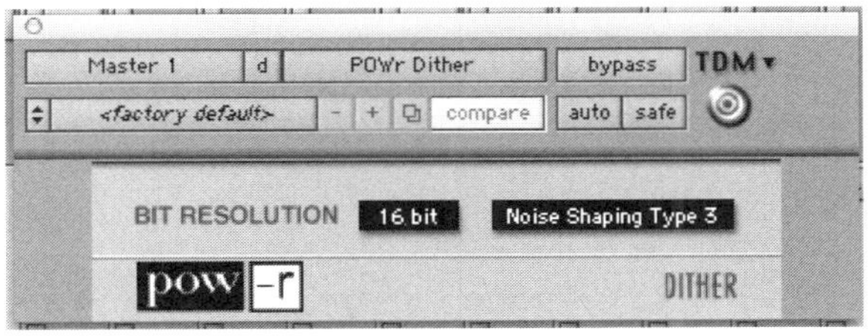

Pow-R Dither

16-bit

Noise shaping type 2

AUTOMATION

A few of the individual tracks in "It Just Comes Natural" contain automation data. The acoustic guitars are raised a bit in the last verse of the song (at the point where the main guitar plays single line fills instead of the busier rhythm part), the fiddle track is automated right before the second verse starts, and the main electric has automation at the same place (though the guitar automation carries on into the second verse). The steel guitar solo has some automation, especially during the solo. The fade-out at the end of the song was written on the submaster buss.

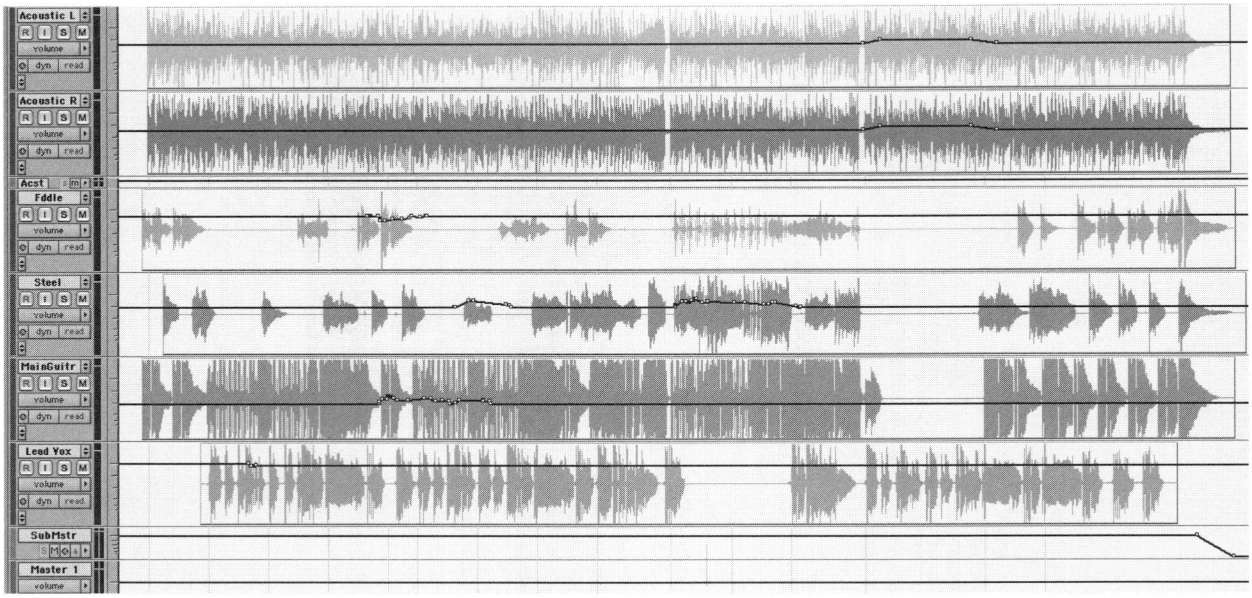

Fig. 4.34. Automation

EDITS

Other than trimming the beginnings of all of the tracks to the point where audio begins, as well as clearing a region in the high BGV between (and during) the solo, no editing was done to any of the tracks on "It Just Comes Natural."

PRINTING MIXES

When printing the mix of each of the songs in this volume, I use a consistent approach: one of the continuous tracks is used to set the final length of the song. (I'll typically use either an acoustic guitar track or the piano track, though on "It Just Comes Natural" the main guitar track was used.) I'll trim the chosen track to just before the first note (by just before, I mean that I'll trim the track to within a single frame, or a thirtieth of a second before the start). Then, at whatever point the fade at the end of the track is completed, I'll trim the back of that same track about a frame after the fade. In Pro Tools, selecting this region and then bouncing the track to the hard drive will cause the Pro Tools to play from the beginning to the end of that track with no excess audio or time either at the beginning or end. In those situations where multiple mixes of a song must be done—for example, if a producer wants vocal up or vocal down versions, TV mixes, or instrumental mixes—all of the versions are the same length, and can be easily lined up for editing.

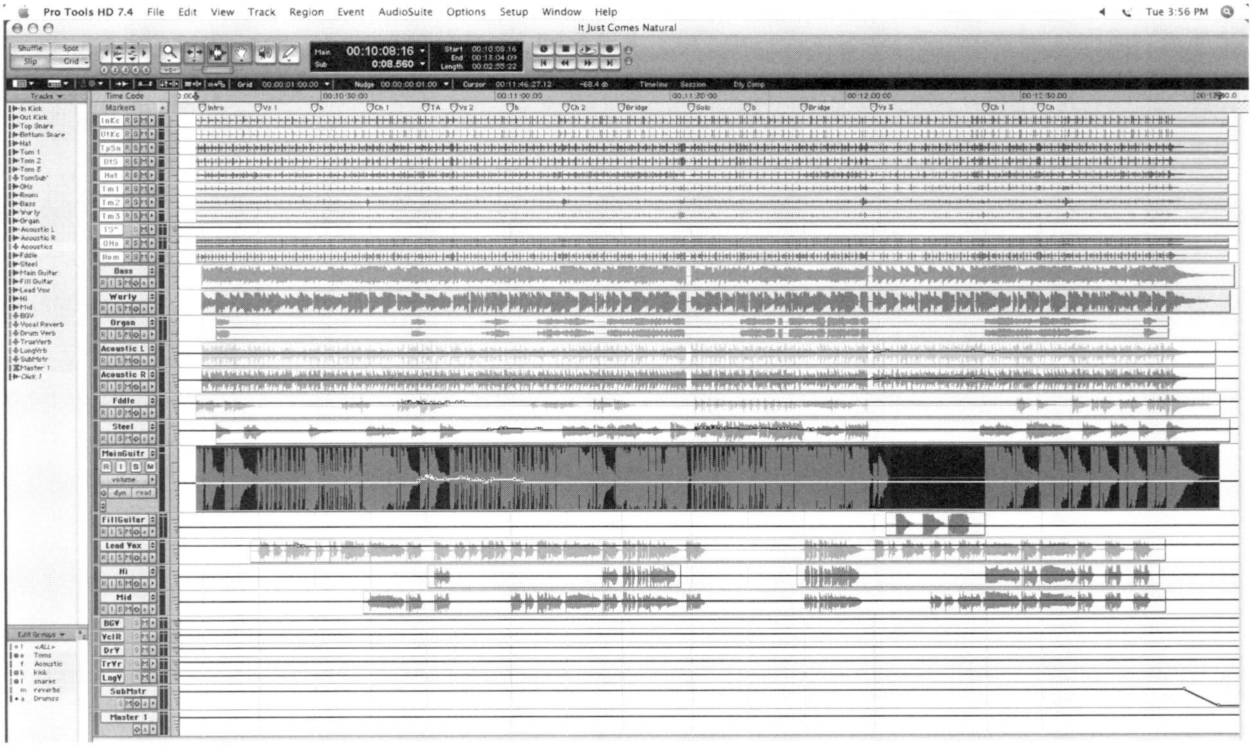

Fig. 4.35. Print Mix

MASTERING

The mix of "It Just Comes Natural" was created with the knowledge that no mastering engineer would see it. While I strongly recommend that my clients who will release their projects commercially should send it to a competent mastering engineer, there are many projects recorded here that are not released commercially, including production music, song demos, and other projects of that nature. The buss processing used on "It Just Comes Natural"—especially the EQ, limiter, and dither plug-ins—would more than likely not be used if these tracks were going to be mastered before release. Remember that the mixes that are delivered for mastering should ideally be 24-bit wave files that are not limited to the point that the mastering engineer's hands are tied. Though I will send out projects for mastering that have been mixed with buss compression, limiting, and EQ, one of the main reasons to send a project to a mastering house is to make the mixes sound as good as they can. If the record has already been squashed, the mastering engineer would have a really hard time trying to "unsquash" it to make it sound good. Those tools are useable at the mixing stage, but they're also easy to overuse.

CHAPTER 5

"My Give a Damn's Busted"

(As Recorded by Jo Dee Messina)

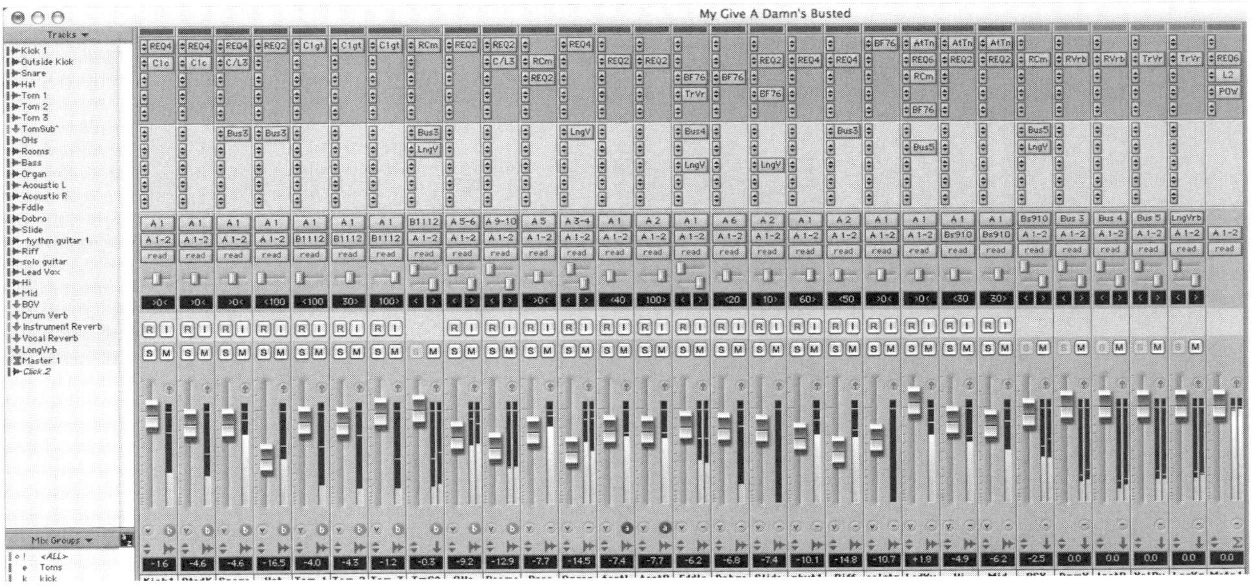

Fig. 5.1. Mix Window

The juxtaposition of instruments that are generally thought of as loud and powerful (drums, electric guitars) with instruments that are typically associated with quieter music (acoustic guitar, dobro, fiddle) gives "My Give a Damn's Busted" an interesting texture—of course, the lyrics (by Joe Diffie, Tom Shapiro, and Tony Martin) are what makes the tune memorable.

DRUMS

The drum tracks on "My Give a Damn's Busted" were recorded in the same manner as the other drum tracks in this volume, without EQ and with little or no compression so that the mixing process could be made a bit more informative. If all the needed processing were done in the tracking stage, then there would be little to talk about concerning the mixing of the drums. Besides that, the lack of processing at the recording stage means that the raw tracks can be manipulated in a bit more creative manner at the mixing stage. "My Give a Damn's Busted" has two kick drum tracks—one track, labeled "In-Kick" was recorded with a Shure Beta 52 microphone placed inside the drum about three inches from the batter head (and recorded through a Daking preamp). Shure's Beta 52 is part of a new generation of microphones that were designed and voiced to get a bit closer to a contemporary kick drum sound; other microphones with a similar design goal include the Audix D6, the AKG D112, and the Sennheiser w602. I find the Beta 52 to be the best of the breed for my own tastes.

Fig. 5.2. Drum Mix

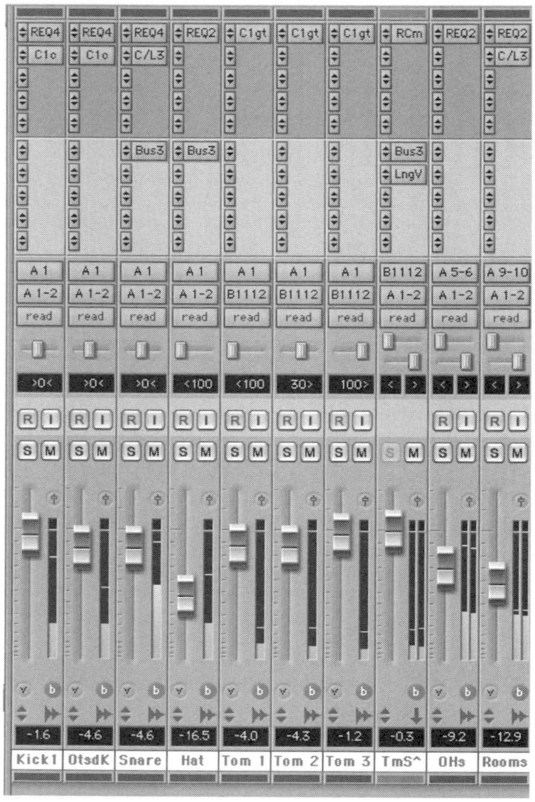

The other kick drum track, labeled "out-kick" was recorded with a CAD Trion mic. The Trion was placed a couple of inches in front of the front head. These two signals sound quite different from each other; most mixing engineers will combine the two sounds while processing each as needed to create the final kick drum sound.

The practice of using two different microphones on the kick drum (with one placed inside the kick and the other placed outside) allows for quite a number of interesting variants in the overall sound of the kick track; and with a large diaphragm condenser like the Trion, there can also be interesting changes in the overall sound of the drum set. For example, the out mic picks up a lot more than just the kick drum—the out mic track also picks up some of the snare drum, the toms, and even some of the cymbals. Sometimes, this open sound is more appropriate than at other times; in those situations, a condenser in front of the kit is an excellent basis for building a drum track. And when it isn't the right sound for a given situation, there are a couple of ways to handle it. The first is to use some fairly radical processing to change the sound of the recorded track so that it does work. The other, naturally, would be to simply mute the track and not use it at all. Both are viable approaches to a problematic track.

Kick Drum

"My Give a Damn's Busted" will take a new (and slightly different) approach to processing the kick drum; both the inside and the outside kick tracks are gated, using the Waves C1 Compressor/Gate. The C1 Compressor/Gate is an expanded version of the C1 Gate used on earlier mixes, with more features and parameters, including a compressor/expander, a 1-band EQ that can be used either in the audio path or in the sidechain of compressor or the gate, and finally, the ability to turn the "look-ahead" function on or off. When a plug-in has a look-ahead function, it essentially delays the audio signal passing through it while not delaying the signal passing though the detection circuitry. This means that the gating and compression circuit can respond to the peaks in the audio signal before they occur. The price for doing that is plug-in delay.

A discussion of the mechanics involved with manual delay compensation took place in earlier chapters. Since the Pro Tools HD3 system used to mix the tracks in this book (as well as many of the other programs used to record and mix in the box) have automatic delay compensation built into the software, that discussion will not be repeated. Just keep in mind that if the particular program you use does *not* have delay compensation built in, the timing of some of the tracks may suffer unless remedial action is taken.

Kick 1

The kick 1 track has two plug-ins inserted: a 4-band Waves Renaissance EQ and the Waves C1 Compressor/Gate. The Renaissance EQ is primarily used for a relatively mild boost at 35 Hz and a larger 4.5 dB boost in the 11 to 3.5 kHz range. You may notice that the third band of the EQ is centered at 39 Hz, while the fourth band, a shelving EQ is centered a bit lower. This isn't an issue; it's simply that while playing with the EQ, the kick sounded better when the shelving frequency was moved lower than the third band of the EQ.

When experimenting with equalization, Waves plug-ins make it easy to simply use a mouse or trackball to adjust both the amount of boost and cut and the center frequency. While these adjustments can be made with the individual band controls by clicking and dragging—and even specific numbers may be entered with a double click—it's usually quicker to simply click and drag the markers in the graph window. This is why frequencies seem to be so specific (for example, band 2 of the kick 1 EQ is at 511 Hz); it doesn't necessarily mean that 505 Hz or 520 Hz wouldn't work—505 Hz was just what came up while moving the center frequency of that particular band.

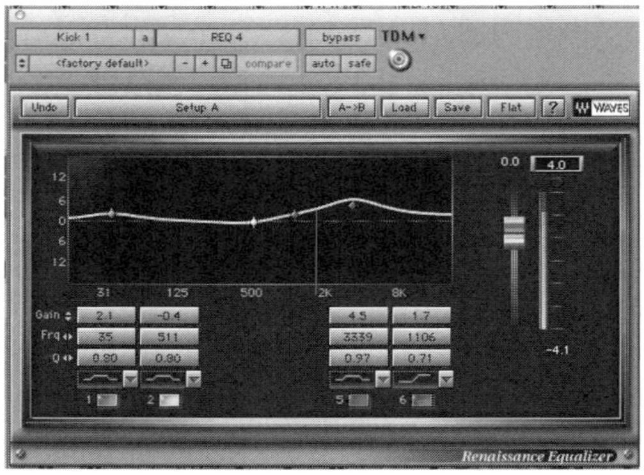

Fig. 5.3. In-Kick EQ

Waves Renaissance REQ-4 Kick 1 Settings				
parameter	**band 1**	**band 2**	**band 3**	**band 4**
gain	+2.1 dB	–0.4 dB	+4.5 dB	+1.7 dB
frequency	35 Hz	511 Hz	3,339 Hz	1,106 Hz
Q	0.80	0.80	0.97	0.71
shape	bell	bell	bell	shelf

The C1 Compressor/Gate that follows the EQ is the first instance of the expanded version of the C1 Gate that's been used on tom tracks for the last couple of mixes (and used on this song as well). On the kick 1 track, the compressor/expander is not active. The EQ band is set as a low-pass filter with a frequency of 854 Hz; the filter is being used as a sidechain on the gate. The sidechain makes the gate detection circuitry more sensitive to those frequencies below 850 Hz; since the goal is to have the gate open when the kick drum hits, higher frequencies (like bleed from the snare drum) are filtered out. This makes the gate less prone to opening at inopportune times.

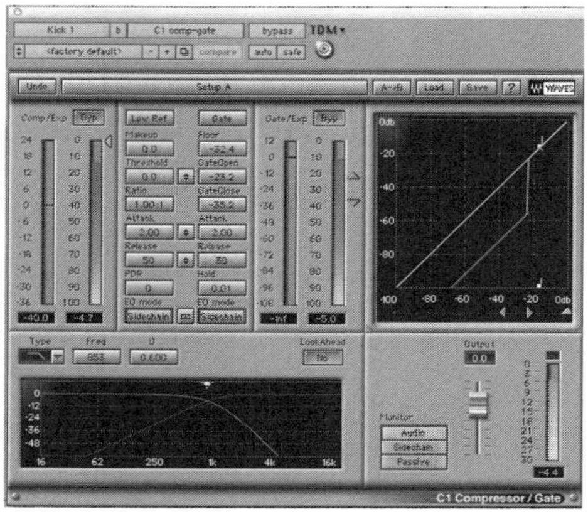

Fig. 5.4. In-Kick Gate

Waves C1 Compressor/Gate Kick 1 Settings	
parameter	**setting**
compressor/expander	(inactive)
makeup	0.0
threshold	0.0
ratio	1.00:1
attack	2.00
release	50
pdr	0
EQ	wideband
GATE	
floor	–32.4 dB
gate open	–23.2 dB
gate close	–35.2 dB
attack	2.00
release	30
hold	0.01
EQ mode	sidechain
EQ type	low pass
frequency	853 Hz
Q	0.60
look ahead	no
output	0 dB

The output level of the Kick 1 track is set at –1.6 dB.

Out-Kick

Because the CAD Trion microphone used as an outside kick was not muffled in any way (it's uncommon to cover the front of the kick drum with a heavy packing blanket when using an outside kick in this manner), the un-processed track is picking up a whole lot of the drums set—not only the snare bleeds into the microphone, but also the toms, the hi-hat, and even the cymbals. It's for this reason that the gates were used on the two kick drum mics; it wasn't necessary for the inside kick, but remember the issue of delay compensation—it's easier to avoid phasing and timing issues between the two kick drum mics if identical processing is used for both tracks.

The Renaissance EQ used on the outside kick track is boosting low frequencies while cutting the highs (the inside kick is taking care of the kick drum's high end just fine). A 5 dB boost at 34 Hz and a 4.8 dB boost at 60 Hz help to warm up a rather unappealing sound, while a low-pass filter at 200 Hz removes the rest of the signal that would otherwise clutter up the outside kick track.

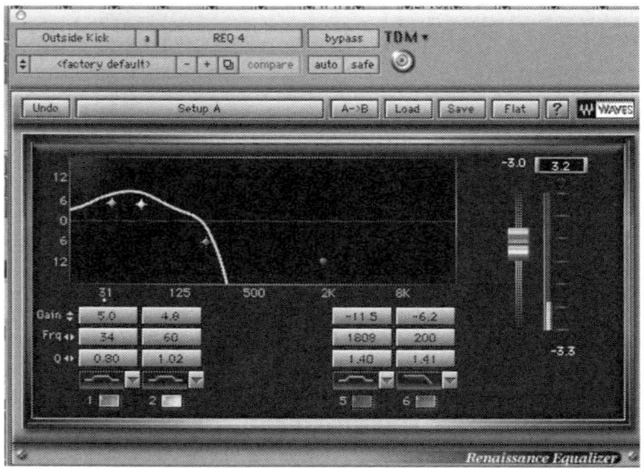

Fig. 5.5. Out-Kick EQ

Waves Renaissance REQ-4 Outside Kick Settings				
parameter	**band 1**	**band 2**	**band 3**	**band 4**
gain	+5.0 dB	+4.8 dB	–11.5 dB	–6.2 dB
frequency	34 Hz	60 Hz	1,808 Hz	200 Hz
Q	0.80	1.02	1.40	1.41
shape	bell	bell	bell (inactive)	shelf

The C1 used on the outside kick track is being used as a compressor and not as a gate; the severe low passing by the EQ section takes care of removing the extraneous noise. The settings on the compressor—specifically, the 2 ms attack time—add a bit of a point to the drum sound. Shortening the attack time would tend to make the point of the kick even stronger (by lowering the level of the kick shortly after the actual strike of the beater against the drum), while raising the attack time past about 30 ms would round off the attack, leaving it more like the sound of the post-EQ'd outside kick. If the attack time of a kick drum compressor is set too fast, the "thump" of the kick drum can change to a "tick" (or, if it's a bit slower, to a "blip"). Conversely, a hit that doesn't have a lot of attack can be changed with a substantial amount of compression (up to 10:1) and a bit slower attack time—this can artificially create a point on the drum hit (the original signal will then be lowered in volume by the compressor).

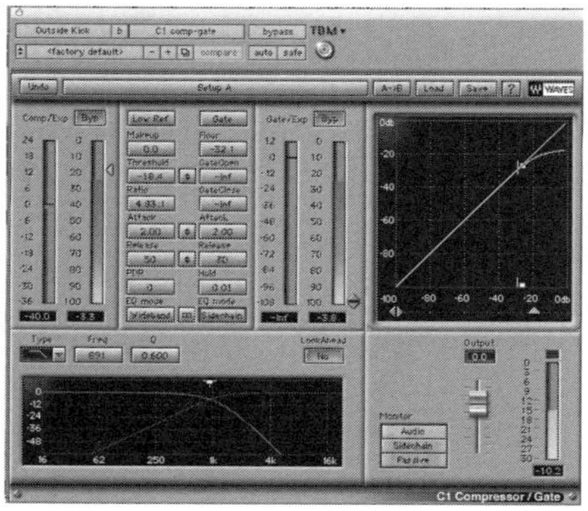

Fig. 5.6. Out-Kick Gate

Remember that lowering the attack and release times of the compressor effectively changes the tone of the outside kick track as well. When you remove that part of the kick sound that sustains (though it's a short sustain), the tone becomes harder and less boomy. (Fun with compressors.)

Waves C1 Compressor/Gate Out-Kick Settings

parameter	setting
compressor/expander	(Inactive)
makeup	0.0 dB
threshold	–18.4 dB
ratio	4.83:1
attack	2.00
release	50
pdr	0
EQ mode	Wideband
gate	(Inactive)
floor	–32.1 dB
gate open	Infinite
gate close	Infinite
attack	2.00
release	30
hold	0.01
EQ mode	Sidechain
EQ type	Low Pass
frequency	891 Hz
Q	0.60
look ahead	No
output	0 dB

The fader level of the outside kick was set at –4.6 dB; according to the fader, only 3 dB below the level of the main kick drum track, but after the plug-ins, quite a bit lower.

Snare

The snare track on "My Give a Damn's Busted" was recorded with the standard SM57. The SM57 is such a recording standard that some folks (at least, those who haven't spent years standing next to a drummer) accept the sound of a snare through an SM57 as the paradigm for what a snare drum should sound like. They're welcome to that belief, of course—as are the folks who feel like rock 'n' roll died with Buddy Holly. The snare track has two plug-ins: a 4-band Renaissance Compressor and a DigiRack Compressor/Limiter.

When adding an EQ plug-in to the snare track, knowledge of where both useful and problem frequencies exist can make mixing a given track much easier. While they are guidelines rather than rules (suggestions, not commandments), keep the following in mind.

Since little other than bleed from the kick drum or room ambience exists below 100 Hz on a snare drum, high passing the snare at somewhere between 80 and 100 Hz is almost never a bad idea. To fatten up a snare drum, the frequencies in the 100 to 350 Hz range are excellent candidates for tweaking. The "boxiness" that can happen with snare tracks can usually be mitigated by cutting frequencies in the 500 to 1,000 Hz range. The 5 kHz to 7 kHz area (with some room for fudging on either side) can add a crispness to the snare track to help it cut through a dense mix, while the 8 to 15 kHz range adds snap or sizzle to the snare.

The DigiRack Comp/Limiter 3 is part of the plug-in bundle that comes with Pro Tools; it's a full-featured plug-in, offering not only the usual adjustable parameters (including an adjustable knee) but also a sidechain option that can be set either to the included EQ filters or to an external key.

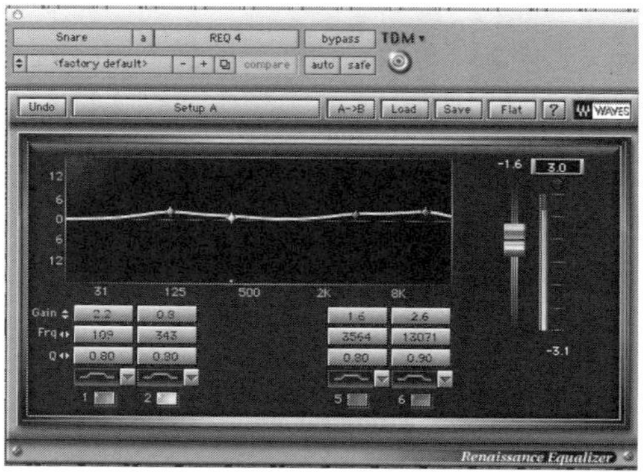

Fig. 5.7. Snare EQ

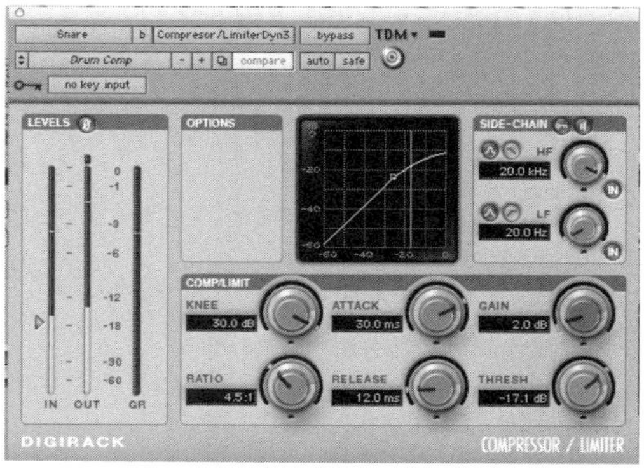

Fig. 5.8. Snare Compressor

Waves Renaissance REQ-4 Snare Settings				
parameter	**band 1**	**band 2**	**band 3**	**band 4**
gain	+2.2 dB	+0.8 dB	+1.6 dB	+2.6 dB
frequency	109 Hz	343 Hz	3,564 Hz	13,071 Hz
Q	0.80	0.80	0.80	0.90
shape	bell	bell	bell	bell

DigiRack Comp/Limiter 3 Snare Settings						
parameter	**knee**	**ratio**	**attack**	**release**	**gain**	**threshold**
setting	30.0 dB	4.5:1	30.0 ms	120 ms	+2.0 dB	–17.1 dB

The output level of the snare track was set at –4.6 dB, and the effects send to the drum reverb was at –10.1 dB.

Hi-Hat

The hi-hat track was panned to the left in keeping with the rest of the drum panning, which is from the drummer's perspective. The output level on the hat was set to –16.5 dB, and for a change, the hi-hat is also being sent (via an effects send at –8.0dB) to the drum reverb.

Also, a 2-band Renaissance EQ was added to the drum track to high pass around 250 Hz. There's also a small 1 dB boost at 8 kHz on the hi-hat track.

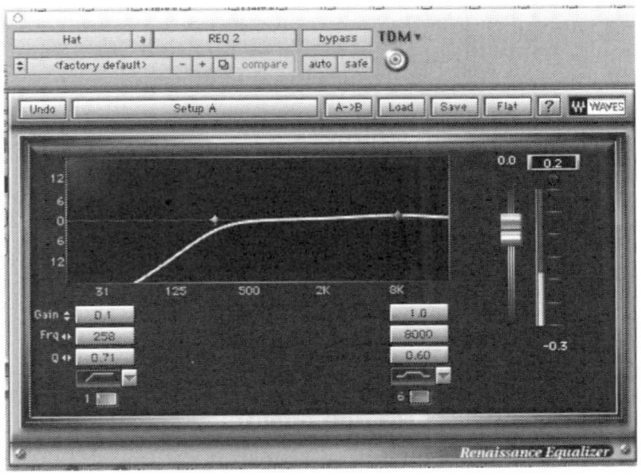

Fig. 5.9. Hat EQ

Waves Renaissance REQ-2 Hi-hat Settings		
parameter	**band 1**	**band 2**
gain	+0.1 dB	+1.0 dB
frequency	258 Hz	8 kHz
Q	0.71	0.60
shape	high pass	bell

Toms

As with the snare, certain frequency ranges tend to be most useable when EQ'ing toms. And also like the snare, there are so many variables, from the tom sizes to the microphones used, the style of music played, and the way that the toms were tuned and played, that these can be no more than suggestions for a starting point.

If using a high-pass filter on the toms, keep in mind that the floor tom is generally quite a bit larger than the rack mounted toms, and has a lot lower frequency range. If I high pass the tom tracks, I tend to start somewhere in the 70 to 80 Hz range with the rack toms and work down to 40 Hz for the floor tom. The meaty sound of toms typically lives in the 80 to 200 Hz area; when there's a need to minimize boxiness, those frequencies would usually be from somewhere in the 250 Hz range to as high as 700 Hz. The 3 to 6 kHz range would define the attack of the toms, and above about 8 kHz is a high-end snap.

While some engineers will, as a matter of course, compress the tom tracks (not that there's anything wrong with that), I usually won't do so. While judicious use of compression can increase sustain on each tom, that amount of compression will also bring up the level of the other drums that are bleeding into the tom mics. In addition to that, the tom hum that was mentioned earlier will also be raised in the track, which could very well necessitate additional processing to minimize the effects. Nevertheless, if you feel that the tom sound could be improved with compression, feel free to experiment. That, after all, is the purpose of this book.

Tom Hum Revisited

Prior chapters have seen two different approaches to dealing the sound that toms make when the drum kit is played—the first couple of mixes were done with the view that tom hum is part of the sound of the kit and is therefore nothing to be concerned about. As one drummer explained, "The hum is the glue that makes it sound like a real drum kit." The next couple of mixes used gates on the tom tracks to eliminate all extraneous noise except when the toms were actually being hit. This has the advantage of removing tom hum as well as all other sounds that bleed into the drum mics, including the sounds of the snare drum and the kick drum. The biggest disadvantage is that if you accept the premise that tom hum is a part of the sound of a kit, the gates also remove the glue. "My Give a Damn's Busted" combines the two approaches used previously—it uses gates while allowing a certain amount of the sounds other than the actual tom hits to pass. But before discussing the settings used for "My Give a Damn's Busted," it would be well to review the essentials of gates.

Gates

It's quite easy to understand the basic concept of a noise gate: it allows signals that are over a given threshold to pass while not allowing signals under that threshold to pass. All gates share a number of parameters, though some offer more controls that can make them more useable for a given application. The basic parameters for a simple gate are: floor, gate open, gate close, attack, release, and hold.

Floor

The floor setting of a gate is the level of the signal that is allowed to pass through the unit when the gate is closed. The lower the number, the less signal is allowed through. An infinite level simply means that nothing at all passed through the gate when it's closed, while 0.0, or unity, means that all of the signal may pass through the gate unchanged—the gate has no effect, whether it's open or closed.

Gate Open

This parameter determines the threshold at which the gate opens. For example, if the "gate open" setting is at –12.0 dB, the gate opens only when the signal exceeds –12.0 dB. Once the gate is open, a number of other settings will determine when the gate closes again.

Gate Close

The first of these is the gate close parameter; all other things being equal, when the signal strength passes below the level of the gate close setting, the gate would close again, and wouldn't open until the signal level once again exceeds the gate open threshold. But things aren't quite equal in this regard; both the gate open and gate close settings can be modified by other parameters.

Attack

The attack setting controls how fast—once the signal strength exceeds the gate open threshold—the gate actually opens. The attack time can vary from a couple of microseconds (very fast) to a number of milliseconds (pretty slow). There are applications where either fast or slower attacks are more appropriate, though with drums, the faster attack times are usually chosen.

Release

As a signal falls below the gate close setting, the release rate determines how fast the gate closes again. Fast release settings would be the sonic equivalent of slamming a door closed while slower settings are gentler, more akin to quietly easing the door closed behind you when sneaking into the house late at night.

Hold

Once the gate opens (when the signal strength passes the gate open threshold), the hold parameter comes into force. The hold setting determines the minimum time that the gate remains open—whether or not the signal strength falls below the gate close threshold during that time. As an example, if the hold setting is at one second, then even if a signal peak opens the gate but immediately falls back below the threshold that would cause the gate to close, it will remain open for the one second determined by the hold parameter.

But back to "My Give a Damn's Busted." The fader levels on Tom 1 were set at –4.0 dB, Tom 2 was set to –4.3 dB, and Tom 3 was set to –1.2 dB. Waves C1 Gates were used on all three toms, which are sent to the stereo tom buss. The three tom tracks are panned hard left, center, and hard right. The floor for all of the tom gates was set at –12.0 dB, meaning that when the gate is closed, the level of the tom tracks is 12 dB quieter than when the gates are open. In this manner, the tom hum is reduced but not eliminated from the mix—overall, an improvement.

Fig. 5.10. Tom Gates

Waves C1 Gate for Tom 1 Settings					
floor	gate open	gate close	attack	release	hold
–12.0 dB	–9.8	–9.8	1.78	545	0.01

Waves C1 Gate for Tom 2 Settings					
floor	gate open	gate close	attack	release	hold
–12.0 dB	–12.1	–12.1	1.78	631	0.01

Waves C1 Gate for Tom 3 Settings					
floor	gate open	gate close	attack	release	hold
–12.0 dB	–15.4	–15.4	1.78	545	0.01

Alternatives to Gates

A couple of methods—each with its own advantages and disadvantages—can be used to minimize or eliminate extraneous noise (tom hum, other drums bleeding into the tom mics) on the tom tracks. One simple approach is to simply clear all audio from the tom tracks except when the toms are actually struck; when either another snare hit occurs or the sustain of the toms dies down to inaudibility within the track, the track can be cleared until the next time the toms are hit. This can be done fairly quickly, because you can see where the tom hits occur in the song. A bit more care needs to be taken at the end of the fill (or single hit) so that the tom sound isn't cut off too abruptly but that another sound like a snare hit isn't heard through the tom mics. If these tracks have been cleared, the snare (heard through the tom mics as well as the snare and overhead tracks) will sound quite different than the snare that isn't heard through the tom tracks. It's generally also a good practice, when clearing unwanted audio, to add a fade at the end of the audio clip, so that the toms fade smoothly rather than being cut out abruptly.

Instead of clearing audio from the tracks, the tracks may simply be muted when silence is the desirable result. There's no functional difference, other than the fact that (in Pro Tools, at least) the muted audio regions are still visible.

A third approach is to simply lower the level of the tom tracks at those times when they shouldn't be heard. This can be done in two ways: by automating the volume of the tom tracks, or by using gates. Gates have been discussed in chapters three and four; chapter six will examine the use of volume automation to lower the level of tom hum.

Automating the volume levels on the tom tracks is quite simple, though the methods of doing so will be slightly different with each of the major software programs. By bringing the volume of the toms down—somewhere between 3 and 20 dB—when no toms are being hit, tom hum and bleed from other drums is minimized rather than eliminated. This practice usually results in a more natural sound (though we must admit that there's nothing "natural" about placing a microphone three inches from a drum—a place where no sane human would place an ear). When taking this approach, I would typically group the three tom tracks together, then write the volume automation on all three tracks at once. In much the same manner as discussed above when clearing audio, the point at which the volume is reduced from its highest levels may need to be tweaked a bit.

Tom Buss

The output of the tom bus was –0.3 dB. Two effects sends were used; the send to the drum reverb was at –7.7 dB, and the long reverb send was at –25.5 dB. A Waves Renaissance Compressor was added to the tom buss, though it will rarely affect the tom sound since the compression ratio is very close to unity.

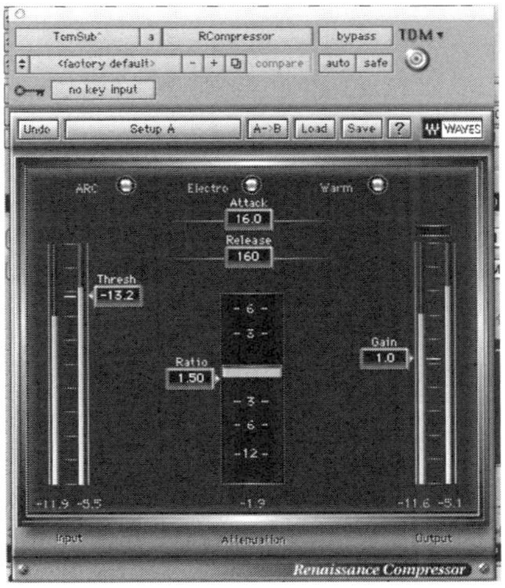

Fig. 5.11. Tom Buss Compressor

Waves Renaissance Compressor Tom Buss Settings				
threshold	attack	release	ratio	gain
–13.2 dB	16.0	160	1.50:1	+1.0 dB

Overheads

The fader levels for the overheads were at –9.2 dB, and a 2-band Waves Renaissance EQ had a 2 dB cut centered at 80 Hz and a very slight boost at 7.2 kHz. In much the same manner as the other mixes in this volume, the overhead microphones were used more to bring cymbal levels to where they needed to be than to serve as the basis for the whole drum mix (which would use close mics simply to reinforce the information coming from the overheads).

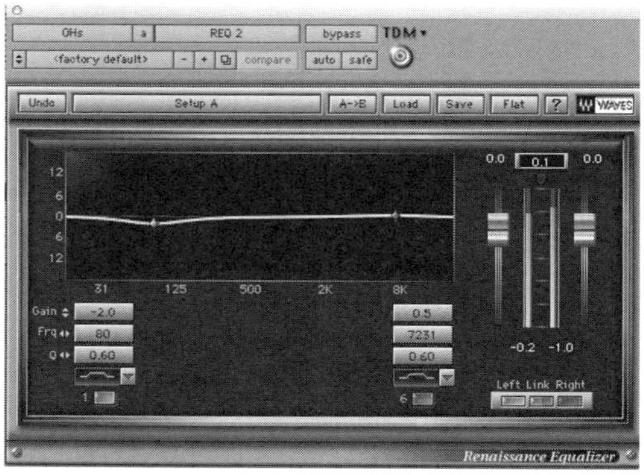

Fig. 5.12. Overhead EQ

Waves Renaissance REQ-2 Overheads Settings		
parameter	band 1	band 2
gain	–2.0 dB	+0.5 dB
frequency	80 Hz	7,231 Hz
Q	0.60	0.60
shape	bell	bell

Room

Because "My Give a Damn's Busted" has a pretty hard-hitting drum track, the stereo room tracks have been processed to reinforce the rocking aspects of the song. There are two plug-ins used on the room mic track: the first is a 2-band Renaissance EQ with a shelving EQ that reduces the level of frequencies below 700 Hz. The other is a DigiRack Compressor/Limiter that's set to 40 dB of gain reduction. It's worth discussing explicitly the differences between compression and limiting, so here goes:

Limiting versus Compressing

Many dynamics plug-ins are called compressors or limiters as though these are two different processes; the truth is that (at least in the analog days), there is no functional difference between compressing and limiting other than the settings used. When compression ratios of less than 10:1 (that is, once the threshold of compression is reached, an additional 10 dB of gain at the input of the compressor results in 1 dB of gain on the output of the compressor), the process is known as compressing. At ratios greater than 10:1, the process is called limiting. Typically, limiters use fast attack and release times, while compressors may be set for slower attack and release times.

The exception to this standard is the "look-ahead" limiter—those plug-ins like Waves' L1, L2, and L3, which are considered to be "brick-wall" limiters. Those have extremely high ratios, and are designed to detect signal peaks before they actually arrive. By delaying the audio a couple of milliseconds, the L1 can detect and react to the incoming signal instantaneously, preventing any transient peaks from passing through the processor.

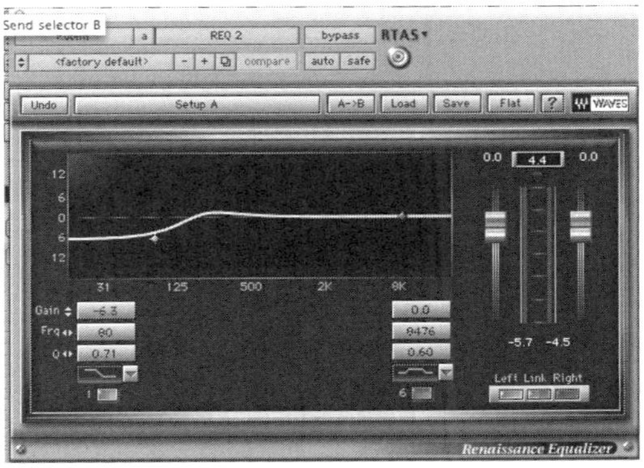

Fig. 5.13. Room Mic EQ

Waves Renaissance REQ-2 Room Mic Settings		
parameter	**band 1**	**band 2**
gain	–6.3 dB	0 dB
frequency	78 Hz	8,646 Hz
Q	0.71	0.60
shape	shelf	bell

The idea with the compressor is to severely limit the signal to the point of distortion. And by making the attack time very short (at 20 microseconds), and the release time at 40 ms, even the kick and the snare will have a bit of the same gritty character. When the room mics are at their most obnoxious, bring them up underneath the drum track—not enough to be noticeable, but just to the point that it adds an interesting ambience to the drum sound.

Fig. 5.14. Room Mic Compressor

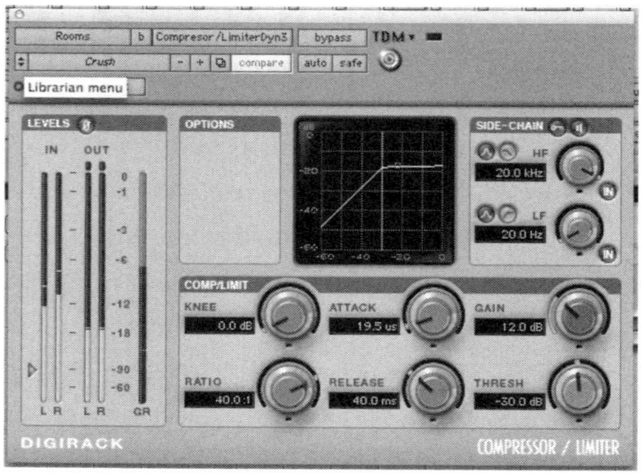

DigiRack Comp/Limiter 3 Room Mic Settings						
parameter	knee	ratio	attack	release	gain	threshold
setting	20.0 dB	40.0:1	20.0 us	40 ms	+12.0 dB	–30.0 dB

The room mic fader level was set to –12.9 dB.

BASS

The bass tracks on "My Give a Damn's Busted" used a Waves Renaissance Compressor and a 2-band Waves Renaissance EQ as plug-ins. The output fader of the bass was set at –7.7 dB. Not a whole lot of gain reduction was used on the bass track; it was added primarily to even out any inequities in the track. The EQ was primarily used to add bottom end to the bass track since the Q setting affects the width of the band. Remember, the lower the number, the wider the frequency range affected by any changes to the level of that band. Even though the center frequency of this EQ band is quite low—not only below the lowest frequency that the bass can create, but lower than the lowest frequency that most consumer speakers can reproduce—the Q setting is wide enough that a fairly wide range of frequencies that *can* be reproduced are affected by this EQ band.

Fig. 5.15. Bass Compressor

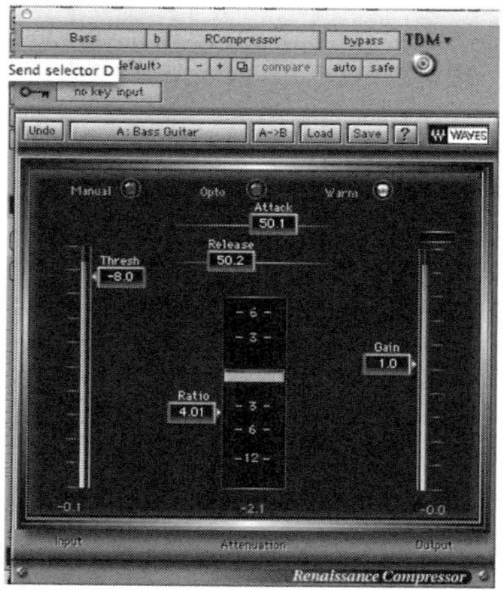

In addition to that, keep in mind that a lot of what is perceived as bass is not necessarily the fundamental note (the low E note on a bass is at 41 Hz, and notes played on the B string are lower than that), but are harmonics an octave (or more) higher than the fundamental note. Boosting the fundamental frequency will also raise the level of the harmonic notes associated with that frequency.

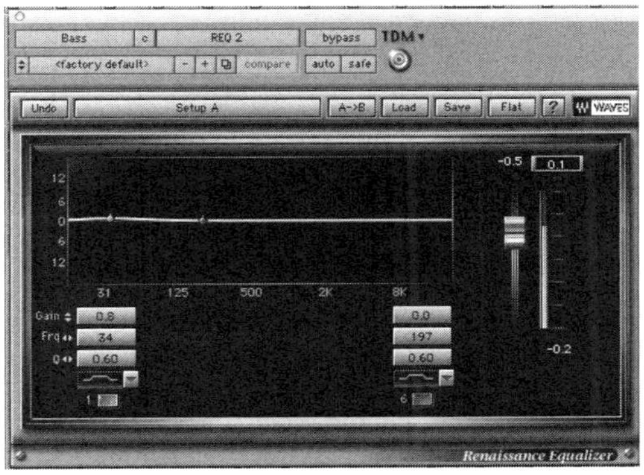

Fig. 5.16. Bass EQ

Waves Renaissance Compressor Bass Settings				
threshold	attack	release	ratio	gain
–8.0	50.1	50.2	4.01:1	+1.0 dB

Waves Renaissance REQ-2 Bass Settings		
parameter	band 1	band 2
gain	+0.8 dB	+0.5 dB
frequency	34 Hz	197 Hz
Q	0.60	0.60
shape	bell	bell

ORGAN

The organ track on "My Give a Damn's Busted" needed little processing; other than a slight boost at 14 kHz and a 2.2 dB rise at 327 Hz, the natural sound of the Hammond C3 used on this track was left alone. The fader level was set at –14.5 dB, and the effects send to the long verb was at –14.8 dB. The Hammond organ is capable of so many different sounds that if the right sound comes from the organ, it's usually very close to what's needed in the final mix. A Renaissance EQ was used for the tonal changes to this track.

Fig. 5.17. Organ EQ

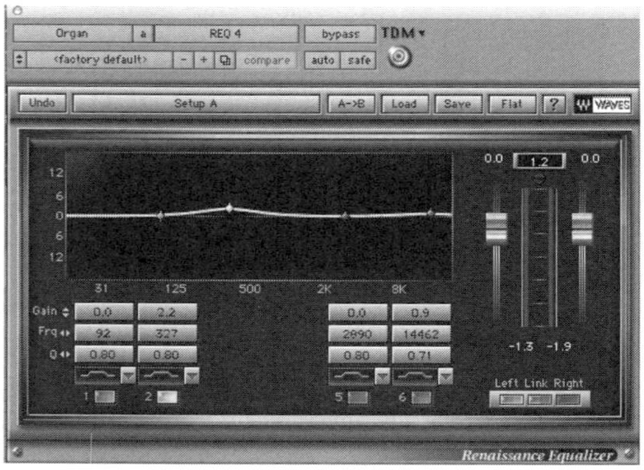

Waves Renaissance REQ-4 Organ Settings				
parameter	**band 1**	**band 2**	**band 3**	**band 4**
gain	0	+2.2 dB	0	+0.9 dB
frequency	92 Hz	327 Hz	2,890 Hz	14,462 Hz
Q	0.80	0.80	0.80	0.71
shape	bell	bell	bell	bell

ACOUSTIC GUITARS

Instead of using a buss EQ on the acoustic guitar tracks—for that matter, instead of routing the acoustic guitar tracks to their own buss, "My Give a Damn's Busted" has a simple 2-band EQ on each of the guitar tracks. The first EQ band was used as a high-pass filter on both of the tracks, clearing away unneeded low frequency information while the second EQ band is used to add a presence peak that allows the acoustic to cut through the mix. The acoustic left track output is at –5.8 dB, while the acoustic right output is at –6.1 dB. No compression was used on the acoustic tracks, under the principle that if it's not needed, it shouldn't be used.

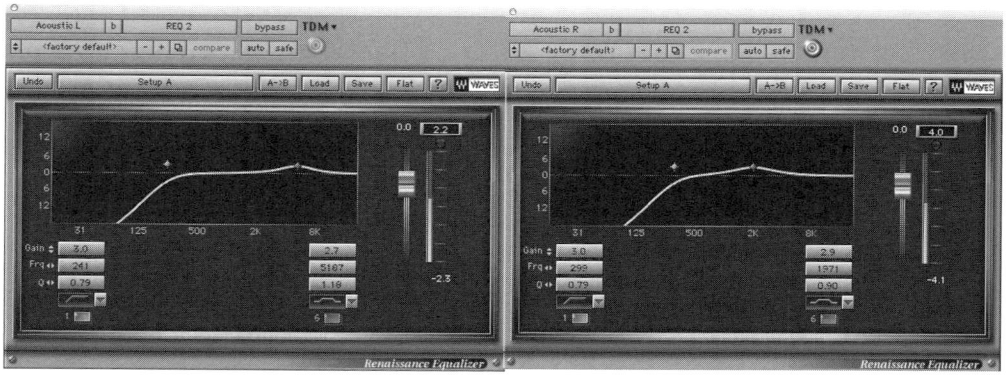

Fig. 5.18. Acoustic Guitar EQ

Waves Renaissance REQ-2 Acoustic L Settings		
parameter	band 1	band 2
gain	+3.0 dB	+2.7 dB
frequency	241 Hz	5,187 Hz
Q	0.79	1.18
shape	high pass	bel

Waves Renaissance REQ-2 Acoustic R Settings		
parameter	band 1	band 2
gain	+3.0 dB	+2.9 dB
frequency	299 Hz	1,971 Hz
Q	0.79	0.90
shape	high pass	bell

FIDDLE

It's not uncommon for fiddle tracks to need no EQ to fit into the overall mix, and the fiddle on "My Give a Damn's Busted" is no different. Nevertheless, when adjustments need to be made, they're typically either in the low range (between 300 to 500 Hz) to add warmth, or above 3 kHz, to minimize any edginess or scratchy sounds coming from the instrument. For this particular mix, a Bomb Factory BF76 compressor was used, along with a Waves TrueVerb Reverb, set to the Rock Guitar Closet preset. Even though a reverb was used as in insert for the fiddle track, effects send also sends the fiddle signal (including the inserted reverb plug-in) to the instrument reverb at –9.8 and to the long reverb at –18.5 dB. The output of the fiddle track was set to –6.2 dB.

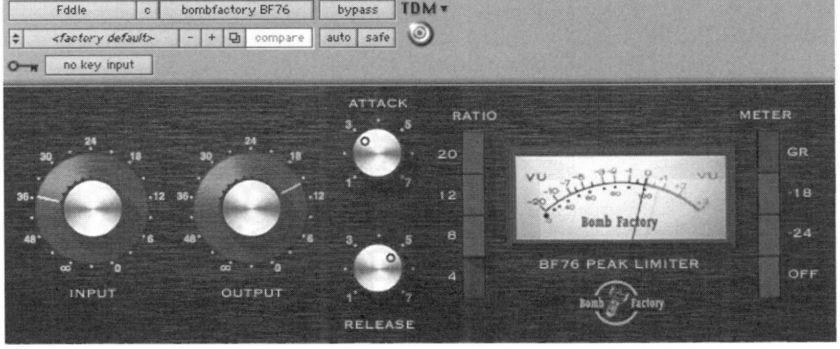

Fig. 5.19. Fiddle Compressor

Bomb Factory BF76 Fiddle Settings				
input	output	attack	release	ratio
36	14.5	3	5	4:1

The Rock Guitar Room preset used here isn't adding reverb per se—it really emulates a rather small acoustic space using the early reflections from the TrueVerb. This effect, by the way, can be done at the recording stage simply by adding a second mic a few feet away from the signal source.

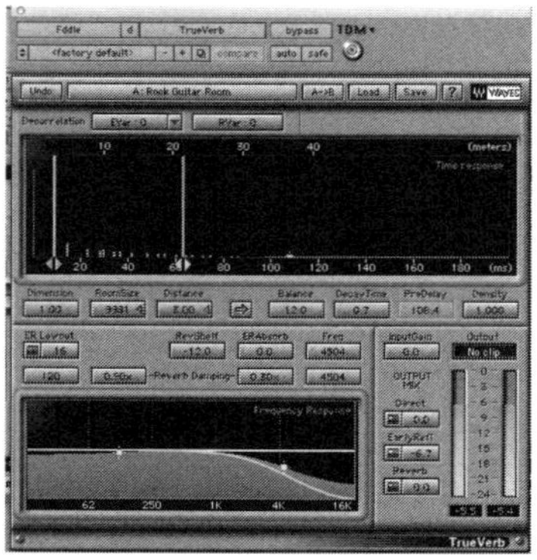

Fig. 5.20. Fiddle Reverb

Waves TrueVerb Fiddle Settings	
parameter	setting
dimension	1.00
room size	9,981
distance	3.00
balance	12.0
decay time	0.7
predelay	108.4
density	1.000
EARLY REFLECTION	
low cut	16
reverb damping frequency low	120
damping	0.90¥
reverb damping frequency high	4,504
damping	0.10¥
reverb shelf	–12.0
ER absorb	0.0
ER absorb freq	4,504
input gain	0.0
direct output	–0.5 dB
early reflection output	–6.7 dB
reverb output	0.0 dB

DOBRO

The dobro track on "My Give a Damn's Busted" is pretty sparse. With just two specific licks in each chorus and fills in the second half of the second verse, it adds a nice bit of flavor to the mix without becoming too familiar through overuse. It's also a nice sonic change from the slide guitar that's used in other parts of the mix.

From a processing viewpoint, I'll tend to use a compressor with a fairly fast attack on a dobro since the transients can sound a bit metallic. The compressor tames the transients. And, with a fairly fast release time, the dobro's sustain isn't impaired. The dobro isn't a particularly full-range instrument—in fact, most of the sonic information is in the midrange—so when EQ needs to be applied, it's usually best to either go for a general tone shaping with a fairly broadband EQ or to do the opposite and use very narrow bands to remove problem frequencies. This particular dobro track has a Bomb Factory BF76 plug-in added, and the output of the track is at –14.1 dB.

Fig. 5.21. Dobro Compressor

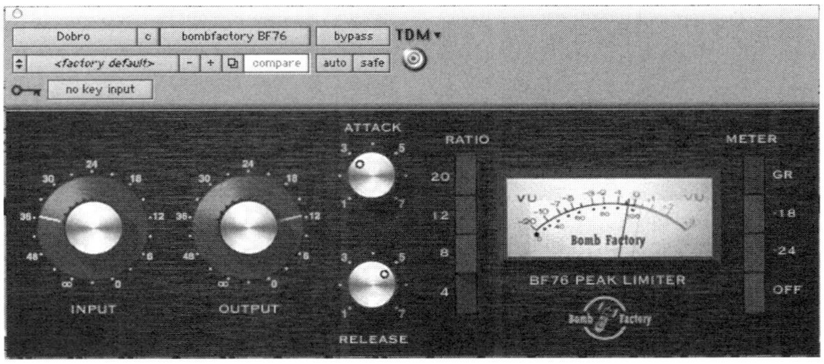

Bomb Factory BF76 Dobro Settings				
input	**output**	**attack**	**release**	**ratio**
36	14.5	3	5	4:1

ELECTRIC GUITARS

The four guitar tracks on this tune are each given space through a combination of panning and EQ. Regarding the panning of the guitars, the rhythm guitar track is panned 60 percent left and the riff guitar track is panned 50 percent right; the slide guitar is panned just to the right of center (as a reflection of the dobro, which is panned just left of the center). The solo guitar is right in the center of the sound field.

Slide Guitar

The slide guitar track uses a 2-band Renaissance EQ for a slight boost around 2.7 kHz and a low-pass filter to remove frequencies at 8.7 kHz. A Bomb Factory BF76 Compressor plug-in adds a bit of tone as level control to the track. The output level is at –7.4 dB, and the effects send to the long reverb is at –14.8 dB.

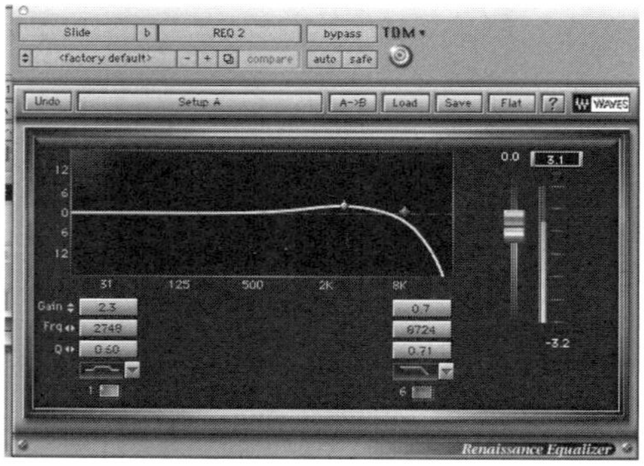

Fig. 5.22. Slide EQ

Waves Renaissance REQ-2 Slide Guitar Settings		
parameter	**band 1**	**band 2**
gain	+2.3 dB	+0.7 dB
frequency	2,748 Hz	8,724 Hz
Q	0.60	0.71
shape	bell	low pass

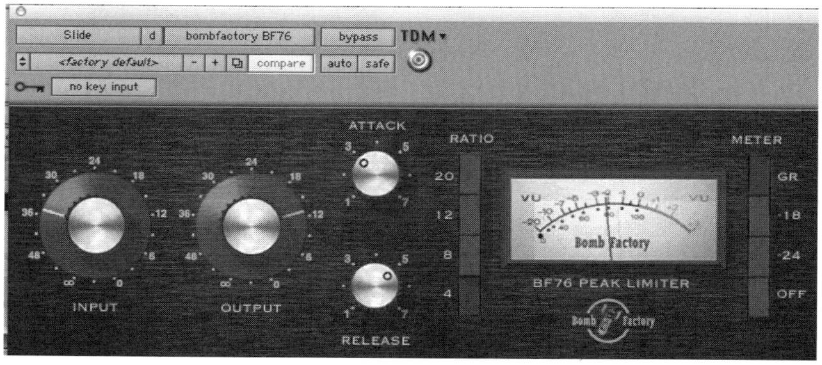

Fig. 5.23. Slide Compressor

Bomb Factory BF76 Slide Guitar Settings				
input	**output**	**attack**	**release**	**ratio**
36	14.5	3	5	4:1

Rhythm Guitar

The 4-band Renaissance EQ has a high-pass filter to remove unwanted low frequencies and to add a slight boost at 200 Hz (to add some body) and at 5.5 kHz. The output level of the rhythm guitar is –10.1 dB.

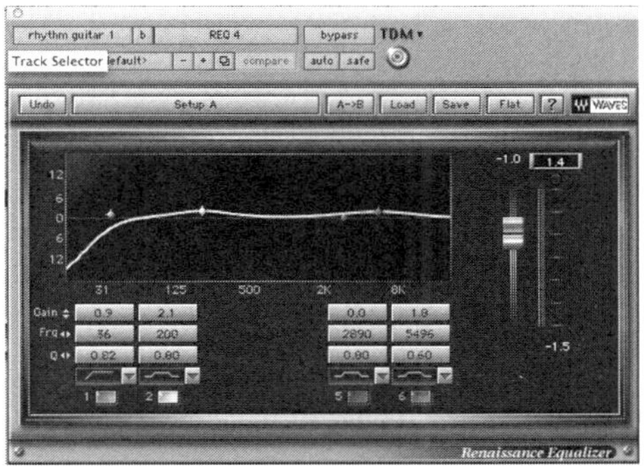

Fig. 5.24. Rhythm Guitar EQ

Waves Renaissance REQ-4 Rhythm Guitar Settings				
parameter	**band 1**	**band 2**	**band 3**	**band 4**
gain	+0.9 dB	+2.1 dB	0 dB	+1.8 dB
frequency	36 Hz	200 Hz	2,890 Hz	5,496 Hz
Q	0.82	0.80	0.80	0.71
Shape	high pass	bell	bell	bell

RIFF GUITAR

Though another 4-band Renaissance EQ is on the riff guitar track, the primary function of the plug-in is to cut the high frequencies around 6.8 kHz by a couple of decibels. The output fader level is at –14.8 dB and there's an effects send to the drum reverb at –14.8 dB.

Fig. 5.25. Riff Guitar EQ

Waves Renaissance REQ-4 Riff Guitar Settings				
parameter	band 1	band 2	band 3	band 4
gain	0 dB	0 dB	+1.1 dB	–2.4 dB
frequency	92 Hz	163 Hz	1,164 Hz	6,825 Hz
Q	0.80	0.80	0.80	0.55
shape	bell	bell	bell	bell

Solo Guitar

No EQ was necessary for the solo guitar, but a Bomb Factory BF76 plug-in was used. The output level of the solo guitar was –10.7.

Fig. 5.26. Solo Guitar Compressor

Bomb Factory BF76 Solo Guitar Settings				
input	output	attack	release	ratio
33	14	3	5	41

LEAD VOCAL

The lead vocal on "My Give a Damn's Busted" has four different processors on it, as well as the aux sends that send the lead vocals to the vocal reverb (in this mix, a Waves TrueVerb). The aux send to the TrueVerb was at –12.0 dB. The output level was set at +1.1 dB. The plug-ins used on this track are Auto-Tune 4, a 6-band Waves Renaissance EQ, a Renaissance Compressor, and a Bomb Factory BF76 compressor.

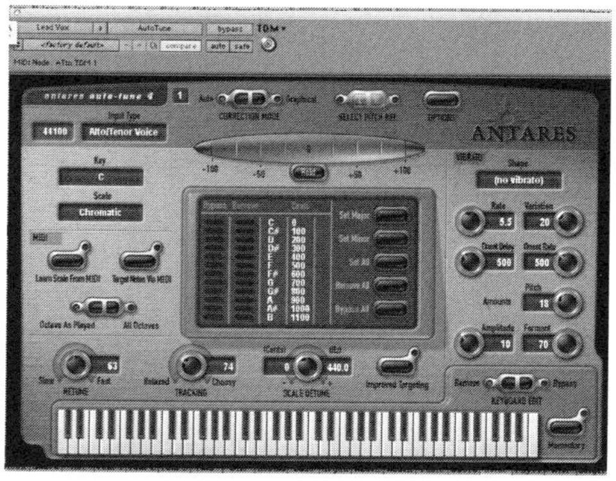

Fig. 5.27. Lead Vocal Auto-Tune

Auto Tune

Retune: 63
Tracking: 74
Input Type: Alto/Tenor Voice

The EQ is used to add a bit of body to the vocals by boosting at 200 Hz, and to brighten up the top end of the track with a shelving EQ at 12 kHz.

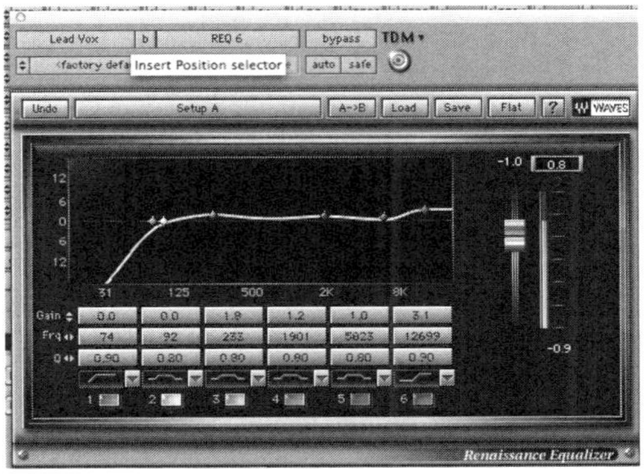

Fig. 5.28. Lead Vocal EQ

Waves Renaissance REQ-6 Lead Vocal Settings						
parameter	**band 1**	**band 2**	**band 3**	**band 4**	**band 5**	**band 6**
gain	0 dB	0 dB	+1.8 dB	+1.2 dB	+1.0 dB	+3.1 dB
frequency	74 Hz	92 Hz	233 Hz	1,901 Hz	5,823 Hz	12,699 Hz
Q	0.90	0.80	0.80	0.80	0.80	0.90
shape	high pass	bell	bell	bell	bell	shelf

The Renaissance compressor is set to a very mild compression ratio—1.2:1. While it adds a nice tone to the vocal track, the primary gain reduction is coming from the BF76. Though the compression ratio on the BF76 is 4:1 (not generally considered to be a high ratio), the BF76 has a tremendous amount of "grab." The meter may indicate only small amounts of gain reduction, but it sounds like there's a lot more.

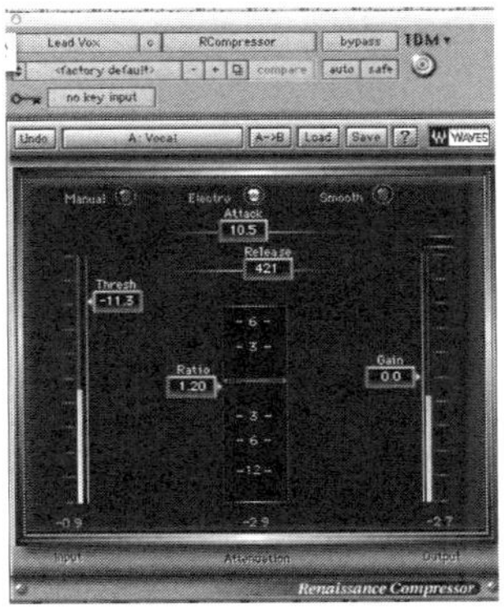

Fig. 5.29. Lead Vocal Compressor

Waves Renaissance Compressor Lead Vocal Settings				
threshold	attack	release	ratio	gain
–11.3 dB	10.5	421	1.13:1	0 dB

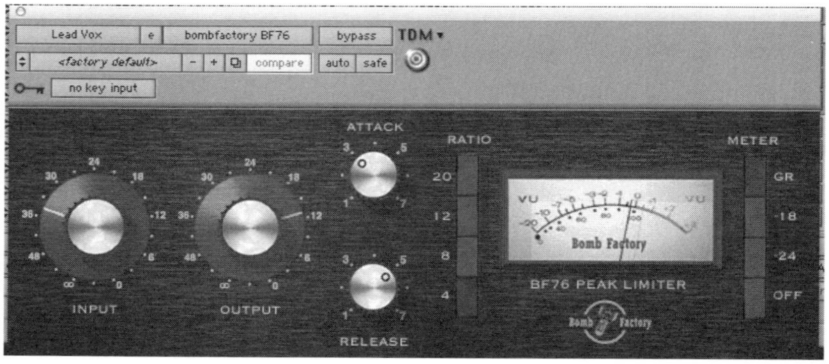

Fig. 5.30. Lead Vocal BF76

Bomb Factory BF76 Lead Vocal Settings				
input	output	attack	release	ratio
34	13.5	3	5	4:1

BACKGROUND VOCALS

The two background vocal (BGV) tracks use the same Auto-Tune 4 settings as the lead vocals. Again, this isn't because the vocals sound out of tune, but because that "tuned" sound has, unfortunately, become a part of the records released in Nashville. The two BGV tracks also have a 2-band Renaissance EQ inserted, with a 2.4 dB boost at 8.5 kHz. The output level of the high BGV is –4.9 dB, and the mid BGV is -6.2 dB.

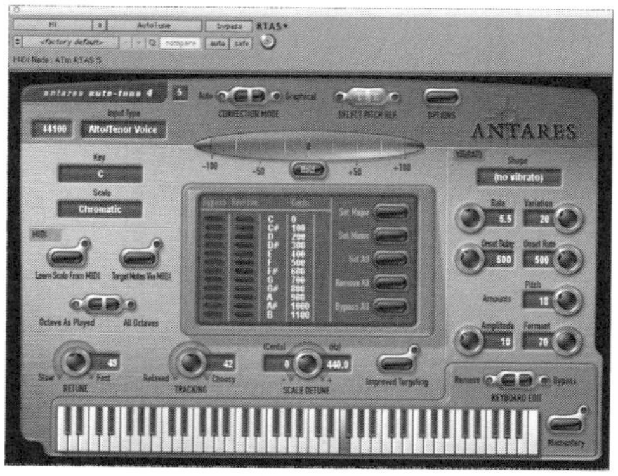

Fig. 5.31. High BGV Auto-Tune

Auto Tune

Retune: 49

Tracking: 42

Input Type: Alto/ Tenor voice

Fig. 5.32. High BGV EQ

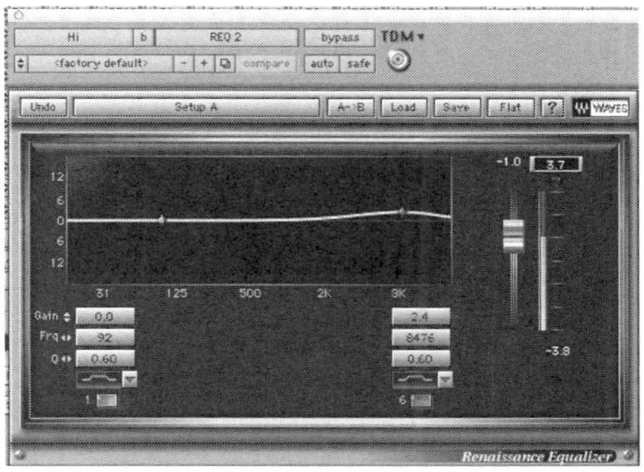

Waves Renaissance REQ-2 High BGV Settings		
parameter	**band 1**	**band 2**
gain	0 dB	+2.4 dB
frequency	92 Hz	8,476 Hz
Q	0.60	0.60
shape	bell	bell

Fig. 5.33. Mid BG Auto-Tune

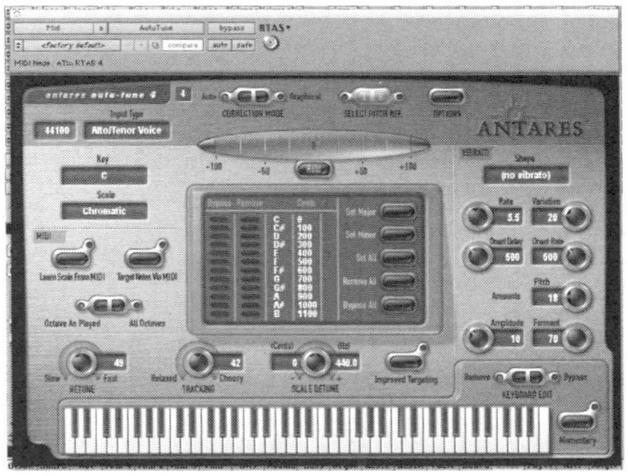

Auto Tune

Retune: 49

Tracking: 42

Input Type: Alto/Tenor Voice

Fig. 5.34. Mid BG EQ

Waves Renaissance REQ-2 Mid BGV Settings		
parameter	band 1	band 2
gain	0 dB	+2.4 dB
frequency	92 Hz	8,476 Hz
Q	0.60	0.60
shape	bell	bell

BGV Buss

The background vocals are sent to the BGV buss, which has a Renaissance compressor plug-in inserted. The output of the BGV buss is –2.5 dB. The send to the vocal reverb is –15.4 dB and the long reverb send is –12.9 dB.

Fig. 5.35. BGV Buss Compressor

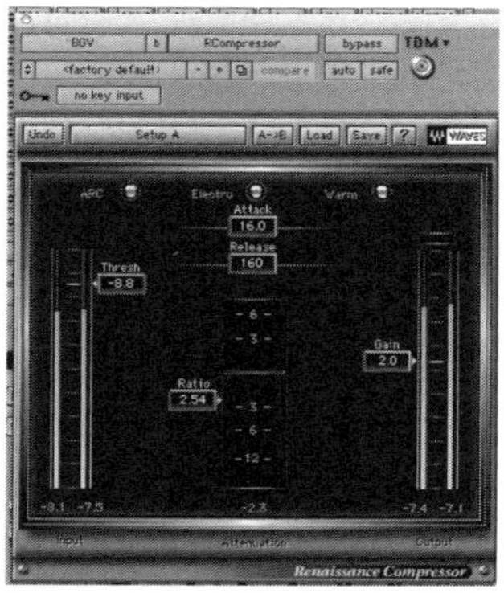

Waves Renaissance Compressor BGV Buss Settings				
threshold	attack	release	ratio	gain
–8.8 dB	16.0	160	2.54:1	+2.0 dB

AUX SENDS AND BUSS PROCESSING

Four reverbs have been set up for this mix; the drum reverb is a Waves Renaissance Reverberator set to a drum plate setting. The instrument reverb is a Waves Renaissance Reverberator set to a medium room setting. The third, named "vocal reverb" has a Waves TrueVerb set to a Nice Plate setting, and the fourth and last reverb is the "long verb" which is a Waves TrueVerb set to a Large Concert setting. Any combination of these four reverbs can be used on any track; the names given to the reverb return is just a matter of convenience. The practice of setting up multiple reverbs of different lengths and flavors is a hold-over from the days of mixing on consoles; well equipped studios in the 1970s would likely have a plate reverb or two (set to different reverb times) and possibly a chamber as well. When mixing, any combination of these would be used to meet a given need.

Though modern workstation technology allows an almost unlimited number of reverbs (subject to the processing power available), in reality, there's seldom a need to go to such lengths. The output of the three reverb returns is set to unity gain or 0 dB.

Fig. 5.36. Aux Busses

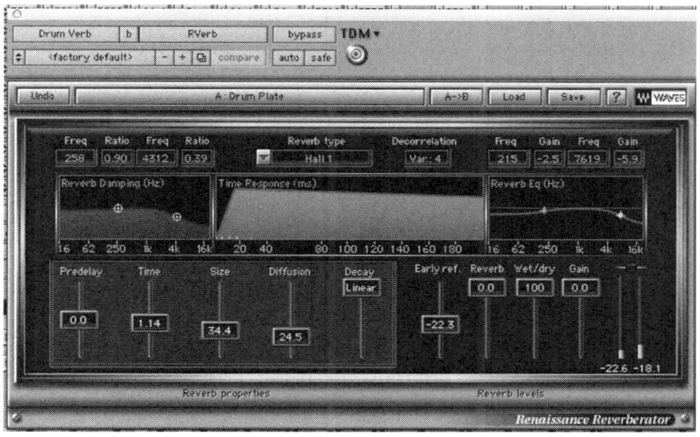

Fig. 5.37. Drum Reverb

Waves Renaissance Reverb Drums Settings	
parameter	**setting**
REVERB DAMPING	
frequency 1	258
ratio 1	0.90
frequency 2	4,312
ratio 2	0.39
reverb type	hall 1
decorrelation	var: 4
REVERB EQ	
frequency 1	215
gain 1	–2.5dB
frequency 2	7,619
gain 2	–5.9 dB
predelay	0.0
time	1.14 sec.
size	34.4
diffusion	24.5
decay	linear
early reflection level	–22.3 dB
reverb	0.0 dB
wet/dry	100%
gain	0

Fig. 5.38. Instrument Reverb

Renaissance Reverb Instrument Settings

parameter	setting
REVERB DAMPING	
frequency 1	29
ratio 1	1.00
frequency 2	4,569
ratio 2	0.76
reverb type	resoverb
decorrelation	var: 1
REVERB EQ	
frequency 1	156
gain 1	0
frequency 2	1,256
gain 2	–4.9 dB
predelay	0.0
time	0.70
size	62.3
diffusion	30
decay	linear
early reflection level	–23.9 dB
reverb	0.0 dB
wet/dry	100%
gain	0

Fig. 5.39. Vocal Reverb

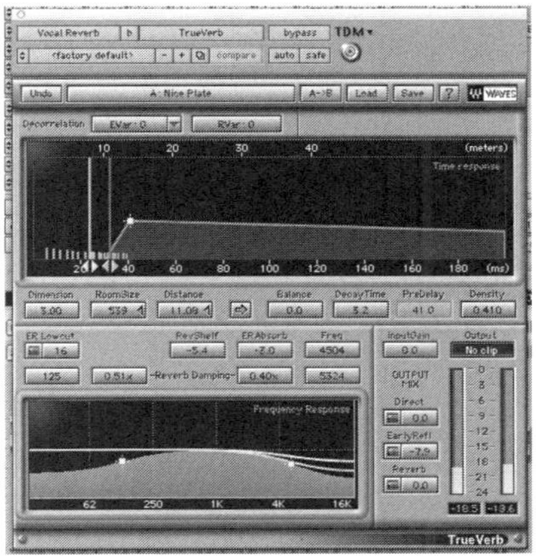

Waves TrueVerb Vocal Reverb Settings	
parameter	**setting**
dimension	3.99
room size	1,024
distance	15.59
balance	6.5
decay time	0.9
predelay	60.4
density	0.975
EARLY REFLECTION (ER)	
low cut	16
reverb damping frequency low	125
damping	0.51 x
reverb damping frequency high	4,504
damping	0.40 x
reverb shelf	–5.4
ER absorb	–3.0
ER absorb freq	5,324
input gain	0.0
direct output	0.0
early reflection output	–7.2
reverb output	0.0

Fig. 5.40. Long Reverb

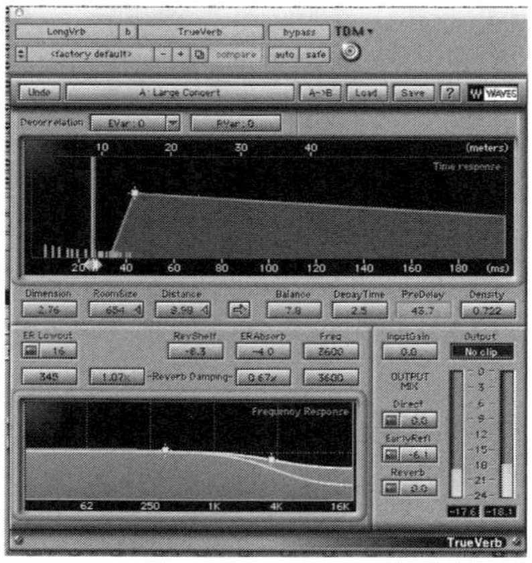

Waves TrueVerb Long Verb Settings

parameter	setting
dimension	2.76
room size	653
distance	8.98
balance	7.8
decay time	2.5
predelay	43.7
density	0.722
EARLY REFLECTION (ER)	
low cut	16
reverb damping frequency low	345
damping	1.07¥
reverb damping frequency high	3,600
damping	0.67¥
reverb shelf	–8.3
early reflection (ER) absorb	–4.0
ER absorb freq	3,600
input gain	0.0
direct output	0.0
ER output	–6.1
reverb output	0.0

MASTER OUTPUT

The master output includes a 6-band Renaissance EQ, a Waves L2 Limiter, and a Pow-R Dither plug-in. The 6-band EQ only uses one band, for a 4.5 dB boost at 17 kHz. The L2 Limiter is set to a 6 dB threshold and an output ceiling of 0.4 dBFS.

Fig. 5.41. Buss EQ

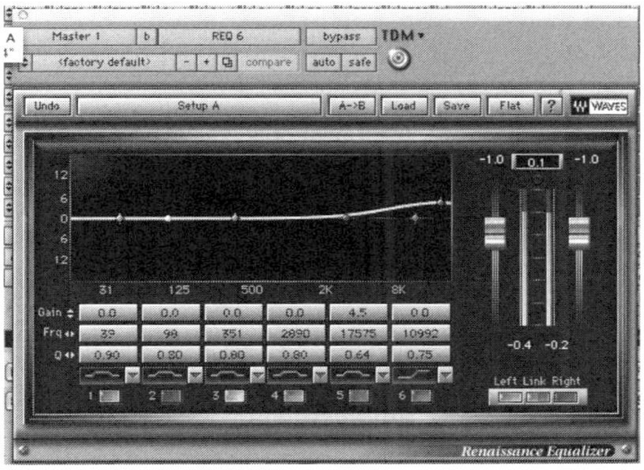

Waves Renaissance REQ-6 Master Output Settings						
parameter	**band 1**	**band 2**	**band 3**	**band 4**	**band 5**	**band 6**
gain	+0.3 dB	0 dB	0 dB	0 dB	+4.5 dB	0 dB
frequency	39 Hz	98 Hz	351 Hz	2,890	17,575 Hz	10,992 Hz
Q	0.90	0.80	0.80	0.80	0.64	0.75
shape	bell	bell	bell	bell	bell	shelving

Fig. 5.42. Buss Limiter

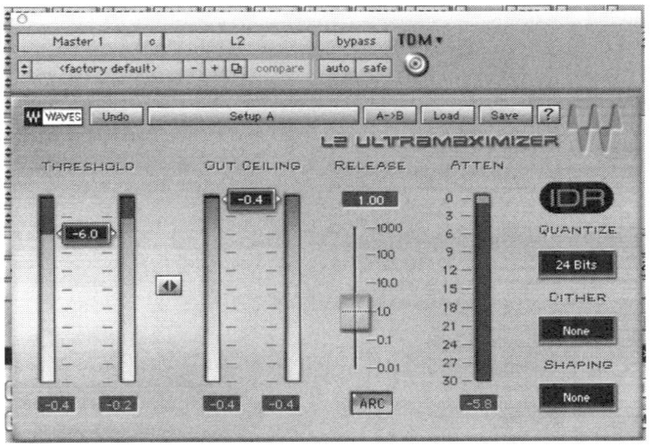

L2 Ultramaximizer

Threshold: –6.0 dB

Out Ceiling: –0.4 dB Release 1.00

The Pow-R Dither plug-in was set to a 16-bit output and used "noise shaping type 3."

Fig. 5.43. Dither

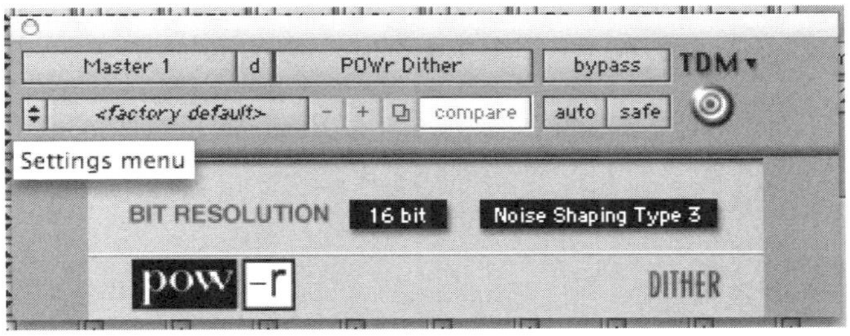

AUTOMATION

Volume automation has been written for a number of the tracks on "My Give a Damn's Busted." In the beginning of the song, the acoustic guitars were turned up for the first few notes, then brought down to the level where they stayed for the rest of the song. The fiddle's volume was adjusted here and there, most notably between the first and second verse, right before (and during) the fiddle solo and at the end of the song. The dobro was changed in the section before and during the second chorus. The slide guitar was adjusted up or down by small amounts for most of the song. Rhythm guitar 1 was turned up at the end of the song, while the riff guitar was boosted in the second verse, where it re-enters in the last chorus, and in the first eight measures of the out section, where it plays the melody. The volume of the solo guitar changes throughout the solo. The lead vocals didn't need any volume changes, but the mid background vocal does change in the fourth verse, when the high background part sits out. The fade-out at the end of the song was written to the master output buss.

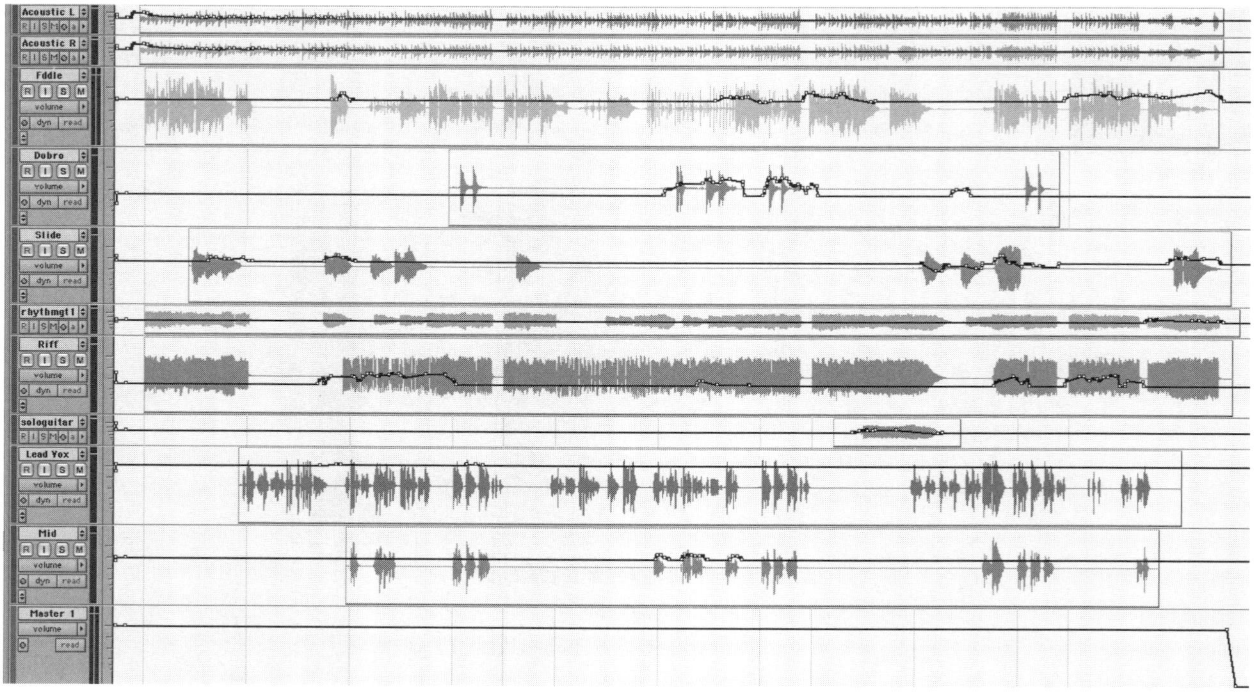

Fig. 5.44. Automation

Edits

Few changes were made to the audio tracks at the mixing stage of "My Give a Damn's Busted." As with many of the other songs included in this volume, each of the tracks were trimmed up to the point that the audio started on that track. For example, the lead vocal was trimmed to the beginning of the first verse and then was cleared until the first chorus where it entered.

Many of the tracks were also trimmed at the end of the song. But all of this is simply for visual clarity; the only actual edit was at 2:04 right before the solo. At that point, some of the drum tracks were cleared because of some residual noise in the break.

Fig. 5.45. Edit

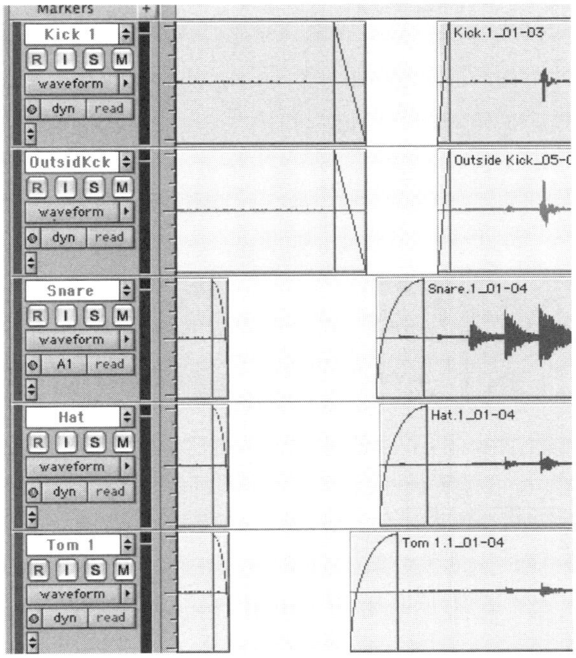

Printing Mixes

When printing the mix of each of the songs in this volume, a consistent approach was used: a track (in this case, a couple of tracks) is used to set the final length of the song. The start and end times for the printed mix of "My Give a Damn's Busted" were set by selecting the overhead track. In Pro Tools, selecting this trimmed track will cause the program to play from the beginning to the end of that track with no excess audio or time at the beginning or end. In those situations where multiple mixes of a song must be done—for example, if a producer wants vocal up or vocal down versions, TV mixes, instrumental mixes—all of the versions are the same length, and can be easily lined up for editing.

Fig. 5.46. Print Mix

CHAPTER 6

"Play Something Country"

(as Recorded by Brooks and Dunn)

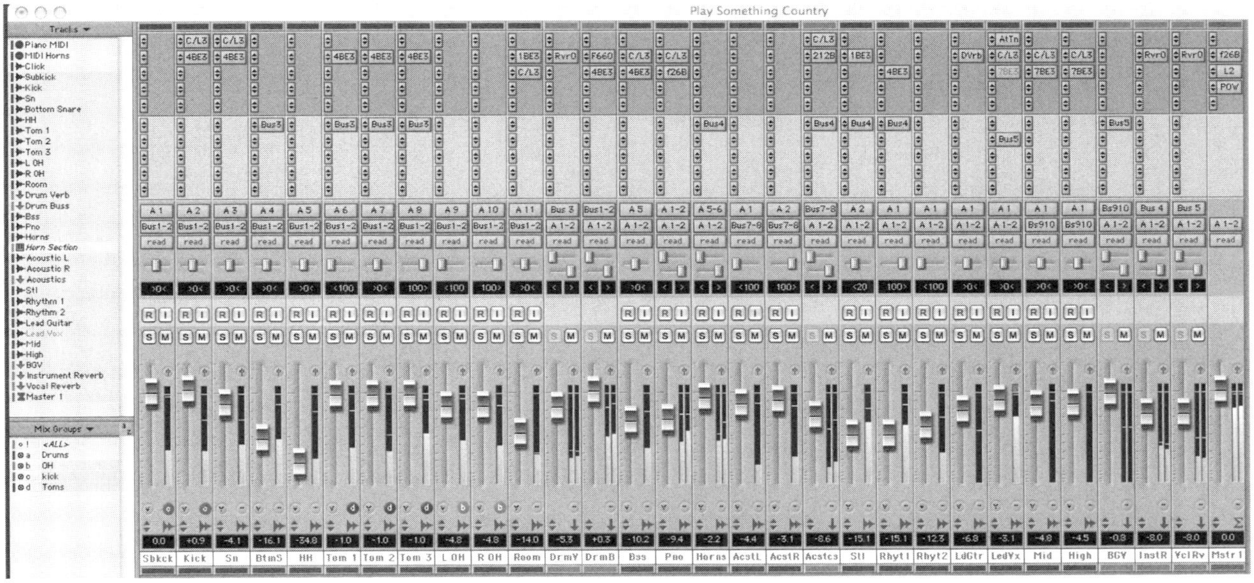

Fig. 6.1. Mix Window

With its distorted rhythm guitars, slide guitar, and a horn section, the southern rock-inflected "Play Something Country" probably owes a debt to both Lynyrd Skynyrd and R&B singer Delbert McClinton. (Has anyone else noticed that whenever a song has the word "country" in the title or the chorus, that song is unlikely to be related to anything that Merle Haggard or Hank Williams would have done? And that any song that has either the word "hillbilly" or "cowboy" in it probably had neither actual hillbillies *nor* cowboys involved at any stage in the production?) In any case, "Play Something Country" is pretty typical of the style, so the mixing possibilities discussed below are applicable to a pretty wide range of material.

Most of the tracks in this volume were mixed using third-party plug-ins—particularly those from Waves. But since those who are just getting into the whole "in the box" thing may hesitate to spend a lot of money on third-party software, the mix of "Play Something Country" used mainly those plug-ins that come for free as part of the Pro Tools software package. While third-party plug-ins can offer some advantages—particularly those that create strange and wonderful effects— the free plug-ins that come with the software packages may certainly be used to good effect.

DRUMS

As a change from the mixes discussed in the last two chapters, "Play Something Country" returns to the practice of assigning the drums to their own stereo buss. While there may be no over-riding sonic advantages to using a drum buss over not using a drum buss, there are also no disadvantages. And creating a stereo drum buss can make certain types of processing—especially parallel processing of the drums—much easier. Parallel processing will be discussed below; it's not an approach that is always necessary or even useable, but it's a nice addition to the mixing engineer's tool kit.

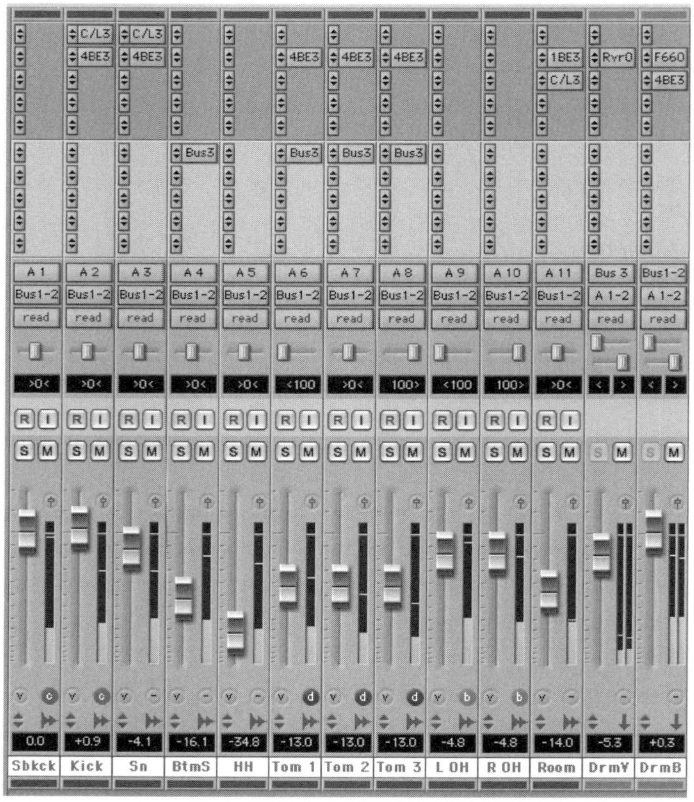

Fig. 6.2. Drum Mix

Kick Drum

Experimenting with the levels of two kick drum tracks to find the best balance (before adding EQ or compression) is usually a good practice, but it's not always worth the time and effort. There are times when you hear the raw tracks and try to find a way to make them useable. In this case, at least one of the kick drum tracks (the subkick) is quite workable with no other processing. There are two kick drum tracks on "Play Something Country." With the subkick left alone, only the main kick track (recorded with a Shure Beta 52) is a viable candidate for processing.

Subkick

The subkick track uses no plug-ins; for its purpose (low frequency kick drum information), the unaltered track is just fine. Therefore, the level of the subkick track was at 0 dB, or unity gain.

Kick

The kick drum, with an output level of –0.9 dB, uses a couple of plug-ins, both part of the DigiRack line by Digidesign. The first in the chain is the DigiRack Compressor/Limiter 3, while the second is the DigiRack 4-Band EQ III. The DigiRack Compressor Limiter is used with a 5:1 compression ratio, with a threshold that results in a maximum of about 3 dB of gain reduction. The attack time of the compressor was set to 100 microseconds (or a tenth of a millisecond). Attack times that short can change the actual tone of the track, as discussed below.

The 4-band EQ III boosts the low end of the kick drum track a bit over 6 dB, cuts the low-mids by 3 dB, then boosts the high-mids by 2.5 dB at 2.7 kHz and the highs +4.9 dB at 6.2 kHz.

Fig. 6.3. Kick Compressor

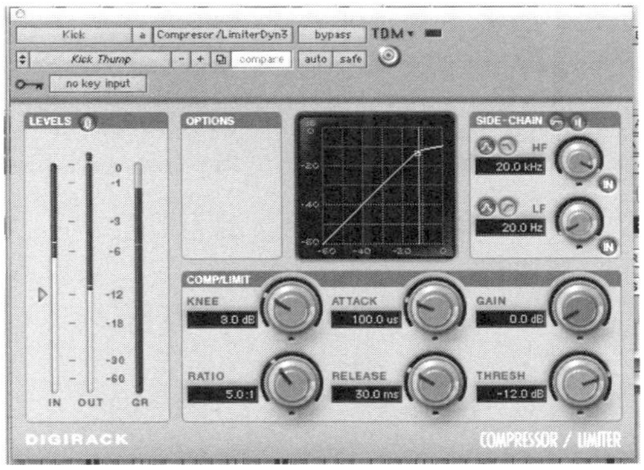

DigiRack Comp/Limiter 3 Kick Drum Settings						
parameter	knee	ratio	attack	release	gain	threshold
setting	8.0 dB	5.0:1	53.0 us	30 ms	0 dB	–6.6 dB

It's been mentioned a number of times that compressors are generally used for one of two reasons—either to even out the musician's performance or to change the tone of the track. A third approach—compressing as an effect—will be discussed at another time. Since it seems that the majority of plug-in compressors are modeled after their analog counterparts, the tone altering attributes of the analog versions are ported over to their digital brethren. When an 1176-type plug-in sounds a lot like the old UREI 1176, or an emulation of an old Fairchild limiter changes the frequency response of the track on which it's used, then inserting that plug-in into the path changes the tone of the signal processed by it.

But that's not the only way to change the tone of a signal with the use of a compressor plug-in—manipulating the attack and release times of the plug-in can alter the tone in other ways. Those signals that deliver most of their energy quickly—drums, for example—can be be altered with a fast attack time so that the characteristic sound of the instrument (such as the initial impact of a drum) is minimized while other tones that are inherent in the drum but are overpowered by the attack can be heard. (These tones may be enhanced by a fast release time, which would bring up the average level of the tones.)

Fig. 6.4. Kick EQ

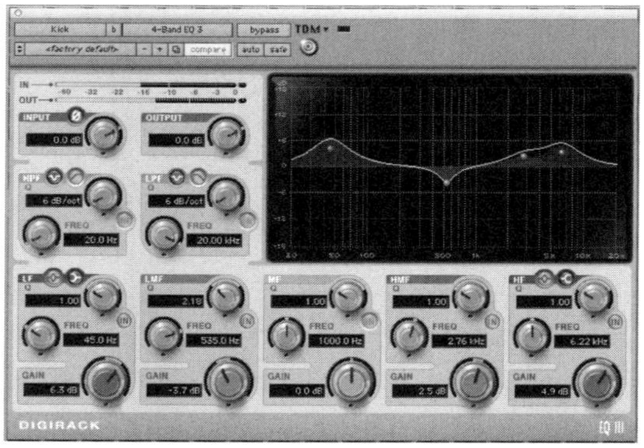

DigiRack 4-band EQ III Kick Drum Settings

parameter	low	low-mid	high-mid	high	input
Q	1.00	2.18	1.00	1.00	0.0
frequency	45.0 Hz	535 Hz	2.76 kHz	6.22 kHz	Output
gain	+6.3 dB	–3.7 dB	+2.5 dB	+4.9 dB	0.0
filter	bell	bell	bell	bell	

Snare

Like the kick drum track, the snare track has a DigiRack Comp/Limiter 3 inserted, followed by a DigiRack 4-band EQ III. The fader level of the snare track was set to –4.1 dB.

When adding an EQ plug-in to the snare track, knowledge of where both useful and problem frequencies exist can make mixing a given track much easier. While these are guidelines rather than recipes, you may want to keep the following in mind:

Since little other than bleed from the kick drum or room ambience exists below 100 Hz on a snare drum, high passing the snare at somewhere between 80 and 100 Hz is almost never a bad idea. To fatten up a snare drum, the frequencies in the 100 to 350 Hz range are excellent candidates for tweaking. The boxiness that can happen with snare tracks can usually be mitigated by cutting frequencies in the 500 to 1000 Hz range. The 5 kHz to 7 kHz area (with some room for fudging on either side) can add a crispness to the snare track to help it cut through a dense mix, while the 8 kHz to 15 kHz range adds snap, or sizzle to the snare.

Fig. 6.5. Snare Compressor

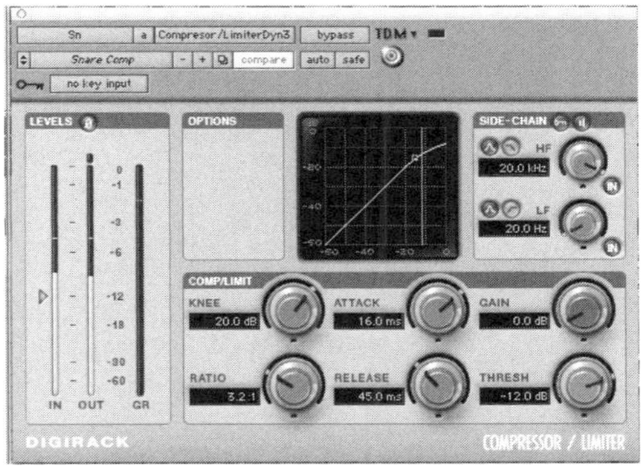

DigiRack Comp/Limiter 3 Top Snare Settings						
parameter	**knee**	**ratio**	**attack**	**release**	**gain**	**threshold**
setting	20.0 dB	3.2:1	16.0 ms	45 ms	0 dB	–12 dB

Fig. 6.6. Snare EQ

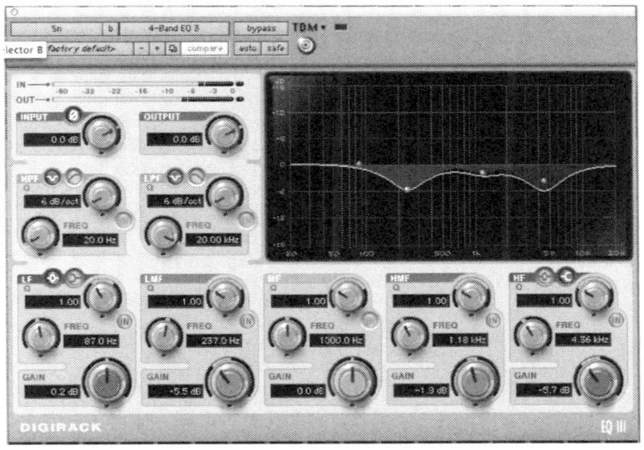

DigiRack 4-band EQ III Top Snare Settings					
parameter	**low**	**low-mid**	**high-mid**	**high**	**input**
Q	1.00	1.00	1.00	1.00	0.0
frequency	87.0 Hz	237 Hz	1.18 kHz	4.36 kHz	output
gain	+0.2 dB	–5.5 dB	–1.8 dB	–1.8 dB	0.0
filter	shelf	bell	bell	bell	shelf

Bottom Snare

The bottom snare track is back—it wasn't used on the song in the previous chapter—but here it is again with an output level of –16.1 dB. For "Play Something Country," the bottom snare track is used for the send to the drum reverb instead of the main snare track; the biggest differences in the two (from the viewpoint of an aux send) are that the bottom snare track has a bit less bleed from the other drums and that the actual drum hits are both brighter and shorter. The send to the drum reverb is at +2.1 dB. This may seem to be quite high, since aux sends with some of the other mixes tended to be in the –8 dB to –20 dB range, but there's a simple explanation: the aux sends are set to be post-fader.

Post-fader sends are the standard approach for aux sends. It means that when the fader levels for a given track are adjusted, the signal sent by the aux send is adjusted as well. This bottom snare track is an excellent example of this; the aux send needs to be high because the fader level is quite low; if the bottom snare was turned up to unity gain, the send would be hot enough to overload the input of the drum reverb.

That doesn't mean that aux sends *must* be post-fader; there are applications where a pre-fader aux send is the preferred approach (sends that go to a headphone mix are one example; it's not a good idea to screw up the musicians' headphone mix just because the producer doesn't want to hear the vocals). There are other situations where a pre-fader aux send would be preferable, but we're getting away from the discussion.

No other processing was used on the bottom snare mic; it fulfills its role by adding a bit of snap to the main snare sound and by providing a signal source for the drum reverb.

Hi-hat

There's little to add to what's been discussed previously; the hi-hat's fader level, at –34.8 dB, helps to add a very little bit of definition to the overall drum track. The hat is panned to the left, in keeping with the drummer's perspective approach to drum mixing that's been used in all of the songs.

Toms

The previous chapter discussed ways to minimize tom hum and bleed from the tom tracks besides using gates. The toms on "Play Something Country" use one of those ways: the three tom tracks are automated so that the volume rises by 12 dB when the toms are played. For most of the song, the tom levels are at –13 dB, but when a tom fill occurs, the level of all three tracks will rise to –1 dB, and then drop back down. This is a quick and convenient way to deal with extraneous noise on the tom tracks. Four-band DigiRack EQ IIIs are used on the three tom tracks, with the particular settings optimized for the various sized drums. The aux sends to the drum reverb are at –8.0 dB for all three toms.

Fig. 6.7. Tom 1 EQ

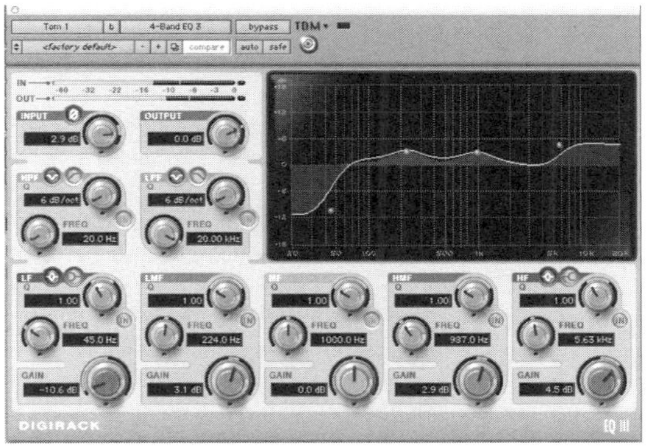

DigiRack 4-band EQ III Tom 1 Settings					
parameter	**low**	**low-mid**	**high-mid**	**high**	**input**
Q	1.00	1.00	1.00	1.00	2.9
frequency	45.0 Hz	224 Hz	987 Hz	5.63 kHz	output
gain	–10.6 dB	+3.1 dB	+2.9 dB	+4.5 dB	0.0
filter	shelf	bell	bell	bell	shelf

Fig. 6.8. Tom 2 EQ

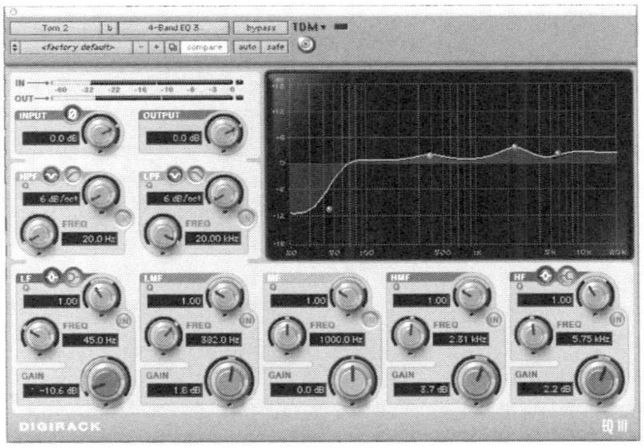

DigiRack 4-band EQ III Tom 2 Settings					
parameter	**low**	**low-mid**	**high-mid**	**high**	**input**
Q	1.00	1.00	1.00	1.00	0.0
frequency	45.0 Hz	382 Hz	2.31 kHz	5.75 kHz	output
gain	–10.6 dB	+1.8 dB	+3.7 dB	+2.2 dB	0.0
filter	shelf	bell	bell	bell	shelf

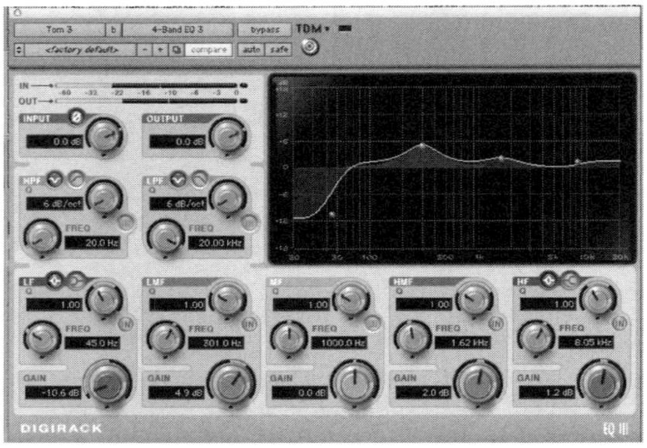

Fig. 6.9. Tom 3 EQ

DigiRack 4-band EQ III Tom 3 Settings					
parameter	**low**	**low-mid**	**high-mid**	**high**	**input**
Q	1.00	1.00	1.00	1.00	0.0
frequency	45.0 Hz	301 Hz	1.63 kHz	8.05 kHz	output
gain	–10.6 dB	+4.9 dB	+2.0 dB	+1.2 dB	0.0
filter	shelf	bell	bell	bell	shelf

Overheads

The overhead tracks, recorded with a pair of Telefunken M16 microphones required no further processing; the left overhead fader level was –5.2 dB, and the right overhead fader level is at –4.8 dB.

Room

All of the songs in this volume have a room mic track; some songs, including "Play Something Country," have a mono room mic (a Telefunken 251) while the others used a pair of Neumann TLM 103s as a stereo room track. The 251 was placed at the far end of the tracking room from the drum set, and was placed around ten feet (a bit less than three meters) above the floor. The mic was set in an omni-directional pattern, which not only means that it was picking up reflected sound from all directions, but that there were no major changes to the low frequencies due to proximity effect. While the 251 was placed in the center of the room, the TLM 103s were set in the far corners of the tracking room, about six feet (two meters) above the ground and pointing towards the ceiling. Though both work fine at adding ambience to the drum sound, the stereo pair can make that ambience seem to be a bit wider.

Though the room mic(s) can be used as-is—brought up judiciously underneath the main drum sound to taste—they can also be processed to use as an effect. For example, try limiting the room mics with a very fast attack and a fast release (and a substantial amount of gain reduction). The idea is to make the attack of the drums disappear, so that just the ambience of the room is emphasized; "uncontrolled pumping" wouldn't be a bad description of the sound once the limiter is set. This is a trick that many attribute to the use of the talkback circuit in the SSL 4000 series console. The circuit included a hard limiter that allowed those who weren't right next to the console to be heard, and some enterprising and creative engineer figured out that if he passed an audio signal through that circuit, interesting things could happen. The Empirical Labs Distressor also has a setting that does the same sort of thing—it's called the "nuke" setting. Though the processed track may sound fairly atrocious when soloed, when it's tucked underneath the normal drum sound, it can add a thickness that's not attainable in any other way. Be careful, though—this is an easy trick to over use. If the processed room track is too loud, the drum sound can quickly get really muddy.

In addition to limiting (or more mildly, compressing) the room mic(s), judicious amounts of equalization may be used to enhance the track. Naturally, a high-pass filter can be used to minimize low frequency information that can make the room mic muddy, but, since the room mics are supposed to be recording the sound of the room as well as the drums, a low-pass filter (set somewhere between 5 kHz and 12 kHz can remove frequencies that are coming directly from the drums and cymbals, effectively allowing the reflected sound of the acoustic space to be more prominent.

The drums on this track were recorded in a space that's approximately twenty-two feet wide and twenty-eight feet long, with the drums on one end of the room. To simulate the sound of a larger room, the room mic can be delayed; the actual amount of delay may vary, but something in the 50–80 millisecond range can be very effective. While longer delays can work, the danger is that the room mics will begin to sound like a slap-back echo and not simply a large room. To minimize the slap-back effect somewhat, try removing high-frequency information from the room track with a low-pass filter; this can be as low as 1kHz or as high as 10 kHz (like many other ideas, the actual frequency is application specific—if it sounds good, it *is* good).

On "Play Something Country," the room mic track is once again used to add a bit of grit to the drum sound that it didn't necessarily have at the tracking stage. A DigiRack Compressor/Limiter 3 and a DigiRack 1-band EQ III were used. The single-band version of the EQ III is used as a high-pass filter at 40 Hz. The Compressor Limiter 3 is used as a hard limiter with a 100:1 compression ratio and a 10-microsecond attack time. The level of the resulting noise is –14.0 dB.

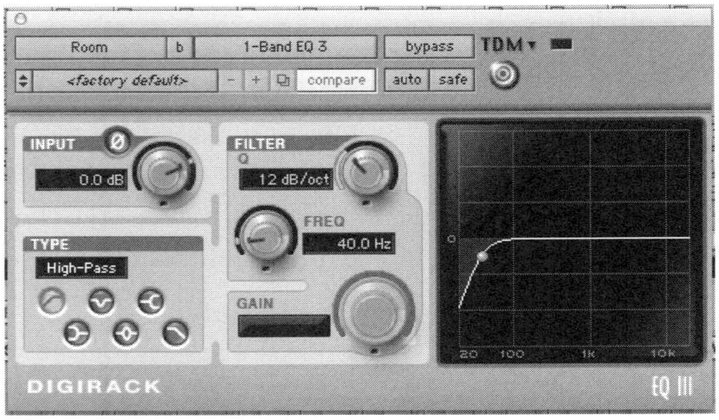

Fig. 6.10. Room EQ

DigiRack 1-band EQ III Room Mic Settings	
parameter	**low**
slope	12 dB/Octave
frequency	40.0 Hz
input	0 dB
filter	high pass

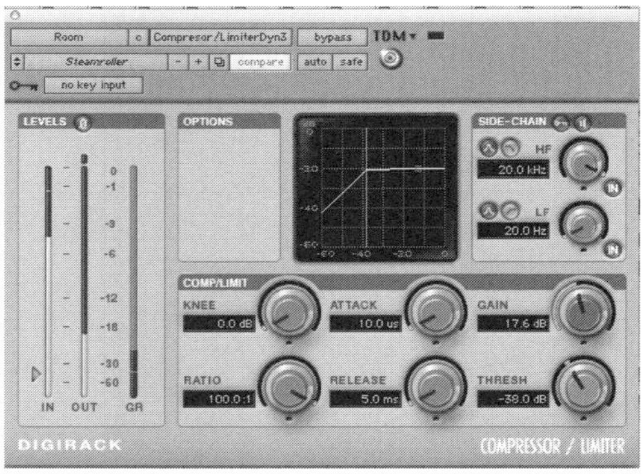

Fig. 6.11. Room Compressor

DigiRack Comp/Limiter 3 Room Mic Settings						
parameter	**knee**	**ratio**	**attack**	**release**	**gain**	**threshold**
setting	0 dB	100.0:1	10.0 μs	5.0 ms	17.6 dB	–38 dB

Drum Routing, Grouping, and Effects

The tracks that make up the drum kit are routed to a stereo buss, so that EQ and a stereo buss compressor can be inserted across the whole kit. Remember, that ultimately, a drum set is a single instrument; each drum in the set is part of the whole. By bussing all of the drum tracks together, you have control over not only the overall level of the kit, but also over any sonic changes that need to affect the whole kit sound.

Fig. 6.12. Drum Groups and Routing

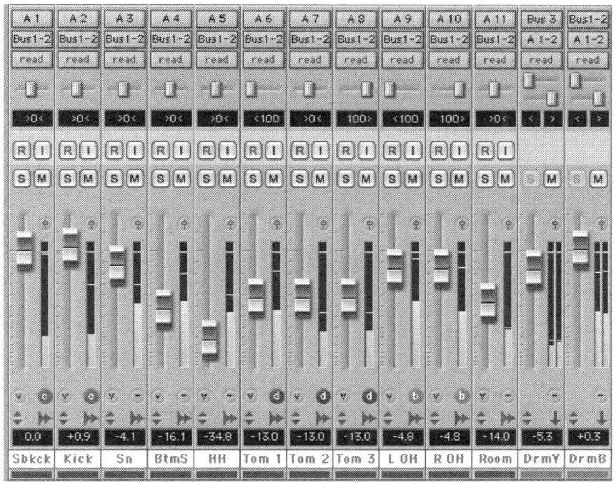

For ease of mixing, I typically create several groups among the drum tracks. I set up three groups for the drums. The first group is the three toms, since once the levels of the toms are set (relative to each other), it's more common to adjust the volumes of all three to adjust their relation to the rest of the kit rather than adjusting each tom individually. The second group is the overhead mics; I put the overheads on two mono tracks rather than one stereo track because it's not uncommon to need to adjust one of the two overhead tracks in order to create the best stereo image. Once the relative levels between the two overhead mics are set, grouping them together so that the relative levels between the two tracks remain the same when turning the overheads up or down makes further adjustments easier and more accurate. The third group is all the tracks that make up the drum kit; though the drum group is usually inactive, it's sometimes convenient to turn all of the tracks up or down to optimize the levels going to the drum buss. The subkick and kick tracks are also grouped to make it easier to adjust the levels of the kick drum once the blend of the two tracks is achieved.

It's usually a good idea to set up an effects buss with some sort of reverb setting for the drums alone; while they might occasionally use the same type of reverb sound as other instruments, it's more common on contemporary records for them to sound as though they were in their own acoustic space. Setting up an effects send just for the drums is quite easy to do. For "Play Something Country," I used a mono auxiliary send that is mostly dedicated to the drums—specifically to the snare and toms. I say "mostly" because in the end, the drum reverb is merely another reverb; if some other track would be enhanced by running it through what's being called the "drum reverb," then that track will be sent to the drum reverb.

The drum buss—that is, the stereo buss where all the drum tracks and the drum reverb end up (before being combined with the other instrument and vocal tracks) are where any processing that applies to the entire drum track are added. On "Play Something Country," a compressor/limiter and an EQ have been added. The compressor, a Fairchild 660 emulation, is only adding mild compression—less than 2 dB—with a fairly slow attack and release time. The EQ, a 4-band DigiRack EQ III, has a shelving EQ at 75 Hz boosting 1.5 dB, and a high frequency shelving EQ boosting 1.4 dB at 9 kHz. The output of the drum buss is at +0.3 dB, and is sent to the master output fader.

Fig. 6.13. Drum Buss Compressor

Fairchild 660 Drum Buss Settings			
control	input gain	threshold	time constant
setting	25	4.8	2

Fig. 6.14. Drum Buss EQ

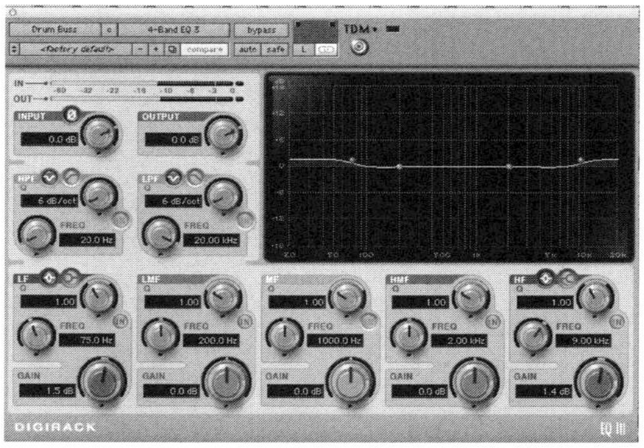

DigiRack 4-band EQ III Drum Buss Settings					
parameter	low	low-mid	high-mid	high	input
Q	1.00	1.00	1.00	1.00	0.0
frequency	75.0 Hz	200 Hz	1 kHz	9.0 kHz	output
gain	+1.5 dB	0 dB	0 dB	0 dB	0.0
filter	shelf	bell	bell	bell	

The drum reverb on "Play Something Country" is a Digidesign Reverb One set to a slightly altered Large Wood Room preset. Digi's Reverb One has many parameters that can be altered to suit the needs of a given track in addition to a whole bunch of presets. Here's a table that shows these settings a bit more clearly:

Fig. 6.15. Drum Reverb

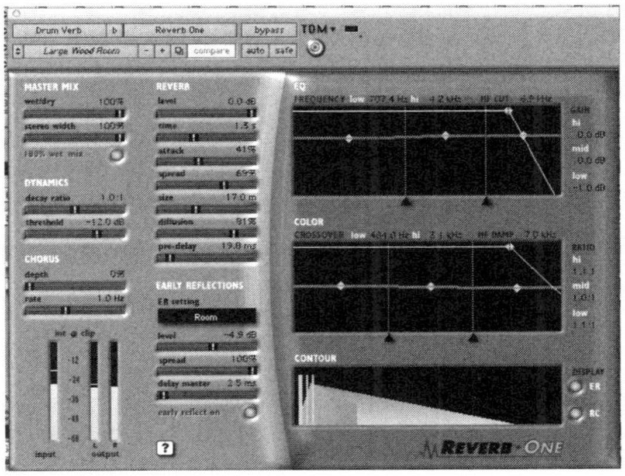

Reverb One Drum Reverb Settings

parameter	setting
wet/dry	100%
stereo width	100%
decay ratio	1.0:1
threshold	–12 dB
reverb level	0 dB
reverb time	1.3 seconds
attack	41%
spread	69%
size	17.0 meters
diffusion	81%
pre-delay	19.8 ms
early reflection (ER) Setting	room
ER level	–4.9 dB
ER spread	100%
ER delay master	2.5 ms

The Reverb One has a number of other parameters available—a 3-band EQ, a high-frequency cut, high-frequency damping, and even a "color" window that offers even more settings to adjust. On the reverb return fader, the output of the drum reverb is set to –5.3 dB, and is routed to the master output fader (and not to the drum buss, which has been the case in some other mixes).

Ambience

Another approach to adding ambience to the drum set is with parallel compression. Conceptually, parallel compression is a simple idea; it's simply duplicating the drum buss, limiting the heck out of the duplicate (with an extremely fast attack time) and then bringing the compressed track up underneath the original track. This method makes it possible to bring a controlled amount of, well, distortion, into the track; parallel compression makes the hum from the toms, the ambience of the room, and even such things as the rattle of the snare drum a useable part of the drum sound. This concept was also discussed in relation to the lead vocal track, but while the point of parallel compression for the lead vocal is to smooth out the dynamic range in a reasonably transparent manner, the point of doing so for drums is to add a sound that's hard to get in any other manner.

BASS

The bass track used a DigiRack Compressor/Limiter 3 and a DigiRack 4-band EQ III for processing. The compressor settings were mild, with a 2.5:1 compression ratio.

Concerning the use of compression on bass tracks: in an ideal world, there would be no need to process electric bass tracks in this manner—for instance, most engineers in the 1960s and 1970s knew that if the legendary Joe Osborn played bass on a track, there was no need to add a compressor to the bass either on the tracking session or when mixing the record. Joe's playing was so consistently even in volume and tone that no compression was needed to make his bass tracks fit perfectly in the final mix. But sadly, this isn't an ideal world, and most of us aren't mixing records that Joe Osborn played on. From time to time, the bass tracks *do* need a bit of help. The tools typically used to tame errant bass tracks are the same ones discussed with other tracks—EQ and compression.

Keep in mind that the low E string on a bass vibrates at around 40 Hz, or 40 cycles per second (those who desire accurate information rather than ease in understanding can feel better by knowing that in an even-tempered tuning with A equaling 440 Hz, the low E is 41.2 Hz). So it might make sense to high pass all bass tracks at 40 Hz—and it would have been high passed before the popularity of 5- and 6-string basses made its way into country music. But notes lower than the low E—all the way down to a low B (and, when the bassist retunes, even B flat and an extremely low A)—are used in contemporary country tracks. So before high passing the bass track, it would be good to know what the lowest note is. Though very few professional monitors are actually flat to below 40 Hz (and most—especially the smaller desktop monitors that are so popular today—don't have an effective range even that low), there's no reason not to mix as though the listener is sitting in the middle of his audiophile sound system. Also, while the monitors don't necessarily reproduce the fundamental frequencies of low notes, harmonics of those notes (especially those an octave higher) are reproduced, and, in fact, are a large part of the bass sound heard on consumer systems. If you high pass the bass track somewhere around 30 Hz, the lowest fundamental frequencies will not be affected (the low B on a 5-string bass vibrates at 30.87 Hz.) In the real world, it's not that critical—high-pass filters aren't typically of the brick-wall type, but roll off frequencies at 6–12 dB per octave. This means those frequencies below the cut-off are attenuated, not removed, and those closest to the cut-off point are attenuat ed less than those farther away.

While any suggestions about adding or subtracting specific frequencies can be no more than broad generalizations, the following general pointers might help to lead in the right direction. If the bass sounds muddy or lacks definition, a cut in the 200–300 Hz area may improve matters. On the other hand, if a bass track sounds thin, boosting a bit in the 100–250 Hz range might help. For more high-end definition, try the frequencies between 450 and 800 Hz, and if you're seeking more brightness, look in the 3–5 kHz range; as a general rule, electric basses don't have much sonic information above 5 kHz.

Though Joe Osborn did not play bass on the songs in this volume, the bass tracks are fairly consistent in level (that is, when the bass gets softer or louder, it's intentional, not accidental). So the compressor used on the track is chosen as much for the tonal changes that the plug-in imparts as for the actual compression. Typical compressor settings are quite mild—ratios in the 2:1 to -4:1 range—with fairly short attack times to catch any peaks (or fingernails) that jump out and they have medium release times. Typically, the threshold will be set so that only a couple of dB of gain reduction take place. The idea is to avoid a squashed bass track; it's usually more natural sounding to have one that breathes a bit.

Sidechaining

One creative option that can be used on the bass (and really, any other instrument) is sidechain compression. With a normal compressor, a simple way to understand what's happening is to visualize that the signal is split at the input of the unit. The signal goes both along the audio path and to a detection circuit, which reads the level of the signal and when that level exceeds a certain threshold, lowers the level of the audio path according to the settings on the compressor. (Software plug-ins more or less emulate this.) Sidechain compression is different in that instead of using the same signal in the detector path as the audio path, a different signal—like a kick drum—is sent to the detector circuit. Using the kick drum as an example, the bass compressor can be sidechained so that the bass level drops when the kick drum is hit, making the attack of the kick drum more audible by essentially moving the bass track out of its way. Another version of sidechaining is common in the broadcast field, where a music track is automatically reduced in level (by sidechaining the announcing mic to a compressor on the music tracks) when the announcer speaks. Having a kick drum trigger a volume reduction in the bass track is the same principle (though, admittedly, a bit more subtle than having the orchestra get quieter when the announcer's voice intones, "Picture a world where apes evolved from men....")

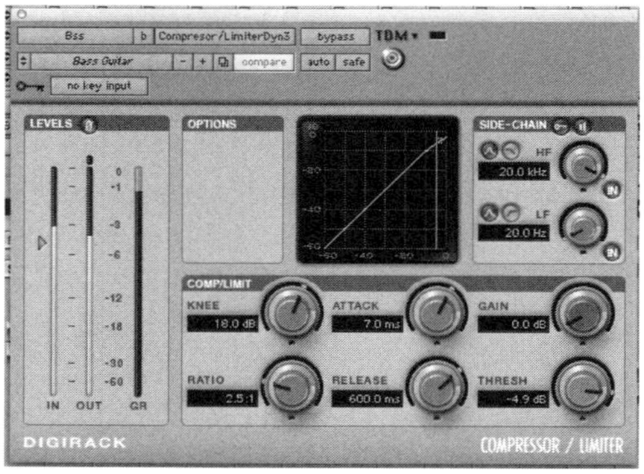

Fig. 6.16. Bass Compressor

DigiRack Comp/Limiter 3 Bass Settings						
parameter	knee	ratio	attack	release	gain	threshold
setting	18.0 dB	2.5:1	7.0 ms	600.0 ms	0 dB	–4.9 dB

The EQ is primarily boosting low-mid frequencies while cutting high-mid frequencies; this is to add a bit of meat to the bass track without causing it to get in the way of the guitars. The output level of the bass track was set to –10.2 dB.

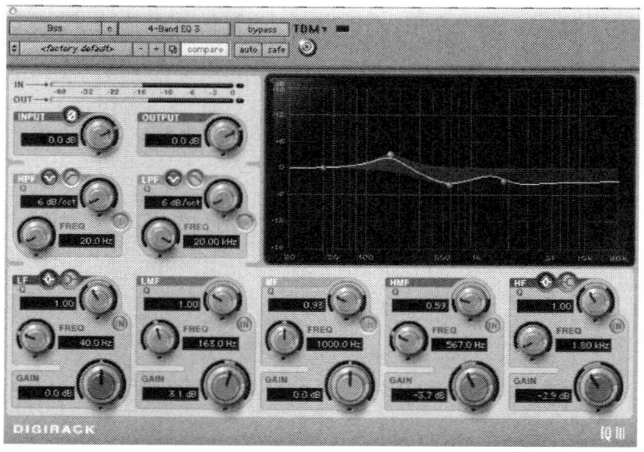

Fig. 6.17. Bass EQ

DigiRack 4-band EQ III Bass Settings					
parameter	low	low-mid	high-mid	high	input
Q	1.00	1.00	.59	1.00	0.0
frequency	40 Hz	160 Hz	567 Hz	1.8 kHz	output
gain	–5.5 dB	+3.1 dB	–3.7 dB	–2.9 dB	0.0
filter	shelf	bell	bell	bell	shelf

PIANO

The piano on "Play Something Country" was not the Yamaha C7 grand piano heard on most of the other tracks in this volume; on this song, the piano sound came from a Kurzweil K2500 rack-mounted unit. By using a number of different piano sounds (created by recording the piano with a variety of different mics: Telefunken 251s, AKG 480 small-diaphragm condensers in an YW pattern or 480s as a spaced pair), a wider range of processing is necessary. This allows for more opportunities to show different EQ needs. The output level of the piano was –9.4 dB.

The usual DigiRack Comp/Limiter 3 was used, with a fairly soft knee and 4:1 compression ratio. But rather than using the EQ III a Focusrite d2 6-band EQ was inserted. Though the piano track sounded fine by itself, it needed to be thinned out a bit to match the piano on the original track. To that end, the high-mids were boosted by 1.5 dB, and a 3 dB boost above 12 kHz was made with a shelving filter.

Fig. 6.18. Piano Compressor

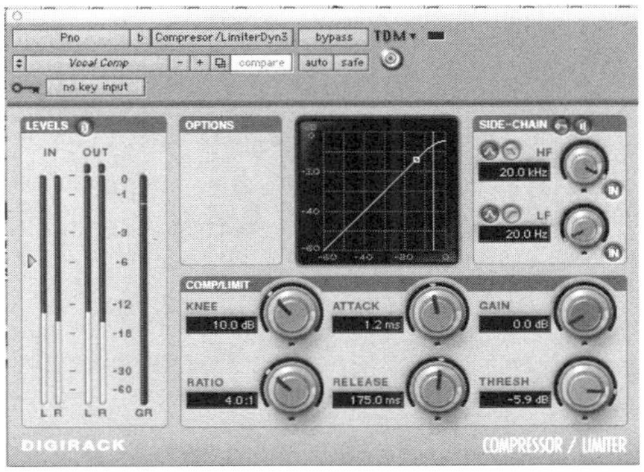

DigiRack Comp/Limiter 3 Piano Settings

parameter	knee	ratio	attack	release	gain	threshold
setting	18.0 dB	4.0:1	1.2 ms	175.0 ms	0 dB	–5.9 dB

Fig. 6.19. Piano EQ

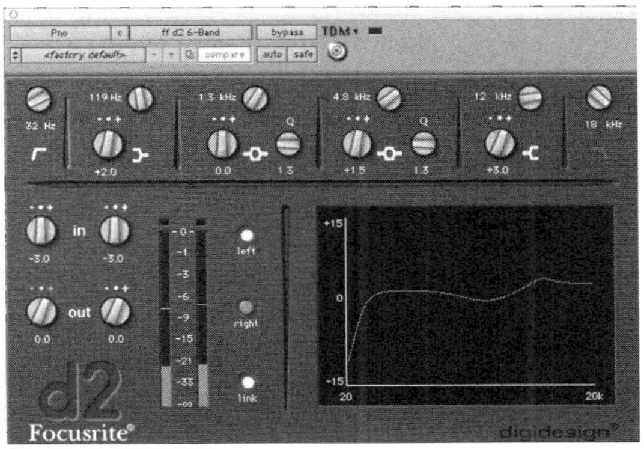

Focusrite d2 6-band EQ Piano Settings						
parameter	hi pass	low	low-mid	high-mid	high	low-pass
frequency	32 Hz	119 Hz	1.3 kHz	4.8 kHz	12 kHz	18 kHz
level		+2.0dB	0 dB	+1.5 dB	+3.0 dB	
Q			1.3	1.3		
filter	in	shelf	bell	bell	shelf	bypass

HORNS

The horn tracks on "Play Something Country" were created with a virtual instrument called "Xpand!" and the specific patch was "natural brass section." While it would be possible (within a Pro Tools session) to mix the track with the virtual horns, they were printed to a stereo track so that those who don't have the Xpand! instrument could still hear the track. The horn volume is automated throughout the track, since the keyboard sensitivity of the plug-in was a bit wider than the keyboardist was accustomed to. An aux send to the instrument reverb was set at –0.3 dB.

Fig. 6.20. Xpand! Horns

ACOUSTIC GUITARS

The acoustic guitar on this song isn't actually a "stereo" track; the two microphones used to record the acoustic were placed with one mic between the sound hole and the neck of the instrument about four inches from the face of the guitar while the other mic was placed approximately even with the guitarist's shoulder and pointing at the lower bout from approximately twelve inches away. These two tracks are generally treated (and processed) as a stereo pair, but since purists would argue that "stereo" has a specific meaning in audio, it might be better to refer to it as a "two-microphone" technique. In any case, the two tracks have a pretty different tone—acoustic A is a bit more direct sounding and has more presence than acoustic B. Nevertheless, these two tracks can be panned to hard left and right, and provide an acoustic guitar sound that sounds quite full.

The level of the left acoustic track (the track from the microphone near the guitar's neck) was set at –4.4 dB, while the right acoustic track was a bit higher at –3.1 dB to more closely match the levels. As with the drums being grouped together, I grouped the acoustic guitar tracks once the relative levels were set correctly. This allows for changes in volume without losing the relationship between the two tracks. These tracks were bussed to their own stereo buss, so that processing could be done to both tracks simultaneously. First, a DigiRack Comp/Limiter 3 was inserted to add a bit of compression. Rather mild settings were used; a 2:1 compression ratio and a soft knee minimized the sound of compression. Even at the loudest part of the song, the compressor was only reducing gain by about 2 dB. After the compressor, a Focusrite d2 2-band EQ was used. A bell-shaped EQ centered at 33 Hz at 06.5 dB rolled off some of the low end from the acoustic guitar tracks while a 4 dB boost at 4.5 kHz brightened the tracks considerably. An aux send at a level of –8.0 dB was used to route the acoustic guitar buss to the instrument reverb.

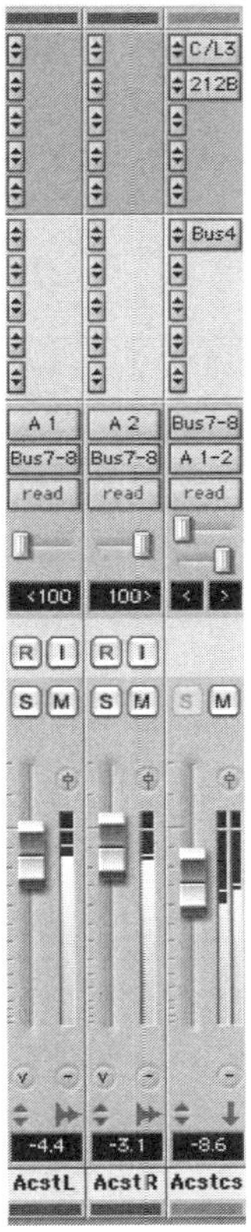

Fig. 6.21. Acoustic Buss

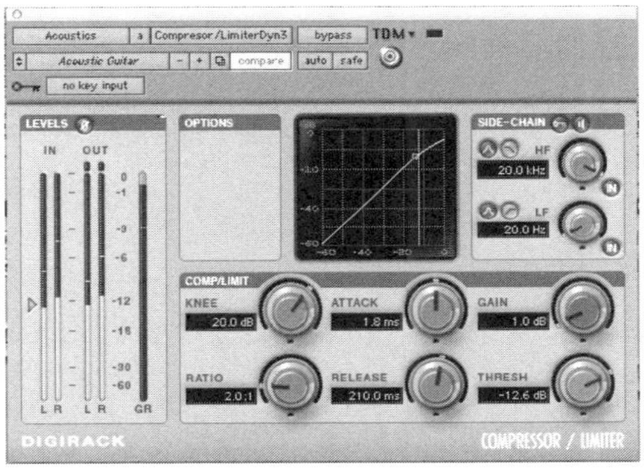

Fig. 6.22. Acoustic Guitar Compressor

DigiRack Comp/Limiter 3 Acoustic Guitar Settings						
parameter	**knee**	**ratio**	**attack**	**release**	**gain**	**threshold**
Setting	20.0 dB	2.0:1	1.8 ms	210.0 ms	+1.0 dB	–12.6 dB

Fig. 6.22a. Acoustic Guitar EQ

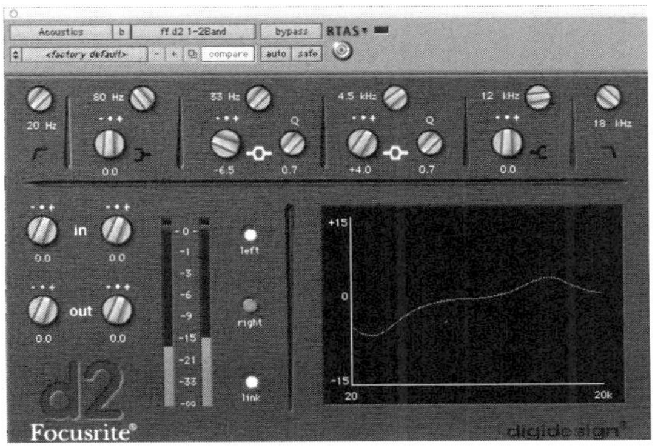

Focusrite d2 2-band EQ Acoustic Guitar Settings		
parameter	low	high
frequency	33 Hz	4.5 kHz
level	–6.5 dB	+4.0 dB
Q	0.7	0.7
filter	bell	bell

STEEL

Though the track is called "steel," the instrument that is actually playing on "Play Something Country" is a lap steel. A number of different instruments are now considered steel in county music; the pedal steel guitar is the most common, but the original lap steel that became popular during the Hawaiian music craze of the 1920s and 1930s is still used on records today. While a few of the non-pedal steel players in Nashville trace their playing style back to the pre-pedal era country musicians like Don Helms (Hank Williams) and Jerry Byrd (Hank Snow), most of the studio musicians who also play a non-pedal steel guitar seem to be more influenced by multi-instrumentalist David Lindley and slide guitarists like Lowell George and Duane Allman. As a point of fact, the lap steel that some of Nashville's busiest sessions players use is, as often as not, a Fender guitar (Telecaster or Stratocaster) that's been set up with specially made nut and extra high action so that it can be played with a steel guitar bar. The lap steel on this track was played with exactly that—an old Fender Tele that had been set up as a lap steel. Despite that, lap steel is a different beast than a slide guitar, which is played with a hollow slide that fits over one of the musician's fingers.

It's pretty common for lap steel tracks to sound as though they're played through an amp that's been turned all the way up—and that's how a lot of the lap steel tracks on today's records have been recorded. But it's equally common for steel players to use an overdrive pedal, like guitarists do. Though regular steel guitar is usually harmonically complex (and therefore doesn't behave well or sound good when distorted), some steel parts—and most lap steel parts—are good candidates for amp simulator plug-ins like Amp Farm of Amplitube. In much the way that guitars—even those recorded with an amp—can use the amp simulator plug-ins, so can steel guitars and lap steels.

Though it's not quite a standard, regular listening to country music on the radio reveals an interesting relationship between the fiddle and the steel guitar; when both instruments are present in a mix, it's far more common for the fiddle to be panned to the left and the steel to the right than the other way. An engineer friend who has mixed dozens of hit records over the last two decades told me one day that he might have started that trend in the late 1980s. He said, "Well, I don't really like the sound of a steel guitar, so I always pan it so it's on the passenger's side in the car. It's farther away from me that way." True or not, it's as good a reason as any for the steel to be on the right side of the stereo field.

Steel guitars can have an exceptionally wide dynamic range as well as sonic range, but I tend to not use any compression on the steel guitar. Because the musician controls his own levels through the use of a volume pedal, using a compressor plug-in to control the attack of a given note is usually unnecessary—steel is more prone to fade into those chords (and back out after, so there's no attack to control). I will, however, use a compressor to change the tone of the instrument, and will also use the output of the plug-in to raise the level when needed. A few dB of gain reduction doesn't hurt—depending, of course, on the specific track. If the steel is playing a smooth pad, where the sound swells in and out, the gain reduction is likely to be unheard; if the steel track includes a lot of fast single-note lines, the compressor may help to even out errant notes.

On this track, the fader level is set to –15.1 dB, and an aux send to the instrument reverb is set at –5.2 dB. The only plug-in on the steel rack is a 1-Band EQ III that's boosting the 2 kHz area by 5.1 dB.

Fig. 6.23. Steel EQ

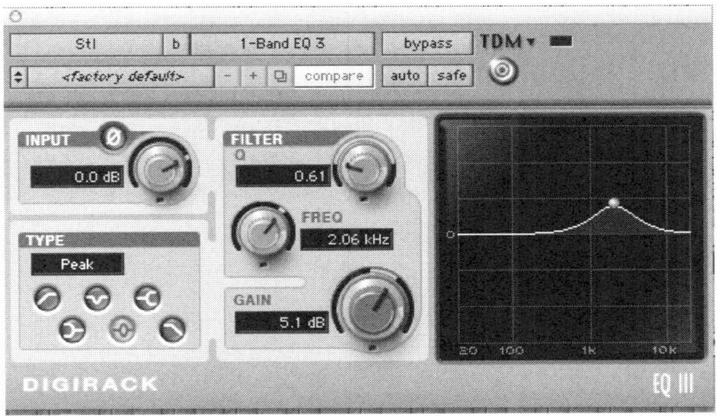

DigiRack 1-band EQ III Lap Steel Settings	
parameter	**settings**
Q	0.61 dB
frequency	2.06 kHz
gain	+5.1 dB
filter	bell

ELECTRIC GUITARS

"Play Something Country" has three guitar tracks: two rhythm tracks and a lead guitar. Rhythm 1 is panned hard right while rhythm 2 is panned hard left. The three guitars are processed a bit differently as well: Rhythm 1 has a DigiRack 4-band EQ III and also has an aux send that goes to the instrument reverb at –9.5 dB, and rhythm 2 has neither plug-ins nor effects sends. The lead guitar, which also plays the melodic part in the intro and turnarounds, uses a DigiRack D-Verb to add ambience. The D-Verb was, for many years a much-reviled reverb—one that caused at least some Pro Tools power users at the time to try third-party reverb plug-ins for the first time. Nevertheless, it has its place, and adding ambience to a guitar track is one of them. The medium room setting that's used on the lead guitar track does the job of creating a bit of space around that track.

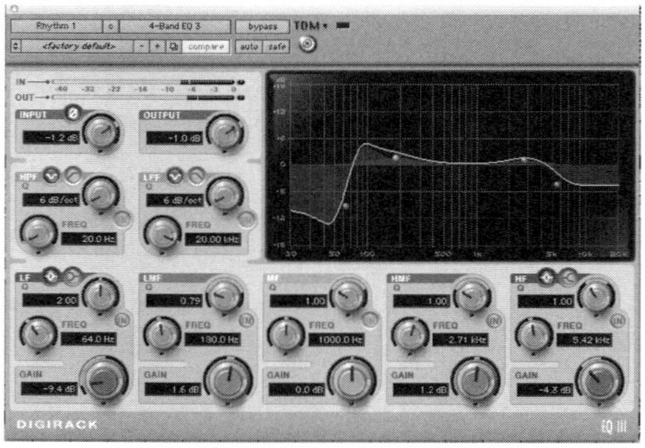

Fig. 6.24. Rhythm 1 EQ

DigiRack 4-band EQ III Rhythm 1 Settings					
parameter	**low**	**low-mid**	**high-mid**	**high**	**input**
Q	2.00	0.79	1.00	1.00	–1.2 dB
frequency	64.0 Hz	180 Hz	2.71 kHz	5.42 kHz	output
gain	–9.4 dB	+1.6 dB	+1.2 dB	–4.3 dB	–1.0 dB
filter	shelf	bell	bell	shelf	

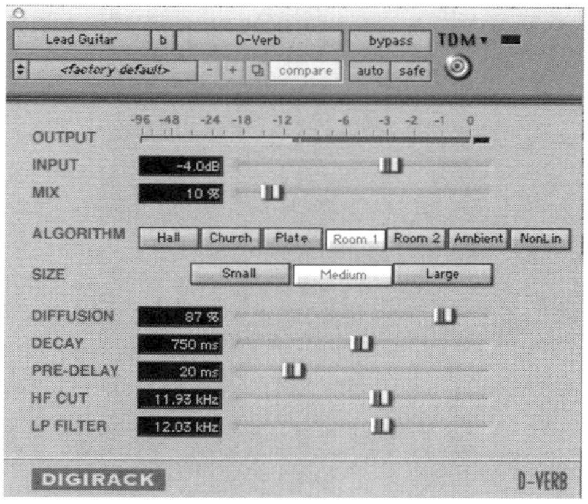

Fig. 6.25. Lead Guitar Reverb

Digidesign D-Verb Lead Guitar Settings	
parameter	**setting**
input	–4.0 dB
mix	10%
algorithm	room 1
size	medium
diffusion	87%
decay	750 ms
predelay	20 ms
HF cut	11.93 kHz
low pass filter	12.03 kHz

LEAD VOCAL

The lead vocal on "Play Something Country" has three processors on it, as well as an effects send that sends the lead (as well as the background) vocals to the vocal reverb.

The first is the Antares Auto-tune 4 plug-in. Since the Auto-Tune plug-in has been discussed *ad nauseum* already, I'll leave it alone for this mix.

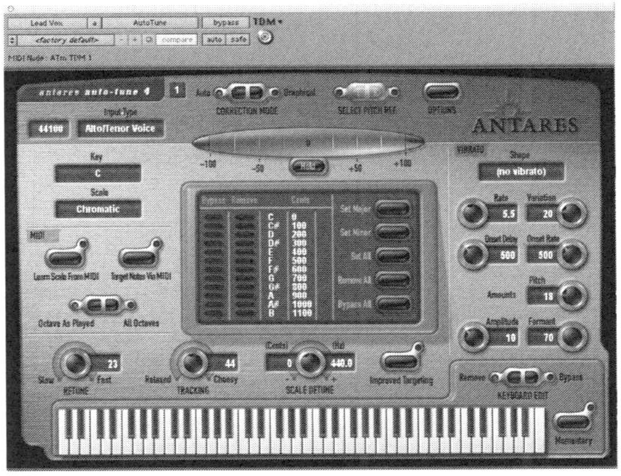

Fig. 6.26. Lead Vocal Autotune

Antares Auto-Tune 4 Settings

Input Type: Alto/Tenor Voice
Retune: 23
Tracking: 44

Next up is a DigiRack Compressor/Limiter 3, which was set to a 4.2:1 compression ratio, a 7.8 dB knee, and a fairly fast attack and release time. The threshold of the compressor was set to –9.3 dB, which results in a gain reduction of approximately 5 dB. Does this make the vocals sound compressed? Sure. But that's part of the sound of records these days.

The final plug-in on the lead vocal track is a DigiRack 7-band EQ III. The high-pass filter is active, with a 12 dB per octave slope beginning at 63 Hz, and the other EQ bands pretty much tilting the frequency response of the track towards the high end. The output fader on the lead vocal track was set at –4.2 dB, and the aux send to the vocal reverb was at –3.1 dB.

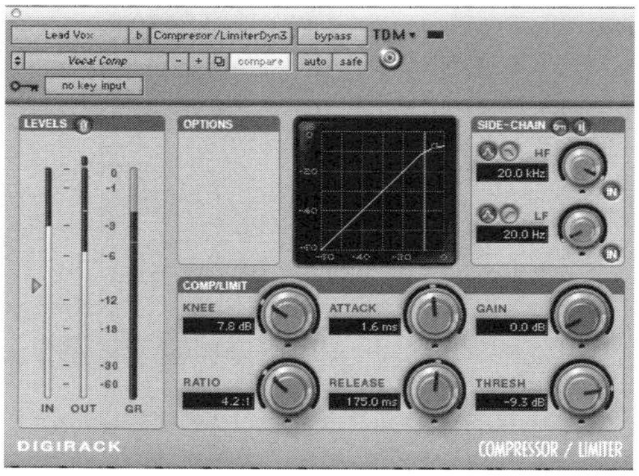

Fig. 6.27. Lead Vocal Compressor

DigiRack Comp/Limiter 3 Lead Vocal Settings						
parameter	knee	ratio	attack	release	gain	threshold
setting	7.8 dB	4.2:1	1.6 ms	175.0 ms	0 dB	–9.3 dB

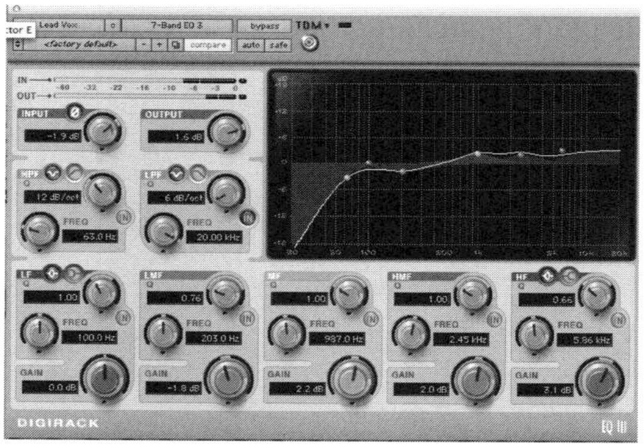

Fig. 6.28. Lead Vocal EQ

DigiRack 7-band EQ III Lead Vocal Settings						
High-pass filter in 63 Hz, 12 dB-per-octave slope						
parameter	low	low-mid	mid	high-mid	high	input
Q	1.00	0.76	100	1.00	0.66	–1.9 dB
frequency	100.0 Hz	203 Hz	987.0	2.45 kHz	5.86 kHz	output
gain	0 dB	–1.8 dB	+2.2 dB	+2.0 dB	+3.1 dB	+3.1 dB
filter	shelf	bell	bell	bell	shelf	

BACKGROUND VOCALS

The two background vocal tracks share identical processing—a DigiRack Comp/Limiter 3 and a DigiRack 7-band EQ III were used on each of the two tracks, and the settings on both plug-ins were identical for each track. The output level on the Mid BGV track was—4.8 dB, and the output level of the High BGV track was -4.5 dB.

Fig. 6.29. Mid BGV Compressor

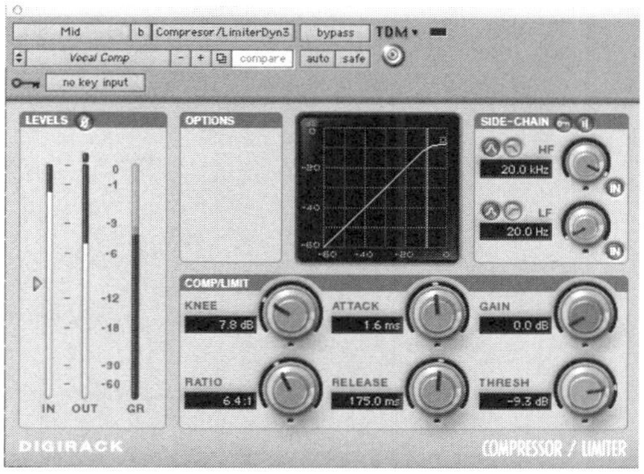

DigiRack Comp/Limiter 3 Mid Background Vocal Settings						
parameter	knee	ratio	attack	release	gain	threshold
setting	7.8 dB	6.4:1	1.6 ms	175.0 ms	0 dB	–9.3 dB

Fig. 6.30. Mid BGV EQ

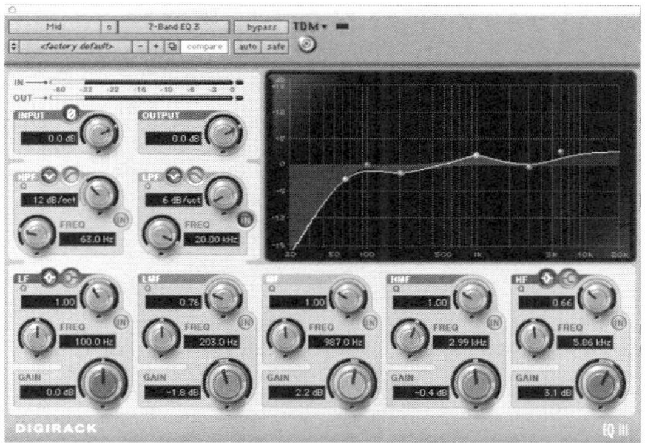

DigiRack 7-band EQ III Mid Background Vocal Settings						
High-pass filter in 63 Hz 12 dB-per-octave slope						
parameter	low	low-mid	mid	high-mid	high	input
Q	1.00	0.76	100	1.00	0.66	–1.7 dB
frequency	100.0 Hz	203 Hz	987.0	2.99 kHz	5.86 kHz	output
gain	0 dB	–1.8 dB	+2.2 dB	–0.4 dB	+3.1 dB	+1.6 dB
filter	shelf	bell	bell	bell	shelf	

The two background vocals were then sent to the BGV buss; no additional processing was used, but a send to the vocal reverb was at –5.2 dB. The BGV buss level was –0.8 dB.

REVERBS

In addition to the drum reverb discussed earlier in the chapter, two more reverbs were used on "Play Something Country." A Digidesign Reverb One was used as the instrument reverb, set to a "medium plate" setting.

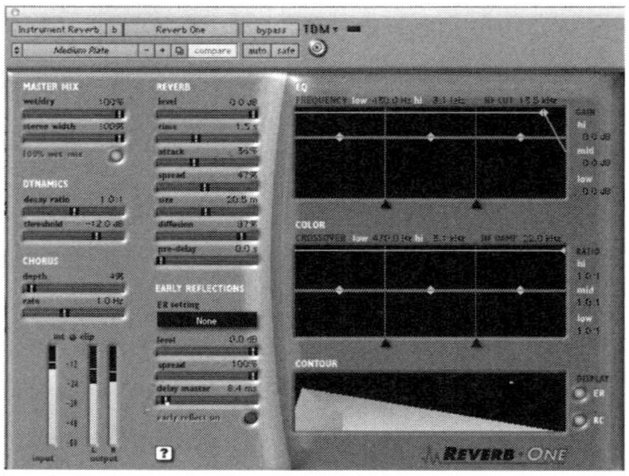

Fig. 6.31. Instrument Reverb

Digidesign Reverb One Instrument Reverb Settings	
parameter	**setting**
wet/dry	100%
stereo width	100%
decay ratio	1.0:1
threshold	–12 dB
reverb level	0 dB
reverb time	1.5 seconds
attack	36%
spread	47%
size	20.5 meters
diffusion	87%
pre-delay	0 ms
early reflection (ER) setting	none
ER level	0 dB
ER spread	100%
ER delay master	8.4 ms

The last reverb, the vocal reverb, was another Digidesign Reverb One, set to a medium wood room.

Fig. 6.32. Vocal Reverb

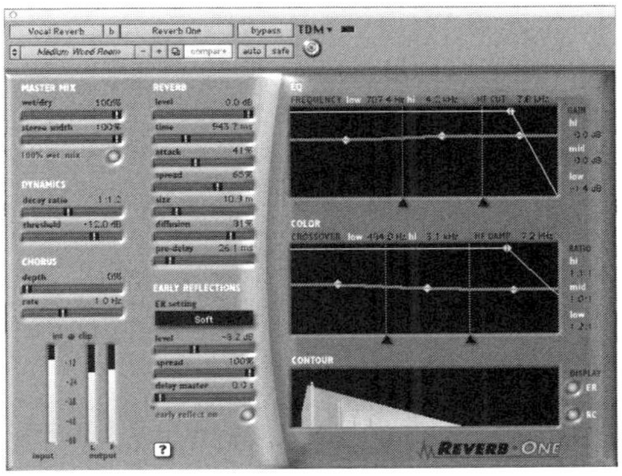

Digidesign Reverb One Vocal Reverb Settings	
parameter	**setting**
wet/dry	100% wet
stereo width	100%
decay ratio	1:1.2
threshold	–12 dB
reverb level	0 dB
reverb time	943.7 ms
attack	41%
spread	65%
size	10.9 meters
diffusion	81%
pre-delay	26.1 ms
early reflection (ER) setting	soft
ER level	–8.2 dB
ER spread	100%
ER delay Master	0 ms

Before leaving the subject of reverb, here are a couple of thoughts to keep in mind when choosing which reverb to use for a given application. There are circumstances when it's appropriate for a reverb to be obvious—big, present, and noticeable—and there are times when it's not. But there are options other than either having reverb or not having reverb. By using the reverb plug-in simply to add a bit of ambience rather than the sound of a concert hall or large plate, the feeling of a bit of space around a signal—even if it's not heard as reverb—is usually quite nice. For those situations, consider starting with a small room preset, or even a chamber (with a short decay).

Pre-delay

You can also try changing the pre-delay setting of the reverb. Pre-delay is the time between the direct sound and the onset of any reflections or reverberation. Judicious use of pre-delay can increase the intelligibility of the direct signal with the added bonus of making the reverb sound as though the space emulated by the reverb sound larger than it is.

EQ'ing

A couple of approaches can be used when EQ'ing reverbs. There are no rules against using an EQ either before the reverb plug-in (which tailors the input signal that enters the input of the reverb plug-in) or after the reverb (which would change the sound of the output of the plug-in). Besides that, a number of reverb plug-ins have the ability to EQ the processed signal as part of the plug-in by adjusting the high frequency dampening setting (which, with most reverbs, effectively darkens the reverb sound). In the world of digital audio workstations, there's seldom (if ever) a need to settle for something that isn't exactly appropriate for a given application or instrument, unless there isn't time to find what you want. If you have the time to experiment, you can almost always find exactly what you need.

Master Output and Buss Processing

All of the audio tracks, busses, and effects returns end up at the Master Output; the Master Output has a Focusrite 6-band EQ and a Waves L2 Limiter (one of the few plug-ins used on this mix that doesn't come with the Pro Tools Software), and ends with a Pow-R Dither plug-in.

The Focusrite EQ includes a high-pass filter at 33 Hz as well as a 1 dB boost at 1.2 kHz and a 2.3 kHz boost at 7.1 kHz. The input of the EQ is at –2.5 dB, which keeps the L2 from being hit too hard.

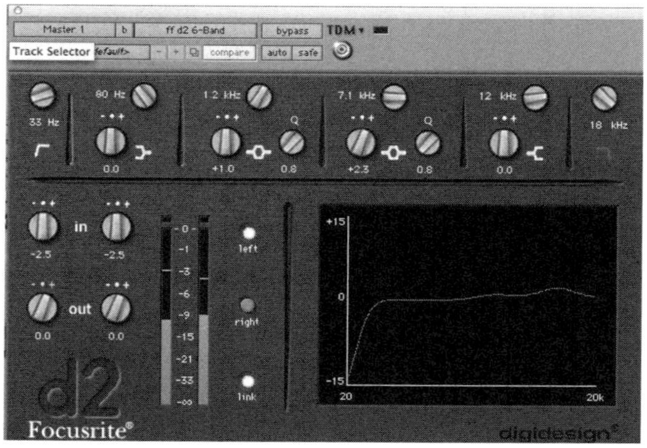

Fig. 6.33. Buss EQ

Focusrite d2 6-band EQ Master Buss Settings						
parameter	hi pass	low	low-mid	high-mid	high	low pass
frequency	33 Hz	80 Hz	1.2 kHz	7.1 kHz	12 kHz	18 kHz
level		0 dB	+1.0 dB	+2.3 dB	0 dB	
Q			0.8	10.8		
filter	in	shelf	bell	bell	shelf	bypass

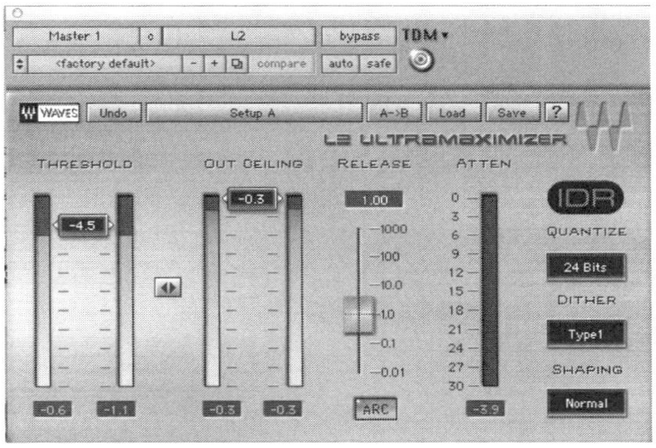

Fig. 6.34. Buss Limiter

The threshold of the L2 is set to –4.5 dB, and the out ceiling is –0.3 dB.

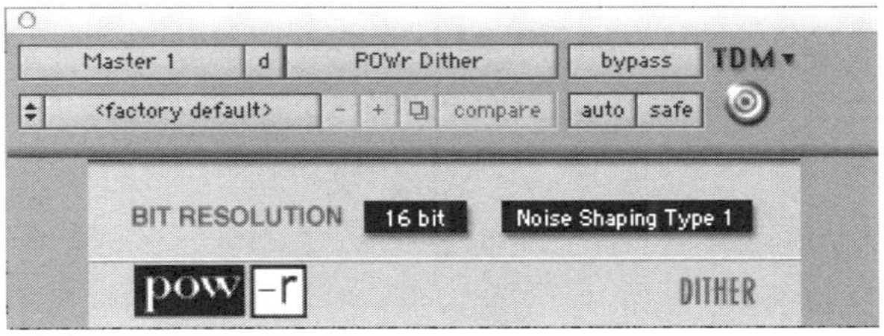

Fig. 6.35. Dither

The Pow-R Dither plug-in is set to 16-bit word length and type 1 noise shaping.

AUTOMATION

Surprisingly little automation was written for this mix of "Play Something Country." Other than the tom tracks, which use volume automation in lieu of noise gates to keep tom hum to a minimum, the only audio track that was automated was the stereo horn track. The master output fader was used to write the fade at the end of the track

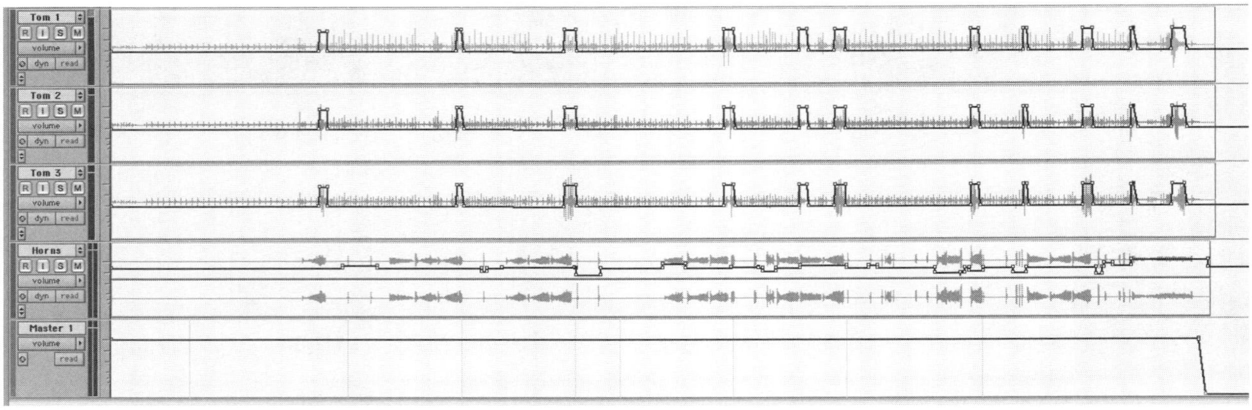

Fig. 6.36. Automation

PRINTING MIXES

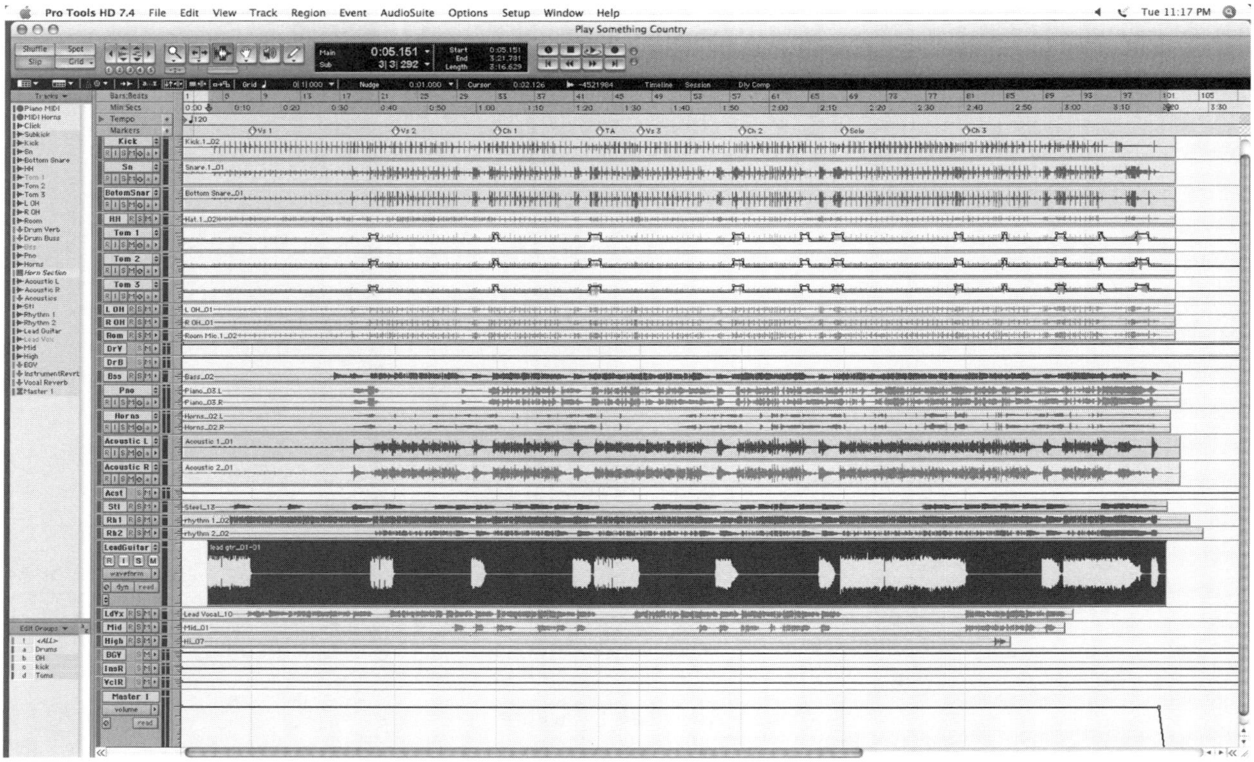

Fig. 6.37. Print Mix

When printing the mix of each of the songs in this book, a consistent approach was used: one of the tracks that is continuous for the full length of the song (I'll typically use either an acoustic guitar track or the piano track) is used to set the final length of the song. I'll trim the chosen track to just before the first note (by "just before," I mean that I'll trim the track to within a single frame, or a thirtieth of a second before the start). Then, at whatever point the fade at the end of the track is completed, I'll trim the back of that same track about a frame after the fade. In Pro Tools, selecting this trimmed track will cause the program to play from the beginning to the end of that track with no excess audio or time at the beginning or end. In those situations where multiple mixes of a song must be done—for example, if a producer wants vocal up or vocal down versions, TV mixes, instrumental mixes—all of the versions are the same length, and can be easily lined up for editing.

MASTERING

The mix of "Play Something Country" was created with the knowledge that it would not be mastered. Because of this, the Focusrite EQ and a limiter were inserted on the Master Output. The dither plug-in was used for the same reason; If this song had been going to a mastering house (a process I strongly suggest for projects intended for commercial release), the processing on this buss would have been removed or at least used in a minimal fashion—especially the L1, L2, and L3—so that the mastering engineer's work would not be hampered or constricted by something that was done in the mixing process. And since the preferred delivery format for audio for mastering is 24-bit WAV files, these mixes wouldn't have needed to be dithered to 16-bit files.

CHAPTER 7

"Redneck Woman"

(as recorded by Gretchen Wilson)

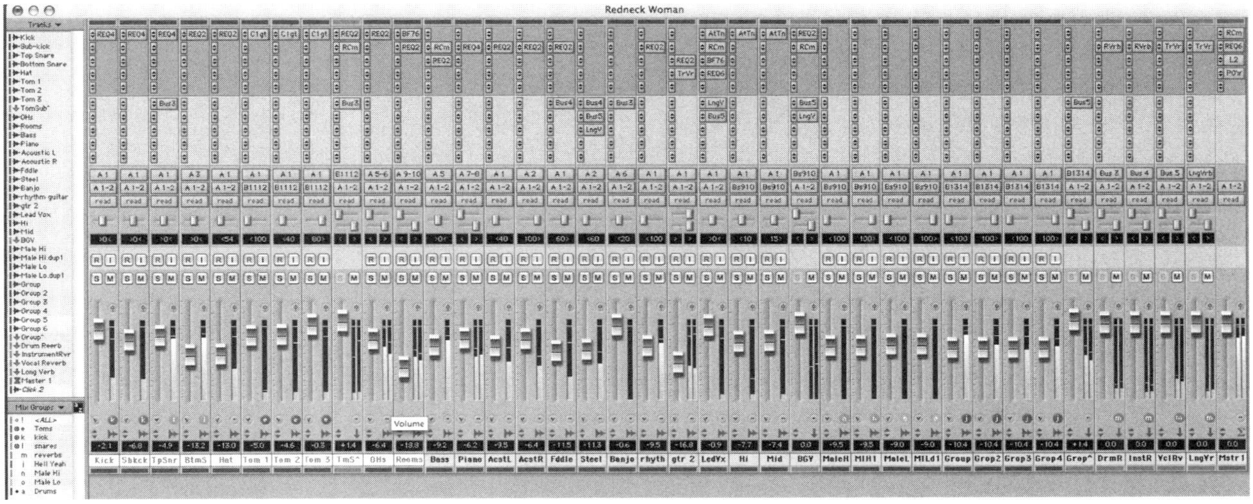

Fig. 7.1. Mix Window

"Redneck Woman" could be characterized as rockin' country—an up-tempo country song with fairly normal instrumentation, though the interesting thing about this track is the need to work with all the background vocals. In addition to the group of female voices, male singers make an appearance.

DRUMS

The drum tracks on "Redneck Woman" were recorded in the same manner as the other drum tracks in this volume, without EQ and with little or no compression so that the mixing process could be made a bit more informative. If all the needed processing was done in the tracking stage, then there would be little to talk about concerning the mixing of the drums. Besides that, the lack of processing at the recording stage means that the raw tracks can be manipulated in a bit more creative manner at the mixing stage. "Redneck Woman" has two kick drum tracks: one, labeled "kick" was recorded with a Shure Beta 52 microphone placed inside the drum about three inches from the batter head while the "subkick" track was recorded with a Yamaha Subkick placed directly in front of the drum. These two signals sound quite different from each other; most mixing engineers will combine the two sounds while processing each as needed to create the final kick drum sound.

Fig. 7.2. Drum Mix

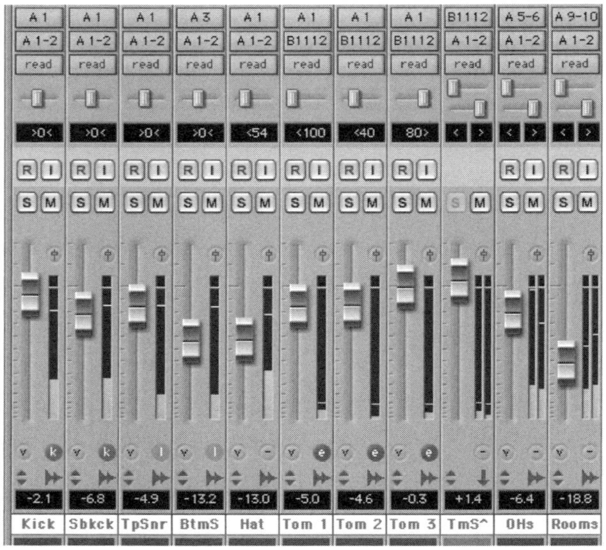

Kick Drum

Neither of the kick drum tracks on "Redneck Woman" used (or needed) a compressor; only a 4-band Waves Renaissance EQ was inserted onto the track. The inside kick track has a 2 dB boost around 35 Hz. Keep in mind that 35 Hz is the center frequency for this EQ band; since that band has a fairly wide Q, those frequencies higher than 35 Hz and up into the useable audio range are also boosted slightly. Two other bands, centered near 4 kHz and around 10 kHz are also boosted. These frequency ranges help to add a bit of a click to the kick drum sound and that helps add definition. The main kick fader level was –2.1 dB, while the outside kick level was set at –6.8 dB.

Fig. 7.3. Kick EQ

Waves Renaissance REQ-4 Kick Settings				
parameter	band 1	band 2	band 3	band 4
gain	+1.5 dB	+3.8 dB	+4.4 dB	+3.4 dB
frequency	35 Hz	944 Hz	3,748 Hz	2 kHz
Q	0.80	0.80	0.80	0.90
shape	bell	bell	bell	shelf

Subkick

The subkick track also has a 4-band Renaissance EQ, with a boost centered at 46 Hz and a 3.5 dB cut around 600 Hz. The subkick was recorded with a Yamaha Subkick; this is a new version of a fairly old idea. The subkick is essentially a speaker that's wired with an XLR connection so that it can be used as a microphone.

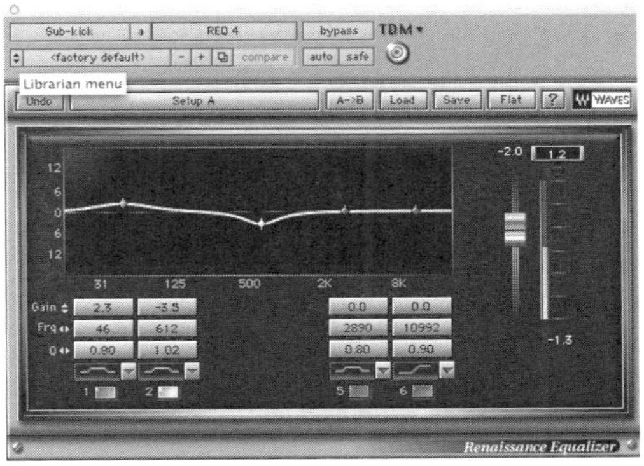

Fig. 7.4. Subkick EQ

Waves Renaissance REQ-4 Out-Kick Settings				
parameter	band 1	band 2	band 3	band 4
gain	+2.3 dB	–3.5 dB	0 dB	0 dB
frequency	46 Hz	612 Hz	2,890 Hz	10,992 Hz
Q	0.80	1.02	0.80	0.90
shape	bell	bell	bell	shelf

Snare Drum

There are two snare drum tracks on "Redneck Woman." One Neumann KM 84 was used on top of the snare and another was used underneath the snare. These are labeled as "top snare" and "bottom snare."

Top Snare

The top snare track has a 4-band Renaissance EQ inserted as a plug-in. The Waves Renaissance EQ is primarily used to add a bit of thump to the track (with about a 2 dB boost around 100 Hz), a bit of snap (with a boost around 2 kHz), and a bit of air (boosting at 12 kHz). The output of the top snare track is at –3.4 dB; the send to the drum reverb is –17.1 dB.

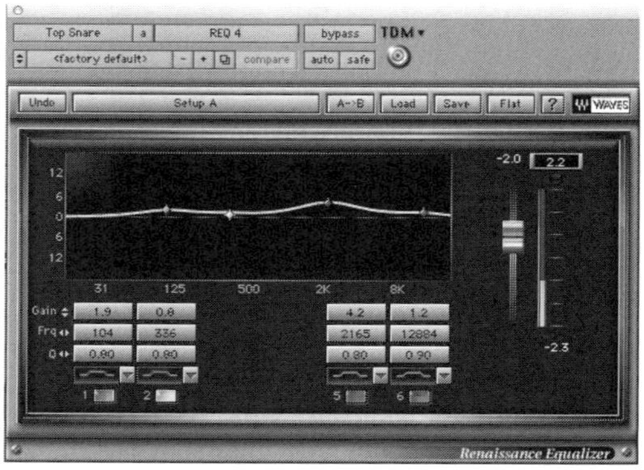

Fig. 7.5. Top Snare EQ

Waves Renaissance REQ-4 Top Snare Settings				
parameter	**band 1**	**band 2**	**band 3**	**band 4**
gain	+1.9 dB	0.0 dB	+4.2 dB	+1.2 dB
frequency	104 Hz	612 Hz	2,165 Hz	12,884 Hz
Q	0.80	1.02	0.80	0.90
shape	bell	bell	bell	bell

Bottom Snare

The bottom snare track has a 2-band Waves Renaissance REQ-2 that's cut by 3.7 dB at 90 Hz and boosted 2.5 dB around 7.8 kHz. The fader level for the bottom snare track is at –13.2 dB. It's interesting to note that quite a number of recording engineers will use a bottom snare mic, but they don't always use it in the mix. There's no rule that requires that every track delivered to be mixed actually be used. By the way, if you don't like the tone imparted by a track—especially something like a bottom snare, an outside kick, or a room mic—then by all means, don't use it.

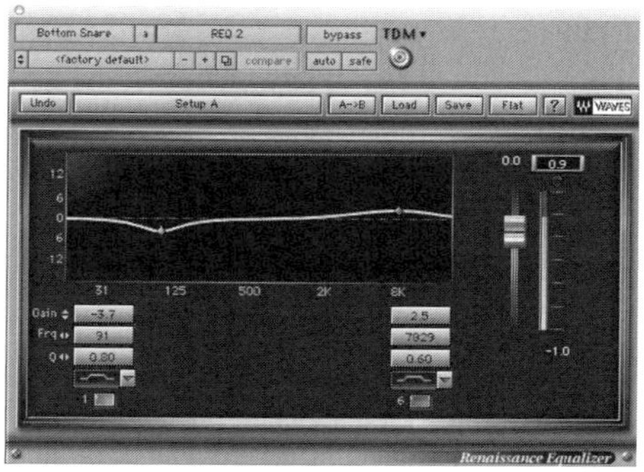

Fig. 7.6. Bottom Snare EQ

Waves Renaissance REQ-2 Bottom Snare Settings		
parameter	band 1	band 2
gain	–3.7 dB	+2.5 dB
frequency	91 Hz	7,829 Hz
Q	0.80	0.60
shape	bell	bell

Hi-Hat

Much like the bottom snare mic, the hi-hat mic can be used or not used, depending on the engineer, the drummer, and the song being mixed. If the hi-hat track is used in the mix, it should be panned to reflect the drum set as a whole. If the drums are mixed from the drummer's perspective, pan the hat to the left; if mixing drums from the audience's perspective, pan the hat to the right. The hi-hat track level is –18.8 dB, loud enough to be heard, but not loud enough to be bothersome. The EQ on the hat track consists of a high-pass filter at 183 Hz, and a boost around 4 kHz of 1.8 dB.

Fig. 7.7. Hat EQ

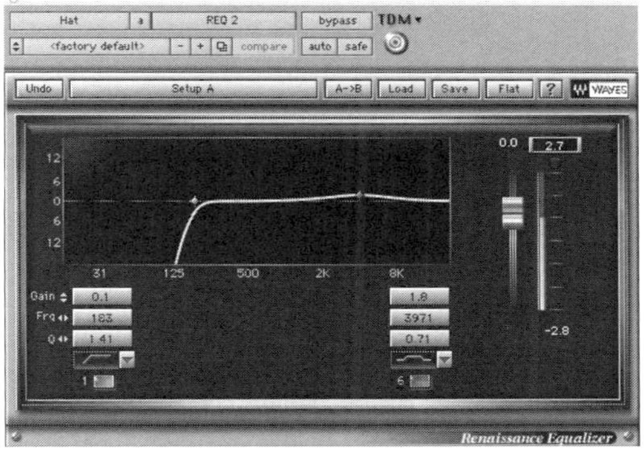

Waves Renaissance REQ-2 Hat Settings		
parameter	band 1	band 2
gain	0 dB	+1.8 dB
frequency	183 Hz	3,971 Hz
Q	1.41	0.71
shape	high pass	bell

Toms

The toms on "Redneck Woman" are handled in much the same was as they were on "My Give a Damn's Busted." They're gated with the Waves C1 Gate, but the floors of the gates are adjusted to allow some of the ringing of the toms to come through. On "My Give a Damn's Busted," the floor was set to

–12 dB but on “Redneck Woman,” the level of the closed gate is reduced a bit, to –23.1 dB—enough that there is still a bit of the glue that holds the drum track together, but not so much that it becomes obtrusive. The output levels of the three tom tracks are: Tom 1 is at –5.0 dB, Tom 2 is at –4.6 dB, and Tom 3 is at –0.3 dB.

Fig. 7.8. Tom Gate

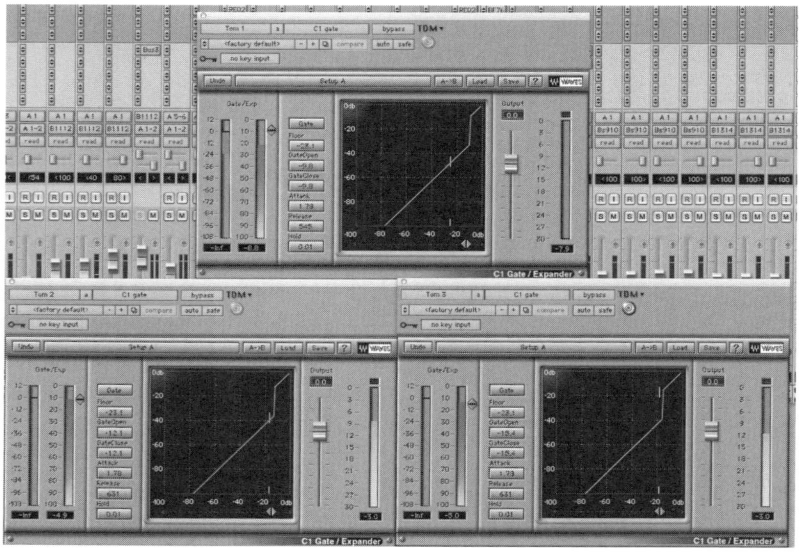

Waves C1 Gate Tom 1 Settings

floor	gate open	gate close	attack	release	hold
–23.1 dB	–9.8	–9.8	1.78	545	0.01

Waves C1 Gate Tom 2 Settings

floor	gate open	gate close	attack	release	hold
–23.1 dB	–12.1	–12.1	1.78	631	0.01

Waves C1 Gate Tom 3 Settings

floor	gate open	gate close	attack	release	hold
–23.1 dB	–15.4	–15.4	1.78	545	0.01

Tom Buss

The three tom tracks are routed to the tom buss; this stereo buss has two plug-ins inserted. The first is a 2-band Waves Renaissance EQ set to add a bit of brightness to the toms, with a 3.5 dB boost at 2.2 kHz and a 1.8 dB boost around 9.3 kHz. The output of the tom buss is set to +3.6 dB, and the send to the drum reverb is at –16.8 dB.

Fig. 7.9. Tom EQ

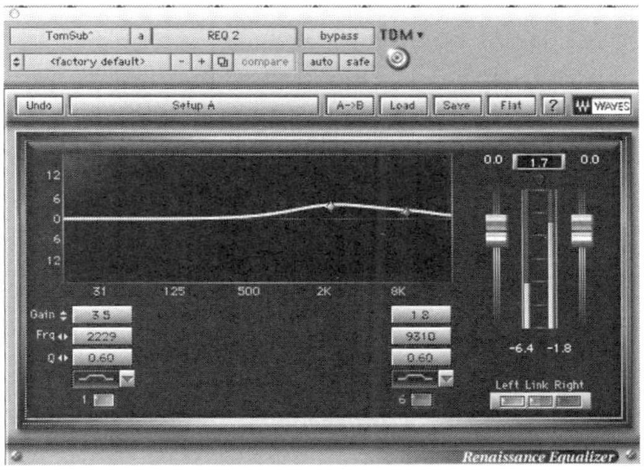

Waves Renaissance REQ-2 Tom Buss Settings		
parameter	**band 1**	**band 2**
gain	+3.5 dB	+1.8 dB
frequency	2,229 Hz	9,310 Hz
Q	0.60	0.60
shape	bell	bell

Fig. 7.10. Tom Compressor

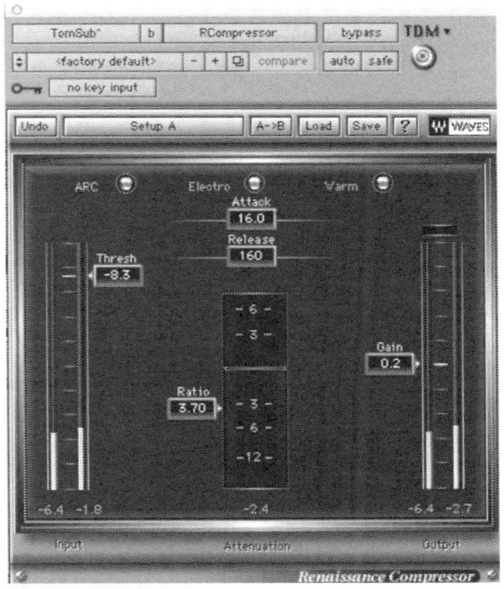

Waves Renaissance Compressor Tom Buss Settings				
threshold	**attack**	**release**	**ratio**	**gain**
–8.3 dB	16.0	160	3.71:1	+0.2 dB

Overheads

There are two major paradigms involving overhead microphones, and choosing one or the other impacts the whole process of mixing drums. The first of these is to think of the overheads as the source of the main drum sound. With this approach, the overhead mics and a kick drum mic contain most of the sonic information from the kit, and the individual drum mics are used simply to beef up anything that isn't present enough in the overheads. The other paradigm is to treat the overhead mics more as cymbal mics that also pick up a lot of snare and toms. With this approach, the main drum sound comes from the individual microphones and the overheads are brought into play just to add the sound of the cymbals. It must be noted, though, that the snare drum is usually louder than cymbals in the overheads no matter where the overheads are placed. Both approaches are viable, though (at least at the time of writing this volume), it's more common to use the individual mics as the main drum sound in contemporary country mixes. That's kind of a shame, too—the overhead mics on this song sound particularly nice. There's no reason that they shouldn't sound nice, though—the overhead tracks on "Redneck Woman" were recorded using a pair of Telefunken 251 microphones with vintage capsules and electronics. These microphones were placed about a foot behind and two feet above the drummer's head, pointing down towards the drum kit.

The 2-band Waves Renaissance EQ high passes the overhead tracks at 40 Hz, and adds a 2.4 kHz boost at 4.4 kHz. The output of the overhead tracks is set at –6.4 dB

Fig. 7.11. Overhead EQ

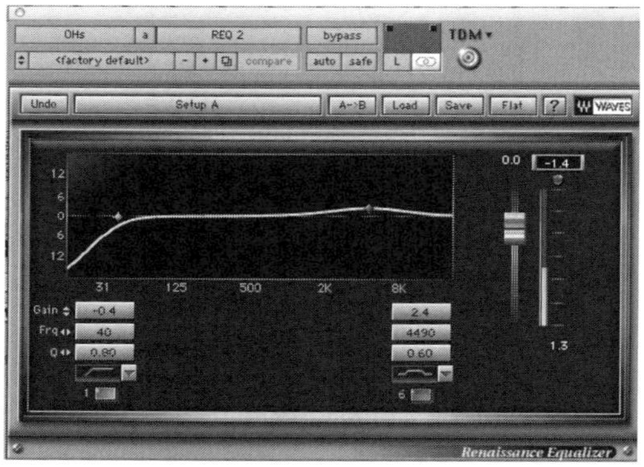

Waves Renaissance REQ-2 Overheads Settings		
parameter	**band 1**	**band 2**
gain	–0.4 dB	+2.4 dB
frequency	40 Hz	4,490 Hz
Q	0.80	0.60
shape	high pass	bell

Room Mics

Though the processing used on the stereo room mic tracks appears to be similar to some of the earlier mixes, that's not actually the case. The Bomb Factory BF76 compressor is only being used to control the levels of the room mics, not to destroy them (a fun approach, but not useful for every song). So, the output of the BF76 is pretty clean, which leads to a different approach with the room mic tracks. For "Redneck Woman," the room track simply adds a bit of ambience to the overall drum track. The fader levels on the room mics are set to –18.8 dB a 2-band Renaissance EQ removed some of the low-end mud from the track with a 5.6 dB cut at 100 Hz, using a shelving EQ. The second band isn't used.

Fig. 7.12. Room Compressor

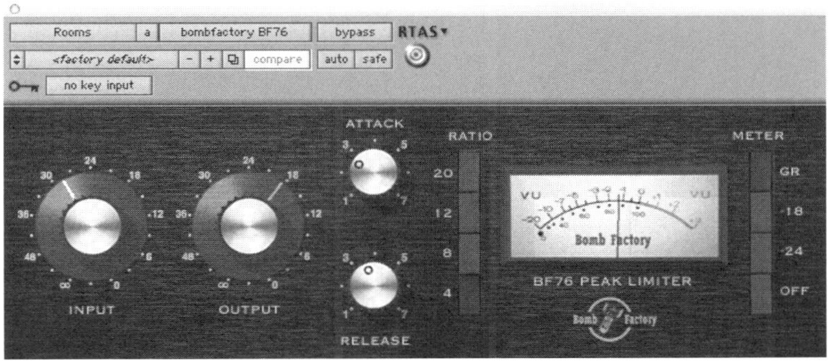

Bomb Factory BF76 Room Mic Settings				
input	**output**	**attack**	**release**	**ratio**
28	18	2.5	3.6	4:1

Fig. 7.13. Room EQ

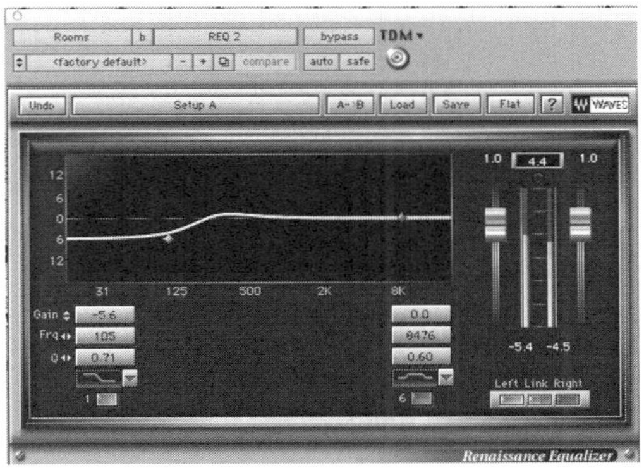

Waves Renaissance REQ-2 Room Mic settings		
parameter	**band 1**	**band 2**
gain	–5.6 dB	0 dB
frequency	105 Hz	8,476 Hz
Q	0.71	0.60
shape	shelf	bell

BASS

The bass track on "Redneck Woman" uses a Waves Renaissance Compressor and a 2-band Waves Renaissance EQ as plug-ins. The output fader of the bass was set at –7.4 dB. Not a whole lot of gain reduction was used on the bass track; it was added primarily to even out any inequities in the performance. The EQ was primarily used to add bottom end to the bass track because the Q setting affects the width of the band—that is, the lower the number, the wider the frequency range affected by any changes to the level of that band. Even though the center frequency of this EQ band is quite low—not only below the lowest frequency that the bass can create, but lower than the lowest frequency that most consumer speakers can reproduce—the Q setting is wide enough that a fairly wide range of frequencies that *can* be reproduced are affected by this EQ band.

In addition to that, keep in mind that a lot of what is perceived as bass is not necessarily the fundamental note (the low E note on a bass is at 41 Hertz, and notes played on the B string are lower than that), but are harmonics an octave (and more) higher than the fundamental. Boosting the fundamental frequency will also raise the level of the harmonic notes associated with that frequency.

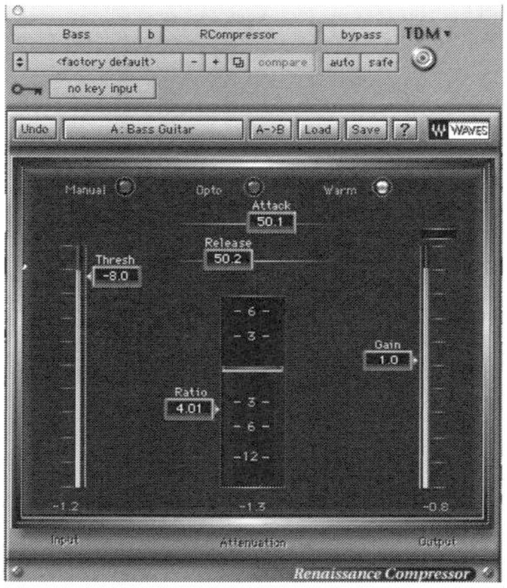

Fig. 7.14. Bass Compressor

Waves Renaissance Compressor Bass Settings				
threshold	**attack**	**release**	**ratio**	**gain**
–8.0 dB	50.1	50.2	4.01:1	+1.0 dB

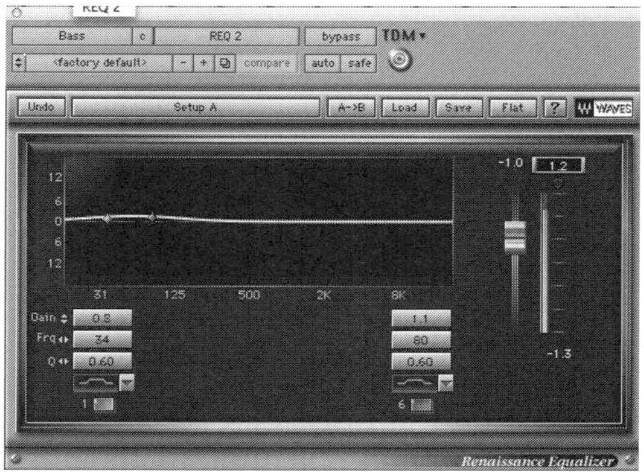

Fig. 7.15. Bass EQ

Waves Renaissance REQ-2 Bass Settings		
parameter	band 1	band 2
gain	+0.8 dB	+1.1 dB
frequency	34 Hz	80 Hz
Q	0.60	0.60
shape	bell	bell

PIANO

"Redneck Woman" is another instance where the sounds from a Kurzweil rack-mounted sampler were used for piano instead of the real piano. (By the way, if you're wondering how the songs that used the sampled keyboards were chosen, it was simply that the pianist was still sitting at the keyboard after finishing a string pass or a bell pass, and I would say, "Why don't you just stay there for the next piano part? We need the variety." Choosing the microphone setup for each song was just about as random. When building the mixes of each song, I'd try to remember what was used on the prior mix in the previous chapter, and then pick something else. The only processing used on the piano was a 4-band Waves Renaissance EQ, which essentially was used to brighten the piano sound to match the original recording. The fader level for the piano was set at –6.2 dB.

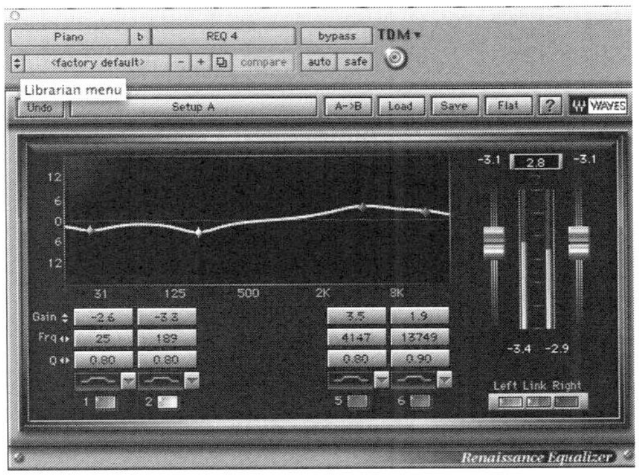

Fig. 7.16. Piano EQ

Waves Renaissance REQ-4 Piano Settings				
parameter	band 1	band 2	band 3	band 4
gain	–2.6 dB	–3.3 dB	+3.5 dB	+1.9 dB
frequency	25 Hz	189 Hz	4,147 Hz	13.7 kHz
Q	0.80	0.80	0.80	0.90
shape	bell	bell	bell	bell

ACOUSTIC GUITAR

The acoustic guitar tracks on this song (for that matter, on all the songs in this volume) were recorded with essentially the same microphone placement: one microphone was pointed at a point midway between the end of the neck and the soundhole a couple of inches below the strings. The mic was placed four to six inches from the body of the guitar. The second microphone pointed down towards the body of the instrument from about ten inches away, from a point more or less even with the guitarist's head. While this isn't the sort of stereo placement that could be used to record a chamber orchestra (or, that would be taught in recording schools), it yields a full and even sound that can be panned in a number of ways to suit the needs of a specific track.

Typically, the two acoustic tracks are panned to hard left and right; the result is a full acoustic guitar sound that doesn't overpower the other instruments, and by itself, sounds quite natural. The close mic (in the left speaker) is brighter and more present, while the track in the right speaker is a bit more ambient, a bit darker, and a bit fuller. In those applications where the acoustic guitar needs to be panned toward one side or the other, panning one of the two tracks to the center keeps the essential qualities of the instrument, while shifting the soundfield from the center of the mix to one side. And even those situations that require the acoustic to be all the way to one side of the stereo field work fine because phase issues are minimized by this style of guitar miking.

While this method of recording acoustic guitars can result in a very natural acoustic guitar sound, that's not always desired; bussing the acoustic guitars to their own stereo submaster allows for the use of stereo EQ and compressor plug-ins that process both tracks simultaneously. This is more important with compression; if a mono compressor is used on each track, the stereo image will shift in an uncontrolled manner as one track or the other gets louder. The use of a stereo compressor helps not only to keep the overall levels of the two acoustic guitars under control, it also helps to keep the relative levels of the two tracks consistent with each other.

When it comes to EQ, a number of approaches can be taken with the acoustic guitar. High passing the acoustic is almost never a bad idea; 100 Hz or even higher can help to clean the acoustic tracks of information that would otherwise muddy the sound. A slight boost at 3-5 kHz can emphasize the attack of the pick, while a boost at 10 kHz, brings out the "sheen" that is a common part of Nashville's acoustic guitar sound.

Occasionally, it's useful to think of the various instruments in a mix as they relate to the drum set. For instance, there's a relationship between the bass and the kick drum, and similarly, there's often a correlation between the electric guitar and the snare. This was more common in R&B records of the '60s and '70s than it is today. Think of the "chink" guitar playing on beats two and four on the old Stax and Motown records. Following this thought onto the acoustic, the acoustic guitar—especially a strummed acoustic—often is related to the hi-hat: the acoustic is commonly playing eighth notes that must match the feel that the drummer plays on the hat.

For "Redneck Woman," the acoustic guitar tracks are not bussed; each track has its own 2-band Waves Renaissance EQ, and no compression was used (or needed). The EQs on each of the two guitar tracks used one of the two bands to high pass the signal, removing low frequency mud, and the other band to add a bit of sparkle to the high end. The left guitar track's output was –9.5 dB while the right guitar track's output was –6.4.

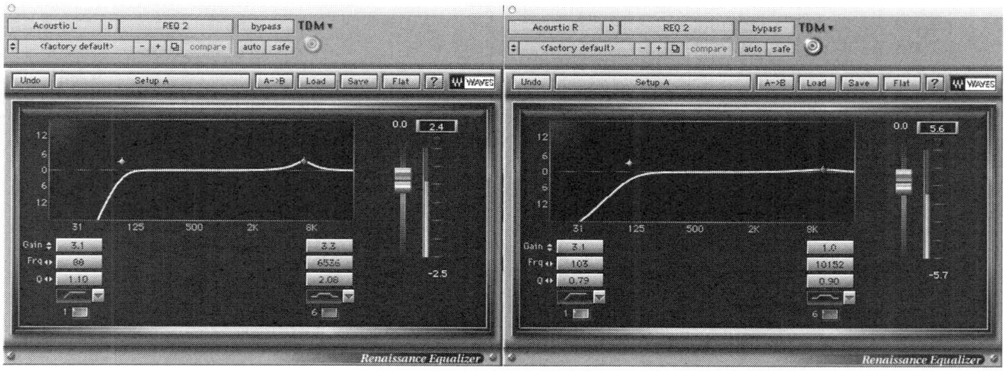

Fig. 7.17. Acoustic Guitar EQ

Waves Renaissance REQ-2 Acoustic L Settings		
parameter	**band 1**	**band 2**
gain	+3.1 dB	+1.0 dB
frequency	88 Hz	6,536 Hz
Q	1.10	2.08
shape	high pass	bell

Waves Renaissance REQ-2 Acoustic R Settings		
parameter	**band 1**	**band 2**
gain	+3.1 dB	+1.0 dB
frequency	103 Hz	10,152 Hz
Q	0.79	0.90
shape	high pass	bell

FIDDLE

The fiddle on "Redneck Woman" plays primarily in the choruses of the song and in the first half of the solo. To leave a bit of room in those choruses for the female vocals (both lead and background vocals are female, and the vocal tracks are fairly bright), the upper midrange of the fiddle track is reduced by 2.4 dB at 8.6 kHz. This type of equalization could be considered as simply moving the fiddle out of the way, though in the greater scheme of things, it might not be that big a deal. The fiddle track also has an aux send to the instrument reverb; the level of the aux send is –10.1 dB. The fiddle is panned 60 percent right, which offsets the steel track that's panned 60 percent left. Though a bit of volume automation is used, the average level of the fiddle track is set to –11.5 dB.

Fig. 7.18. Fiddle EQ

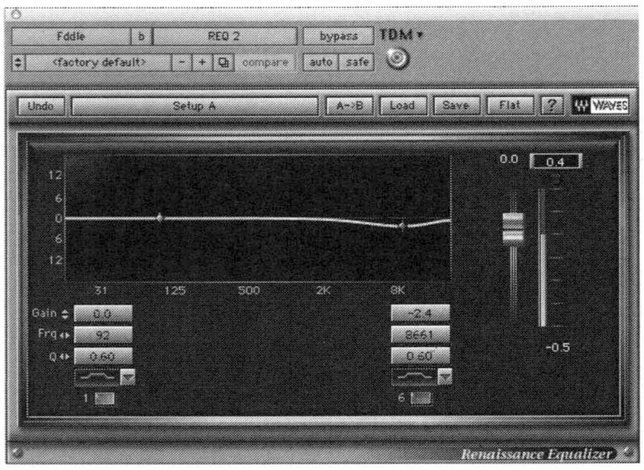

Waves Renaissance REQ-2 Fiddle Settings		
parameter	band 1	band 2
gain	0 dB	–2.4 dB
frequency	92 Hz	8,661 Hz
Q	0.60	0.60
shape	bell (inactive)	bell

STEEL

The steel guitar on "Redneck Woman" was recorded with no effects, no reverb, and no delay. Because of this, reverb needed to be added to the steel track at the mixing stage. Three different reverbs (at three different levels) were combined to create the ambience surrounding the steel: the instrument reverb (at –11.3 dB), the vocal reverb (at –10.7 dB), and the long verb (at –14.8 dB) were used. The output of the steel was –11.3 dB.

BANJO

Though the banjo only plays for five measures in "Redneck Woman," those five measures are very cool, and the banjo contributes greatly to the overall feel of the song during those five measures. As an aside, I must disagree with those who denigrate the banjo as merely a "drum with strings." It's an instrument worthy of respect. In light of that professed respect, I don't have a good explanation for why the drum reverb was used for the banjo track. I guess things just worked out that way. The output level of the banjo track is –0.6 dB, and the send to the drum reverb is at –18.2 dB.

ELECTRIC GUITARS

The two electric tracks on "Redneck Woman," labeled "rhythm guitar" and "gtr 2" have different roles to play. The rhythm guitar (which is panned to the left) plays the signature riffs and is generally the key to the feel of the song, while guitar 2, when playing rhythm, is doing a simple offbeat rhythm part for most of its track, but it's also playing the slide guitar part.

It's often easier to put each of the different electric guitar sounds and parts onto their own tracks—even if these sounds were recorded in a single pass—so that processing may be applied to suit each of the sounds and their placement within the song; however, that wasn't done for the guitar 2 pass of "Redneck Woman." This is partly because the sound of the instrument, the panning, and the levels didn't change when that guitar was playing rhythm versus the slide, but the other reason is that the slide and rhythm are intertwined into a single performance; it should be treated as one.

Rhythm Guitar

The rhythm guitar track used a 2-band Waves Renaissance EQ with a slight boost at 100 Hz to add some body to the sound; since this guitar does the signature lick in the intro, turnarounds, and at the end of the song, it is a bit more dominant in the mix. The rhythm guitar is panned to the left and the output level is at –9.5 dB where volume automation isn't used.

Fig. 7.19. Rhythm Guitar EQ

Waves Renaissance REQ-2 Rhythm Guitar Settings		
parameter	**band 1**	**band 2**
gain	+0.7 dB	0 dB
frequency	107 Hz	3,858 Hz
Q	0.82	0.60
shape	bell	bell (inactive)

Guitar 2

The second guitar, playing rhythm and slide, is panned to the right side (where the slide doesn't conflict with the steel guitar that's panned to the left). The fader level is at –17.2 dB, and a 2-band Renaissance EQ was used to add some meat to the low end of what is a fairly thin Telecaster sound. In addition, the Waves TrueVerb was used to add a bit of ambience to the track, set to the Rock Guitar Room preset.

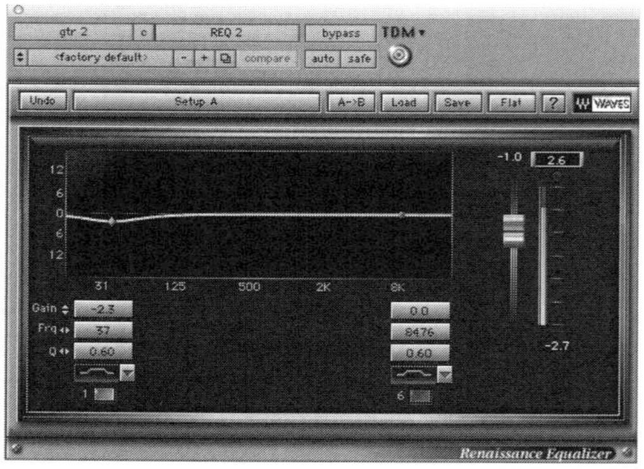

Fig. 7.20. Guitar 2 EQ

Waves Renaissance REQ-2 Solo Guitar Settings

parameter	band 1	band 2
gain	–2.3 dB	0 dB
frequency	37 Hz	8,746 Hz
Q	0.60	0.60
shape	bell	bell (inactive)

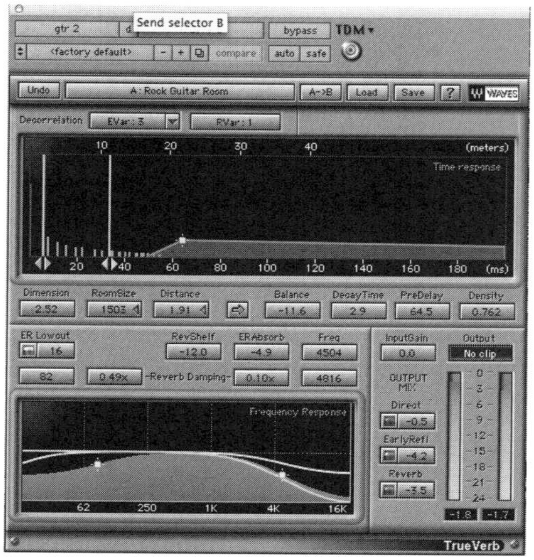

Fig. 7.21. Guitar 2 Reverb

Waves TrueVerb Solo Electric Settings	
parameter	**setting**
dimension	2.52
room size	1,503
distance	1.91
balance	–11.6
decay time	2.9
predelay	64.5
density	0.762
EARLY REFLECTION (ER)	
low cut	16
reverb damping frequency low	82
damping	0.49 x
reverb damping frequency high	4,816
damping	0.10 x
reverb shelf	–12.0
ER absorb	–4.9
ER absorb freq	4,504
input gain	0.0
direct output	–0.5 dB
early reflection output	–4.2 dB
reverb output	–3.5

LEAD VOCAL

The lead vocal track on "Redneck Woman" is fairly straightforward from a mixing viewpoint; other than a need to raise the volume a bit during some of the verse lines, it sits well without much automation. The average fader level was at +0.9 dB, and two reverbs were used: the long reverb level was set at –32.3 dB and the vocal reverb was at –17.1 dB. There were four plug-ins used on the lead vocal track: Auto-Tune 4, Renaissance Compressor, Bomb Factory BF76, and Renaissance EQ-6.

It's been mentioned before, so here's the auto-tune recap: it's used on these mixes not so much because the vocals need to be tuned, but because the sound of auto-tune has become a part of the sound of contemporary country records. Given the choice between listening to a classic George Jones or Kitty Wells recording and one of the current crop of contemporary songs, I would choose the classic every time. But that's just one person's opinion. As has been the norm for the other tracks in this volume, auto-tune is set to quite mild settings. The retune parameter is set to 63, and the tracking speed is at 74, which is quite relaxed.

Fig. 7.22. Lead Vocal Auto-Tune

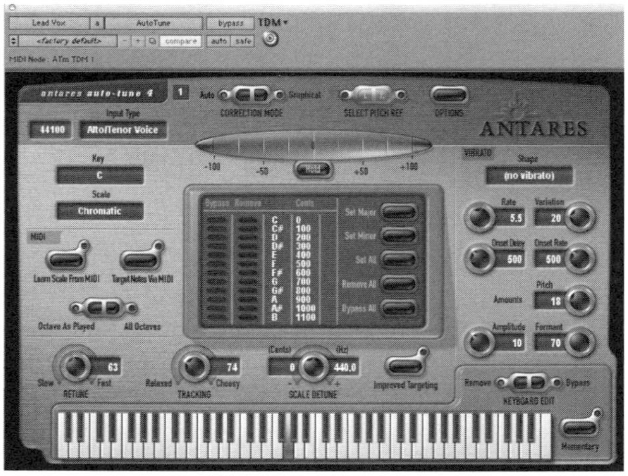

Antares Auto-Tune 4 Settings

Input Type: Alto/Tenor Voice
Retune: 63
Tracking: 74

The Renaissance Compressor is set to a threshold of –2.5 dB and a compression ratio of 3.28:1. The maximum gain reduction from the Renaissance Compressor is 2.8 dB, which isn't a great amount. A bit more compression comes from the Bomb Factory BF76 Compressor. The BF76, like the UREI 1176 upon which it is based, is a fast-acting compressor. With a 4:1 compression ratio and less than 3 dB of gain reduction, the BF76 does very well at controlling the levels of the track.

Fig. 7.23. Lead Vocal Compressor 1

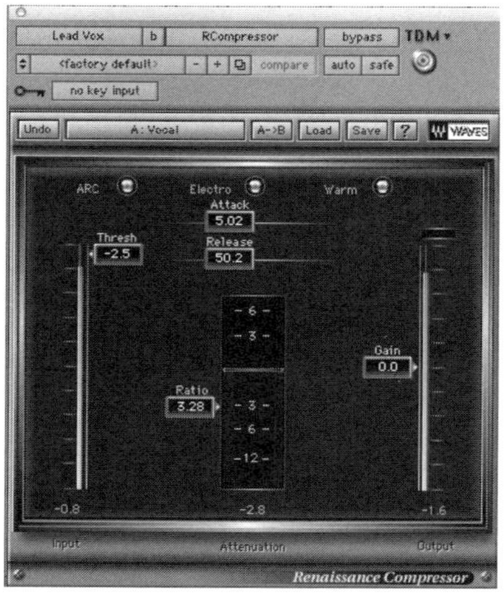

Waves Renaissance Compressor Lead Vocal Settings				
threshold	**attack**	**release**	**ratio**	**gain**
–2.5 dB	5.02	50.2	3.28:1	0 dB

Fig. 7.24. Lead Vocal Compressor 2

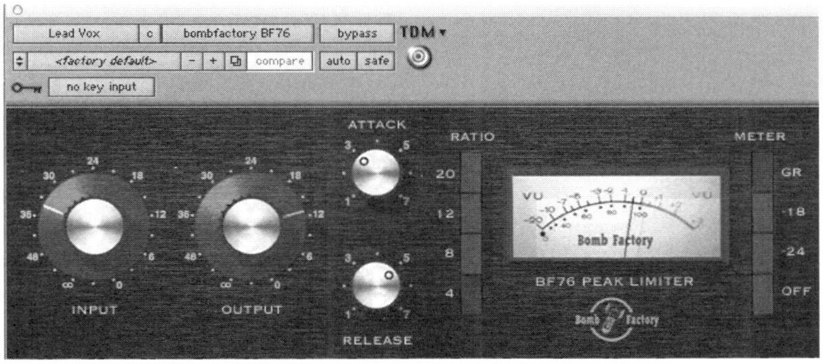

Bomb Factory BF76 Lead Vocal Settings				
input	**output**	**attack**	**release**	**ratio**
34	11.5	3	5	4:1

The last plug-in in the lead vocal chain is a Renaissance EQ-6. A high-pass filter removes frequencies below 74 Hz, and a boost of approximately 2 dB around 250 Hz adds some body to the track. The other EQ bands simply tilt the top end of the vocals up a bit, with a 1.2 dB boost at 1.8 Hz, a 3 dB boost at 6.2 kHz, and a 3 dB boost from a shelving EQ at 12 kHz.

Fig. 7.25. Lead Vocal EQ

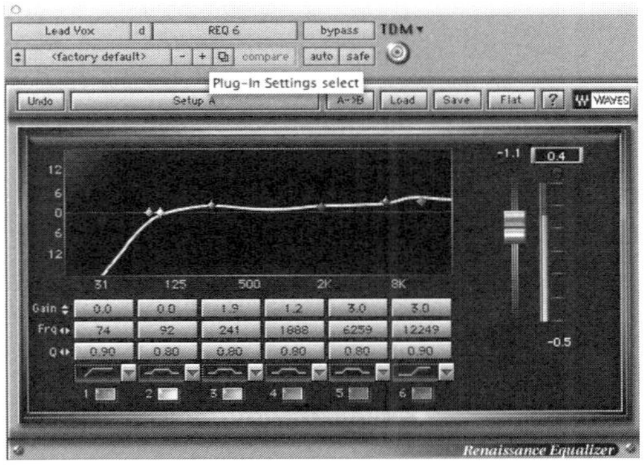

Waves Renaissance EQ-6 Lead Vocal Settings						
parameter	**band 1**	**band 2**	**band 3**	**band 4**	**band 5**	**band 6**
gain	0 dB	0 dB	+1.9 dB	+1.2 dB	+3.0 dB	+3.0 dB
frequency	74 Hz	92 Hz	241 Hz	1,888 Hz	6,259 Hz	12,249 Hz
Q	0.90	0.80	0.80	0.80	0.80	0.90
shape	high pass	bell	bell	bell	bell	shelf

BACKGROUND VOCALS

The background vocals are where "Redneck Woman" gets interesting; from a mixing perspective, there are three separate groups of background vocals. The first group is the one that does the most; a high-background part and a mid-background part that sing with the lead vocalist for the most part (though in the second verse, there are some lines that they sing as a counterpoint to the lead vocal). It's not uncommon for songs to have two background vocals (BGVs) on some of the lines and only one background part on some other lines; these typically mix themselves, since the single BGV doesn't need to be as loud in the mix as those with two parts.

Fig. 7.26. BGV Auto-Tune

The output level of the high background vocal is –7.7 dB, and the mid vocal is at –7.4 dB. The Auto-Tune 4 plug-in was used on these two BGV tracks; the retune and tracking parameters were the same on each track: set at 49 and 42 respectively. Volume automation was written to both of these BGV parts in the last chorus, but it was not needed at any other points in the mix. The high- and mid-background tracks were routed to the BGV buss, where a Renaissance EQ and a Renaissance Compressor were inserted. The output level of the BGV buss (which is sent to the master output) is set to unity gain, or 0 dB.

The Renaissance EQ has a 1.2 dB boost at 92 Hz and a 2.4 dB boost at 8.4 kHz. The Renaissance Compressor's maximum gain reduction is –1.6 dB; the compression ratio is 2.54:1, and the attack and release times are fairly slow, with a 16-millisecond attack time and a 160-millisecond release time.

Fig. 7.27. BGV Buss EQ

Waves Renaissance REQ-2 Background Buss Settings		
parameter	**band 1**	**band 2**
gain	+1.0 dB	+2.4 dB
frequency	92 Hz	8,746 Hz
Q	0.60	0.60
shape	bell	bell

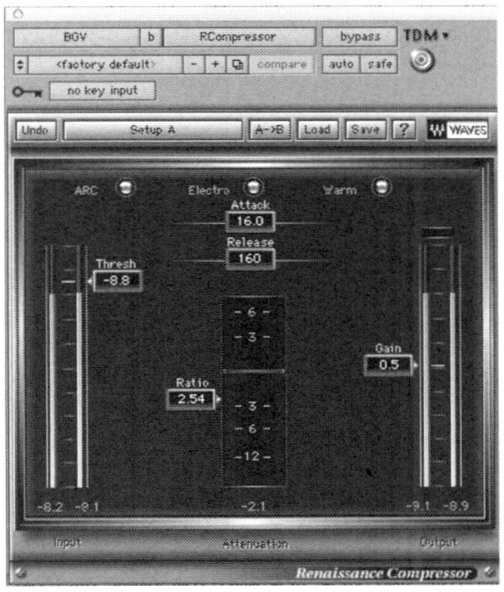

Fig. 7.28. BGV Buss Compressor

Waves Renaissance Compressor BGV Buss Settings				
threshold	**attack**	**release**	**ratio**	**gain**
–2.5 dB	5.02	50.2	3.28:1	0 dB

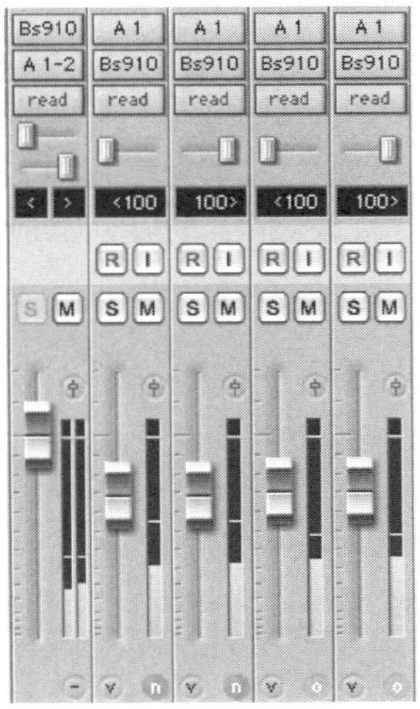

Fig. 7.29. Male BGV

Male Vocals

The second group of background vocals is made up of the male vocals that are only present during the first part of the last chorus. There are four tracks of male vocals; two of the tracks have the singer singing a low F sharp (the key of the song) while the other two are an F sharp an octave higher. The two parts are doubled (that is, each of the parts is sung twice). The higher parts are at –9.5 dB, while the lower parts are at –9.0 dB. The male vocals are also bussed to the BGV buss. The two high tracks are panned hard left and right, and the two low tracks are panned in the same manner.

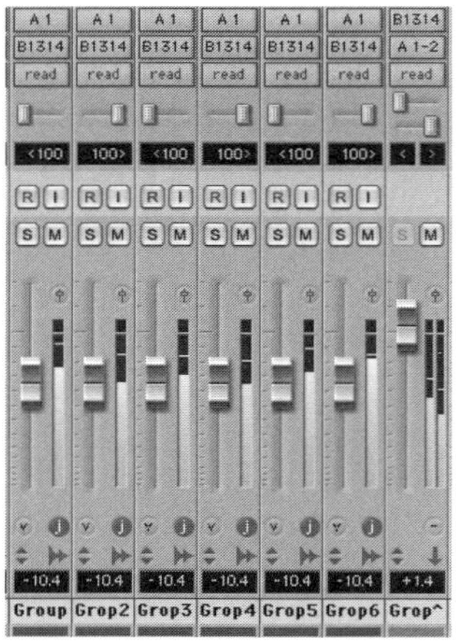

Fig. 7.30. Group Vocals

Group Vocals

There are six tracks of group vocals, which are intended to emulate the crowd singing along on the original version of "Redneck Woman." Each of the two tracks has two female vocalists (really, the same two vocalists are doing each track), so there are a total of twelve voices singing—or shouting—"Hell Yeah!" The individual fader levels are set at –10.4 dB, and the tracks are sent to a group buss, not the BGV buss. This was done because the group vocals needed a reverb to help them sound like a big group shouting in a large room. The other background tracks—the male voices and the main background vocals—needed different reverb sends, so the group buss was set up separately from the BGV buss. The output level of the group buss was +1.4 dB, while the vocal reverb send was at –12.6 dB.

Aux Sends and Buss Processing

Four reverbs were used for this mix of "Redneck Woman." They're labeled drum reverb, instrument reverb, vocal reverb, and long reverb.

The drum reverb used was a Waves Renaissance Reverberator set to Drum Plate and the output level of the drum plate was at unity gain, or 0 dB.

Fig. 7.31. Aux Sends and Buss

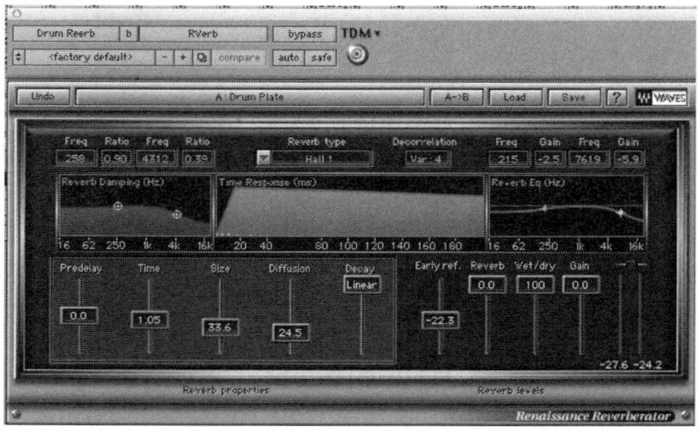

Fig. 7.32. Drum Reverb

Waves Renaissance Reverberator Drum Reverb Settings	
parameter	**setting**
REVERB DAMPING	
frequency 1	258
ratio 1	0.90
frequency 2	4,312
ratio 2	0.39
reverb type	hall 1
decorrelation	var: 4

REVERB EQ	
frequency 1	215
gain 1	–2.5 dB
frequency 2	7,619
gain 2	–5.9 dB
predelay	0.0
time	1.05 seconds
size	33.6
diffusion	24.5
decay	linear
early reflection level	–22.3 dB
reverb	0.0 dB
wet/dry	100%
gain	0

The instrument reverb used for this mix was another Renaissance Reverberator, which was set to a Medium Room preset; the output level of the reverb was set to unity gain, or 0 dB.

Fig. 7.33. Instrument Reverb

Waves Renaissance Reverberator Instrument Reverb Settings

parameter	setting
REVERB DAMPING	
frequency 1	29
ratio 1	1.00
frequency 2	4,569
ratio 2	0.76
reverb type	Resoverb
decorrelation	Var:1

Waves Renaissance Reverberator Instrument Reverb Settings	
parameter	**setting**
REVERB EQ	
frequency 1	156
gain 1	0
frequency 2	1,256
gain 2	–4.9dB
predelay	0.0
time	0.70
size	62.3
diffusion	30
decay	linear
early reflection level	–23.9dB
reverb	0.0dB
wet/dry	100%
gain	0

The vocal reverb used for this mix was a Waves TrueVerb, which was set to a Nice Plate preset; the output level of the reverb was set to unity gain, or 0 dB.

Fig. 7.34. Vocal Reverb

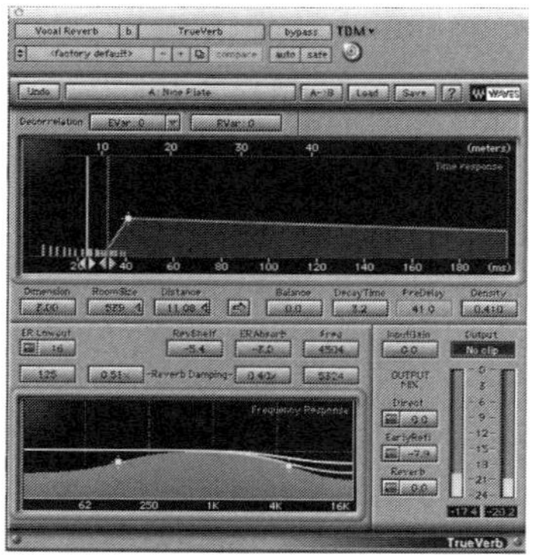

Waves TrueVerb Vocal Reverb Settings	
dimension	3.00
room size	539
distance	11.08
balance	0.0
decay time	3.2
predelay	41.0
density	0.410

EARLY REFLECTION (ER)	
low cut	16
reverb damping frequency low	125
damping	0.51x
reverb damping frequency high	5,324
damping	0.40 x
reverb shelf	–5.4
ER absorb	–3.0
ER absorb freq	4,504
input gain	0.0
direct output	0.0
early reflection output	–7.9
reverb output	0.0

The long reverb was a Waves TrueVerb set to a Large Concert preset; the output level of the reverb was set to unity gain, or 0 dB.

Fig. 7.35. Long Reverb

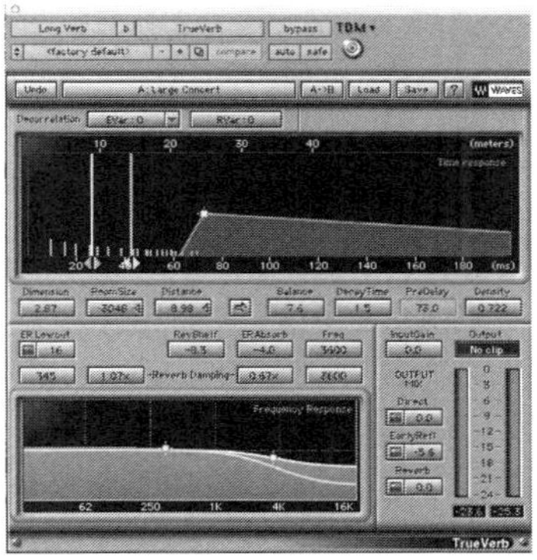

Waves TrueVerb Long Reverb Settings

parameter	setting
dimension	2.87
room size	3,048
distance	8.98
balance	9.4
decay time	2.8
predelay	73.0
density	0.722
EARLY REFLECTION (ER)	
low cut	16
reverb damping frequency low	345

Waves TrueVerb Long Reverb Settings	
parameter	**setting**
damping	1.07 x
reverb damping frequency high	3,600
damping	0.67 x
reverb shelf	–8.3
ER absorb	–4.0
ER absorb freq	3,600
input gain	0.0
direct output	0.0
early reflection output	–5.6
reverb output	0

Master Output

The master output includes a Waves Renaissance Compressor, a 6-band Renaissance EQ, a Waves L2 Limiter, and a Pow-R Dither plug-in. The compressor's threshold is set to –2.2 dB, the attack is 10.7 ms, and the release is 683 ms. The compression ratio is 2.511. The 6-band EQ uses one band for a slight boost at 39 Hz and another for a 4.5 dB boost at 17 kHz. The L-2 Limiter is set to a –4.1 dB threshold and an output ceiling of –0.3 dBFS. The Pow-R Dither plug-in is set to a 16-bit output and uses noise-shaping type 3.

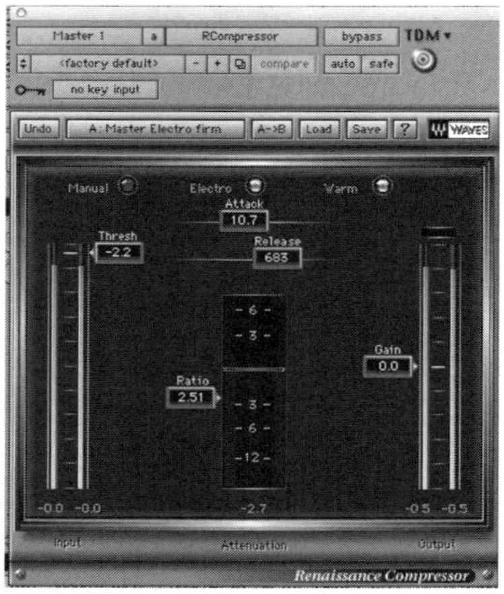

Fig. 7.36. Output Compressor

Waves Renaissance Compressor Master Output Settings				
threshold	**attack**	**release**	**ratio**	**gain**
–2.2 dB	10.7	683	2.51:1	0 dB

Fig. 7.37. Output EQ

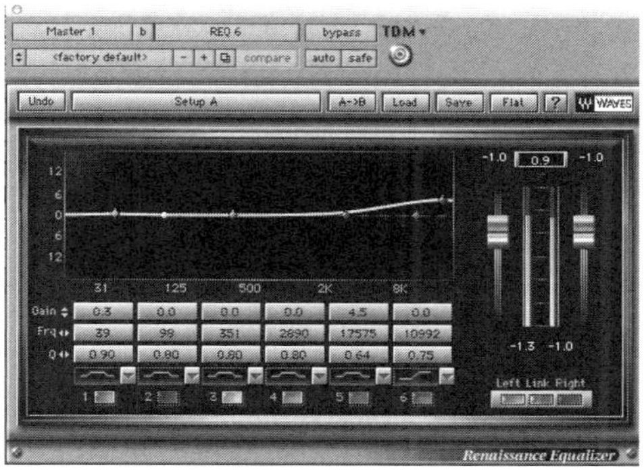

Waves Renaissance EQ-6 Master Output Settings						
parameter	**band 1**	**band 2**	**band 3**	**band 4**	**band 5**	**band 6**
gain	+0.3 dB	0 dB	0 dB	0 dB	+4.5 dB	0 dB
frequency	39 Hz	98 Hz	351 Hz	2,890 Hz	17.5 Hz	11 kHz
Q	0.90	0.80	0.80	0.80	0.80	0.90
shape	bell	bell	bell	bell	bell	shelving

Fig. 7.38. Buss Limiter

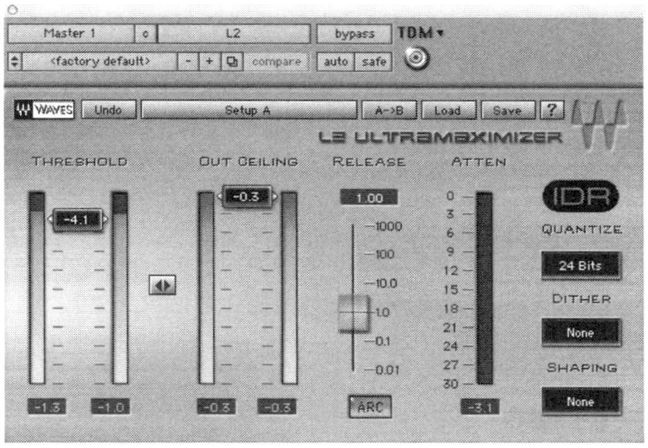

Waves L2

Threshold: –4.1 dB

Out Ceiling: –0.3 dB

Release: 1.00

Fig. 7.39. Dither

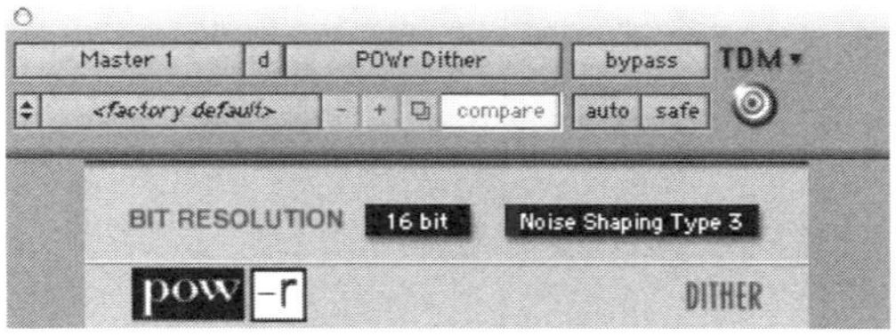

Pow-R Dither

16 bit

Noise Shaping Type 3

AUTOMATION

Volume automation has been written for a number of the tracks on "Redneck Woman." In the second verse, the piano has been raised a bit while it plays some fills. The fiddle track is also increased in volume in the first chorus and in the solo section. In the same manner as the fiddle, the steel track was raised a bit in the first chorus and during its solo. Both of the guitars were adjusted during the course of the song as well, with the rhythm guitar lowered during the steel solo and guitar 2 changed a bit throughout the tune. The lead vocal automation was primarily in the verses where it was raised a bit to meet the needs of the song, and the two main background parts were raised during the down section of the last chorus.

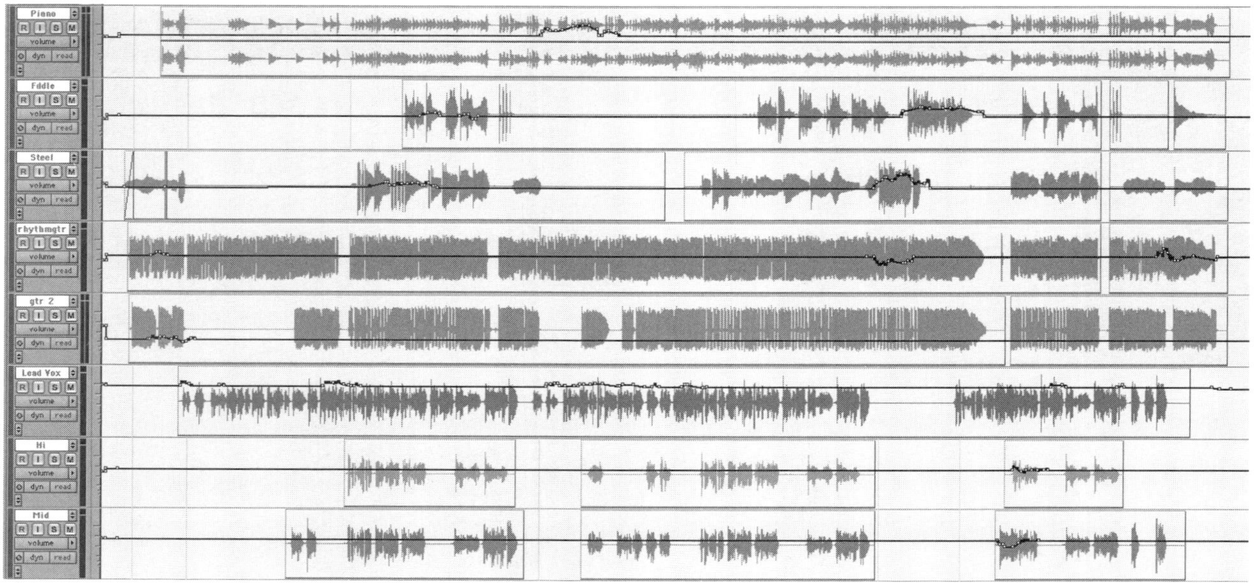

Fig. 7.40. Automation

No automation was written on the master output for the fade at the end of the song; as a change, faders were written to the audio tracks themselves; by choosing the drum tracks when printing the mix, the fades worked in the same manner as writing the fade-out on the master output would have. The goal is to have a clean and controlled fade to nothing at the end of the track—whether that is done with a master fader or in another manner is, to a certain extent, irrelevant.

EDITS

A few changes were made to the audio tracks at the mixing stage of "Redneck Woman." Those included on the DVD are the same ones that were used in this mix, but from time to time, it's easier to use a non-destructive edit to achieve a desired goal. To begin with, all of the tracks in the session were trimmed to the start of the audio (with the exception of the steel track, discussed below). Then, those audio tracks that were still present at the time the song should end (drums and bass) were trimmed to the appropriate times and then fades were created on all. The fade length was 1.16 seconds.

Some mixers prefer to clear those regions of the audio tracks where no audio is present; they feel that this practice makes it easier to see what's happening at any given point in the song. That practice was partially followed on "Redneck Woman" mostly in regards to those regions before the first entrance of the instrument on any given track. To illustrate, the piano was cleared from the beginning of the track up to the point halfway through the intro where it enters, while the banjo track isn't visible until just before the last chorus. The background vocal tracks are treated the same way, with some additional clearing of the audio tracks in those sections where nothing is going on.

Other edits to the audio tracks were made to clear unwanted audio; while these changes could have been done by using volume automation, or by selecting the appropriate regions and making them inactive, simply selecting and then clearing the selected areas was the quickest and easiest approach.

Fig. 7.41. Clearing to Remove Noise

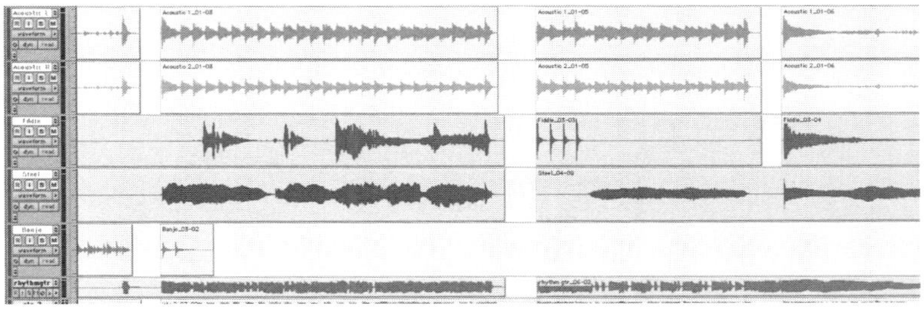

At a 1:47 ratio, a piece of the steel track was cleared; this was done because the steel player started to play something that shouldn't have been there. Removing it by selecting and then clearing it was the easiest way to get rid of the offending note. At 2:51, the acoustic guitar, banjo and guitar 2 tracks were cleared to eliminate noise from what should be silence in the track. The same thing was done at 3:09, with the acoustic, fiddle, steel, and rhythm guitar 1, and the acoustic, and fiddle tracks were cleared at 3:22. All of the clearing was done for the same reason—to get rid of noise on the track that shouldn't be there.

Fig. 7.42. Steel Intro Note

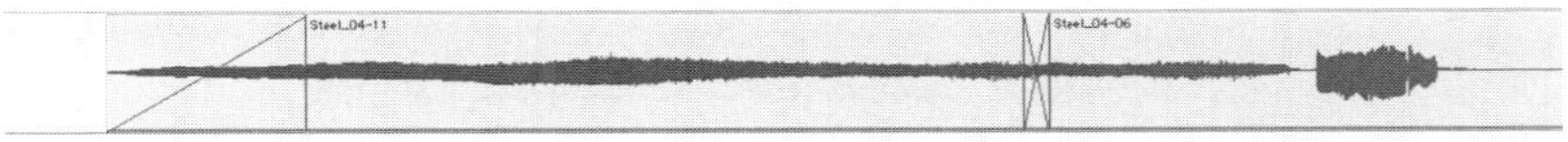

And finally, "Redneck Woman" begins with a steel guitar note that rises in volume; the steel track started a bit later than what sounded best in the mix. To remedy this, two changes were made: first, the held note that begins the steel track was separated and moved forward. This left a spot where the steel was not played, which wasn't the goal. So from the separation on the original track, the audio was shifted forward to meet what had been moved, and then the point where the original and the moved track met was blended together with a fade. Once that was done, a fade was added to the audio track at the beginning of the note. Since this was done after the drum track fades were created, selecting the length of the printed mix involved (in Pro Tools) choosing the edited steel track (for a start time) and then holding the shift key while selecting one of the drum tracks (for the end time).

Printing Mixes

When printing the mix of each of the songs in this volume, a consistent approach was used: a track (in this case, a couple of tracks) is used to set the final length of the song. The start time of "Redneck Woman" was set by selecting the steel track, and the ending time of the mix was chosen by selecting one of the drum tracks. In Pro Tools, selecting this trimmed track will cause the program to play from the beginning to the end of that track with no excess audio or time at the beginning or end. In those situations where multiple mixes of a song must be done—for example, if a producer wants vocal up or vocal down versions, TV mixes, instrumental mixes—all of the versions are the same length, and can be easily lined up for editing.

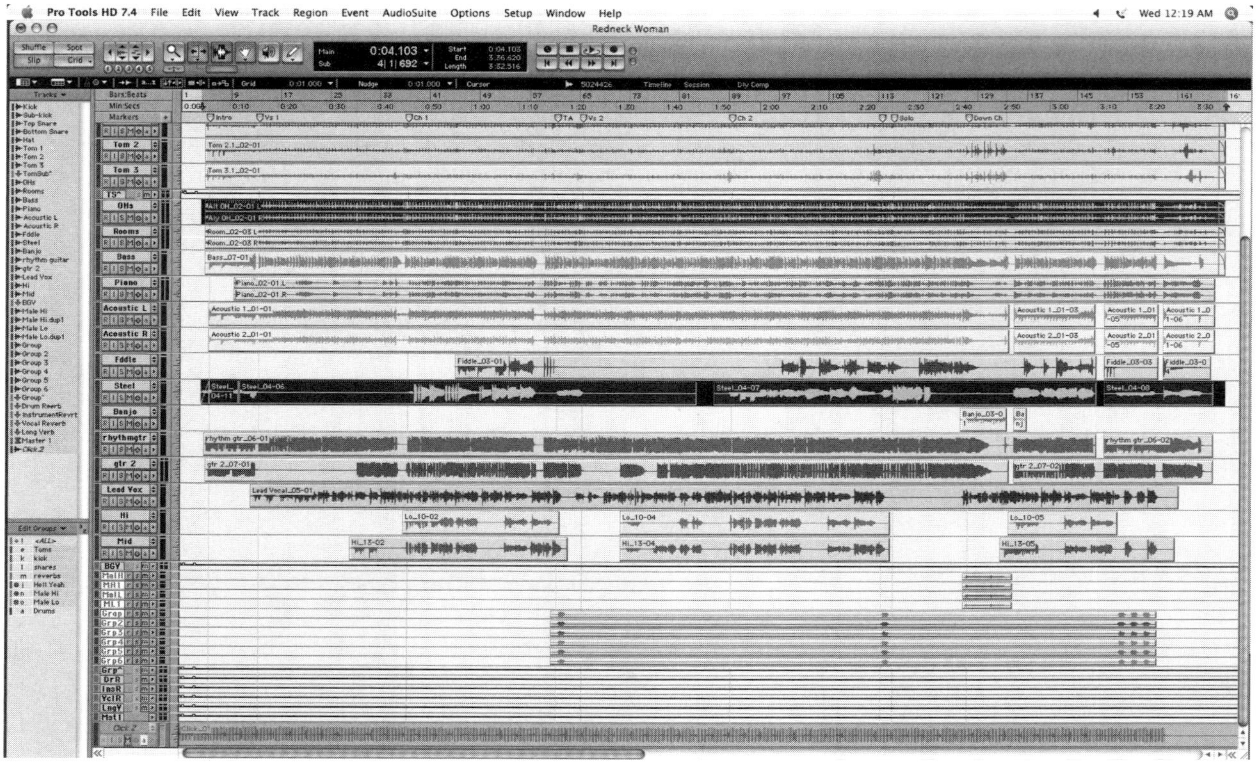

Fig. 7.43. Print Mix

CHAPTER 8

"Stealing Kisses"

(As Recorded by Faith Hill)

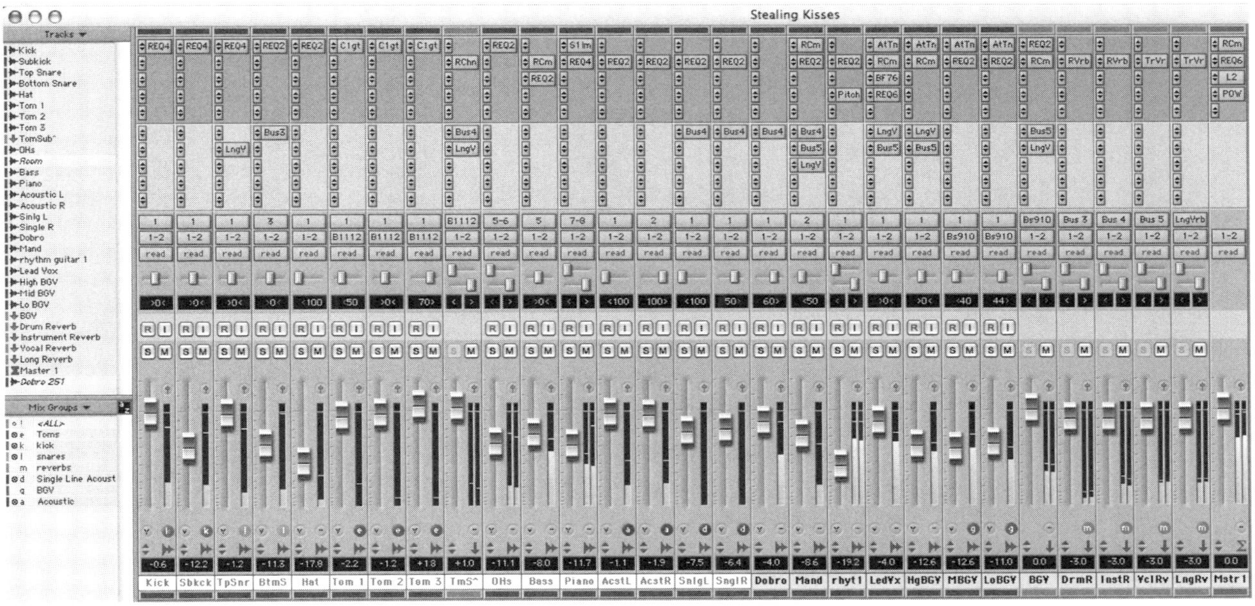

Fig. 8.1. Mix Window

Faith Hill's "Stealing Kisses" is a remake of the Lori McKenna song; in fact, comparing the two is an educational study in the differences between contemporary country and contemporary acoustic pop production. Hill's "Stealing Kisses" uses drums played with brushes and has a more open and spacious mix than many of the songs in this set.

DRUMS

The drum tracks on "Stealing Kisses" were recorded in the same manner as the other drum tracks in this volume, without EQ and with little or no compression so that the mixing process could be made a bit more informative. If all the needed processing was done in the tracking stage, then there would be little to talk about concerning the mixing of the drums. Besides that, the lack of processing at the recording stage means that the raw tracks can be manipulated in a bit more creative manner at the mixing stage. There are two kick drum tracks on "Stealing Kisses"—one, labeled "kick" (though the actual audio track is called "alt kick") was recorded with an Electro-Voice RE20 placed inside the drum about three inches from the batter head. For many years, the RE20 was a standard kick drum microphone in studios around the country. The "sub-kick" track was recorded with a Yamaha Subkick placed directly in front of the drum. These two signals sound quite different from each other; most mixing engineers will combine the two sounds while processing each as needed to create the final kick drum sound.

Fig. 8.2. Drum Mix

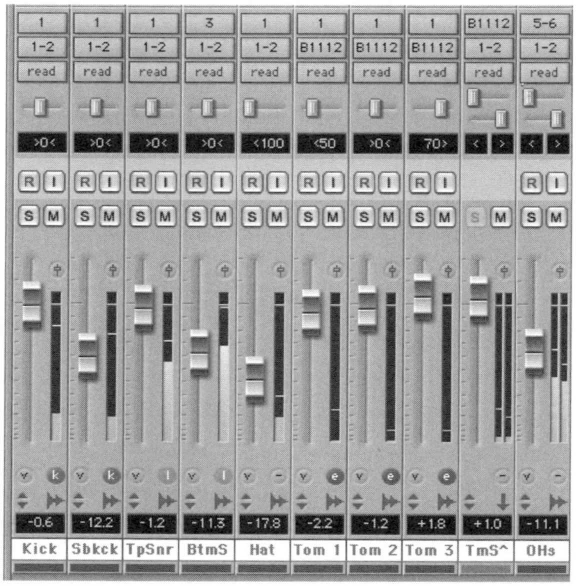

Kick Drum

The main kick drum track was boosted 1.5 dB at 31 Hz (to add some bottom), cut by 4.8 dB at 482 Hz to remove the cardboard box sound, boosted 4.5 dB at 3.8 kHz to add a bit of snap. A shelving filter at 10 kHz was boosted by 2.2 dB. The output level of the kick drum was –0.6 dB. No compression was used on either of the kick drum tracks.

Fig. 8.3. Kick Drum EQ

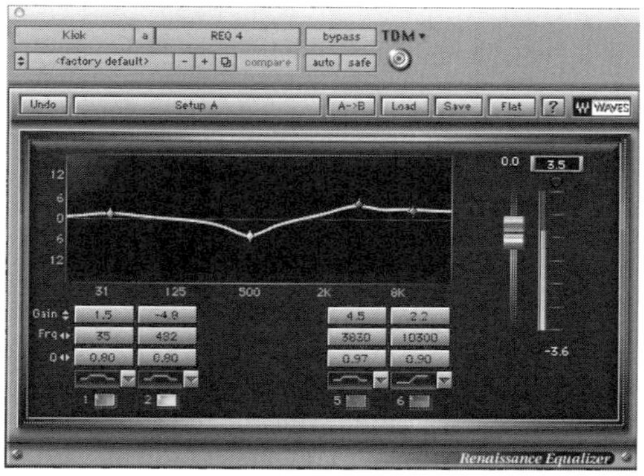

Waves Renaissance REQ-4 In-Kick Settings				
parameter	band 1	band 2	band 3	band 4
gain	+1.5 dB	–4.8 dB	+4.5 dB	+2.2 dB
frequency	31 Hz	482 Hz	3,830 Hz	10,300 Hz
Q	0.80	0.80	0.97	0.90
shape	bell	bell	bell	shelf

Subkick

The subkick track also has a 4-band Renaissance EQ, with a boost centered at 44 Hz and a 3.5 dB cut around 600 Hz. The subkick was recorded with a Yamaha Subkick; this is a new version of a fairly old idea. The subkick is essentially a speaker that's wired with an XLR connection so that it can be used as a microphone. The output level of the "sub kick" track is –12.2 dB.

Fig. 8.4. Subkick EQ

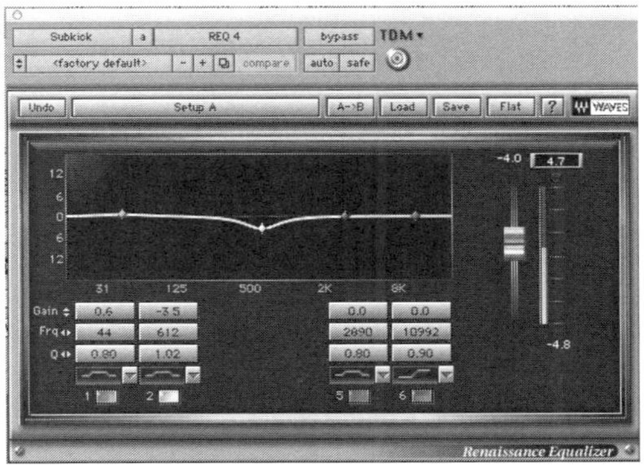

Waves Renaissance REQ-4 Subkick Settings				
parameter	band 1	band 2	band 3	band 4
gain	+0.6 dB	–3.5 dB	+0 dB	0 dB
frequency	44 Hz	612 Hz	2,890 Hz	10,992 Hz
Q	0.80	1.02	0.80	0.90
shape	bell	bell	bell	shelf

Snare Drum

There are two snare drum tracks on "Stealing Kisses." A Neumann KM 84 was used on top of the snare and another KM 84 was used underneath the snare. These are labeled in the mixing session as "Top Snare" and "Bottom Snare."

Top Snare

The top snare track has a 4-band Renaissance EQ inserted as a plug-in. The Waves Renaissance EQ is primarily used to add a bit of thump to the track (with about a 2 dB boost around 100 Hz), a bit of snap (with a boost around 2 kHz) and a bit of air (boosting at 12 kHz). The output of the top snare track is at –1.2 dB; the send to the long reverb is –12.3 dB.

The snare on "Stealing Kisses" was a Ludwig 6 .5-inch Supraphonic snare drum—this may well be the most recorded drum of the last forty years; the 5-inch deep snare was the standard snare that came with Ludwig's drum sets for many years, and then an English guy named John Bonham started using a 6.5-inch deep snare, and every rock drummer wanted that sound.

Fig. 8.5. Top Snare EQ

Waves Renaissance REQ-4 Top Snare Settings

parameter	band 1	band 2	band 3	band 4
gain	+2.2 dB	+1.6 dB	+3.3 dB	+3.3 dB
frequency	109 Hz	341 Hz	3,830 Hz	14,778 Hz
Q	0.80	1.02	0.80	0.90
shape	bell	bell	bell	bell

Bottom Snare

The bottom snare track has a 2-band Waves Renaissance EQ2 that rolls off with a high-pass filter at 92 Hz and is boosted by 0.4 dB around 10 kHz. The fader level for the bottom snare track is at –11.3 dB. It's interesting to note that quite a number of recording engineers will set up a bottom snare mic for every recording session, but they don't always use it in the mix. It's been mentioned earlier that there's no rule requiring that every track delivered to be mixed actually be used. For "Stealing Kisses," the bottom snare is used for an effects send to the drum reverb.

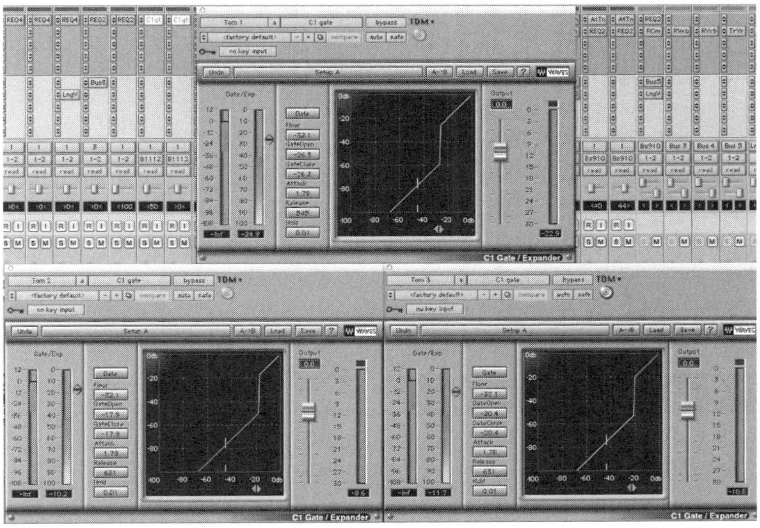

Fig. 8.6. Bottom Snare EQ

Waves Renaissance REQ-2 Bottom Snare Settings		
parameter	**band 1**	**band 2**
gain	0 dB	+0.4 dB
frequency	92 Hz	9,935 Hz
Q	0.71	0.60
shape	high pass	bell

Hi-hat

Precious little can be added to the other discussions of the hi-hat track—use it if you wish, don't if you don't think it adds anything. I used it, with a high pass at 92 Hz and a 0.0 dB boost around 8.3 kHz. Fader Level: –17.3 dB.

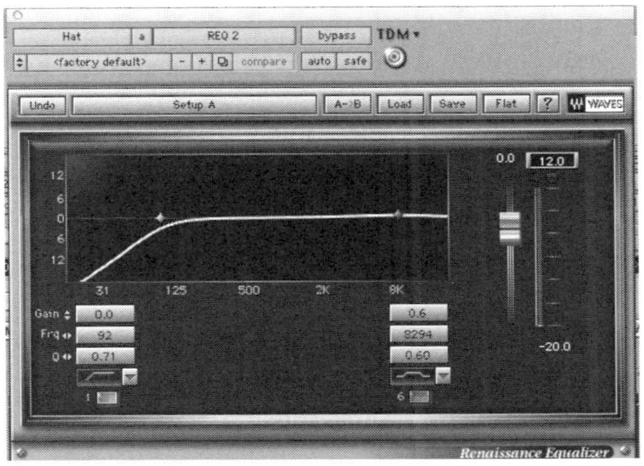

Fig. 8.7. Hat EQ

Waves Renaissance REQ-2 Hi-hat Settings		
parameter	band 1	band 2
gain	0 dB	+0.6 dB
frequency	92 Hz	8,294 Hz
Q	0.71	0.60
shape	high pass	bell

Toms

The three tom tracks were again bussed to their tom buss and gated to minimize noise. The fader levels on Tom 1 were set at –2.2 dB, Tom 2 was set to –2.2 dB, and Tom 3 was set to –2.2 dB. Waves C1 Gates were used on all three toms, which are sent to the stereo tom buss. The three tom tracks are panned hard left, center, and hard right. The floor for all of the tom gates was set at –32.1 dB, meaning that when the gate is closed, the level of the tom tracks is 32.1 dB quieter than when the gates are open.

Fig. 8.8. Tom Gates

Waves C1 Gate Tom 1					
floor	gate open	gate close	attack	release	hold
–34.5 dB	–26.3 dB	–26.3 dB	1.78	545	0.01

Waves C1 Gate Tom 2					
floor	gate open	gate close	attack	release	hold
35.2	–17.9 dB	–17.9 dB	1.78	631	0.01

Waves C1 Gate Tom 3					
floor	**gate open**	**gate close**	**attack**	**release**	**hold**
35.2	–20.4 dB	–20.4 dB	1.78	631	0.01

Fig. 8.9. Tom Processing

Tom Buss

Two different reverbs are used on the tom buss—the vocal reverb send is at –8.6 dB while the long verb send is at –16.5 dB. Instead of using a separate Renaissance EQ for the tom buss, a Renaissance Channel was inserted. The Renaissance Channel may be considered as simply a combination of a 4-band EQ and a compressor, but it's actually more full-featured than that. In the case of the Renaissance Channel, an expander is available. Additionally, the Renaissance Channel offers parameters that aren't available with the single function versions, including, sidechain filters on both the compressor and the gate, as well as a phase reverse switch that inverts the polarity of the signal passing through it. In this instance, the polarity switch is activated, which simply means that the toms sounded better (especially in relation to the overheads) with the switch engaged than when it wasn't.

Waves Renaissance Channel EQ Buss Settings				
parameter	**band 1**	**band 2**	**band 3**	**band 4**
gain	+2.5 dB	0 dB	0 dB	+0.1 dB
frequency	135 Hz	110 Hz	2,134 Hz	50,401 Hz
Q	0.80	1.00	0.66	0.90
shape	bell	bell	bell	bell

Waves Renaissance Channel Compressor Buss Settings				
Phase reverse on				
threshold	**attack**	**release**	**ratio**	**gain**
–3.0	3.60	240	3.7:1	+1.1 dB

Overheads

The overhead tracks were recorded using a pair of Telefunken M16 microphones. Though they were recorded to two mono tracks, for the mix of "Stealing Kisses," they were moved to a stereo track for ease of mixing (some engineers are used to seeing the overheads as a stereo track;

anything that helps the mixing engineer to do his job in an expedient manner is a good thing—but more on that later. The overheads have a Waves Renaissance EQ plug-in with a broad 3.6 dB cut on the low end and a 7.4 dB boost in the high end. A bell-shaped filter centered at 20 Hz provided the low-end cut, but the Q (that is, the width) of that filter (0.26) means that frequencies over 100 Hz were also slightly attenuated. In the same manner, the high-end EQ also had a fairly wide Q, so that even though it was centered at 26.5 kHz, frequencies as low as 2 kHz were affected.

Fig. 8.10. Overhead EQ

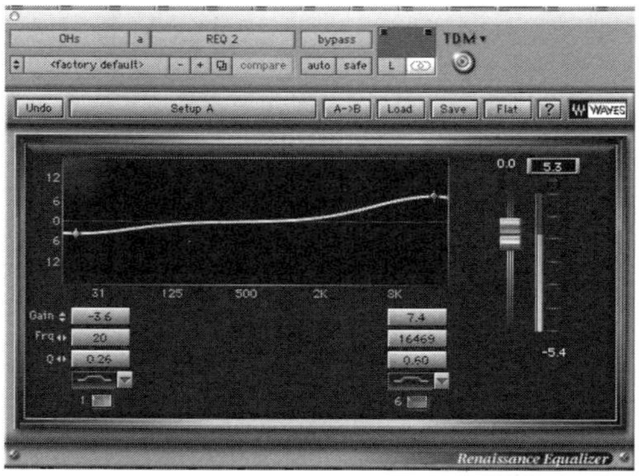

Waves Renaissance REQ-2 Overhead Settings		
parameter	band 1	band 2
gain	–3.6 dB	+7.4 dB
frequency	20 Hz	16,469 Hz
Q	0.26	0.60
shape	bell	bell

Room Mic

It's been mentioned before that you can always choose not to use a given audio track when mixing; that decision was made with the room mic on "Stealing Kisses." Since the sound of the room didn't add anything to the mix, it was turned off.

BASS

The bass track on "Stealing Kisses" used a Waves Renaissance Compressor and a 2-band Waves Renaissance EQ as plug-ins. The output fader of the bass was set at –8.0 dB. Not a whole lot of gain reduction was used on the bass track; it was added primarily to even out any inequities in the track.

The EQ was primarily used to add bottom end to the bass track. The Q setting affects the width of the band—the lower the number, the wider the frequency range affected by any changes to the level of that band. Even though the center frequency of this EQ band is quite low—below not only the lowest frequency that the bass can create, but also the lowest frequency that most consumer speakers can reproduce—the Q setting is wide enough that an audible range of frequencies is affected by this EQ band.

In addition to that, keep in mind that a lot of what is perceived as bass is not necessarily created by the fundamental note (the low E note on a bass is at 41 Hertz, and notes played on the B string are lower than that), but by harmonics an octave (and more) higher than the fundamental. Boosting the fundamental frequency will also raise the level of the harmonic notes associated with that frequency.

Fig. 8.11. Bass Compressor

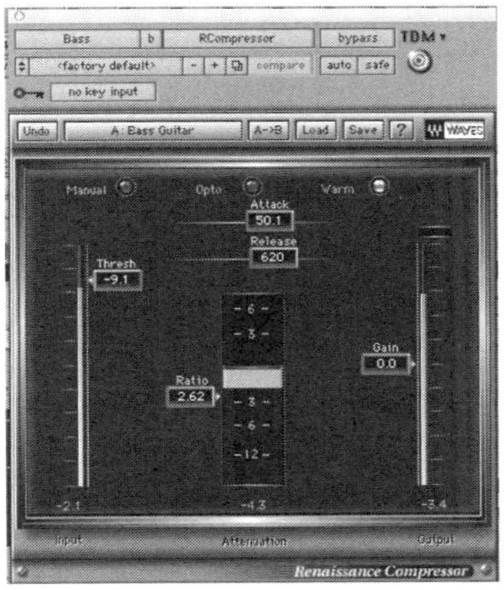

Waves Renaissance Compressor Bass Settings				
threshold	**attack**	**release**	**ratio**	**gain**
–9.1 dB	50.1	620	2.62:1	0 dB

Fig. 8.12. Bass EQ

Waves Renaissance REQ-2 Bass Settings		
parameter	**band 1**	**band 2**
gain	+0.8 dB	0 dB
frequency	34 Hz	197 Hz
Q	0.60	0.60
shape	bell	bell

PIANO

Though piano tracks are almost always panned hard left and right, the term "stereo" would probably be a misnomer. When the piano microphones are placed inside the piano, one is usually towards the foot of the instrument over the bass strings while the other is closer to the keys and centered over the higher strings—not what they teach you in recording school as one of the stereo placements. Nevertheless, we'll refer to them as "stereo" simply because it's easier that typing "the two tracks of piano." Of course, it's not always necessary (or even desirable) to pan the piano to hard left and right; like everything else associated with mixing, piano panning is application specific. For example, if a mix has many hard-panned tracks (like doubled rhythm guitars, or fiddle on the left and steel on the right), keeping the piano more in the center of the stereo field may well lead to better results. The best way to do this is *not* to pan the two piano tracks to the center; phase cancellation between the two tracks would likely change the sound of the piano in a drastic manner. Instead, pan them to 60–75 percent of hard left and right; this will collapse the image without doing as much damage.

There are also applications when you may want the piano to be more on one side of the stereo field. For instance, if another keyboard (like a Wurlitzer electric piano or an organ) is on the other side, separating the instruments in the sound field may yield better results.

An acoustic piano is capable of producing a huge dynamic range as well a huge tonal range; though most serious pianists understand how to use this range to enhance the music being played, it's sometimes necessary to use compression to narrow that dynamic range to something suitable for contemporary country (and pop) music.

If the piano needs compression to even out the performance on the track, the style of the piano track will help to determine the appropriate plug-in. A slower compressor (one that emulates an electro-optical compressor like the Teletronix LA-2A) may work very well when the track that doesn't include a lot of isolated peaks. When the piano is played in a more percussive manner, a plug-in based on a faster compressor (for example, one of the many 1176 emulation plug-ins) might well be the ticket since a faster attack and release time can help to control transients while releasing quickly enough to control the next transient. A good starting point would be to set the attack time in the 15- to 25-millisecond range and the release time in the 100- to 150-millisecond range. This setting would capture more transients (especially with a compression ratio above 4:1) than a slower electro-optical emulation that presets the attack times in the 50-millisecond (or longer) range and release times in excess of 250 ms. Of course, if the track sounds better when the attack of each note comes through, then raising the compressor's attack time (to 50 or even 150 ms) is the best approach.

When it comes to adding EQ to a piano track, the only reliable guide is your ear. Because most country records have a large number of instruments, it's often necessary to try to keep the piano from masking other instruments, or conversely, it may be required to use equalization to make the piano stand out from other instruments that would otherwise be masking it. Even when a song uses piano as the primary (or only) instrument, some amount of EQ may be appropriate. For example, if the piano track is pretty bright, the track might be improved by darkening it a bit (with a shelving EQ set in the 12–15 kHz range). Adding the "sheen" that seems to be popular these days (a brightness that some folks say is a characteristic of Yamaha C7s with hard hammers), you may wish to boost that same range. There's a limit to how much boost a real piano track will make, because the piano's sustain pedal controls dampers that stop the strings from ringing. When these dampers lift up off of the string, there's a bit of a noise that is usually not heard in the context of a mix. Boosting the high frequencies can (and usually will) make this sound much more audible. There's also a low-frequency component to the damper system; should you wish to enhance the low end of the piano (by boosting the 100–250 Hz range), you may run into the same issue. Frequencies in the 2–5 kHz area may be used to either emphasize or de-emphasize the piano's attack, and it seems that the 250–2 kHz range brings out the body of the piano sound.

On "Stealing Kisses," the piano's fader level was set at −11.7 dB, and two different plug-ins were used. The Waves S1 Imager is first, and was inserted to widen the piano image. The S1 works by adding out-of-phase information to the audio track. Though this can affect the mono compatibility of the mix, which generally doesn't become a problem unless extreme settings are used. After the S1, a Renaissance 4-band EQ was used to brighten the piano sound so it comes closer to the sound of the piano used on the original track.

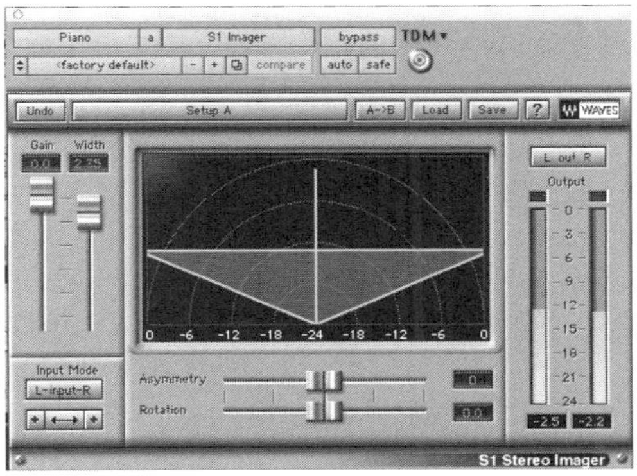

Fig. 8.13. Piano Imager

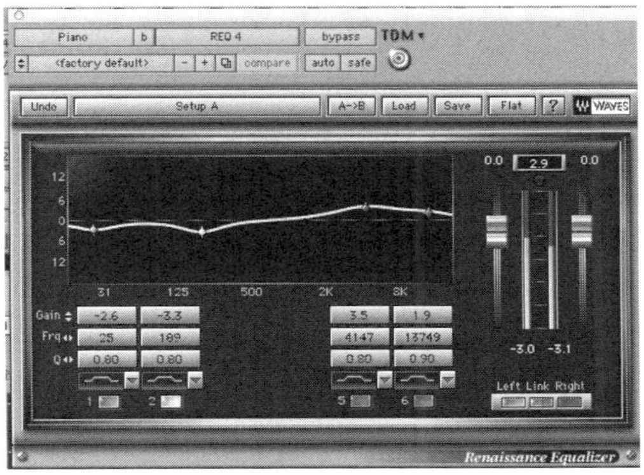

Fig. 8.14. Piano EQ

Waves Renaissance REQ-4 Piano Settings				
parameter	band 1	band 2	band 3	band 4
gain	–2.6 dB	–3.3 dB	+3.5 dB	+1.9 dB
frequency	25 Hz	189 Hz	4,147 Hz	13,749 Hz
Q	0.80	0.80	0.80	0.90
shape	bell	bell	bell	bell

ACOUSTIC GUITARS

"Stealing Kisses" has two guitars. There are four acoustic guitar tracks, but that's because of the miking technique used to record them. The two microphones used to record the acoustic were placed as follows: one mic points a couple of inches below the area between the soundhole and the neck of the instrument with the mic about four inches from the face of the guitar; the other mic was placed approximately even with the guitarist's shoulder and pointing at the lower bout from approximately twelve inches away. These two tracks are generally treated (and processed) as a stereo pair, but since purists would argue that "stereo" has a specific meaning in audio, it might be better to refer to it as a "two-microphone" technique. In any case, the two tracks have a drastically different tone: "acoustic L" is a bit more direct sounding and has more presence than "acoustic R".

The second pair of acoustic guitar tracks contain the melodic lines that occur throughout the song; in the mix session for this song, the two guitars are labeled as "acoustic" L and R, and "single line" L and R. The main acoustic guitar (that is, "acoustic L" and "acoustic R") has the left fader level at –1.1 dB and the right fader level at –1.9 dB. A 2-band Waves Renaissance EQ was used on each track, each with a high-pass filter to remove unwanted low frequencies and a boost to help the high frequencies cut through the track.

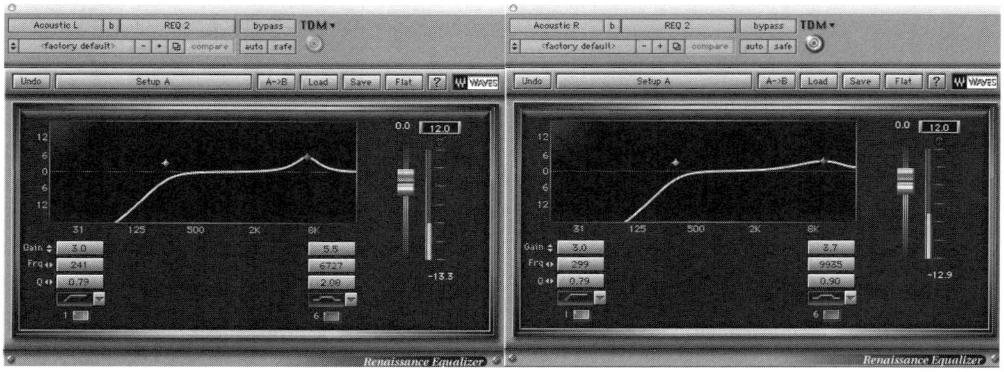

Fig. 8.15. Acoustic EQ

Waves Renaissance REQ-2 Acoustic L Settings		
parameter	band 1	band 2
gain	+3.0 dB	+5.5 dB
frequency	241 Hz	6,727 Hz
1.28	0.79	2.08
shape	high pass	bell

Waves Renaissance REQ-2 Acoustic R Settings		
parameter	band 1	band 2
gain	+3.0 dB	+3.7 dB
frequency	299 Hz	9,935 Hz
1.28	0.79	0.90
shape	high pass	bell

The second pair of acoustic guitar tracks, "single line" L and R, have the left fader level at –7.5 dB and the right fader level at –18.5 dB. A 2-band Waves Renaissance EQ was used on each track, each with a high-pass filter to remove unwanted low frequencies and a boost to help the high frequencies cut through the track. A send to the instrument reverb was added to the single line acoustic tracks, with the aux level for the instrument reverb set at –18.5 dB for the left side and –17.8 dB for the right side of the single line acoustic.

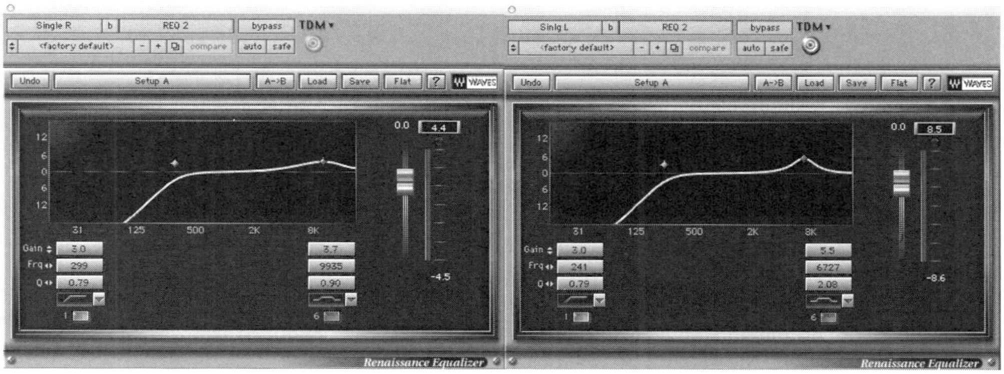

Fig. 8.16. Single Line EQ

Waves Renaissance REQ-2 Single Line Acoustic L Settings		
parameter	band 1	band 2
gain	+3.0 dB	+5.5 dB
frequency	241 Hz	6,727 Hz
1.28	0.79	2.08
shape	high pass	bell

Waves Renaissance REQ-2 Single Line Acoustic R Settings		
parameter	band 1	band 2
gain	+3.0 dB	+3.7 dB
frequency	299 Hz	9,935 Hz
1.28	0.79	0.90
shape	high pass	bell

DOBRO

The dobro track has no processing other than the instrument reverb (the aux send level to that reverb is –12.3), but the dobro track is of interest for another reason: it also has a track that is left unused in this mix. The dobro on "Stealing Kisses" was recorded with two microphones: a Telefunken 251 was pointed approximately at the spot where the neck meets the body of the instrument from about one foot away, and a Crowley and Tripp Naked Eye ribbon microphone was placed over the resonator of the instrument (also about one foot away). At the mixing stage, it was decided that the Telefunken track by itself offered everything that was needed in the way of a dobro sound, so the Crowley and Tripps track was made inactive and not used at all. Readers of this book may listen to both tracks (one is called "dobro 251" and the other is "dobro Naked Eye") and decide for themselves. The output level of the dobro is set at –4.0 dB, and the send to the instrument reverb is at –12.3 dB.

MANDOLIN

Since the mandolin is tuned like a fiddle and has F-holes like a fiddle, and is the same size as a fiddle, it seems logical that you can mix it like a fiddle. So much for logic; I find that where a warm sound works best for fiddles—whose notes have a slow attack time—mandolins are much more percussive. So when adding compression to a mandolin track, faster attack and release times tend to be more successful at containing transient peaks.

Mandolins can be mixed (and also recorded) in a manner that emphasizes the high frequencies of the instrument; Nickel Creek's Chris Thiele most often has a sound like this. But mandolins can also produce a strong midrange sound that allows it to drive a track along, much the same as a rhythm guitar. Check out some of the classic Bill Monroe tracks; Monroe's mandolin sound is completely different from the delicate textures that are more common these days. The mandolin on "Stealing Kisses" was recorded with a microphone that does emphasize the high end of the instrument a bit, and by placing the mic at a greater than normal distance, the proximity effect that would otherwise warm up the low register of the instrument is absent.

The mandolin track has two plug-ins inserted in the chain: a Renaissance Compressor and a 2-band Renaissance EQ. The compressor has a 3.24:1 compression ratio and a fairly fast 5-millisecond attack time. This attack time allows the mandolin's attack to be emphasized, and the threshold setting of –11.0 dB results in a maximum of 5 dB of gain reduction. The first band of the EQ boosts the 2.5 kHz area by a bit over 2 dB, while a low-pass filter set a bit under 16 kHz removes some extremely high frequencies. The output of the mandolin is at –8.6 dB and three different reverbs are used on the track. The send to the instrument reverb is at –4.0 dB, the send to the vocal reverb is at –18.5 dB, and the send to the long reverb is at –8.3 dB.

Fig. 8.17. Mandolin Compressor

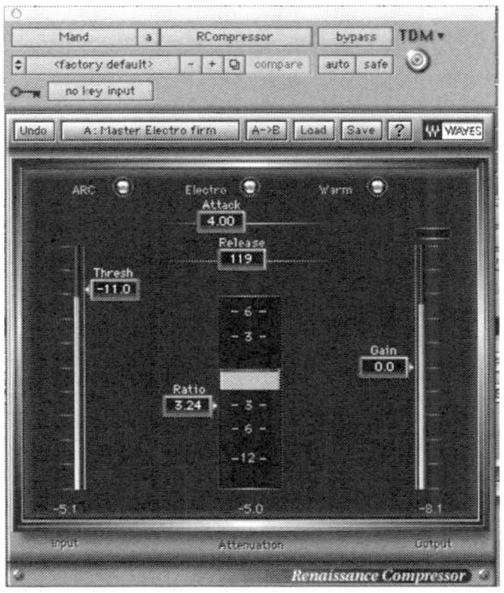

Waves Renaissance Compressor Mandolin Settings				
threshold	**attack**	**release**	**ratio**	**gain**
–11.0 dB	4.00	119	3.24:1	0 dB

Fig. 8.18. Mandolin EQ

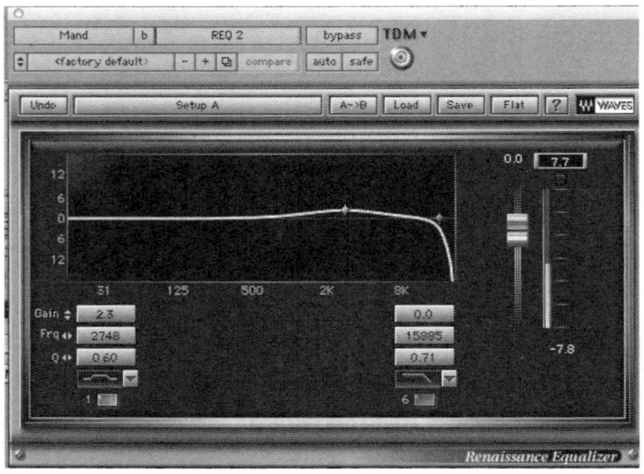

Waves Renaissance REQ-2 Mandolin Settings		
parameter	**band 1**	**band 2**
gain	+2.3 dB	0 dB
frequency	2,478 Hz	15,885 Hz
1.28	0.60	0.71
shape	bell	low pass

ELECTRIC GUITAR

The electric guitar track has one bit of processing for tone and one plug-in that is more of an effect. A 2-band Renaissance EQ has a low-pass filter set at 92 Hz and a 1.8 dB boost around 5.5 kHz. The tremolo was recorded with the track; it is not something added during the mixing process. The effect mentioned just now is a DigiRack plug-in called Pitch—Digidesign's pitch-shifting program. For this track, the plug-in has converted the mono electric guitar track to stereo and the right side is pitched up one cent (one hundred cents is equal to a half step in pitch and 1,200 cents is an octave). This effect—which can be done to other instruments including vocals—will add a spacious quality to the track. The output level of the electric guitar is set at –19.2 dB.

Fig. 8.19. Rhythm Guitar EQ

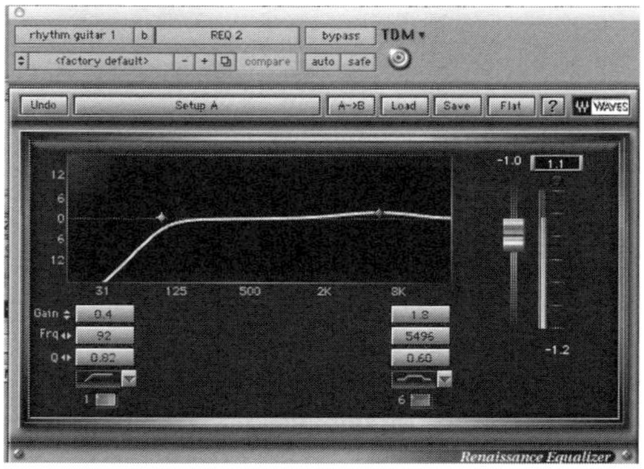

Waves Renaissance REQ-2 Electric Guitar Settings		
parameter	**band 1**	**band 2**
gain	+0.4 dB	+1.8 dB
frequency	92 Hz	5,496 Hz
1.28	0.82	0.60
shape	high pass	bell

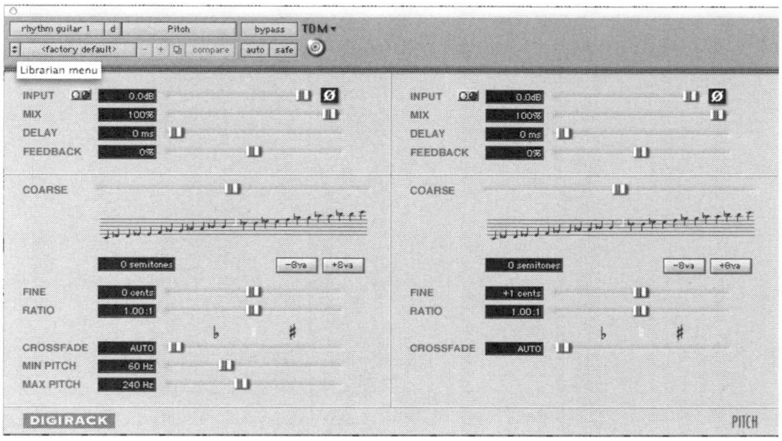

Fig. 8.20. Rhythm Guitar Pitch

VOCALS

It seems that one of the characteristic elements of contemporary country tracks is heavily processed lead vocals. Taking a cue from the pop songs of the '90s, country vocals are often heavily compressed or limited (sometimes both); then EQ'd; then processed again with something like a de-esser to get rid of the artifacts introduced by the compression and equalization. The levels of the vocal tracks are usually automated—sometimes syllable by syllable and sometimes line by line—to bring them into line with the tracks. In addition to this type of processing, it's not uncommon for EQ as an effect to be used whether it's the radio/telephone voice that seems to show up from time to time, or something a bit subtler like a high-pass filter that simply thins out the voice to emphasize certain lines.

LEAD VOCAL

The lead vocal track on "Stealing Kisses" uses four plug-ins: an Auto-Tune 4, a Renaissance Compressor, a Bomb Factory BF76 compressor, and a 6-band Waves Renaissance EQ. The fader is set at –5.2 dB, and two reverbs were used. The send to the long reverb is set at –16.1 dB, and the vocal reverb send is set at –13.9 dB.

The Auto-Tune 4 plug-in's Retune parameter was set to 63 (slow) and the tracking parameter was at 74 (relaxed). The Renaissance Compressor's compression ratio was set at 4.35:1, and the attack and release times were set at 5 ms and 50 ms respectively. The threshold setting on the Renaissance Compressor was at –4.9 dB which, with this particular track, gave a maximum gain reduction of around 4.5 dB. The output of the Renaissance Compressor was reduced by 1.4 dB, which helps to prevent overloads on the next plug-in in the chain, a Bomb Factory BF76. The BF76 added a maximum of another 3 dB of gain reduction to the lead vocal track. The two compressors working together give the lead vocal track the polished, processed sound that comes close to the sound of the original Faith Hill version upon which this mix is based.

Fig. 8.21. Lead Vocal Auto-Tune

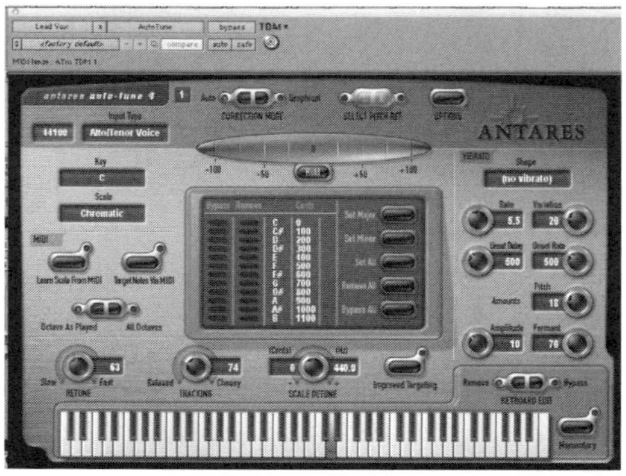

Antares Auto-Tune 4 Settings

Input Type: Alto/Tenor Voice
Retune: 63
Tracking: 74

Fig. 8.22. Lead Vocal Compressor

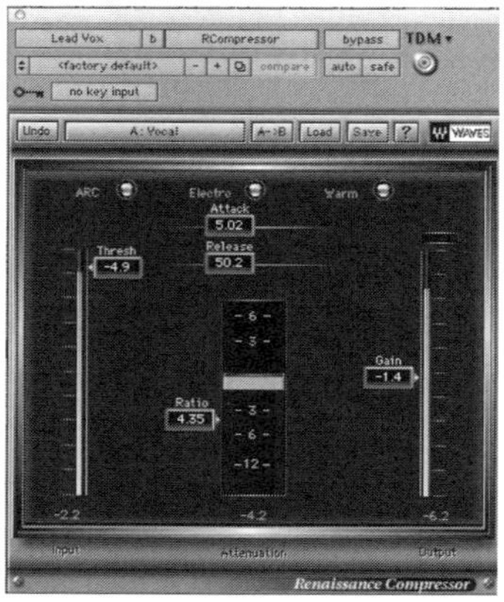

Waves Renaissance Compressor Lead Vocal Settings				
threshold	attack	release	ratio	gain
–4.9 dB	5.02	50.2	4.35:1	–1.4 dB

Fig. 8.23. Lead Vocal BF76

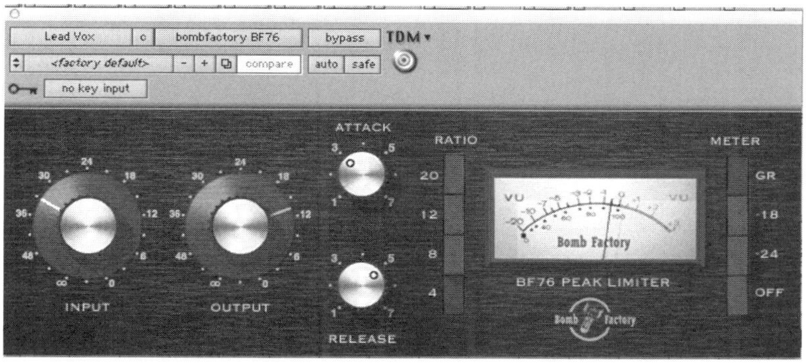

Bomb Factory BF76 Lead Vocal Settings				
input	**output**	**attack**	**release**	**ratio**
33	14	3	5	4:1

The last plug-in in the lead vocal chain is a 6-band Renaissance EQ. A high-pass filter removes frequencies below 74 Hz, and a cut of 0.7 dB at 287 Hz removes some boxiness in the track. The other EQ bands simply tilt the top end of the vocals up a bit, with a 0.6 dB boost at 1.9 Hz, a 1.3 dB boost at 5.5 kHz, and a 1.3 dB boost from a shelving EQ at 10 kHz.

Fig. 8.24. Lead Vocal EQ

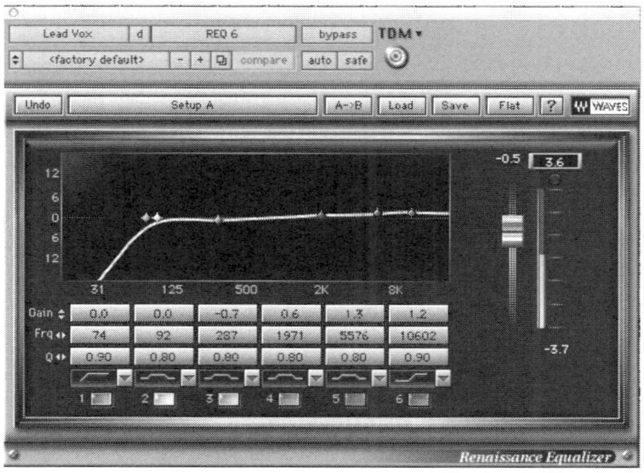

Waves Renaissance EQ-6 Lead Vocal Settings						
parameter	**band 1**	**band 2**	**band 3**	**band 4**	**band 5**	**band 6**
gain	0 dB	0 dB	–0.7	+0.6 dB	+1.3 dB	+1.2 dB
frequency	74 Hz	92 Hz	287 Hz	1,971 Hz	5,576 Hz	10,602 Hz
Q	0.90	0.80	0.80	0.80	0.80	0.90
shape	high pass	bell	bell	bell	bell	shelving

BACKGROUND VOCALS

Though there are three background vocal (BGV) tracks, the reality of this mix is that there's one main background vocal with two other tracks that only show up in the bridge section of the song. So for "Stealing Kisses," the high BGV is bussed to the master output in the same manner as the lead vocal while the mid and low BGVs are bussed to the BGV buss. The reason for doing this is because of the processing—the high BGV has different reverb settings as well as a different compressor setting.

The high BGV has an Auto-Tune plug-in with the retune parameter at 98 (so slow as to essentially being off) and the tracking parameter at 62 quite relaxed. The output level was set at –9.5 dB; the send to the long reverb was at –17.1 dB, while the send to the vocal reverb was at –10.7. A Renaissance Compressor was also added to the high BGV track; the threshold of –6.1 dB when combined with the 4.09:1 compression ratio, gave the track a bit more than 4.5 dB of gain reduction.

Fig. 8.25. High BGV Auto-Tune

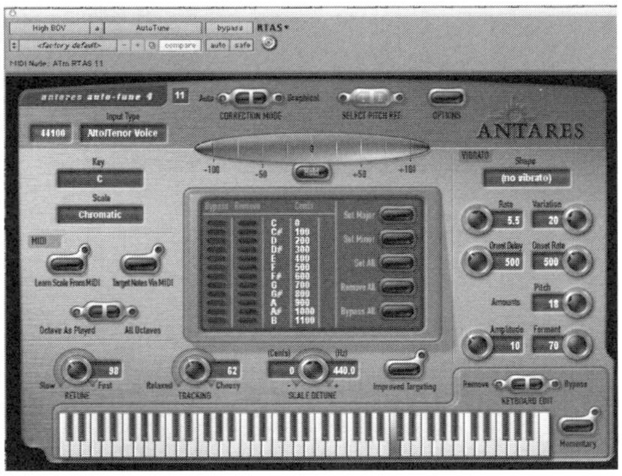

Auto-Tune

Retune: 98

Tracking: 62

Scale detune: 0 cents

Input Type: Alto/Tenor Voice

Fig. 8.26. High BGV EQ

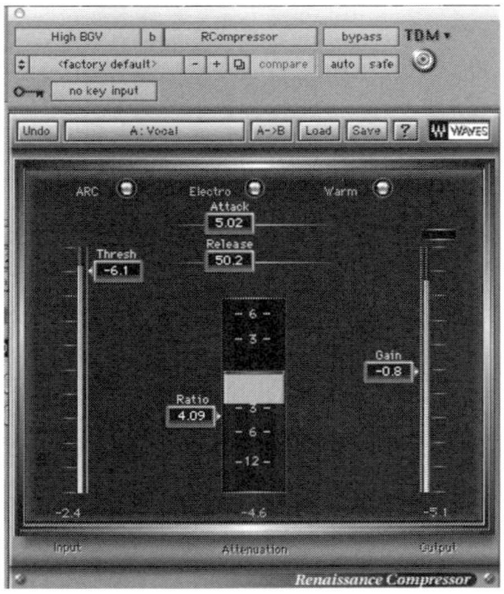

Waves Renaissance Compressor High BGV Settings

threshold	attack	release	ratio	gain
–6.1 dB	5.02	50.2	4.09:1	–0.8

The low and the mid BGV tracks have identical processing: Auto-Tune plug-ins with fairly mild settings, and 2-band Renaissance EQs with 1.5 dB cuts at 91 Hz. The fader level of the mid BGV was –9.9 dB and the low BGV was at –8.3 dB.

Fig. 8.27. Mid BGV Auto Tune

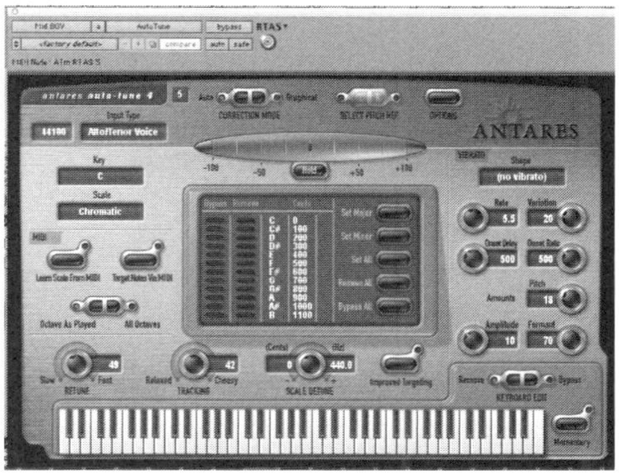

Auto-Tune 4

Retune: 49

Tracking: 42

Scale detune: 0 cents

Input Type: Alto/Tenor Voice

Fig. 8.28. Mid BGV EQ

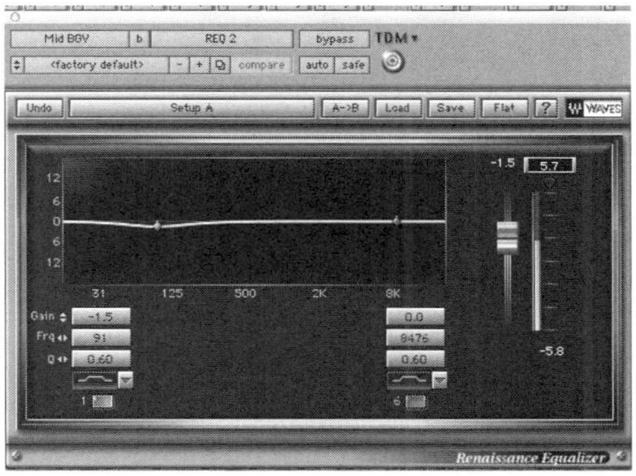

Waves Renaissance REQ-2 Mid BGV Settings

parameter	band 1	band 2
gain	–1.5 dB	0 dB
frequency	91 Hz	8,476 Hz
Q	0.60	0.60
shape	bell	bell

Fig. 8.29. Low BGV Auto-Tune

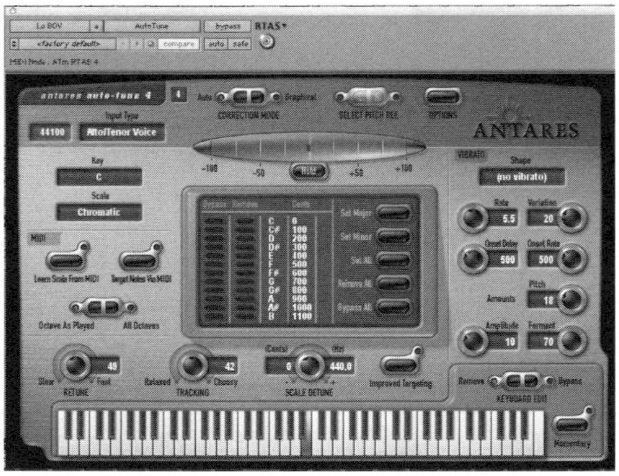

Auto-Tune 4

Retune: 49
Tracking: 42
Scale detune: 0 cents
Input Type: Alto/Tenor Voice

Fig. 8.30. Low BGV EQ

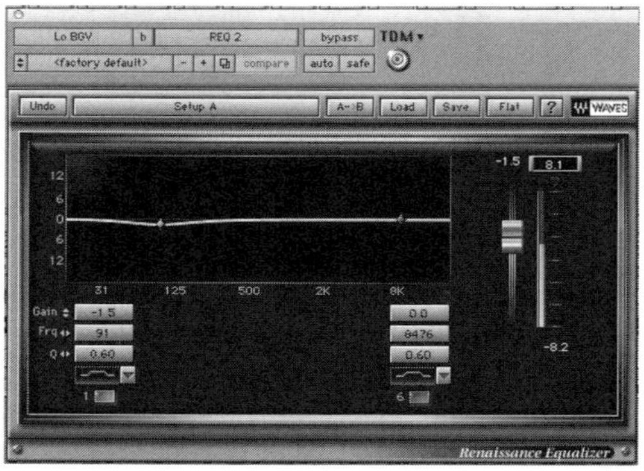

Waves Renaissance REQ-2 Mid BGV Settings

parameter	band 1	band 2
gain	–1.5 dB	0 dB
frequency	91 Hz	8,476 Hz
Q	0.60	0.60
shape	bell	bell

BGV Buss

The BGV buss fader was at unity gain, or 0 dB. Two reverb sends are on the BGV buss; the vocal reverb level is –12.3 db and the long reverb level is –12.9 dB. A 2-band Renaissance EQ and a Renaissance Compressor were inserted on the BGV buss; only one band of the EQ is active, and that adds a 2.4 dB boost around 8.5 kHz. The Renaissance Compressor settings were quite mild; the compression ratio was 2.54:1 and the maximum gain reduction on this plug-in was only a tenth of a dB.

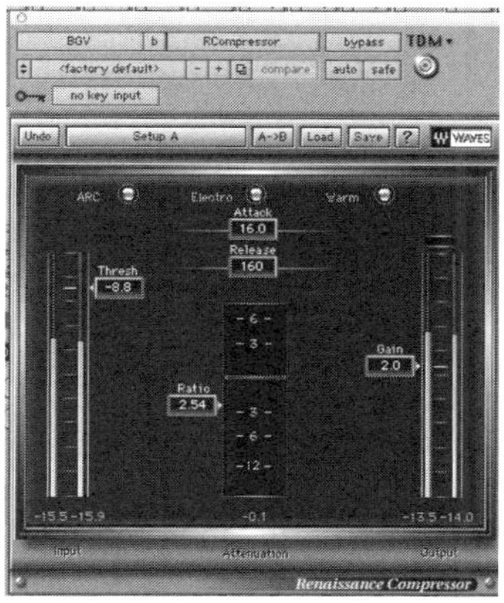

Fig. 8.31. BGV Buss Compressor

Waves Renaissance REQ-2 BGV Buss Settings		
parameter	band 1	band 2
gain	0 dB	+2.4 dB
frequency	92 Hz	8,476 Hz
Q	0.60	0.60
shape	bell	60

Fig. 8.32. BGV Buss EQ

Waves Renaissance Compressor BGV Buss Settings				
threshold	attack	release	ratio	gain
–8.8 dB	16.0	160	2.54:1	+2.0 dB

AUX SENDS AND BUSS PROCESSING

Four reverbs were used for "Stealing Kisses." They're labeled "drum reverb," "instrument reverb," "vocal reverb," and "long reverb."

The drum reverb used was a Waves Renaissance Reverberator set to a Drum Plate preset; the output level of the drum reverb was at –3 db.

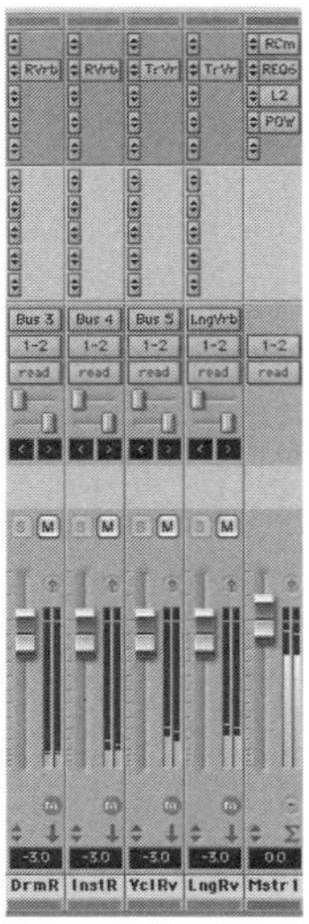

Fig. 8.33. Aux Sends

Fig. 8.34. Drum Reverb

Waves Renaissance Reverberator Drum Reverb Settings	
parameter	**setting**
REVERB DAMPING	
frequency 1	258
ratio 1	0.90
frequency 2	4,312
ratio 2	0.39
reverb type	hall 1
decorrelation	var: 4
REVERB EQ	
frequency 1	215
gain 1	–2.5 dB
frequency 2	7619
gain 2	–5.9 dB
predelay	0.0
time	1.14 seconds
size	34.4
diffusion	24.5
decay	linear
early reflection level	–22.3 dB
reverb	0.0 dB
wet/dry	100%
gain	0

The instrument reverb used for this mix was another Renaissance Reverberator, which was set to a Large Plate setting; the output level of the reverb was set to –3 dB.

Fig. 8.35. Instrument Reverb

Waves Renaissance Reverberator Instrument Reverb Settings	
parameter	**setting**
REVERB DAMPING	
frequency 1	527
ratio 1	1.23
frequency 2	4312
ratio 2	0.80
reverb type	plate 1
decorrelation	var: 4
REVERB EQ	
frequency 1	203
gain 1	0 dB
frequency 2	2447
gain 2	–6.5 dB
predelay	0.0
time	2.63 seconds
size	100.0
diffusion	30.0
decay	linear
early reflection level	0.0 dB
reverb	0.0 dB
wet/dry	100%
gain	0

The vocal reverb used for this mix was a Waves TrueVerb, which was set to a Nice Plate preset; the output level of the reverb was set at –3 dB.

Fig. 8.36. Vocal Reverb

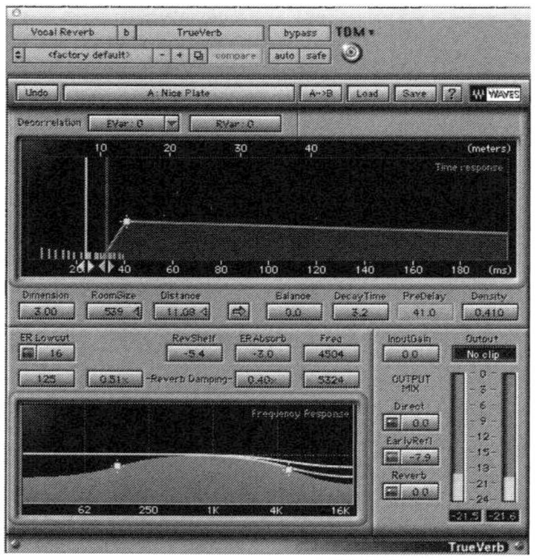

Waves TrueVerb Vocal Reverb Settings	
parameter	**setting**
dimension	3.00
room size	539
distance	11.08
balance	0.0
decay time	3.2
predelay	41.0
density	0.410
EARLY REFLECTION (ER)	
low cut	16
reverb damping frequency low	125
damping	0.51¥
reverb damping frequency high	5324
damping	0.40¥
reverb shelf	–5.4
ER absorb	–3.0
ER absorb freq	4,504
input gain	0.0
direct output	0.0
early reflection output	–7.9
reverb output	0.0

The vocal reverb used for this mix was a Waves TrueVerb, which was set to a Large Concert preset; the output level of the reverb was set at –3 dB.

Fig. 8.37. Long Reverb

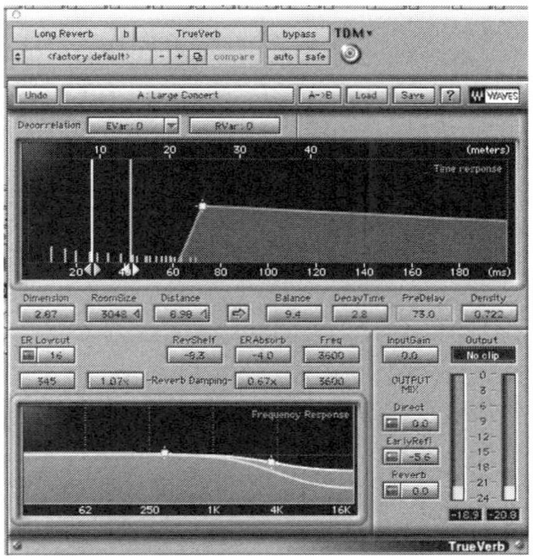

Waves TrueVerb Long Reverb Settings	
parameter	**setting**
dimension	2.87
room size	3048
distance	8.98
balance	9.4
decay time	2.8
predelay	73.0
density	0.722
EARLY REFLECTION (ER)	
low cut	16
reverb damping frequency low	345
damping	1.07¥
reverb damping frequency high	3600
damping	0.67¥
reverb shelf	–8.3
ER absorb	–4.0
ER absorb freq	3,600
input gain	0.0
direct output	0.0
early reflection output	–5.6
reverb output	0

MASTER OUTPUT

The master output includes a Waves Renaissance Compressor, a 6-band Renaissance EQ, a Waves L2 Limiter and a Pow-R Dither plug-in. The compressor, which has a maximum gain reduction of –3 dB, has a slow attack time (at 12 ms) and a slow release time. The compression ratio is 2.51:1, and threshold was set at –4.4 dB. The 6-band EQ has a slight cut (0.6 dB) at 39 Hz and a 4 dB boost at 17 kHz. The L2 Limiter is set to a –4.0 dB threshold and an output ceiling of –0.3 dBFS.

The Pow-R Dither plug-in is set to a 16-bit output and used noise shaping type 3.

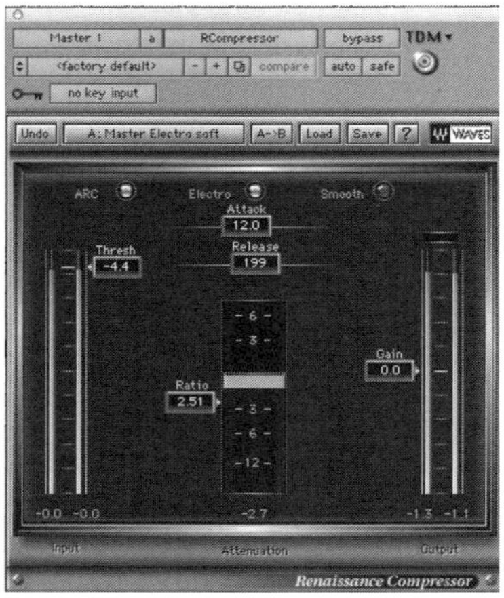

Fig. 8.38. Buss Compressor

Waves Renaissance Compressor Submaster Settings				
threshold	attack	release	ratio	gain
–4.4 dB	12.0	199	2.51:1	0 dB

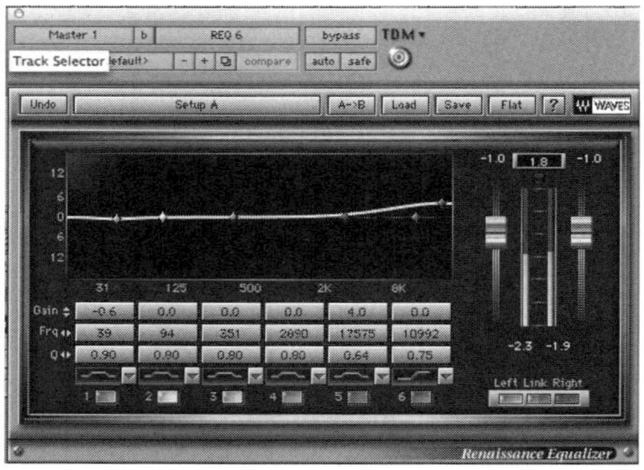

Fig. 8.39. Buss EQ

Waves Renaissance REQ-6 Submaster Settings						
parameter	band 1	band 2	band 3	band 4	band 5	band 6
gain	– 0.6 dB	0 dB	0 dB	0 dB	+4.0 dB	0 dB
frequency	39 Hz	94 Hz	351 Hz	2,890	17,575 Hz	10,992 Hz
Q	0.90	0.80	0.80	0.80	0.64	0.90
shape	bell	bell	bell	bell	bell	shelving

Fig. 8.40. Buss Limiter

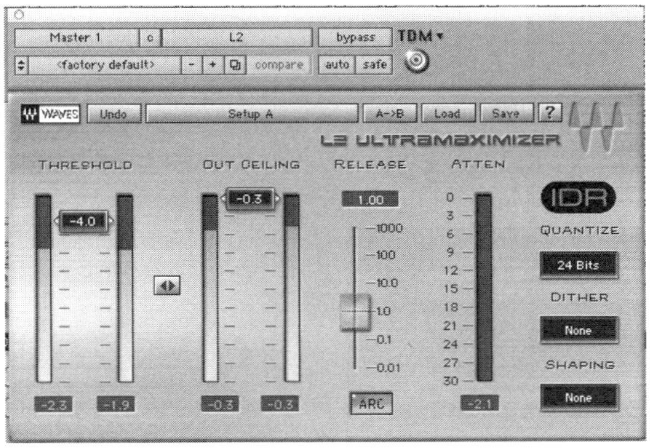

L2 Ultramaximizer

Threshold: –4.0 dB

Out Ceiling: –0.3 dB

Release: 100

Fig. 8.41. Buss Limiter

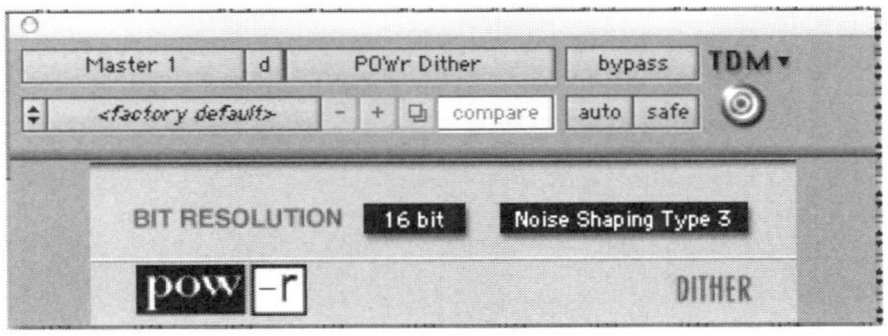

AUTOMATION

Volume automation has been written for a number of the tracks on "Stealing Kisses." The dobro was lowered a bit at the point where it enters, and then raised right before the last chorus. The mandolin track was raised a bit in the first verse, then lowered for the tremolo that happens in the first verse, then raised again for the melody figure it plays immediately afterwards. The mandolin track was also raised a bit in the build that precedes the last chorus. The rhythm guitar was lowered a bit in the intro of the song (and faded out at the end of the intro), but was otherwise unaltered.

The lead vocal track was primarily changed during the bridge, where it was raised above the levels of the BGVs, during the build before the last chorus and for the last two lines, where it was raised a bit. The BGV volume levels were ridden during the bridge section (of course, two of the three parts were only present during the bridge section). The high BGV also needed to be raised a bit in the last chorus.

No automation was written on the master output for the fade at the end of the song; as a change, faders were written to the audio tracks themselves. By choosing the drum tracks when printing the mix, the fades worked in the same manner as writing the fade-out on the master output would have. The goal is to have a clean and controlled fade to nothing at the end of the track—whether that is done with a master fader or in another manner is irrelevant to a certain extent.

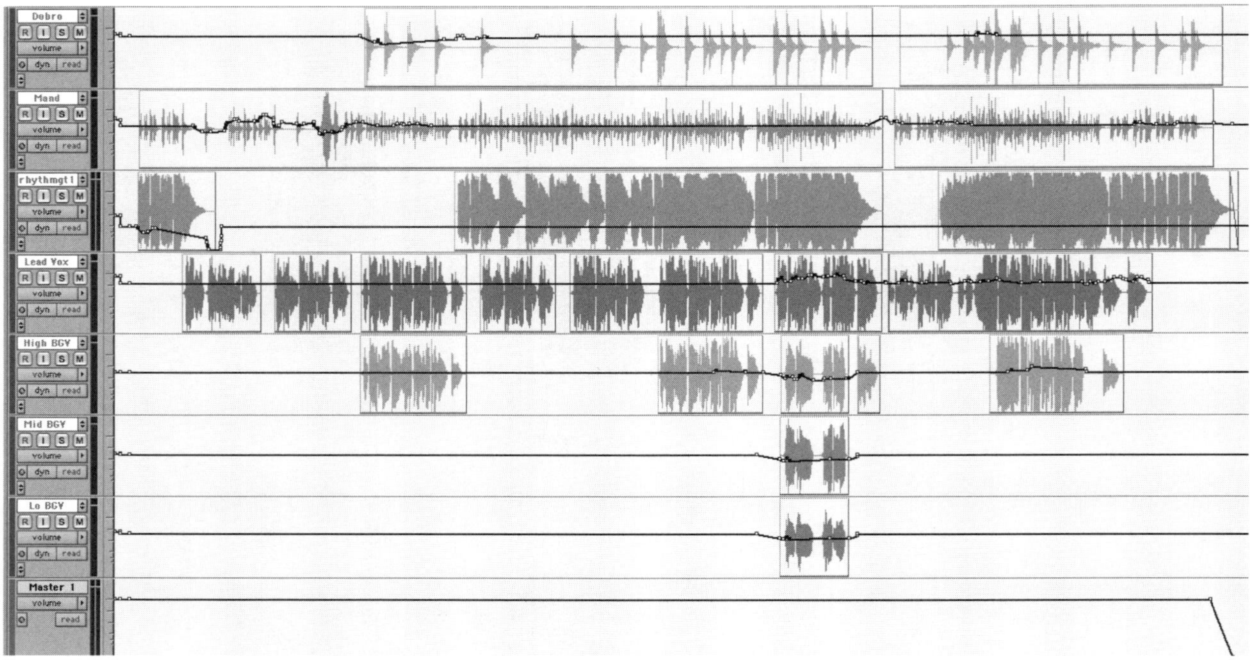

Fig. 8.42. Automation

EDITS

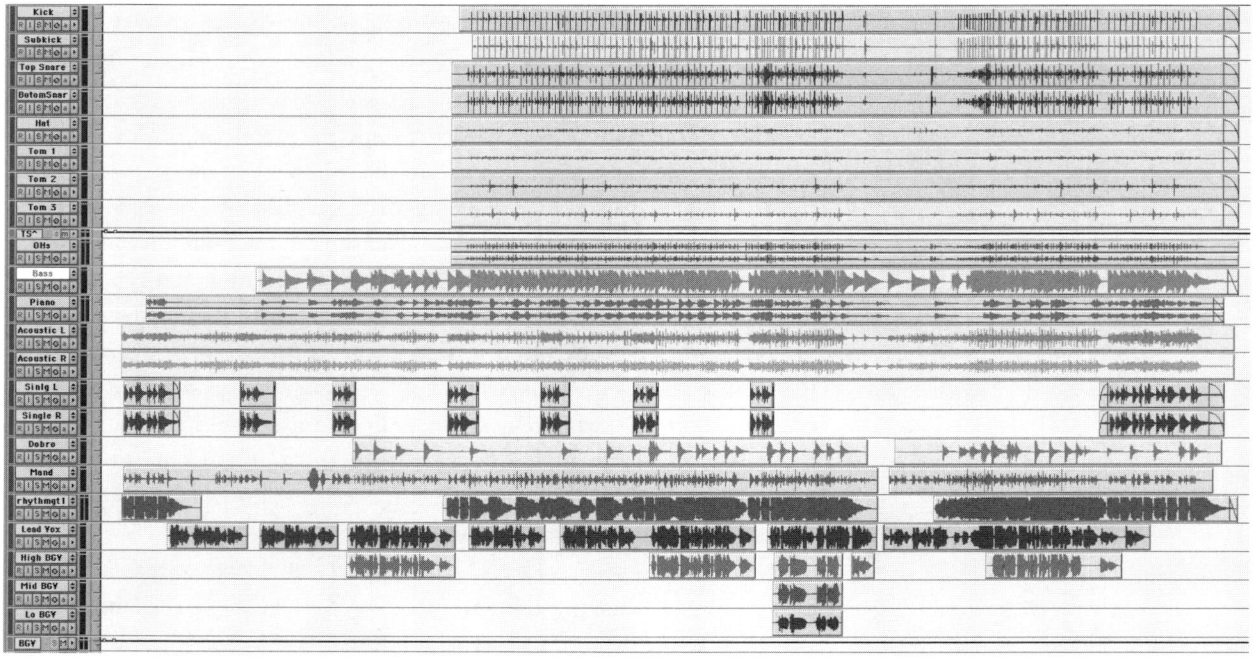

Fig. 8.43. Edits

A few changes were made to the audio tracks at the mixing stage of "Stealing Kisses." To start with, all of the tracks were cleared from the beginning of the session to the point where the instruments on each of those tracks entered. For example, the drum tracks were cleared from the beginning of the session to the point where they begin playing. In addition to that, fades were created on the drum tracks at the end of the song. Fades were also created at the end of the bass, piano, single line guitar, and rhythm guitar tracks. More for visual convenience than any other reason, the single line acoustic track was separated into regions that contain audio data; those parts of the track that don't contain audio data were cleared, and fades were created at the beginning and end of each of those regions. For the same reasons, the electric guitar and vocal tracks were also cleared during those areas that don't contain audio.

About three minutes in, the song has a moment that's close to silent; the dobro, mandolin, electric guitar, and lead vocal tracks were cleared (for varying lengths of time) at that point, mostly to remove extraneous noises that would otherwise be heard.

Fig. 8.44. Clear Audio

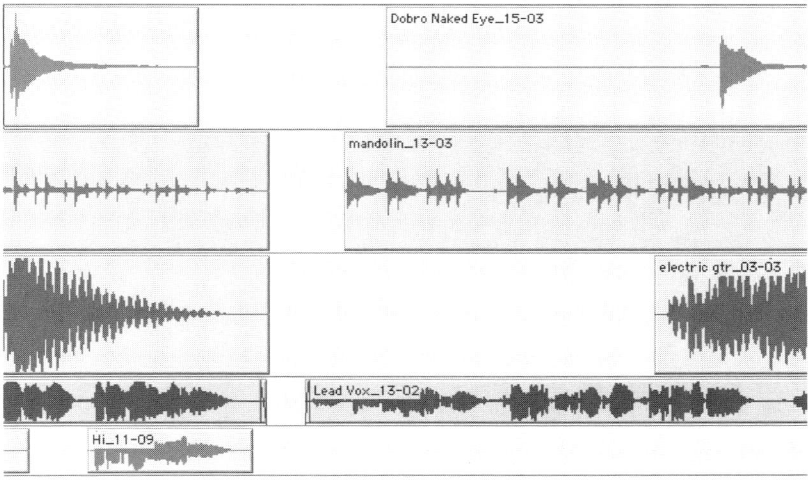

PRINTING MIXES

When printing the mix of each of the songs in this volume, a consistent approach was used: a track is used to set the final length of the song. The start and end times for printing the mix of "Stealing Kisses" were set by selecting the acoustic guitar track. In Pro Tools, selecting this trimmed track will cause the program to play from the beginning to the end of that track with no excess audio or time at the beginning or end. In those situations where multiple mixes of a song must be done—for example, if a producer wants vocal up or vocal down versions, TV mixes, instrumental mixes—all of the versions are the same length, and can be easily lined up for editing.

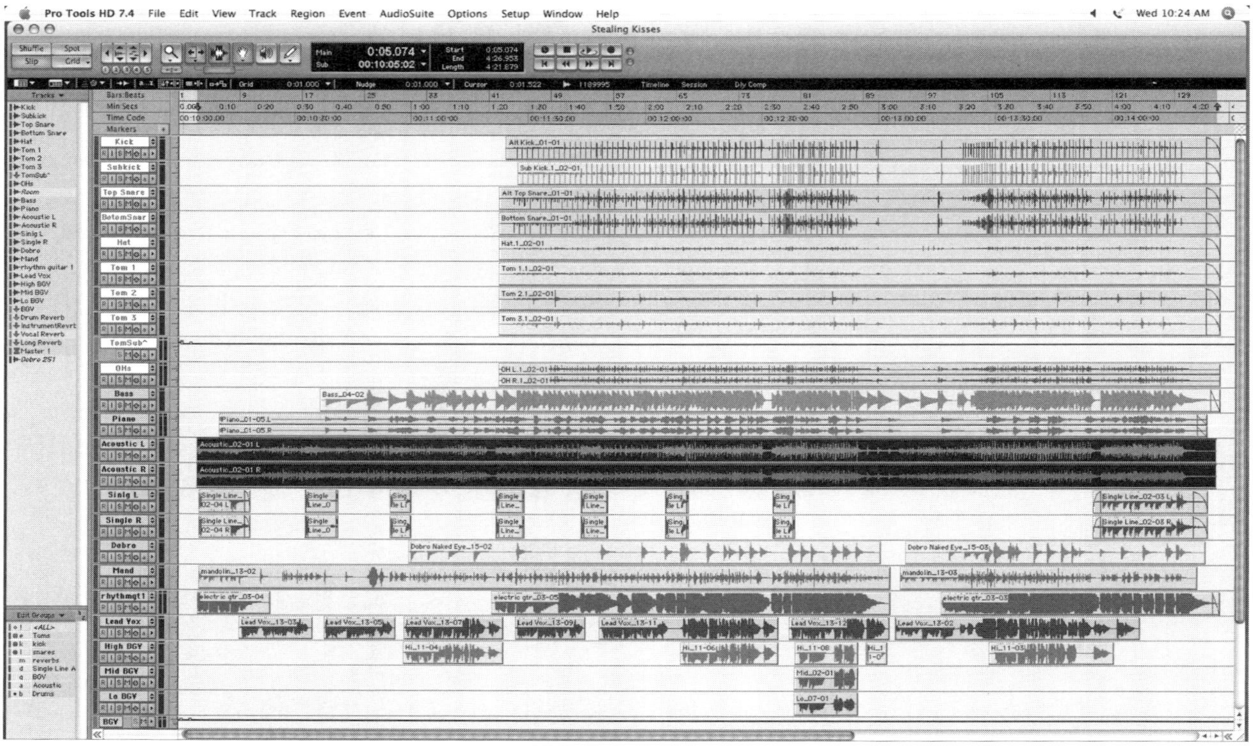

Fig. 8.45. Print Mix

CHAPTER 9

"Summertime"

(As Recorded by Kenny Chesney)

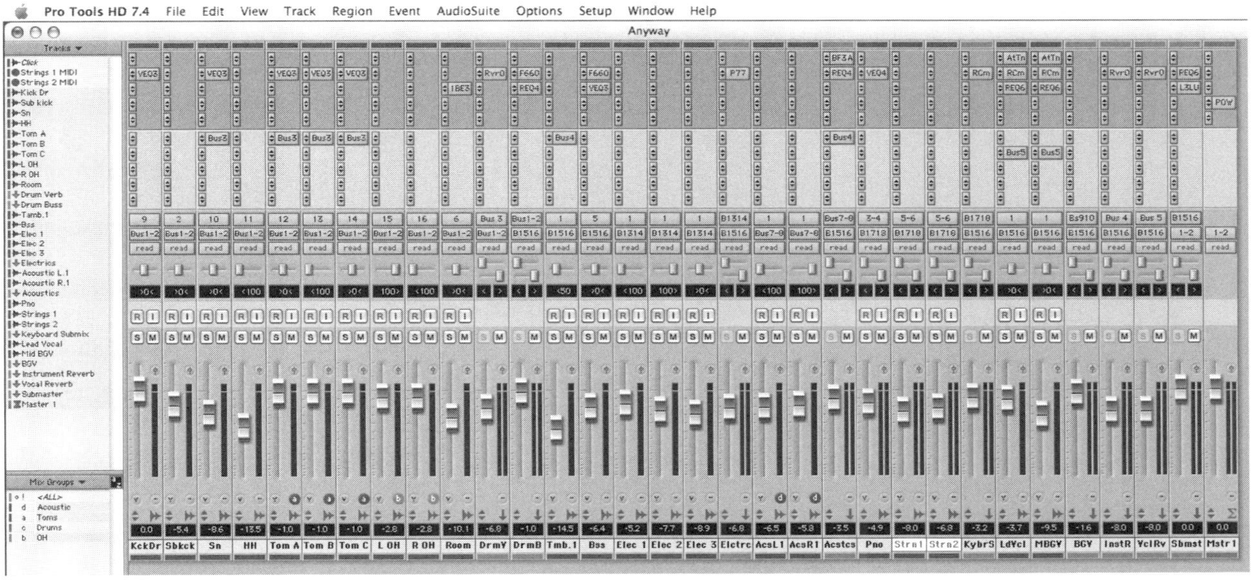

Fig. 9.1. Mix Window

"Summertime" is another song with so much stuff going on that finding space for it all can be a bit of a trick. Banjo, big drums, wah-wah guitar, and even a whispered background vocal track give "Summertime" its distinctive sound.

DRUMS

The drum tracks on "Summertime" were recorded without EQ and with little or no compression so that the mixing process could be made a bit more informative; if all the needed processing was done in the tracking stage, then there would be little to talk about concerning the mixing of the drums other than pushing the faders up to the appropriate levels. Besides that, the lack of processing at the recording stage means that the raw tracks can be manipulated in a bit more creative manner at the mixing stage. "Summertime," has two kick drum tracks: one, labeled "kick," was recorded with a Shure Beta 52 microphone placed inside the drum about three inches from the batter head while the "subkick" track was recorded with a Yamaha Subkick placed directly in front of the drum. These two signals sound quite different from each other; most mixing engineers will combine the two sounds while processing each as needed to create the final kick drum sound.

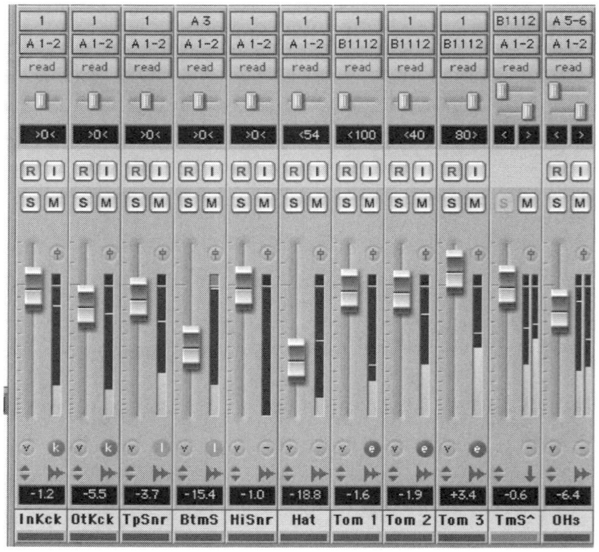

fig. 9.2. Drum Mix

In addition to the two kick tracks, there are a total of three snare tracks in this mix—a top and bottom snare track for the main snare drum as well as a track for a high, or "popcorn," snare that's used as an accent to the main snare.

Kick Drum

The inside kick drum track did not need a lot of processing, so only a 4-band Waves Renaissance EQ was used. The EQ provided a small (0.4 dB) rise at 44 Hz, a 3.2 dB boost at 644 Hz and a substantial boost of around 4.5 dB at 1.4 and 3.7 kHz. The main kick fader level was –1.2 dB.

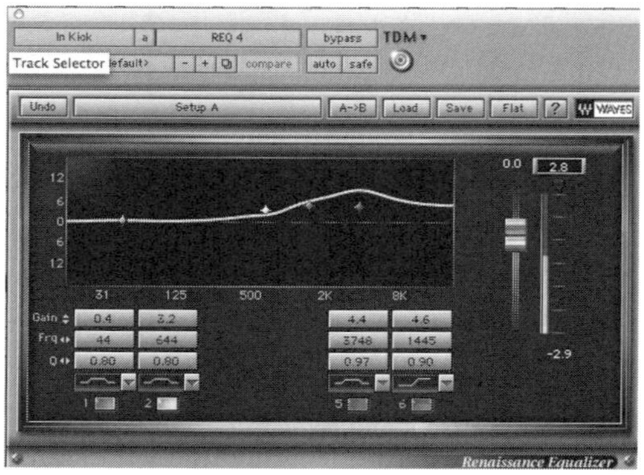

Fig. 9.3. In-Kick EQ

Waves Renaissance REQ-4 In-Kick Settings				
parameter	**band 1**	**band 2**	**band 3**	**band 4**
gain	+0.4 dB	+3.2 dB	+4.4 dB	+4.6 dB
frequency	44 Hz	644 Hz	3,748 Hz	1,445 Hz
Q	0.80	0.80	0.97	0.90
shape	bell	bell	bell	shelf

Subkick

The Yamaha Subkick was again used for the outside kick drum track. The subkick is essentially a speaker that's wired with an XLR connection so that it can be used as a microphone. Of course, a speaker is a pretty inefficient microphone, and it doesn't handle high frequencies well. That's what makes it perfect for this application, where high sound pressure levels are the norm and high frequencies aren't wanted. The 4-band Renaissance EQ was boosted by 2.3 dB at 46 Hz and cut by 2 dB at 536 Hz. The output level of the out-kick track was –5.5 dB.

Fig. 9.4. Out-Kick EQ

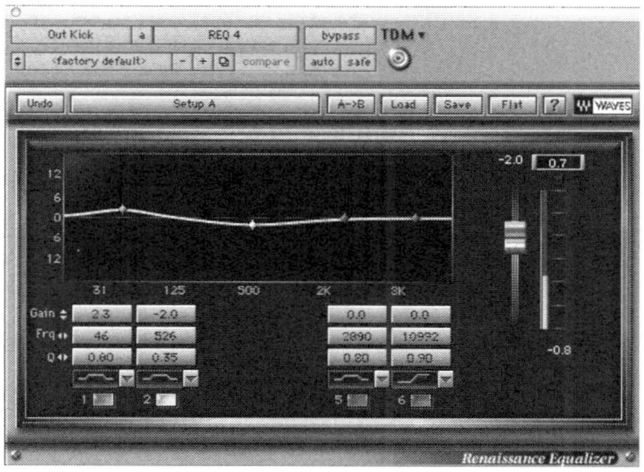

Waves Renaissance REQ-4 Out-Kick Settings				
parameter	**band 1**	**band 2**	**band 3**	**band 4**
gain	+2.3 dB	–2.0 dB	0 dB	0 dB
frequency	46 Hz	526 Hz	2,890 Hz	10,992 Hz
Q	0.80	1.02	0.80	0.90
shape	bell	bell	bell	shelf

Snare Drum

The snare drums on “Summertime” were a Gretsch 5-inch maple snare that was used as the main snare and a Legend Phosphor Bronze 3.5” ¥ 14” snare drum that was used as the high snare. It’s not at all uncommon, by the way, for session drummers to bring as many as a half dozen different snare drums to a session; by doing so, they can be reasonably sure that they have the appropriate snare drum for any song. The engineers don’t tell them, “We’re going to EQ the snare tracks so they all sound the same …”

Top Snare

Partly to help to differentiate the sounds of the main and high snare drums, a Shure SM57 was used on the main snare (the other reason the SM57 was used was because the KM 84 that has been used on some of the other songs in this volume was moved over to the high snare for this song). The output level of the top snare track was –3.7 dB. Two reverb sends were used for the top snare—the drum reverb level was at –9.2 dB and the gate reverb level was –6.2 dB.

Fig. 9.5. Top Snare EQ

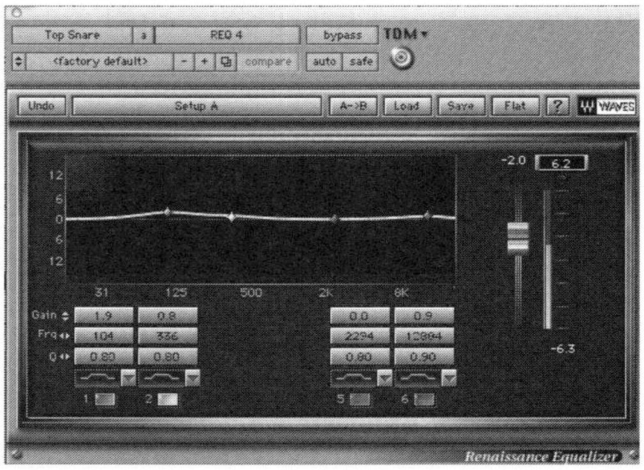

Waves Renaissance REQ-4 Top Snare Settings				
parameter	band 1	band 2	band 3	band 4
gain	+1.9 dB	+0.8 dB	0 dB	+0.9 dB
frequency	104 Hz	336 Hz	2,294 Hz	12,884 Hz
Q	0.80	1.02	0.80	0.90
shape	bell	bell	bell	bell

Bottom Snare

A Neumann KM 84 was used for the bottom snare track. There’s a 2-band Renaissance EQ on the track that high passes the bottom snare track at 93 Hz while the other EQ band slightly boosts at 8.7 kHz. The output of the bottom snare track is –15.4 dB.

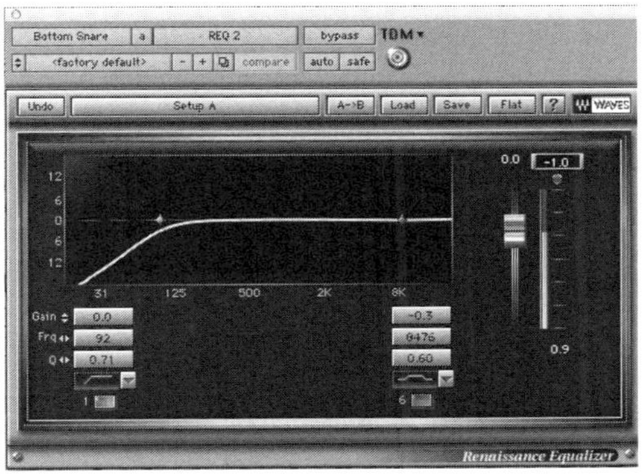

Fig. 9.6. Bottom Snare EQ

Waves Renaissance REQ-2 Bottom Snare Settings		
parameter	**band 1**	**band 2**
gain	0 dB	–0.3 dB
frequency	92 Hz	8,746 Hz
Q	0.71	0.60
shape	high pass	bell

High Snare

As discussed earlier, the high snare track was recorded using a Neumann KM 84; this is a small diaphragm condenser microphone that has, in the years since it went out of production, become one of the most highly regarded microphones in the Neumann line. There's some question as to whether this respect is based solely on the sound of the KM 84, or if it's partly a reflection of how bad most of the current small diaphragm mics sound. In any case, the high snare was set up on the drummer's left—to the left of the hi-hat. The high snare track uses a 4-band Renaissance EQ and a Waves C1 Gate. The output level of the high snare is –1.0 dB.

Notice that some fairly radical equalization is taking place; besides the low frequency cut, the 300 Hz range is boosted by 302 dB and there's a 9.4 dB boost at 3.1 kHz along with a high frequency shelving boost at 12.6 kHz. This kind of EQ can affect not only the high snare, but also the other drum sounds due to bleed into the mic—especially the hi-hat, since that was physically quite close to the high snare. To minimize the tonal changes caused by bleed into the high snare microphone, two remedial actions were taken—the first was the insertion of the Waves C1 gate on the high snare track; this removed most of the problem. The rest was removed from the high snare track by the expedient of clearing all of the audio from the track itself, leaving only the high snare hits. Either clearing the unneeded audio or using the gate would work for this track; both were done to show alternative approaches.

Fig. 9.7a. High Snare Gate

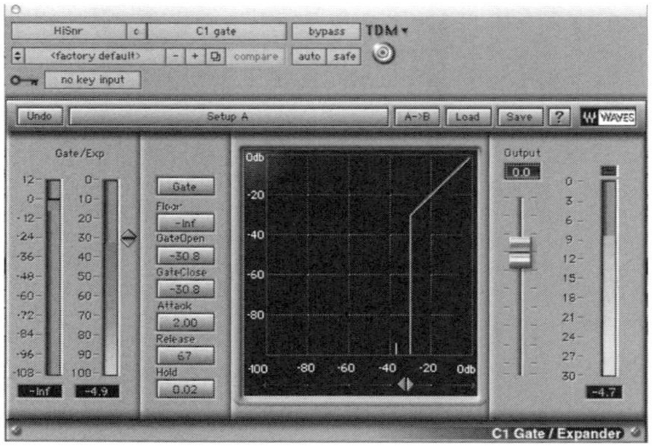

Waves Renaissance REQ-4 High Snare Settings				
parameter	**band 1**	**band 2**	**band 3**	**band 4**
gain	–10.9 dB	+3.2 dB	+9.4 dB	+1.1 dB
frequency	25 Hz	339 Hz	3,107 Hz	12,608 Hz
Q	0.30	1.63	0.63	0.90
shape	bell	bell	bell	bell

Fig. 9.7b. High Snare EQ

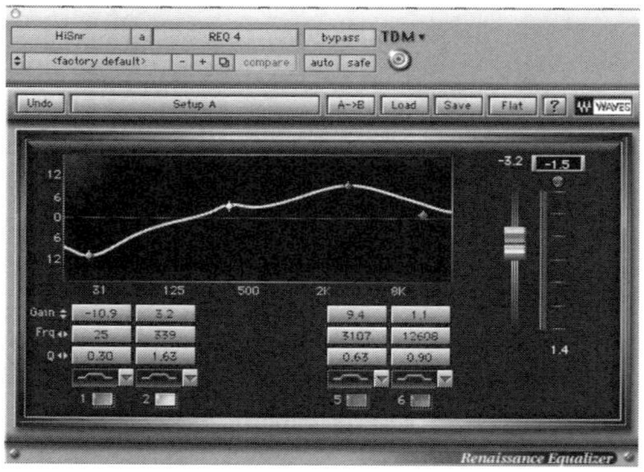

Waves C1 Gate for High Snare Settings					
floor	**gate open**	**gate close**	**attack**	**release**	**hold**
infinite	–30.8 db	–30.8 db	2.00	67	0.02

Hi-hat

The 2-band Renaissance EQ on the hi-hat track has two purposes: the first is to high pass those frequencies below 274 Hz, while the other is to add a slight 0.4 dB boost at 813 kHz. The output level of the hi-hat track is –18.8 dB.

Fig. 9.8. Hat EQ

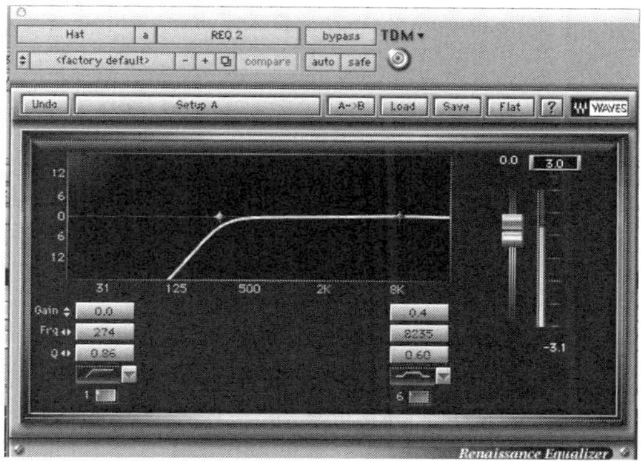

Waves Renaissance REQ-2 Hat Settings		
parameter	**band 1**	**band 2**
gain	0 dB	+0.4 dB
frequency	274 Hz	8,325 Hz
Q	0.86	0.60
shape	high pass	bell

Toms

A number of different approaches to minimizing hum and bleed in the tom tracks have been discussed in this book. On some mixes, the bleed and tom hum were accepted and even celebrated, so it was left alone to be what it is. With other mixes, the toms were gated to remove such things. The levels of the tom tracks have been automated to reduce the level of hum. For "Summertime," a new approach is used; the audio will be cleared from the tom tracks except for those places where the toms are actually used. This action can primarily be done visually, and here's how:

First, I'll group the three tom tracks (if they're not already grouped) so that any action done to one track is done to all three tracks. Looking at the three tom tracks, it's easy to note where the tom fills take place; I put the cursor within a beat of the first tom hit (on any track) and select the audio from that point to a place a couple of beats after the last tom hit. I separate that region (the keyboard shortcut with a Mac-based Pro Tools system is Command+E) and then move to the next place where a tom is used, and then repeat the process. Once all the tom fills have been separated, the regions without tom fills are selected and cleared from the track (the keyboard shortcut is Command+B).

Finally, the beginning and ending of each of the remaining regions need to have fades added, so that there will be no pops or clicks as the regions begin and end. There are two ways to add the fades to multiple regions: the fast way and the good way. The fast way is to select all of the regions in the track and hit Command+F; this adds a short fade to the beginning and end of each region that will eliminate pops and clicks. But it will also cause the audio on the track to go from off to full volume very fast; having the audio come to a quick end at the end of each region (where the final tom hit is fading down) will be audible (and most likely distracting). Therefore, it will sound better to add manual fades to the end of each of the tom fill regions.

By zooming in on a single region and selecting an area before the first hit (approximately one beat) and using the Command+F keystroke, I can create a longer fade. Alternatively, the Pro Tools Smart Tool will create fades when it's placed at the top of the audio track at the beginning of the region. Typically, though, it's not the beginning of the tom fills that need a long fade—it's the end of each fill. The idea is for the fade at the end of the region to blend with the decay of the toms, or if the fade lasts longer than the tom decay, to use the fade to blend the region back into the rest of the drum track without an audible change in the sound of the drums.

Fig. 9.9. Tom Edit

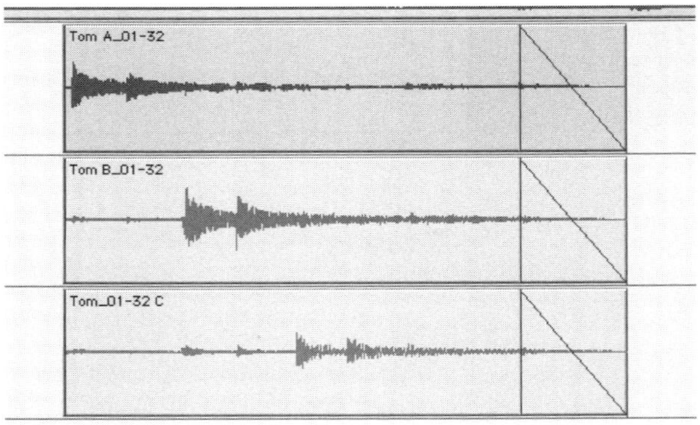

The fader level of the first tom is –1.6 dB, the second tom is –1.9 dB, and the third tom is +3.4 dB. The three tom tracks are sent to the tom buss, where a 4-band Renaissance EQ and a Renaissance compressor are inserted.

Tom Buss

A 4-band Waves Renaissance EQ and a Renaissance Compressor are used on the tom buss; the EQ boosts 60 Hz by 2.4 dB, 2.2 kHz by 3.5 dB, and 9.3 kHz by 1.8 dB. The Renaissance Compressor has a 3.7:1 compression ratio and a threshold of –8.3 dB; the maximum gain reduction from the compressor is less than 3 dB. The relatively slow 16-millisecond attack time allows the transient peaks to be heard, and the output of the compressor was raised by 2 dB. The output of the tom buss (which is sent to the master output) is –0.6 dB, and a send to the drum reverb is at –12 9 dB.

Fig. 9.10. Tom Buss EQ

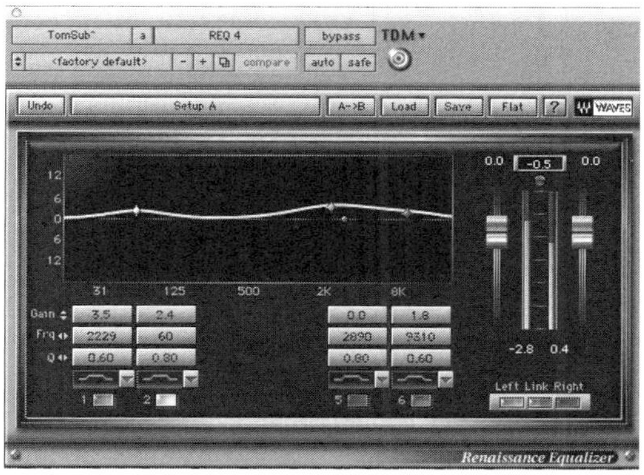

Waves Renaissance REQ-4 Tom Buss Settings				
parameter	**band 1**	**band 2**	**band 3**	**band 4**
gain	+3.5dB	+2.4 dB	0 dB	+1.8 dB
frequency	2,229 Hz	60 Hz	2,890 Hz	9,310 Hz
Q	0.60	0.80	0.80	0.60
shape	bell	bell	(inactive)	bell

Fig. 9.11. Tom Buss Compressor

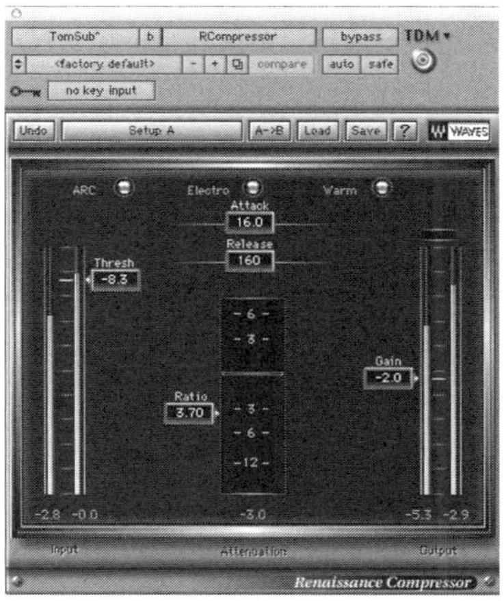

Waves Renaissance Compressor Tom Buss Settings				
threshold	**attack**	**release**	**ratio**	**gain**
–8.3 dB	16.0	160	3.70:1	+2.0 dB

Mics

Overhead and room mics were used on this song.

Overheads

The overhead tracks (recorded with a pair of Telefunken M-16 microphones through a Phoenix DRS-2 preamp) escaped further processing on "Summertime," and the output level of the overhead track was –0.6 dB.

Room

Like the overheads, the room mic was not processed at the mix stage; the output fader level was set to –19.9 dB. This level of the room mic can add a bit of the tracking room's ambience to the mix without becoming overly "roomy." As discussed in other chapters, various amounts of processing can be added to the room track, converting it from a subtle ambience to an over-the-top crunch; the appropriate direction in which to take the room track is generally song specific.

BASS

The bass track used a Waves Renaissance Compressor and a 2-band Waves Renaissance EQ as plug-ins. The output fader of the bass was set at –4.0 dB. Not a whole lot of gain reduction was used on the bass track; the compressor was added primarily to even out any inequities in the bass, while the EQ was primarily used to add warmth to the low end of the track. The maximum gain reduction from the Renaissance Compressor used on the bass track was less than 2 dB.

You may notice that the low band of the Renaissance EQ is centered at 31 Hz; remember that since the Q setting affects the width of an EQ band—that is, the lower the number, the wider the frequency range affect by any changes to the level of that band. Even though the center frequency is quite low—below the cut-off point for most speakers—the Q setting is quite wide. This means that a fairly wide range of frequencies that *can* be reproduced are also affected by the first EQ band. The second band cut 2.6 dB centered at 114 Hz.

Fig. 9.12. Bass Compressor

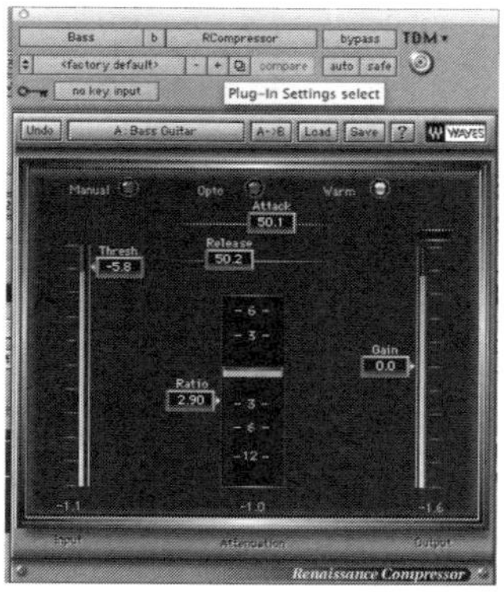

Waves Renaissance Compressor Bass Settings				
threshold	attack	release	ratio	gain
–5.8 dB	50.1	50.2	2.90:1	0 dB

Fig. 9.13. Bass EQ

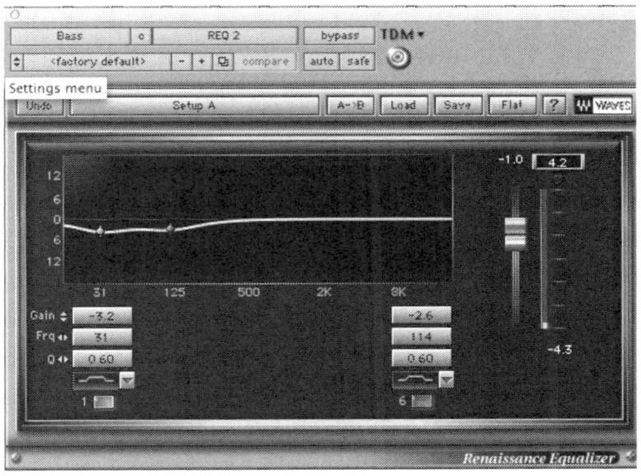

Waves Renaissance REQ-2 Bass Settings

parameter	band 1	band 2
gain	–3.2 dB	–2.6 dB
frequency	31 Hz	114 Hz
Q	0.60	0.60
shape	bell	bell

BANJO

Banjos, like violas and accordions, are another of those often maligned and mistreated instruments. People make jokes about banjos and banjo players almost as often and they make jokes about accordions and their owners. (Q. What's the difference between a banjo and a trampoline? A. You take your shoes off to jump on a trampoline.) A good banjo is really loud, by the way—and percussive; the transient peaks can require the use of a limiter (with a compression ratio in excess of 10:1 to control banjo tracks that aren't played by an extremely competent musician. In the case of "Summertime," the banjo was played by an extremely competent musician so a compressor wasn't needed.

When recording banjo, I normally need the rhythmic effect of the instrument, along with the upper mid range and high end of the tone. A single small diaphragm mic tends to be my mic of choice for a banjo; a tube mic like the Neumann/Gefell M-582 works great here, as does a Neumann KM 84. When I use an equalizer plug-in on a banjo track, I'm typically rolling off unnecessary low end; a high-pass filter set somewhere between 100 and 300 Hz works well, though high passing can be a bit drastic. On "Summertime," a shelving EQ centered at 46 Hz with a wide Q removed the appropriate amount of low frequency information. If the banjo seems excessively bright, a low-pass filter or a shelving EQ can lower the levels of the high end. But on "Summertime," a boost of 1.4 dB at 8.7 kHz was deemed to be the best solution. The output of the banjo track was set to −10.4 dB, with a send to the drum reverb of −18.2 dB.

Though they aren't all that common, a number of hybrid instruments with banjo bodies are available—a Banjolin has a mandolin neck on a banjo body (with mandolin strings and mandolin tuning), a Gitjo (also called a banjitar) is a guitar with a banjo body, and so forth. When these appear (as the guitjo does, from time to time), they're generally mixed in more or less the same way as a banjo.

Fig. 9.14. Banjo EQ

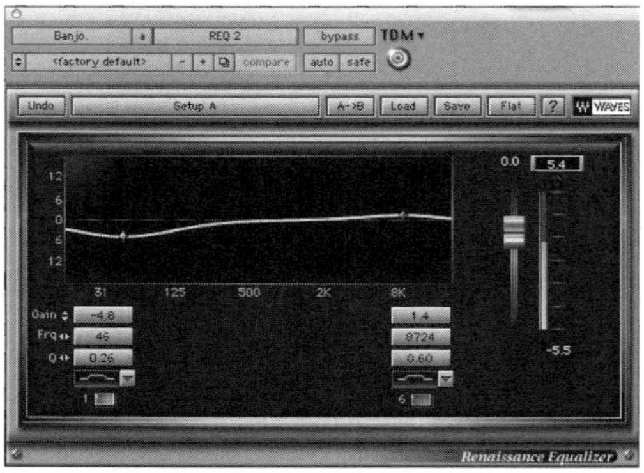

Waves Renaissance REQ-2 Banjo Settings		
parameter	**band 1**	**band 2**
gain	–4.8 dB	+1.4 dB
frequency	46 Hz	8,724 Hz
Q	0.26	0.60
shape	bell	bell

PIANO

Unlike some of the other tracks included with this volume, the piano is used primarily as a rhythm instrument (in other words, there are no sections where the piano is playing fills). Its role in the mix is to add body and fullness, not necessarily for the piano part to be heard through the mix. The output level of the piano was set at –8.0 dB, and a 4-band Waves Renaissance EQ was used on the track. The EQ settings brightened the piano track as a whole by reducing low frequencies with a 2.6 dB cut at 25 Hz and a 3.3 dB cut at 189 Hz, and boosting high frequencies—a 3.5 dB boost at 4 kHz and a 1.9 dB boost a little below 14 kHz ensured that the piano track would be bright.

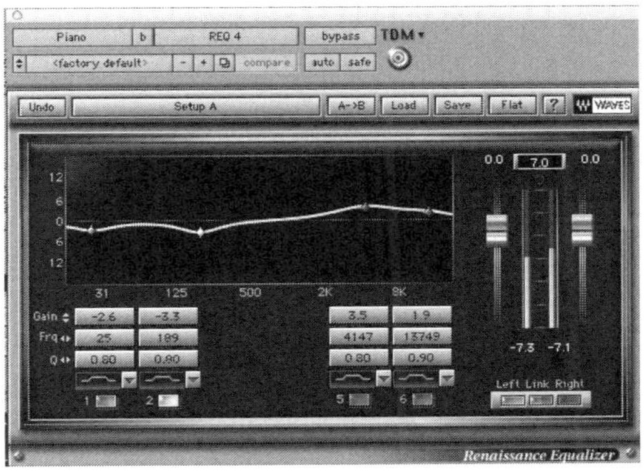

Fig. 9.15. Piano EQ

Waves Renaissance REQ-4 Piano Settings				
parameter	**band 1**	**band 2**	**band 3**	**band 4**
gain	–2.6 dB	–3.3 dB	+3.5 dB	+1.9 dB
frequency	25 Hz	189 Hz	4,147 Hz	13,749 Hz
Q	0.80	0.80	0.80	0.90
shape	bell	bell	bell	bell

ORGAN

The organ used on all of the tracks in this volume, a 1957 Hammond C-3 with a Leslie 21H cabinet, was recorded in a consistent manner—with a pair of AEA R84s at two corners of the cabinet to capture the upper rotor, and an Electro-Voice RE20 capturing the lower rotor. The three microphones were bussed to a stereo track with the R84s panned hard left and right and the RE20 panned in the middle. The relative levels between the upper rotor and the lower rotor were determined at the stereo buss at the recording stage. For "Summertime," the organ track had the high frequencies boosted with a 2.8 dB rise at 14 kHz. Though in some circumstances, a 2.8 dB boost may be considered as substantial, in the case of the Hammond/Leslie combination, this boost is more of a subtle tonal chance, since there's very little information coming out of the Leslie cabinet that high. In addition, the ribbon microphones used to record the Leslie have a high frequency roll-off that begins around 4 kHz, and is down by 304 dB at 14 kHz. Nevertheless, the boost at 14 kHz is subtle but audible. The output level of the organ track was –12.3 dB.

Fig. 9.16. Organ EQ

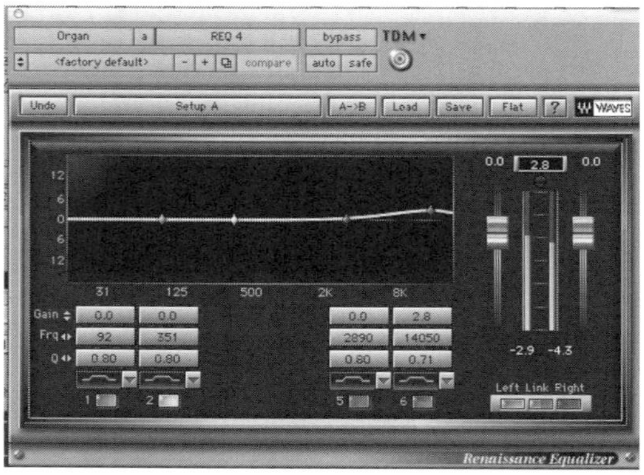

Waves Renaissance REQ-4 Piano Settings				
parameter	**band 1**	**band 2**	**band 3**	**band 4**
gain	0 dB	0 dB	0 dB	+2.8 dB
frequency	92 Hz	351 Hz	2,890 Hz	14,050 Hz
Q	0.80	0.80	0.80	0.90
shape	bell	bell	bell	bell

ACOUSTIC GUITARS

"Summertime" uses a simple 2-band EQ on each of the two acoustic guitar tracks. The first EQ band on each track was used as a high-pass filter, clearing away unneeded low frequency information while the second EQ band is used to add a presence peak that allows the acoustic to cut through the mix. The acoustic left track output is at –8.0 dB, while the acoustic right output is at –6.8 dB. No reverb was necessary on the acoustic guitar tracks.

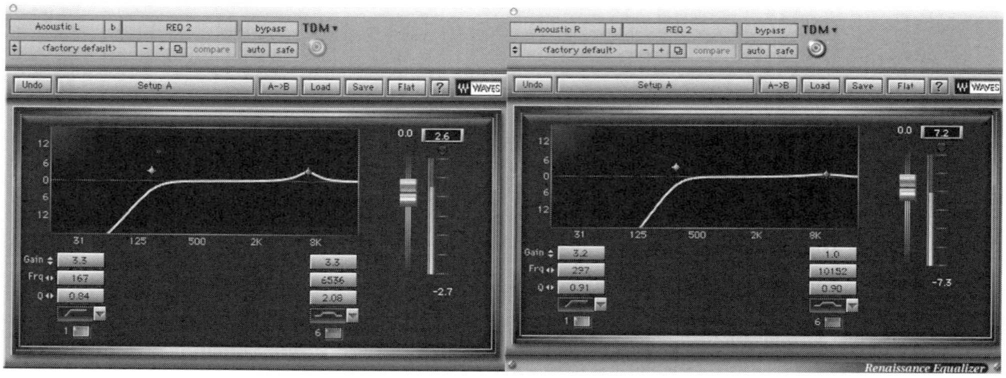

Fig. 9.17. Acoustic Guitar EQ

Waves Renaissance REQ-2 Acoustic L Settings		
parameter	band 1	band 2
gain	+3.3 dB	+3.3 dB
frequency	167 Hz	6,536 Hz
Q	1.10	2.08
shape	high pass	bell

Waves Renaissance REQ-2 Acoustic R Settings		
parameter	band 1	band 2
gain	+3.2 dB	+1.0 dB
frequency	297 Hz	10,152 Hz
Q	0.91	0.90
shape	high pass	bell

ELECTRIC GUITAR

Though electric guitars have been a part of country music since the mid-1940s when Ernest Tubb became the first Grand Ole Opry member to regularly feature the instrument, the role of the guitar has changed dramatically in many ways since then. Though there are some contemporary recordings where the electric is playing in what we'd now consider a "country" style, it's a lot more common for the electric guitar to have a role with roots in '80s rock than in the Grand Ole Opry. This is quite fitting, of course, since the same thing has happened with the other instruments used on country records these days.

When dealing with electric guitars at mix time, it's much more common to add an EQ plug-in to an electric guitar track than a compressor; it's in the nature of tube guitar amps to effectively compress the signal—and even more so when big distorted guitars are part of the track. It's also very common for electric guitarists to use a compressor box between their guitars and amplifiers. When the guitar sound is already compressed before it is recorded, the biggest reason to use yet another compressor plug-in when mixing is for the tone that the compressor imparts—unless the compressor is used as an effect rather than for level control.

When EQ'ing electric guitar, a high-pass filter at 100 Hz is a good idea—unless you're dealing with drop-tuned guitars, there's not a lot of useable information below 100 Hz. Even if there is, high passing at 100 Hz and then boosting around 120 Hz will add punch to a chunky rhythm. If the electric guitar sounds boxy, try working with the frequencies in the 200 to 300 Hz range. Adding (or reducing) bite requires adjustments in the 2 to 3 kHz range. Most guitar amps have little usable sonic information above 5 kHz, though some guitar tracks (especially those that are not distorted) may actually benefit from a bit of a boost in the 5 kHz range. The rest will likely be better served by rolling off those frequencies above 5 kHz.

The last few years have seen the introduction of a number of worthwhile amp simulators—Amp Farm, Amplitube, the Waves GTR stuff—though in most cases, these work best when the guitar is recorded through a DI. They can also be put to good use to change the tone of a recorded guitar, or to add effects that were not recorded. Typically, I'll start with one of the cleaner amp emulations (since adding more distortion to a distorted guitar seems a bit silly). An amp simulator can change the tone of a recorded guitar in ways that an EQ plug-in can't duplicate, so they should be kept in mind as usable mixing tools for exactly that reason. While none of the guitar tracks on "Summertime" were processed using an amp simulator—the tones were created while recording— the practice is becoming more common.

Talk Box Guitar

The talk box guitar track on "Summertime" was recorded using a Rocktron Banshee talk box. The talk box is essentially a driver attached to a length of surgical tubing; the output of a guitar goes to an amplifier, which sends a signal to the driver. The sound from the driver travels up the tubing to the guitarist's mouth, which shapes the sounds. A microphone picks up the sounds from the tube after they are modulated by the guitarist's mouth cavity.

The talk box was made famous by '70s rocker Peter Frampton, who used a tall box designed by legendary PA designer Bob Heil. The Rocktron Banshee, unlike the earlier Heil talk box, doesn't require an external amplifier (making it much more practical to use). A Shure SM58 was used to capture the sound of the talk box.

The level of the talk box track is –12.9 dB, and one band of a 2-band Waves Renaissance EQ was used to lower 8.6 kHz by 2.4 dB. A send to the instrument reverb was at –10.1 dB.

Fig. 9.18. Talk Box EQ

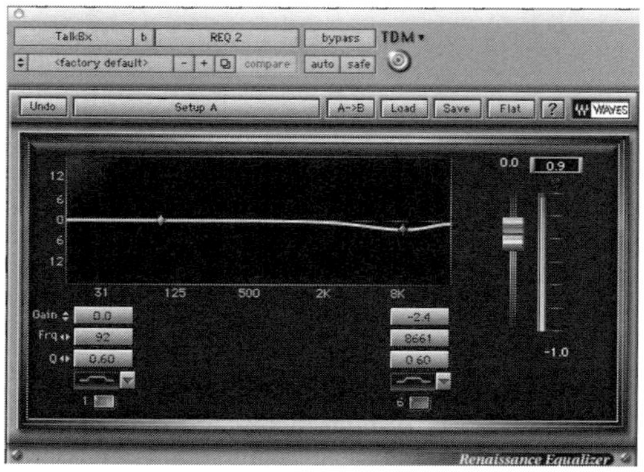

Waves Renaissance REQ-2 Talk Box Guitar Settings		
parameter	band 1	band 2
gain	0 dB	–2.4 dB
frequency	92 Hz	8,661 Hz
Q	0.60	0.90
shape	bell	bell

Arpeggio Guitar

This guitar is playing broken chords or arpeggios. The arpeggio guitar track also used one band of a 2-band Renaissance EQ; this EQ band lowered 14.2 kHz by 7.3 dB, taking some of the edge off of the guitar sound. Three different reverbs were used with the arpeggio guitar: the send to the instrument reverb was at –18.3 dB, the send to the vocal reverb was at –10.7 dB, and the gate reverb send was at –14.8 dB.

Fig. 9.19. Arpeggio Guitar EQ

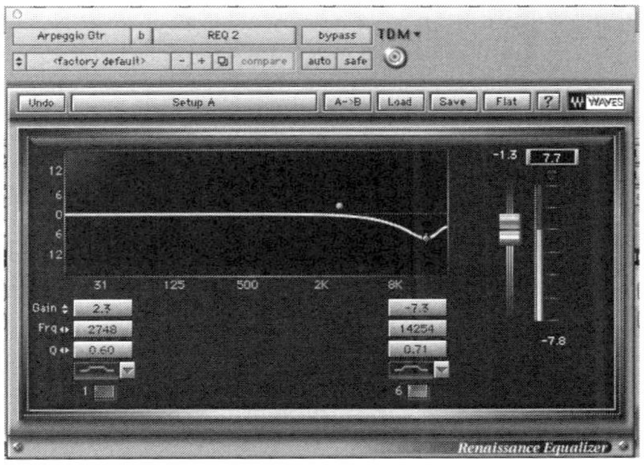

Waves Renaissance REQ-2 Arpeggio Guitar Settings		
parameter	band 1	band 2
gain	+2.3 dB	–7.3 dB
frequency	2,748 Hz	14,254 Hz
Q	0.60	0.71
shape	inactive	bell

Rhythm Guitar

The rhythm guitar track consists of two different parts: during the verses, the guitar is dead-strummed, so that it functions as a percussive instrument, and during the choruses, it plays a more normal rhythm part. A 2-band Renaissance EQ was used to lower the 70 Hz area by 4.4 dB, which keeps the dead-strummed part from taking up too much room in the mix. The output of the rhythm guitar was set to –13.5 dB.

Fig. 9.20. Rhythm EQ

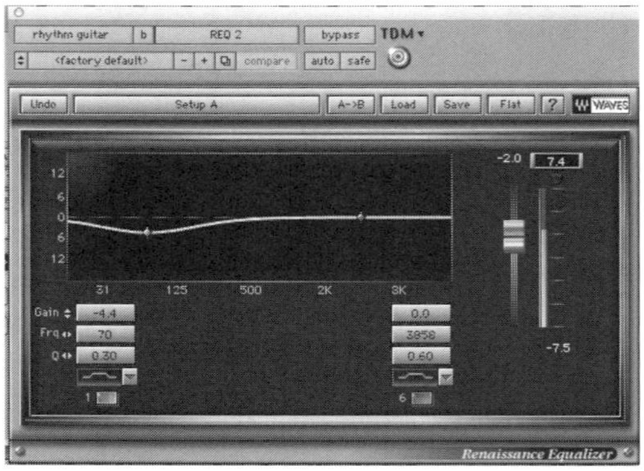

Waves Renaissance REQ-2 Rhythm Guitar Settings		
parameter	**band 1**	**band 2**
gain	–4.4 dB	0 dB
frequency	70 Hz	3,858 Hz
Q	0.30	0.60
shape	bell	bell

Solo Guitar

The solo guitar has a 2-band Renaissance EQ reducing low frequencies by a little over 2 dB, and a Waves TrueVerb set to a modified Rock Guitar Room preset. Where other instances of the Rock Guitar Room preset were fairly dry (with the early reflections as the primary goal), this particular instance raises the reverb level substantially. The plug-in was used as an insert rather than as an auxiliary effect in large part because this particular sound is only used on the solo guitar.

Fig. 9.21. Solo Guitar EQ

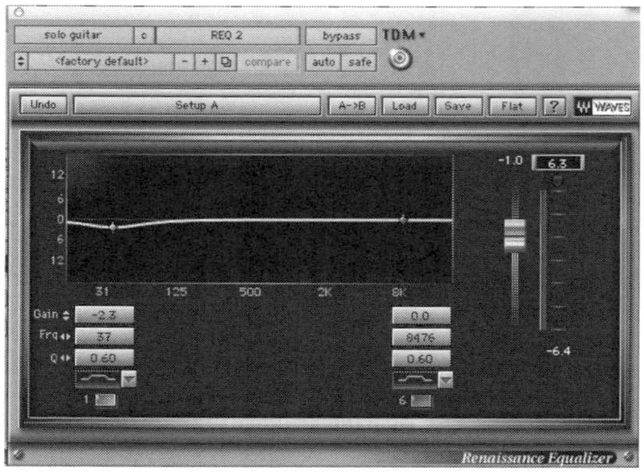

Waves Renaissance REQ-2 Rhythm Guitar Settings		
parameter	**band 1**	**band 2**
gain	–2.3 dB	0 dB
frequency	37 Hz	8,756 Hz
Q	0.60	0.60
shape	bell	bell

Fig. 9.22. Solo Guitar Reverb

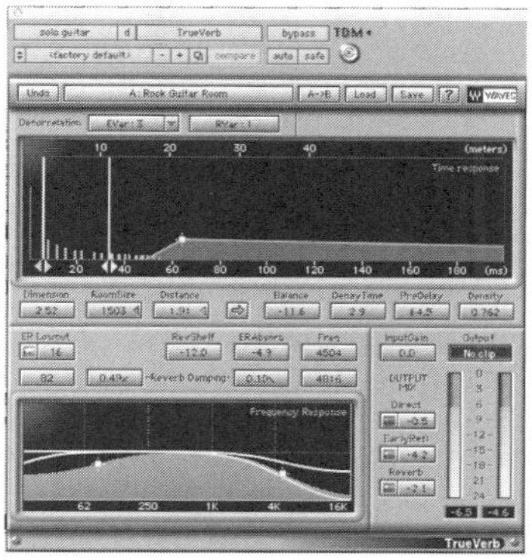

Waves TrueVerb Solo Guitar Settings	
parameter	**setting**
dimension	2.52
room size	1503
distance	1.91
balance	–11.6
decay time	2.9
predelay	64.5
density	0.762
EARLY REFLECTION (ER)	
low cut	16
reverb damping frequency low	82
damping	0.49x
reverb damping frequency high	4816
damping	0.10x
reverb shelf	–12.0
ER absorb	–4.9
ER absorb freq	4504
input gain	0.0
direct output	–0.5 dB
early reflection output	–4.2 dB
reverb output	–2.1 dB

LEAD VOCAL

Four plug-ins were used on the lead vocal chain for this mix: a Trim plug-in, Auto-Tune 4, a Renaissance Compressor, and a 6-band Renaissance EQ.

The trim plug-in hasn't been used on the lead vocal track before now; there are two reasons for using the trim in this manner; the first is to avoid overloading plug-ins that follow it in the signal chain. The second reason (and for some mixers, the primary reason) for using it is that once all of the needed automation is written to a track, that track as a whole may end up being too loud for the rest of the mix. While a "too loud" track can be remedied in a number of ways, inserting a trim plug-in can be the simplest answer to the problem. With Digidesign's Pro Tools, these remedies include reducing the output level of one or more of the plug-ins as well as reducing the overall level of the track in the edit window. The trim setting is at –1.9 dB.

Fig. 9.23. Lead Vocal Trim

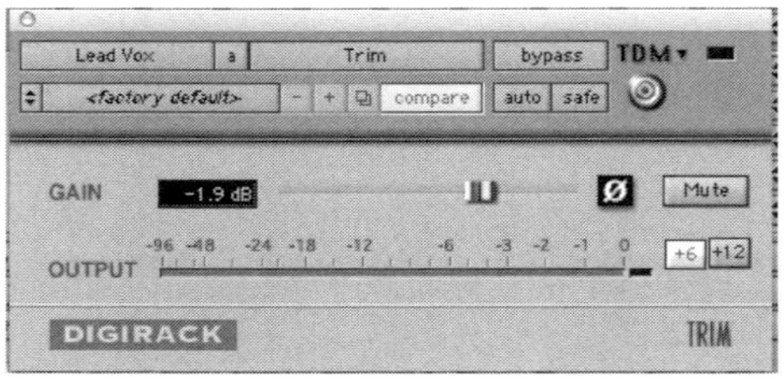

Following the trim plug-in is an instance of Auto-Tune 4, with mild settings; the retune speed is set to 63, and the tracking parameter is at 74. For a discussion of Auto-Tune in contemporary country mixes, please refer to previous chapters.

Next up is a Waves Renaissance Compressor, used in a somewhat different manner than in the past. In this case, the compressor is used as an expander, restoring a bit of the dynamic range that may have been lost in the recording process.

Expansion

Compression ratios—that is, any compression ratio greater than 1:1—reduce the gain of any signals which exceed the threshold (this is the onset of compression). So a 4:1 compression ratio means that for every 4 dB that the signal exceeds the threshold, the output of the compressor will only increase by one decibel. An 8:1 compression ratio means that a signal that is 8 dB over the threshold will increase by 1 dB, so the higher the ratio, the greater amount of signal reduction.

When the compression ratio is less than 1:1, the inverse happens. At a ratio of 0.5:1, for every half of a decibel of the signal over the threshold, the output of the compressor increases by 1 dB. For example, at the 0.5:1 ratio, a signal that exceeded the threshold by 2 dB would be increased by 4 dB at the output of the compressor. Expansion is not used as often as compression; nevertheless, it's a powerful tool for re-gaining dynamics in a track that has lost them.

The final plug-in in the lead vocal chain is a 6-band Renaissance EQ. The Renaissance EQ tilts the frequency response of the lead vocal track towards the high end with a high-pass filter at 70 Hz and a 0.3 dB cut at 100 Hz along with boosts to the 2.8 kHz and 6 kHz regions and a shelving EQ around 12 kHz. The output of the lead vocal track is around 0.6 dB, though volume automation will cause the output to vary. A send to the vocal reverb is at –18.5 dB.

Fig. 9.24. Lead Vocal Auto-Tune

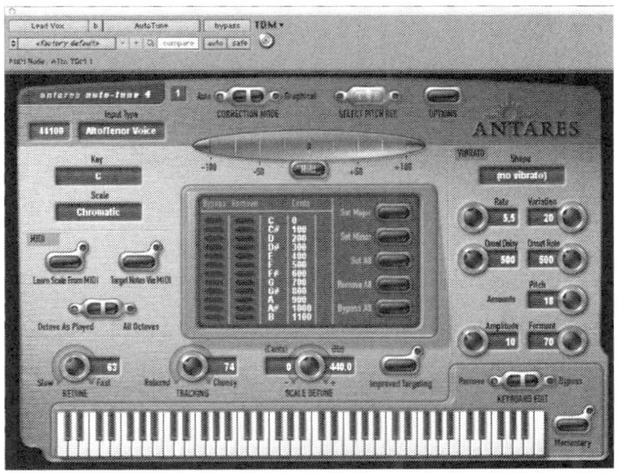

Auto-Tune

Retune: 63

Tracking: 74

Scale detune: 0

Input Type: Alto/Tenor Voice

Fig. 9.25. Lead Vocal Compressor

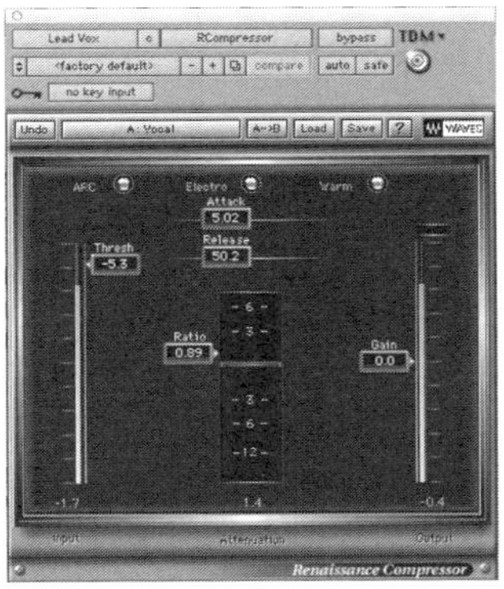

Waves Renaissance Compressor Lead Vocal Settings				
threshold	attack	release	ratio	gain
–5.3 dB	5.02	50.2	0.89:1	0 dB

Fig. 9.26. Lead Vocal EQ

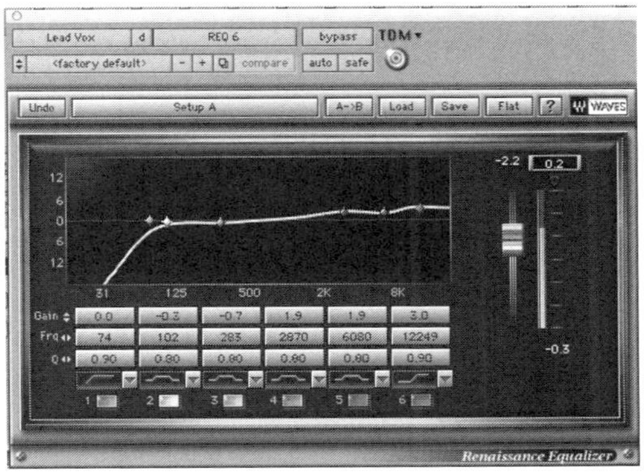

Waves Renaissance REQ-6 Lead Vocal Settings						
parameter	**band 1**	**band 2**	**band 3**	**band 4**	**band 5**	**band 6**
gain	0 dB	–0.3 dB	–0.7 dB	+1.9 dB	+1.9 dB	+3.0 dB
frequency	74 Hz	102 Hz	283 Hz	2,870 Hz	6,080 Hz	12,249 Hz
Q	0.90	0.80	0.80	0.80	0.80	0.90
shape	high pass	bell	bell	bell	bell	shelf

BACKGROUND VOCALS

There are three background vocal tracks on "Summertime" labeled as high, mid and "yoo hoo." The high and mid tracks sing together for most of the song, while the yoo hoo track adds a third part to, well, the yoo hoos. The yoo hoo track is also used for the single-line harmony in the verse and in the whispered background vocals.

In the bridge of "Summertime," the three BGV tracks answer the lead vocal in a whisper; by using three parts in this whisper section, no automation needs to be written to make those parts audible in the track. The output of the high track is set at –5.2 dB; the mid track is also at –5.2 dB and the yoo-hoo track level is at –6.4 dB. The background vocals were sent to the BGV Buss, which was set at –1.0 dB. A 2-band Renaissance EQ and a Renaissance Compressor were used on the BGV buss. The EQ provided a boost of 2.4 dB at 8.7 kHz, and the compressor provided a maximum gain reduction of less than 2 dB to the BGVs.

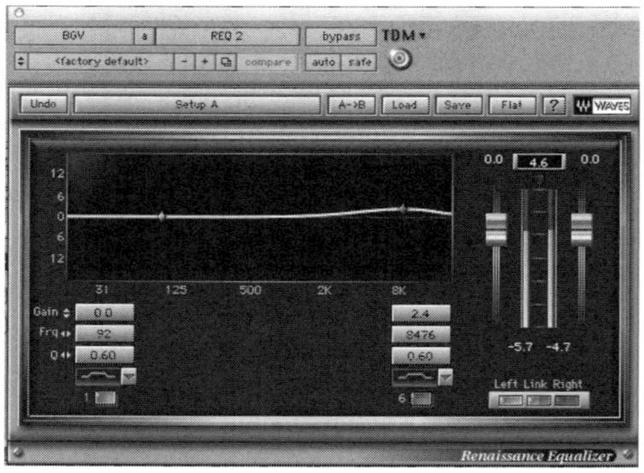

Fig. 9.27. BGV Buss EQ

Waves Renaissance REQ-2 Background Buss Settings		
parameter	**band 1**	**band 2**
gain	0 dB	+2.4 dB
frequency	92 Hz	8,746 Hz
Q	0.60	0.60
shape	bell	bell

Fig. 9.28. BGV Buss Compressor

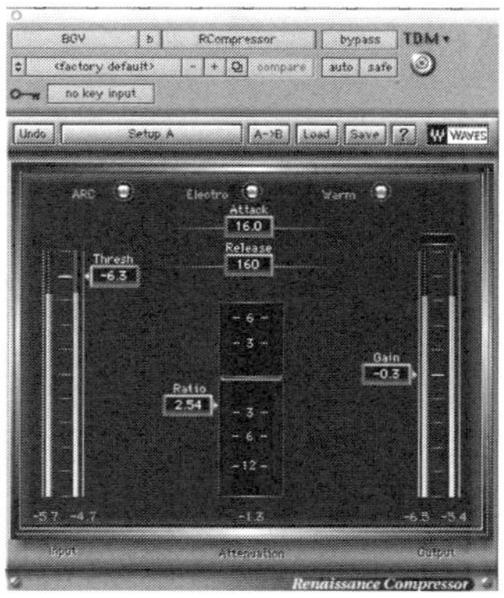

Waves Renaissance Compressor BGV Buss Settings				
threshold	**attack**	**release**	**ratio**	**gain**
–6.3 dB	16.0	160	2.54:1	–0.3 dB

AUX SENDS AND BUSS PROCESSING

Four separate reverbs were used for this mix; they're labeled "drum reverb," "instrument reverb," "vocal reverb," and "long reverb."

The drum reverb used was a Waves Renaissance Reverberator set to a drum plate setting; the output level of the drum plate was at unity gain, or 0 dB.

Fig. 9.30. Drum Reverb

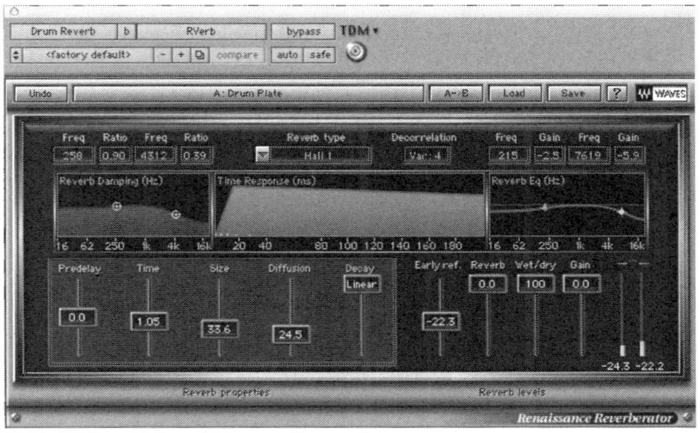

Fig. 9.29. Aux Sends

Waves Renaissance Reverb Drums Settings	
parameter	**setting**
REVERB DAMPING	
frequency 1	258
ratio 1	0.90

Waves Renaissance Reverb Drums Settings continued	
parameter	**setting**
frequency 2	4312
ratio 2	0.39
reverb type	Hall 1
decorrelation	Var:4
REVERB EQ	
frequency 1	215
gain 1	–2.5 dB
frequency 2	7619
gain 2	–5.9 dB
predelay	0.0
time	1.05 seconds
size	33.6
diffusion	24.5
decay	linear
early reflection level	–22.3 dB
reverb	0.0 dB
wet/dry	100%
gain	0

The instrument reverb used for this mix was another Renaissance Reverberator, which was set to a Medium Room preset; the output level of the reverb was set to unity gain, or 0 dB.

Fig. 9.31. Instrument Reverb

Waves Renaissance Reverberator Instrument Reverb Settings	
parameter	**setting**
REVERB DAMPING	
frequency 1	29
ratio 1	1.00
frequency 2	4569
ratio 2	0.76
reverb Type	resoverb
decorrelation	var:1
REVERB EQ	
frequency 1	156
gain 1	0
frequency 2	1256
gain 2	–4.9 dB
predelay	0.0
time	0.70
size	62.3
diffusion	30
decay	linear
early reflection level	–23.9 dB
reverb	0.0 dB
wet/dry	100%
gain	0

The vocal reverb used for this mix was a Waves TrueVerb, which was set to a Nice Plate preset; the output level of the reverb was set to unity gain, or 0 dB.

Fig. 9.32. Vocal Reverb

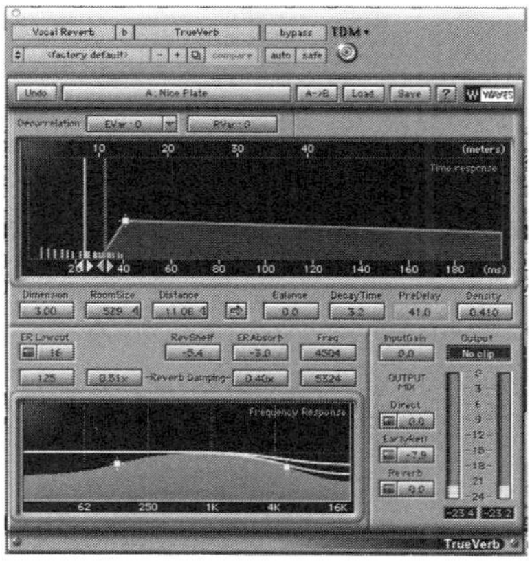

Waves TrueVerb Vocal Reverb Settings	
parameter	**setting**
dimension	3.00
room size	539
distance	11.08
balance	0.0
decay time	3.2
predelay	41.0
density	0.410
EARLY REFLECTION (ER)	
low cut	16
reverb damping frequency low	125
damping	0.51¥
reverb damping frequency high	5,324
damping	0.40¥
reverb shelf	–5.4
ER absorb	–3.0
ER absorb freq	4504
input gain	0.0
direct output	0.0
early reflection output	–7.9
reverb output	0.0

The gate reverb was a DigiRack D-Verb plug-in, set to a medium nonlinear reverb setting. A Waves C1 gate that chopped off the reverb followed the D-Verb.

Fig. 9.33. Gate Reverb

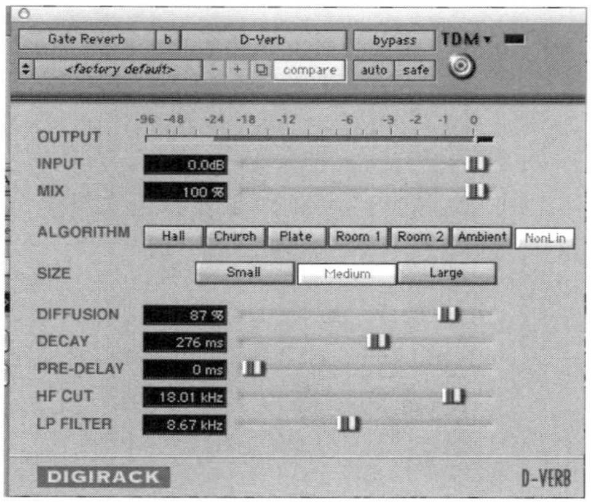

Digidesign D-Verb Long Reverb Settings	
parameter	**setting**
input	0 dB
mix	100%
algorithm	non-linear
size	medium
diffusion	87%
decay	276 ms
predelay	0 ms
HF cut	18.01 kHz
low pass filter	8.67 kHz

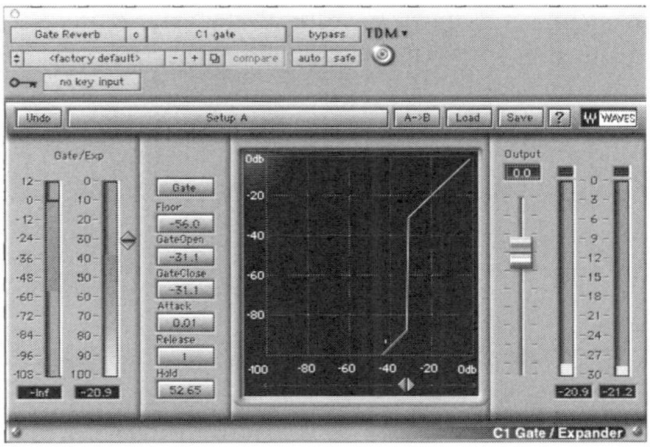

Fig. 9.34. Reverb Gate

Waves C1 Gate for Tom 1 Settings					
floor	**gate open**	**gate close**	**attack**	**release**	**hold**
–56.0 dB	–31.1 dB	–31.1 dB	0.01	1	52.65

MASTER OUTPUT

The master output on "Summertime" includes a Renaissance Compressor, a 6-band Renaissance EQ, a Waves L2 Limiter, and a Pow-R Dither plug-in. The compressor, with a ratio of 2.09:1, is set for less than 3 dB of gain reduction. The Renaissance EQ cuts less than 1 dB at 39 Hz and at 98 Hz and adds a broad boost centered at 20 kHz. This band, though it's a bell filter, functions much like a shelving filter, raising the frequencies above about 4 kHz.

The L2 Limiter is set to a –4.3 dB threshold with an output ceiling of –0.3 dBFS, and the Pow-R Dither plug-in is set to a 16-bit output and used noise shaping type 3.

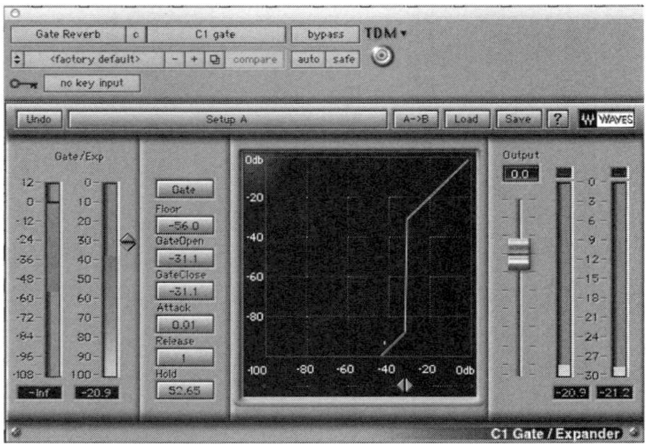

Fig. 9.34. Reverb Gate

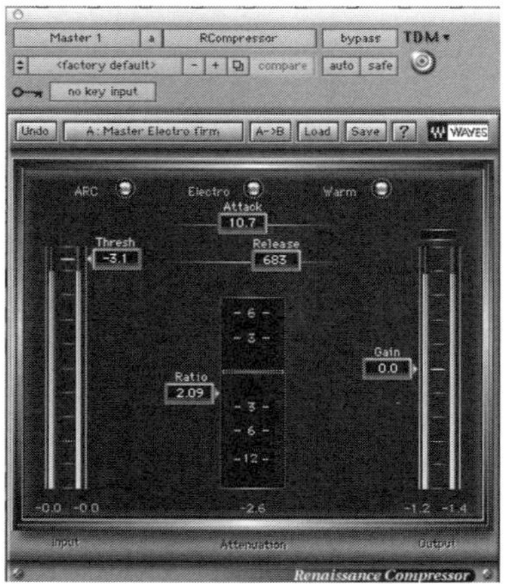

Fig. 9.35. Buss Compressor

Waves Renaissance Compressor Master Output Settings				
threshold	attack	release	ratio	gain
–3.1 dB	10.7	683	2.09:1	0 dB

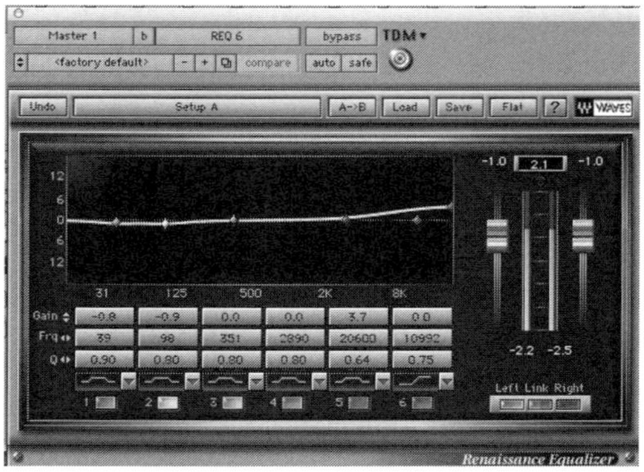

Fig. 9.36. Buss EQ

Waves Renaissance REQ-6 Master Output Settings						
parameter	**band 1**	**band 2**	**band 3**	**band 4**	**band 5**	**band 6**
gain	–0.8 dB	–0.9 dB	0 dB	0 dB	+3.7 dB	0 dB
frequency	39 Hz	98 Hz	351 Hz	2,890	20,600 Hz	10,992 Hz
Q	0.90	0.80	0.80	0.80	0.64	0.75
shape	bell	bell	bell	bell	bell	shelving

Fig. 9.37. Buss Limiter

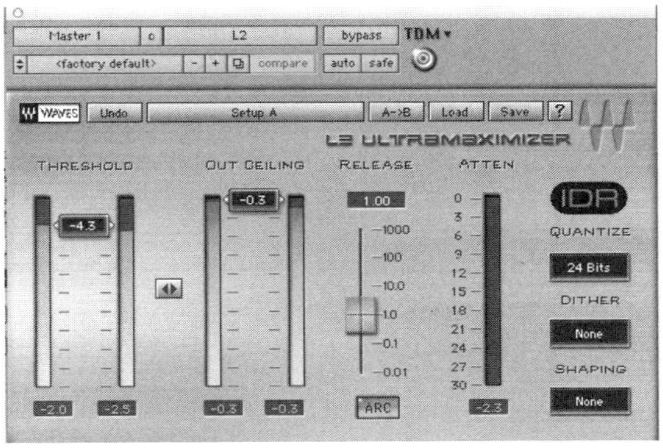

Waves L2
Threshold: –4.3 dB
Out Ceiling: –0.3 dB
Release: 1.00

Fig. 9.38. Dither

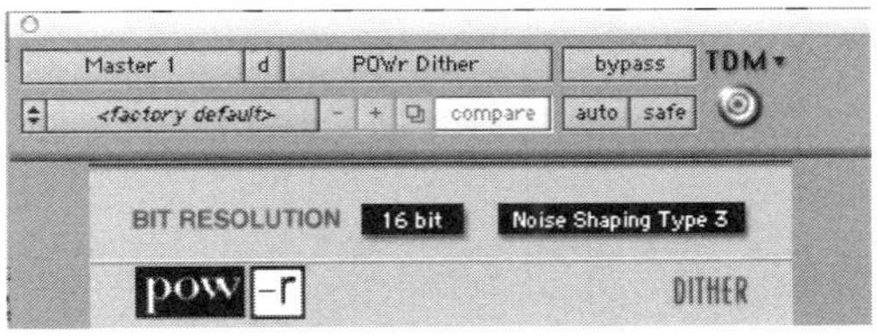

Pow-R Dither
16 bit
Noise Shaping Type 3

AUTOMATION

Volume automation has been written for a number of the tracks on "Summertime." In the second verse, the organ track has been raised a bit while it plays some fills. The talk box electric guitar was also manipulated a bit in the second verse, where the level on the original track had dropped a bit. The arpeggio guitar was turned up in the intro, then turned down when the first verse started, and the volume was adjusted through all of the solo guitar solos.

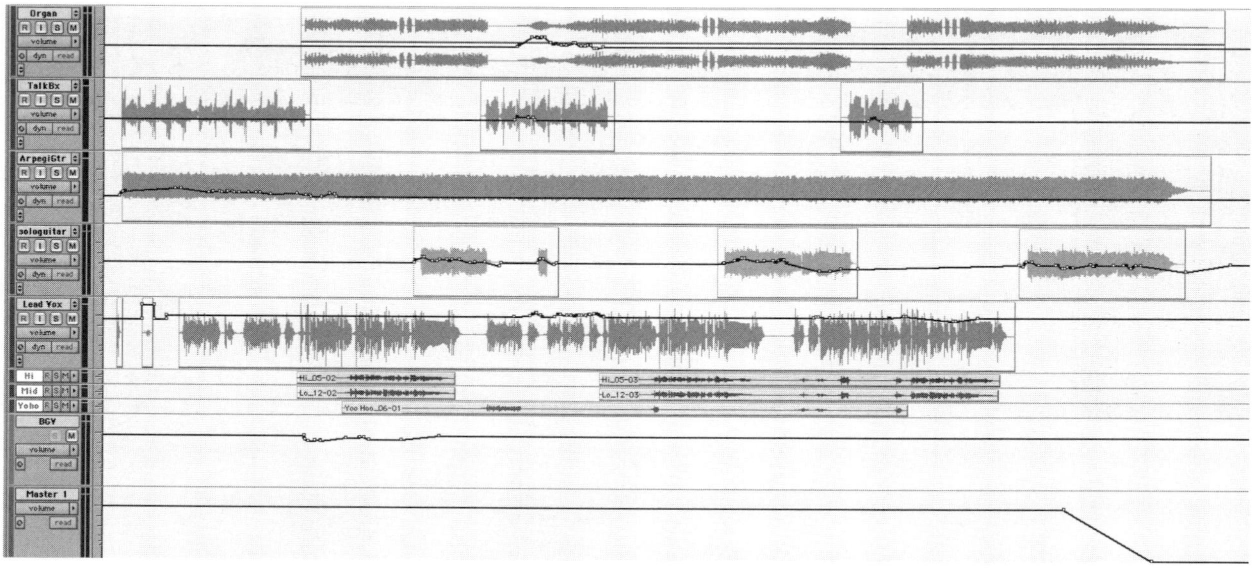

Fig. 9.39. Automation

The lead vocal track had volume automation written in the second verse and in the back half of the last chorus. A bit of volume adjustments were made to the BGV buss during the first chorus, but no automation was written for the individual tracks of BGVs.

A medium length fade was written on the master output for the fade-out that ends "Summertime."

EDITS

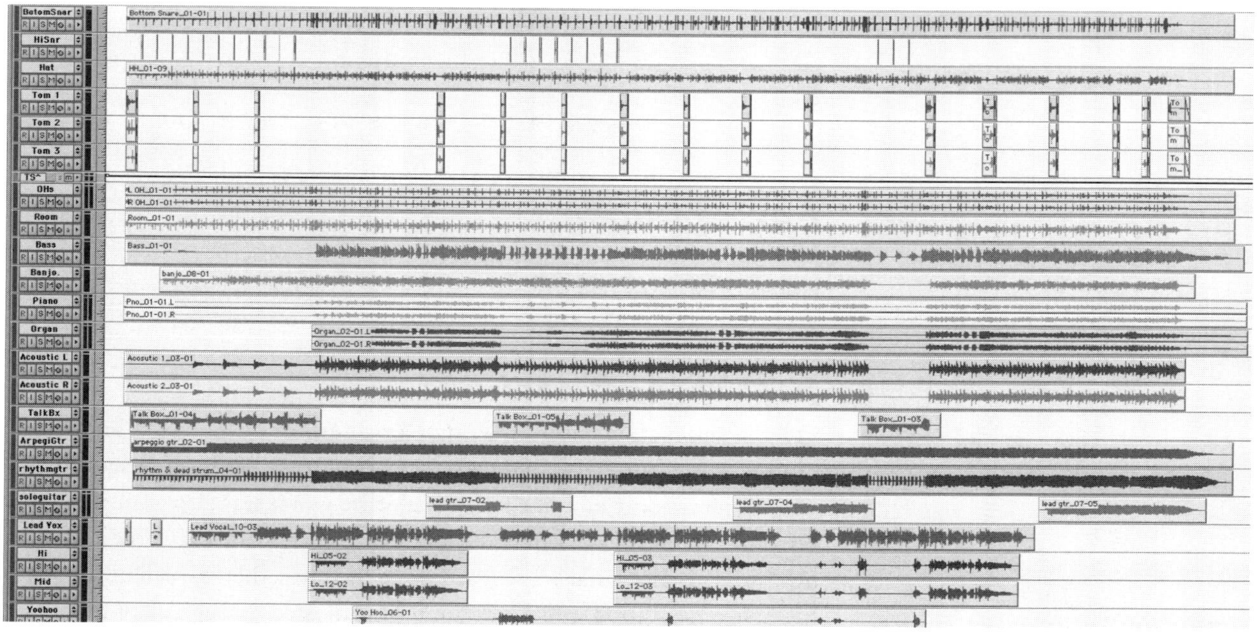

Fig. 9.40. Edits

All of the audio tracks in "Summertime" were trimmed from the beginning of each track to the beginning of the song, and those audio tracks that didn't start at the beginning of the song were trimmed up to the point that they began.

As mentioned earlier, the high snare track was separated into regions for each of the hits on the high snare. The rest of the track was cleared. The same thing took place with the tom tracks; the fills where any of the three toms were hit were separated from the rest of the track (and the rest of the track was cleared from the edit window). A short fade was created at the front of each of the tom fill sections, and a longer fade about an eighth note long was created at the end of each tom fill to let the toms ring out. For all the tom fills, the fade was completed before the next snare hit.

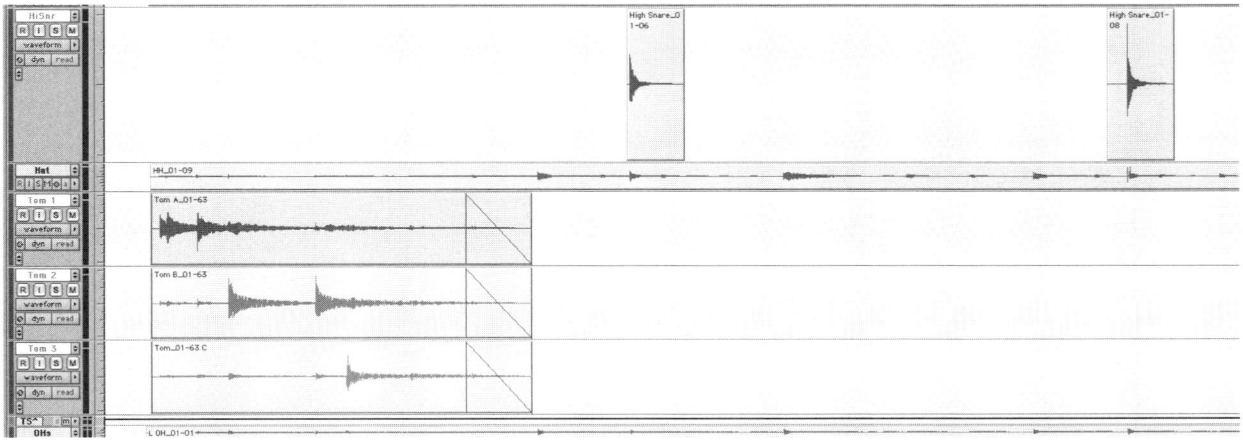

Fig. 9.41. Toms and High Snare

Some other tracks were cleared of blank portions, including the talk box guitar, the solo guitar, and the background vocals. Also, the phrase "kick it" and the laugh that precedes the first verse were separated from the rest of the lead vocal tracks. The only reason that these tracks were cleared of audio is to make it easier for the mixer to see what's going on. Sometimes the visual aspect of mixing in the box becomes important, and if this helps an engineer to see what's happening, then it's worth doing. These clearings, by the way, are not destructive. Though the audio tracks were separated into regions in the mixing session, the actual audio tracks are unchanged.

PRINTING MIXES

When printing the mix of each of the songs in this volume, a consistent approach was used: a track is used to set the final length of the song. The start and end times for "Summertime" were set by selecting the acoustic guitar track. In Pro Tools, selecting this trimmed track will cause the program to play from the beginning to the end of that track with no excess audio or time at the beginning or end. In those situations where multiple mixes of a song must be done—for example, if a producer wants vocal up or vocal down versions, TV mixes, instrumental mixes—all of the versions are the same length, and can be easily lined up for editing.

Fig. 9.42. Print Mix

CHAPTER 10

"Would You Go With Me"

(As Recorded by Josh Turner)

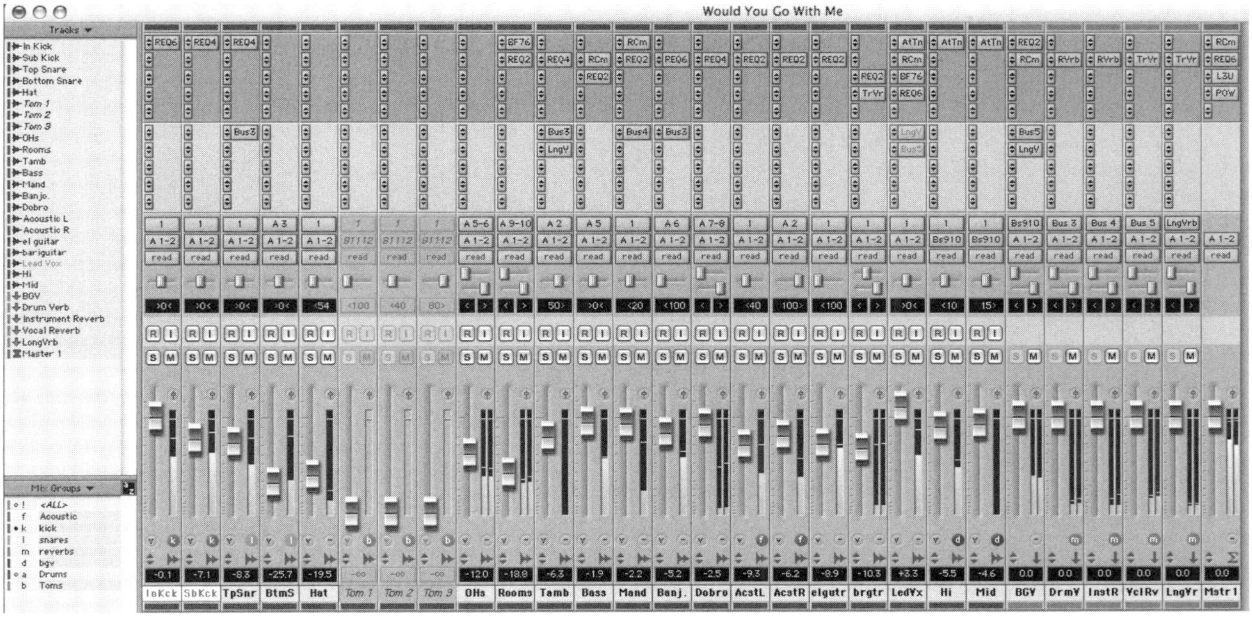

Fig. 10.1. Mix Window

"Would You Go With Me" reflects another one of Nashville's commercial production approaches. Rather than recording the song either with an acoustic (in this case, bluegrass) sensibility or a standard country rhythm section, the producer of this song essentially chose to do both. The song has a full rhythm section (including both electric guitar and a baritone guitar) and then adds a bluegrass quartet (mandolin, dobro, banjo, fiddle) on top of that. Though it was commonly stated by various Music Row executives that the hit *O Brother, Where Art Thou?* soundtrack had nothing to do with Nashville's version of country music, the months that followed the movie's release saw a huge upswing in this sort of production. From a mixing standpoint, one of the primary goals is to find room for all of those instruments.

DRUMS

The drum kit on "Would You Go With Me" is played with Pro Mark plastic brushes, so the timbre of the kit is quite different than the sound on some of the other tracks in this volume. It's the same kit that was used on the other nine songs, but the performance is what makes it sound different. Notice that the tom tracks look different (in the mix window screenshot); they've been made inactive. And in the drum screen shot, they've been hidden so that they aren't cluttering up the mix window.

Fig. 10.2. Drum Mix

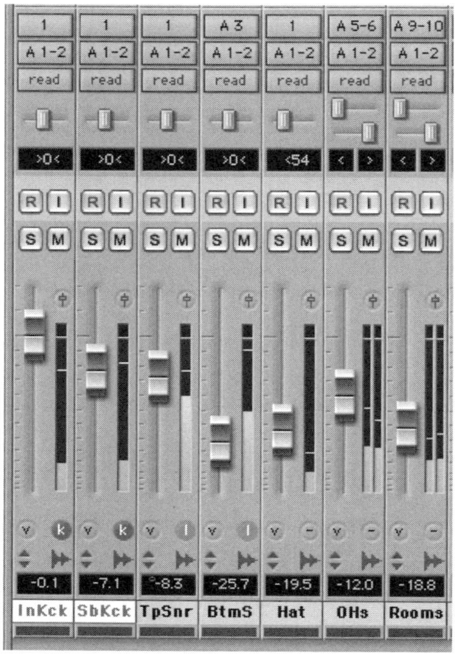

Kick Drum

The in-kick track has only a 6-band Waves Renaissance EQ inserted in the signal path; the EQ boosts 110 Hz by 3.5 dB, cuts 469 Hz by 2.3 dB, boosts 1.4 kHz by 4.1 dB, 3.3 kHz by 6.5 dB, and 5.6 kHz by 10 dB. The output of the in-kick track was at –0.1 dB.

Fig. 10.3. In-Kick EQ

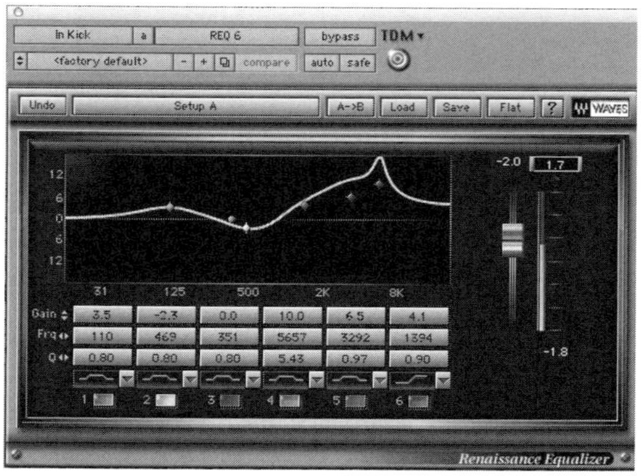

Waves Renaissance REQ-6 Inside Kick Settings						
parameter	band 1	band 2	band 3	band 4	band 5	band 6
gain	+3.5 dB	–2.3 dB	0 dB	+10.0 dB	+6.5 dB	+4.1 dB
frequency	110 Hz	469 Hz	351 Hz	5,657 Hz	3,292 Hz	1,394 Hz
Q	0.80	0.80	0.80	5.43	0.97	0.90
shape	high pass	bell	bell	bell	bell	shelving

Subkick

The Yamaha Subkick was again used for the outside kick drum track. A 4-band Renaissance EQ was used to enhance the low frequencies; 46 Hz was boosted by 2.3 dB and 248 Hz was boosted by 2.8 dB. The output of the subkick track was at –7.1 dB.

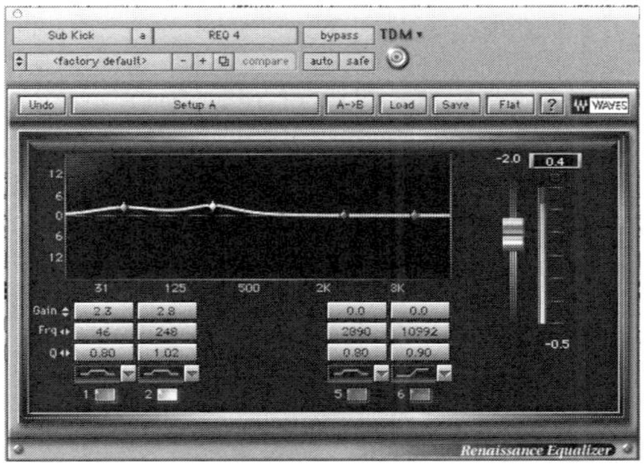

Fig. 10.4. Subkick EQ

Waves Renaissance REQ-4 Out-Kick Settings				
parameter	band 1	band 2	band 3	band 4
gain	+2.3 dB	–2.8 dB	+0 dB	0 dB
frequency	46 Hz	248 Hz	2,890 Hz	10,992 Hz
Q	0.80	1.02	0.80	0.90
shape	bell	bell	bell	shelf

Snare

The snare drum used on "Would You Go With Me" was the same Legend Phosphor Bronze 3.5" ¥ 14" snare that was used as the high snare on "Summertime" (discussed in the last chapter). For "Would You Go With

Me," a plastic donut ring was put on the snare drum to cut down on the amount of ring coming from the drum. A 4-band Renaissance EQ was used on the top snare track; it was used to boost 104 Hz by 1.9 dB, 336 Hz by 0.8 dB, 2.1 kHz by 3.1 dB, and 12.8 kHz by 1.2 dB. The output of the top snare track was set at –8.2 dB, and a send to the drum reverb was set at –17.1 dB. The bottom snare mic was set at –25.7 dB; no processing was used on the bottom snare mic.

Fig. 10.5. Top Snare EQ

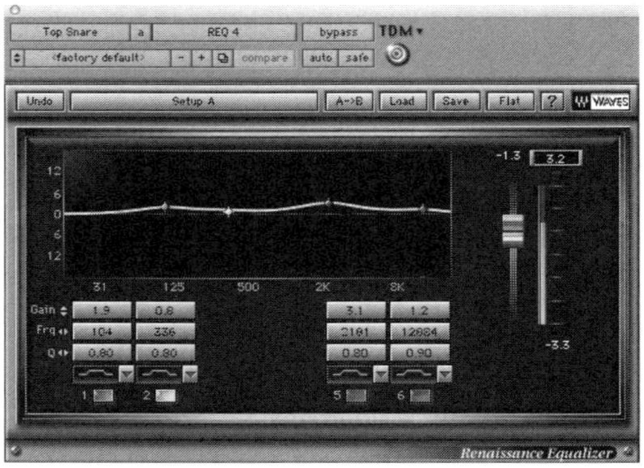

Waves Renaissance REQ-4 Top Snare Settings				
parameter	band 1	band 2	band 3	band 4
gain	+1.9 dB	+0.8 dB	+3.1 dB	+1.2 dB
frequency	104 Hz	336 Hz	2,181 Hz	12,884 Hz
Q	0.80	0.80	0.80	0.90
shape	bell	bell	bell	bell

Hi-hat

The hi-hat level was set at –19.5 dB, and no plug-ins were used on the track.

Toms

A couple of earlier chapters mentioned the truism that if a given track is not needed for a mix, there's no reason to use it. That's the case with the tom tracks on "Would You Go With Me." The toms are not used in the song, so the tom tracks are muted (and made inactive).

Overheads

In keeping with what has become a rather minimalist drum mix, the overhead microphones follow the trend of using no plug-ins. The output of the overhead tracks is –12.0 dB.

Room Mics

Though the processing used on the stereo room mic tracks appear to be similar to some of the earlier mixes, the Bomb Factory BF76 compressor is only being used to control the levels of the room mics. The output of the BF76 is pretty clean, which leads to a different approach with the room mic tracks. For "Would You Go With Me," the room track simply adds a bit of ambience to the overall drum track. The fader levels on the room mics are set to –18.8 dB a 2-band Renaissance EQ removed some of the low-end mud from the track with a 5.6 dB cut at 100 Hz, using a shelving EQ. The second band isn't used.

Fig. 10.6. Room Compressor

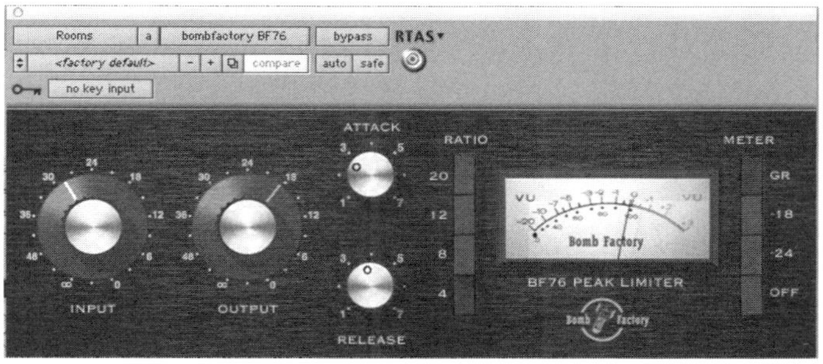

Bomb Factory BF76 Room Mic Settings				
input	**output**	**attack**	**release**	**ratio**
28	18	2.5	3.6	4:1

Fig. 10.7. Room EQ

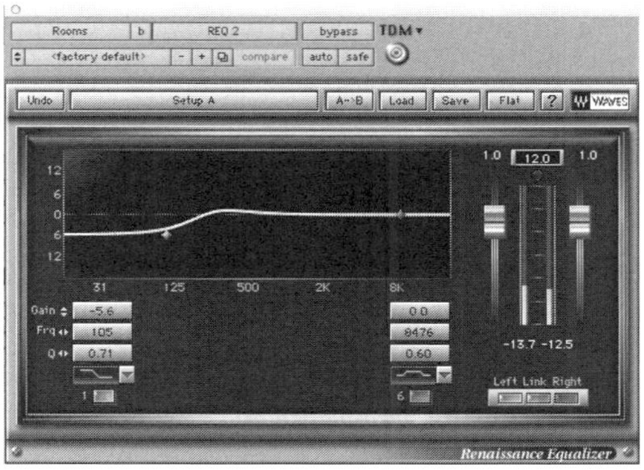

Waves Renaissance REQ-2 Room Mic Settings		
parameter	**band 1**	**band 2**
gain	–5.6 dB	0 dB
frequency	105 Hz	8,476 Hz
Q	0.71	0.60
shape	shelf	bell

PERCUSSION

It's common practice to run some sort of a click track when recording in Nashville. Not only does this allow all of the musicians to know where the downbeats should be, the click track ends up as part of the final mix. The reason is that some Nashville drummers prefer to use a percussion loop as their click track—they feel that it's more fun than a simple eighth note shaker or cowbell. That loop would be printed as part of the tracking session (in much the same way that a click track would be printed). If the mixer or producer feels that the percussion loop adds to the song, it ends up being used in the song. Of course, more often, a loop will be created after the fact and added to the session (since workstations can build a grid map that's locked to the tempo of the song). It's a simple matter to do this even after the fact.

When percussion is added to a song, a decision has to be made about whether to use live percussion (especially shakers and tambourines) or to use sampled percussion either in the mixing stage with virtual instruments or at the tracking stage with a tool like Roland's Handsonic box—an electronic multi-pad sample player. The Handsonic can also be used to generate a click track. The biggest functional difference from a mixing viewpoint is that the sampled/looped percussion can be technically perfect from the viewpoint of both timing (when it's locked to a grid) and levels (then each instrument can play at precisely the same level). On the other hand, live percussion, with all the minor variances in timing and level, can sound more live. In addition to that, it's often quicker to simply play a part than it is to program one that sounds natural.

When recording live percussion, a lot of the sounds that the mixer receives are determined at the recording stage. For example, there are dozens of different kinds of shakers available, from simple egg shakers to handmade shakers (dried lentils in a soft drink can sounds very different from dried peas in a coffee can) to a plethora of commercially made shakers. Tambourines are similar; dozens of varieties are available, and each one has a characteristic sound. With hand drums (congas, bongos, djembes) more subtleties can be created on actual drums than by using sampled versions. In any case, both live and sampled versions are used on contemporary country records.

Percussion can be panned in ways that accentuate the drums (or other instruments), or they can be panned in ways that contrast with the other instruments. A shaker, for example, can be panned to the same side of the soundfield as the hi-hat, creating a rhythmic part that seems to contain elements of both. Or it can be panned to the opposite side of the soundfield, where its character can easily be distinguished from the hat. Since a tambourine may be shaken in a way that duplicates the drummer's playing on the hi-hat or ride cymbal (playing eighth notes or sixteenth notes), it's possible to put the tambourine low enough in the mix that the tambourine is indistinguishable from what the drummer's playing. Or it can be hit on the second and fourth beat of the song accentuating a snare drum. In either case, the percussion level and position will determine whether it becomes a major part of the sound or simply a part that shows up when it's not overpowered by other elements of the mix.

When drum loops are used as part of a country mix, pretty much any processing is allowed; drum loops can be filtered, band-passed, distorted, pitch-shifted, and otherwise abused to make them fit into the producer's vision of the final mix. That being said, the percussion on "Would You Go With Me" is limited to a simple tambourine part.

TAMBOURINE

The tambourine is used in an interesting way in this song—where it would be much more typical for the tambourine to emphasize the second and/or fourth beats of the measure, in "Would You Go With Me," it's used to imply the second and fourth beat in half time, or half of the tempo played by the rest of the rhythm section. This is very nice for a couple of reasons: the big one is that it soothes what could otherwise be thought of as a fairly frenetic tempo. Another reason is that by playing in a place that isn't normal it gives the rhythm tracks an interesting twist. The output of the tambourine is at –6.3 dB, and both the drum reverb and the long reverb are used for the tambourine tracks. The drum reverb send is at –4.0 db and the long reverb send is at –6.8 dB.

A 4-band Waves Renaissance EQ was inserted on the tambourine track; and added a 5.9 dB boost at 1,221 Hz, a 3.6 dB boost at 625 Hz, and a 3.1 dB cut around 7.2 kHz.

Fig. 10.8. Tambourine EQ

Waves Renaissance REQ-4 Tambourine Settings

parameter	band 1	band 2	band 3	band 4
gain	0 dB	+5.9 dB	+3.6 dB	–3.1 dB
frequency	92 Hz	121 Hz	625 Hz	7,179 Hz
Q	0.80	0.80	0.80	0.55
shape	bell	bell	bell	bell

BASS

The bass tracks on "Would You Go With Me" are much like others in this volume of songs; a Waves Renaissance Compressor and a 2-band Waves Renaissance EQ as plug-ins. The output fader of the bass was set at –1.9 dB. Not a whole lot of gain reduction was used on the bass track; it was added primarily to even out any inequities in the performance. The maximum amount of gain reduction from the Renaissance Compressor is 1.3 dB; the compression ratio was 3.13:1 and the threshold was set to –9.3 dB. The output of the Compressor was boosted by 0.7 dB. The low band of the Renaissance EQ cut 2.1 dB at 105 Hz and boosted 1.2 dB around 4.5 kHz.

Fig. 10.9. Bass Compressor

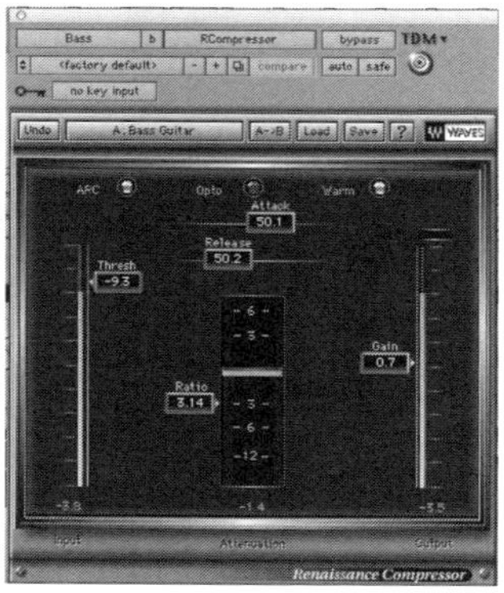

Waves Renaissance Compressor Bass Settings				
threshold	attack	release	ratio	gain
–9.3 dB	50.1	50.2	3.14:1	+0.7 dB

Fig. 10.10. Bass EQ

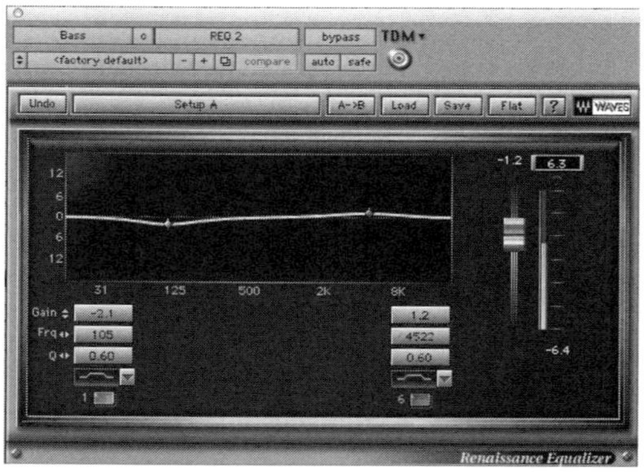

Waves Renaissance REQ-2 Bass Settings		
parameter	band 1	band 2
gain	–2.1 dB	+1.2 dB
frequency	105 Hz	4,522 Hz
Q	0.60	0.60
shape	bell	bell

MANDOLIN

Since the mandolin plays a fairly substantial part in "Would You Go With Me," boosting its EQ in the upper range, around 9.2 kHz, allows it to live in a frequency range where the other instruments are not dominant. This 4.1 dB boost gives the mandolin an airy quality that isn't necessarily what the instrument sounds like in the room, but is certainly part of the sound that people associate with the mandolin in contemporary music. The wide (and deep) cut in the low frequencies helps to reinforce the high end as well. The mandolin track also includes the Renaissance Compressor plug-in with a very mild compression ratio (of 1.38:1); though the threshold is set low enough (at –10.6) that the maximum gain reduction is on the order of 3 dB. The output level of the mandolin is –2.2 dB, and an aux send to the instrument reverb is set to –16.1 dB.

Fig. 10.11. Mandolin Compressor

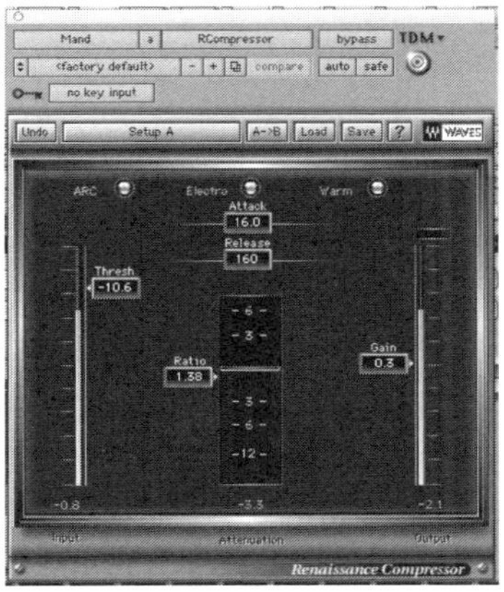

Waves Renaissance Compressor Mandolin Settings				
threshold	**attack**	**release**	**ratio**	**gain**
–10.6 dB	16.0	160	1.38:1	+0.3 dB

Fig. 10.12. Mandolin EQ

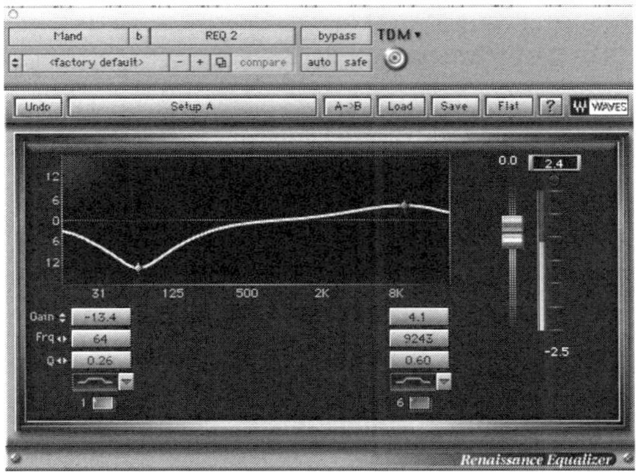

Waves Renaissance REQ-2 Mandolin Settings		
parameter	band 1	band 2
gain	–13.1 dB	+4.1 dB
frequency	64 Hz	9,243 Hz
Q	0.26	0.60
shape	bell	bell

BANJO

The banjo track really drives "Would You Stay With Me," and to make sure that it's heard, a 6-band Renaissance EQ is used. The low end of the banjo is rolled off with a wide 5 dB cut centered at 98 Hz, while 1.5 kHz is boosted by half a decibel. The top end of the banjo track is enhanced quite a lot with a 3.1 dB boost at 8.2 kHz and an 8.3 dB boost with a shelving EQ at 4.2 kHz. Interestingly enough, the 3.1 dB boost actually modifies the 8.3 dB shelving EQ as the screen shots demonstrate.

Fig. 10.13. Banjo EQ

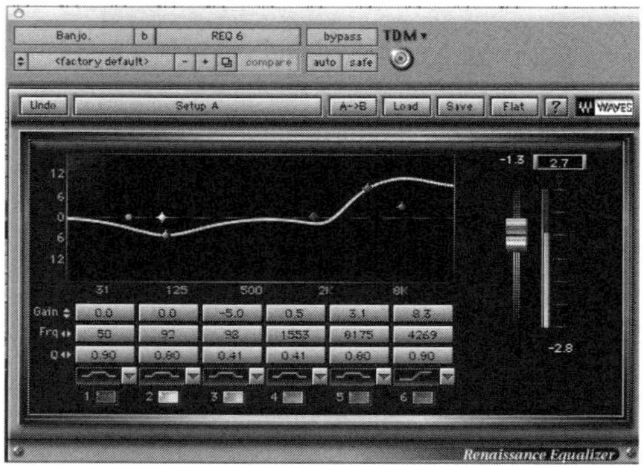

Waves Renaissance REQ-6 Banjo Settings						
parameter	band 1	band 2	band 3	band 4	band 5	band 6
gain	0 dB	0 dB	–5.0 dB	+0.5 dB	+3.1 dB	+8.3 dB
frequency	50 Hz	92 Hz	98 Hz	1,533 Hz	8,175 Hz	4,269 Hz
Q	0.90	0.80	0.41	0.41	0.80	0.90
shape	inactive	bell	bell	bell	bell	shelving

DOBRO

Dobro is an instrument that may not be quite as common as some of the others in this volume (or it might be—you never know who's reading). If you aren't familiar with it, it's more or less a square-necked resonator guitar. The strings cross over the bridge of the instrument, which rests on an aluminum cone (think of a shallow 12-inch speaker with a raised center on which the bridge rests; that's the resonator). The bodies of dobros are sometimes all metal or they or may be made of wood, but the resonator is always metal. Round-necked models can be played as slide guitars (a number of blues players played dobros), or they may be finger-picked (Chet Atkins has played a Del Vecchio resonator on several albums). Square-necked models have the strings raised around a half inch and are played with a bar (much like a steel guitar) and with thumb and finger picks.

The dobro can be recorded in a number of different ways. The two songs with dobro in this volume were done differently: one was a single microphone (a Telefunken U 47). The other was recorded with a Crowley and Tripp Naked Eye (a ribbon mic) about a foot above the resonator while a Telefunken 251 was about a foot over the point where the neck joins the body of the instrument. The single mic captures a rich, full tune from the dobro, but the two-mic combination seems to be a bit more natural sounding. The dobro track has a 4-band Renaissance EQ added to the signal path. The EQ is set to cut at 25 Hz by 2.6 dB, cut at 189 Hz by 3.3 dB, boost at 4.1 kHz by 3.5 dB, and boost around 14 kHz by almost 2 dB. The dobro track's output level is at –0.4 dB.

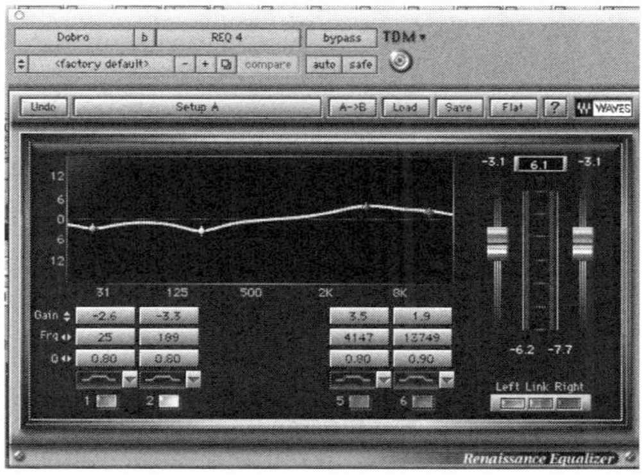

Fig. 10.14. Dobro EQ

Waves Renaissance REQ-4 Dobro Settings

parameter	band 1	band 2	band 3	band 4
gain	–2.6 dB	–3.3 dB	+3.5 dB	+1.9 dB
frequency	25 Hz	189 Hz	4,147 Hz	13,749 Hz
Q	0.80	0.80	0.80	0.90
shape	bell	bell	bell	bell

ACOUSTIC GUITARS

High passing the acoustic is almost never a bad idea; the acoustic guitars on every song in this volume were high passed. One-hundred Hz or even higher can help to clean the acoustic tracks of information that would otherwise muddy the sound. A slight boost at 3-5 kHz can emphasize the attack of the pick, while a boost at 10 kHz, brings out the sheen that is a common part of Nashville's acoustic guitar sound.

Occasionally, it's useful to think of the various instruments in a mix as they relate to the drum set; for instance, there's a relationship between the bass and the kick drum, and similarly, there's often a correlation between the electric guitar and the snare. Following this thought to the acoustic, the acoustic guitar—especially a strummed acoustic—often is related to the hi-hat: the acoustic is commonly playing eighth notes that must match the feel that the drummer plays on the hat.

For "Would You Go With Me," the acoustic guitar tracks are not bussed; each track has its own 2-band Waves Renaissance EQ. The EQs on each of the two guitar tracks used one of the two bands to high pass the signal to remove low frequency mud and the other to add a bit of sparkle to the high end. The left guitar track's output was –9.3 dB while the right guitar track's output was –6.2 dB.

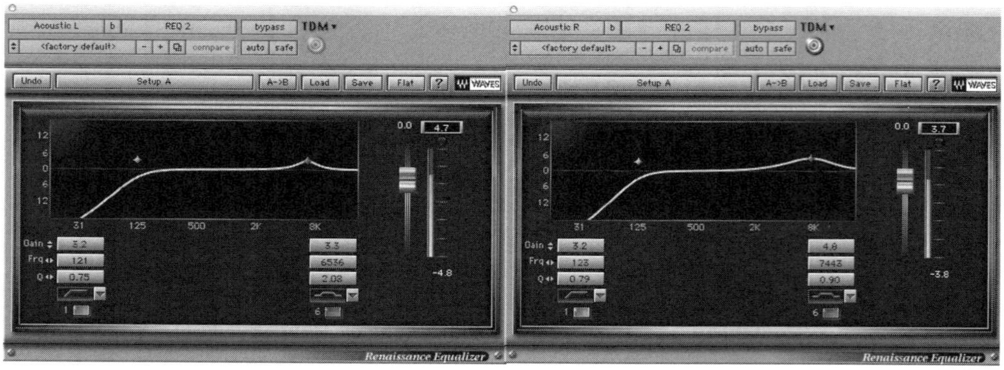

Fig. 10.15. Acoustic Guitar EQ

Waves Renaissance REQ-2 Acoustic L Settings		
parameter	**band 1**	**band 2**
gain	+3.2 dB	+3.3 dB
frequency	121 Hz	6,536 Hz
Q	0.75	2.08
shape	high pass	bell

Waves Renaissance REQ-2 Acoustic R Settings		
parameter	band 1	band 2
gain	+3.2 dB	+4.8 dB
frequency	123 Hz	7,443 Hz
Q	0.79	0.90
shape	high pass	bell

ELECTRIC GUITAR

The electric guitar on "Would You Go With Me" has a 2-band Renaissance EQ with one of those two bands boosting 100 Hz by a modest 0.7 dB. The output level of the electric guitar track is –8.9 dB.

Fig. 10.16. Electric Guitar EQ

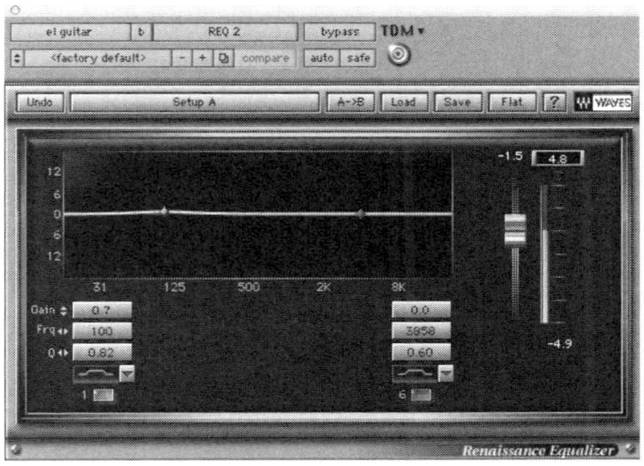

Waves Renaissance REQ-2 Rhythm Guitar Settings		
parameter	band 1	band 2
gain	+0.7 dB	0 dB
frequency	100 Hz	3,858 Hz
Q	0.82	0.60
shape	bell	bell (inactive)

BARITONE GUITAR

"Would You Go With Me" marks the first appearance in this book of the baritone guitar. Although this varies, the baritone guitar is an instrument that is typically tuned a 4th lower than a standard guitar. Baritone guitars are sometimes tuned so that the lowest note is a C, some will drop the tuning so that the lowest note is an A. A number of companies have made baritone guitars over the years, but the one that's generally used (and, in fact, is used on this track) is the Danelectro Baritone. The Danelectro has quite a distinctive sound, both because of Masonite used to construct the body of the instrument and because of the lipstick pickup used on it. In any case, this baritone guitar track has a 2-band Renaissance EQ and a Waves TrueVerb (with the Rock Guitar Room preset) as plug-ins. The Renaissance EQ boosts 78 Hz by 3.2 dB and has a 1 dB cut at 5.3 kHz. The TrueVerb is used both to add ambience from early reflections and to add a short reverb to the baritone guitar sound.

Fig. 10.17. Baritone Guitar EQ

Waves Renaissance REQ-2 Baritone Guitar Settings		
parameter	band 1	band 2
gain	+3.2 dB	–1.0 dB
frequency	78 Hz	5,339 Hz
Q	0.60	0.60
shape	bell	bell (inactive)

Fig. 10.18. Baritone Guitar Reverb

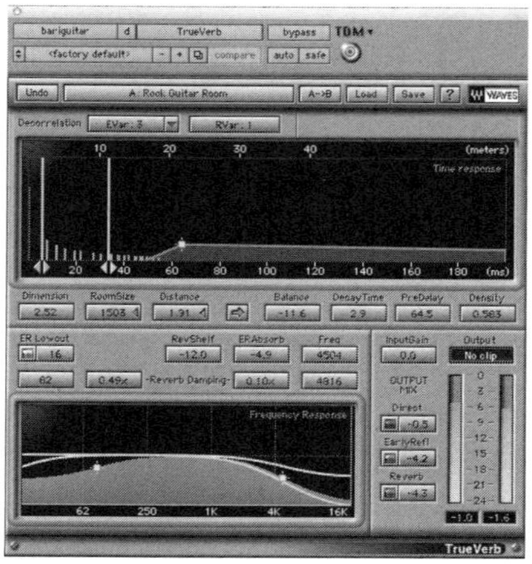

Waves TrueVerb Solo Electric Settings	
parameter	**setting**
dimension	2.52
room size	1,503
distance	1.91
balance	–11.6
decay time	2.9
predelay	64.5
density	0.762
EARLY REFLECTION (ER)	
low cut	16
reverb damping frequency low	82
damping	0.49 x
reverb damping frequency high	4,816
damping	0.10 x
reverb shelf	–12.0
ER absorb	–4.9
ER absorb Freq	4,504
input gain	0.0
direct output	–0.5 dB
early reflection output	–4.2 dB
reverb output	–3.5

LEAD VOCAL

It seems that one of the characteristic elements of contemporary country tracks is the heavily processed lead vocals. Taking a cue from the pop songs of the '90s, country vocals are often heavily compressed or limited (sometimes both), then EQ'd, then processed again with something like a de-esser to get rid of the artifacts introduced by the compression and equalization. The levels of the vocal tracks are usually automated—sometimes syllable by syllable and sometimes line by line, to bring them into line with the tracks. In addition to this type of processing, it's not uncommon for EQ as an effect to be used whether it's the radio/telephone voice that seems to show up from time to time, or something a bit more subtle like a high-pass filter that simply thins out the voice to emphasize certain lines.

The average output level for the lead vocal track on "Would You Go With Me" was at +2.6 dB, and two reverbs were used. The long reverb level was set at –32.3 dB and the vocal reverb was at –16.8 dB. There were four plug-ins used on the lead vocal track; Auto-Tune 4, a Renaissance Compressor, Bomb Factory's BF76 and a 6-band Renaissance EQ.

The Auto-Tune 4's retune parameter was 63 and the tracking parameter was 74 (relaxed). The Renaissance Compressor was also fairly mild; with an attack time of 5 ms, a release time of 50 ms and a compression ratio of 3.28:1, the maximum gain reduction from the Renaissance Compressor was around 2 dB. The Bomb Factory BF76 that followed added possibly another decibel of gain reduction.

The Renaissance EQ was set up a bit differently for the lead vocal track on "Would You Go With Me." In order to support the lowest notes in the song, after a high-pass filter at 29 Hz, 90 Hz was boosted by 3.1 dB and 221 Hz was boosted by 0.1 dB. Then, to brighten up the lead vocal, 2 kHz was boosted by 4.1 dB, 5.3 kHz was boosted by 5.5 dB, and shelving filter raised everything above 9.7 kHz by 7.8 dB.

Fig. 10.19 Lead Vocal Auto-Tune

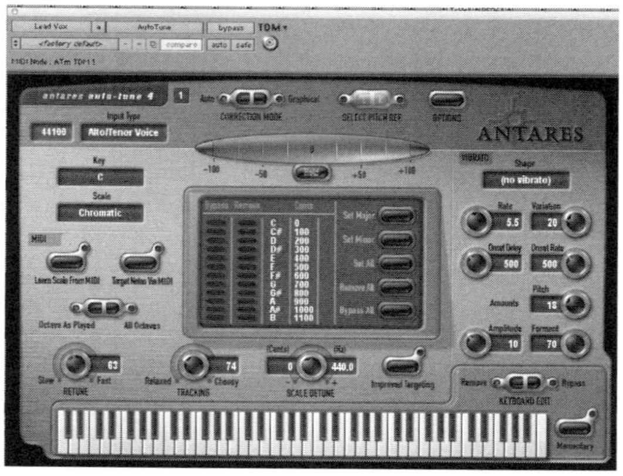

Auto-Tune
Retune: 63
Tracking: 74
Scale detune: 0
Input Type: Alto/Tenor Voice

Fig. 10.20. Lead Vocal Compressor

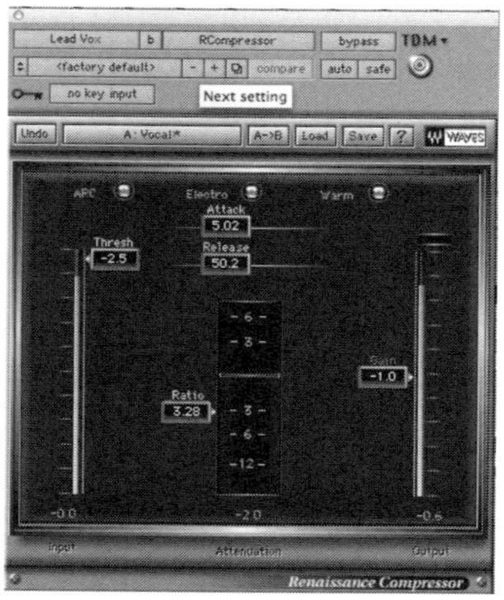

Waves Renaissance Compressor Lead Vocal Settings

Threshold	Attack	Release	Ratio	Gain
–2.5 dB	5.02	50.2	3.28:1	–1.0 dB

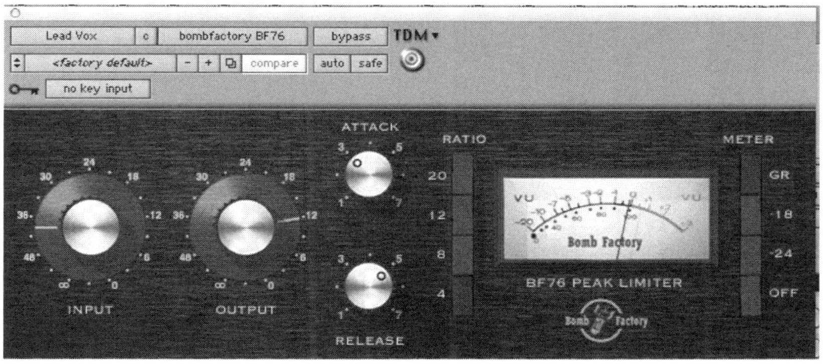

Fig. 10.21. Lead Vocal BF76

Bomb Factory BF76 Lead Vocal Settings

Input	Output	Attack	Release	Ratio
40	12	3	5	4:1

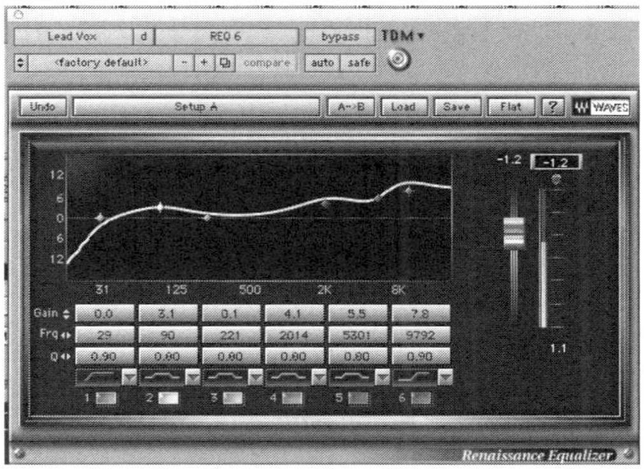

Fig. 10.22. Lead Vocal EQ

Waves Renaissance REQ-6 Lead Vocal Settings

parameter	band 1	band 2	band 3	band 4	band 5	band 6
gain	0 dB	+3.1 dB	+0.1 dB	+4.1 dB	+5.5 dB	+7.8 dB
frequency	29 Hz	90 Hz	221 Hz	2,014 Hz	5,301 Hz	9,792 Hz
Q	0.90	0.80	0.80	0.80	0.80	0.90
shape	high pass	bell	bell	bell	bell	shelf

BACKGROUND VOCALS

There are two background vocal (BGV) tracks on "Would You Go With Me"—a high track and a mid track. Both of the BGV tracks had an Auto-Tune 4 plug-in on them with identical settings; the retune parameter was set at 49 and the tracking parameter was set at 42. The output of the High BGV was –7.7 dB and the output of the mid BGV was –7.4 dB. The two background vocals were bussed to the BGV buss, which was at unity gain. A 2-band Renaissance EQ and a Renaissance Compressor were used on the BGV buss. The EQ had a 1-decibel cut at 41 Hz and a 4.4 dB boost at 6.8 kHz. The compressor's maximum gain reduction was less than 2 dB. The aux sends from the BGV buss were set at –16.1 dB to the Vocal Reverb and –41.8 dB to the Long Reverb.

Fig. 10.23. High BGV Auto-Tune

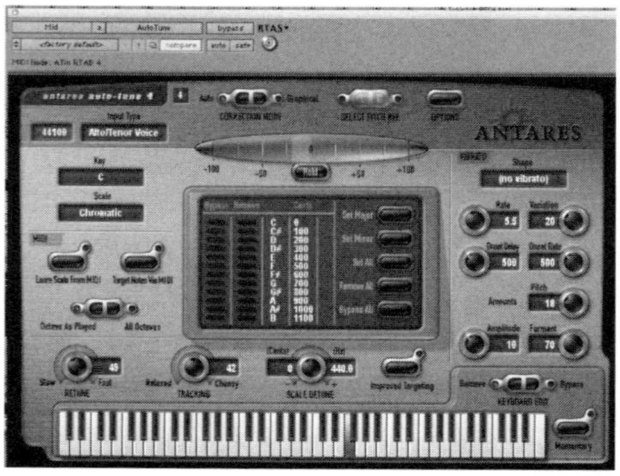

Auto-Tune

Retune: 49
Tracking: 42
Scale detune: 0

Fig. 10.24. Mid BGV Auto-Tune

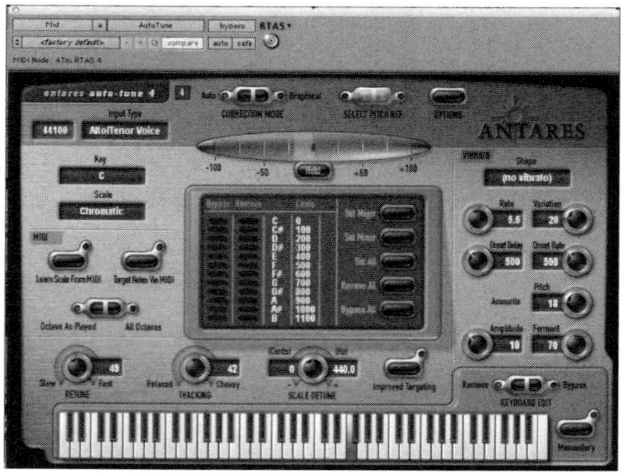

Auto-Tune

Retune: 49
Tracking: 42
Scale detune: 0

BGV Buss

Fig. 10.25. BGV Buss EQ

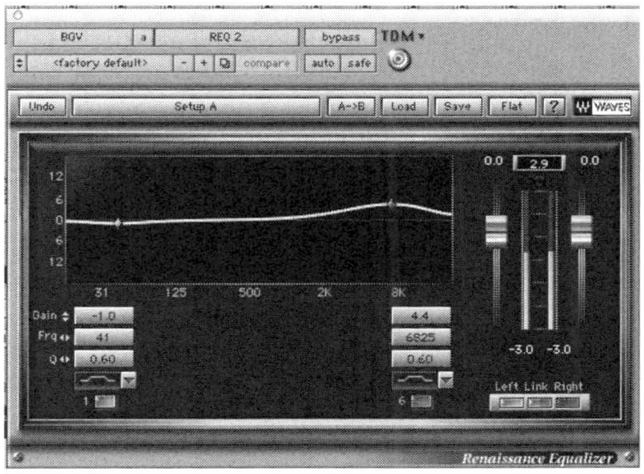

Waves Renaissance REQ-2 Background Buss Settings		
parameter	**band 1**	**band 2**
gain	–1.0 dB	+4.4 dB
frequency	41 Hz	6,825 Hz
Q	0.60	0.60
shape	bell	bell

Fig. 10.26. BGV Buss Compressor

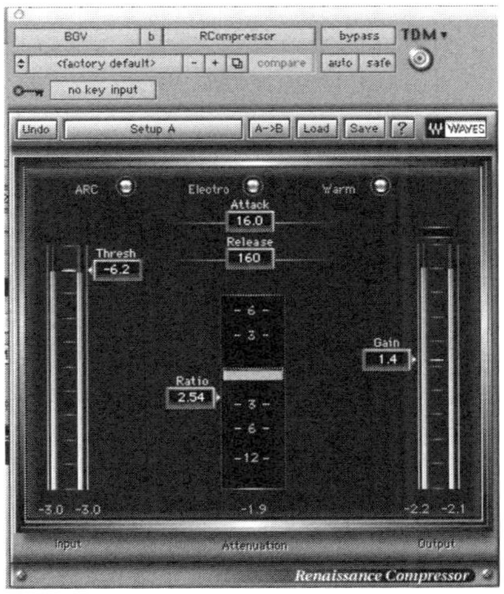

Waves Renaissance Compressor BGV Buss Settings				
threshold	**attack**	**release**	**ratio**	**gain**
–6.2 dB	16.0	160	2.54:1	+1.4 dB

AUX SENDS AND BUSS PROCESSING

Four reverbs were used for this mix of "Would You Go With Me"; they're labeled "drum reverb," "instrument reverb," "vocal reverb," and "long reverb." The drum reverb used was a Waves Renaissance Reverberator set to a Drum Plate preset; the output level of the drum plate was at unity gain, or 0 dB.

Fig. 10.27. Aux Sends

Fig. 10.28. Drum Reverb

Waves Renaissance Drum Reverb Settings	
parameter	**setting**
REVERB DAMPING	
frequency 1	258
ratio 1	0.90
frequency 2	4,312
ratio 2	0.39
reverb type	hall 1
decorrelation	var:4
REVERB EQ	
frequency 1	215
gain 1	–2.5 dB
frequency 2	7,619
gain 2	–5.9 dB
predelay	0.0
time	1.05 Seconds
size	33.6
diffusion	24.5
decay	linear
early reflection level	–22.3 dB
reverb	0.0 dB
wet/dry	100%
gain	0

The instrument reverb used for this mix was another Renaissance Reverberator, which was set to a Medium Room preset; the output level of the reverb was set to unity gain, or 0 dB.

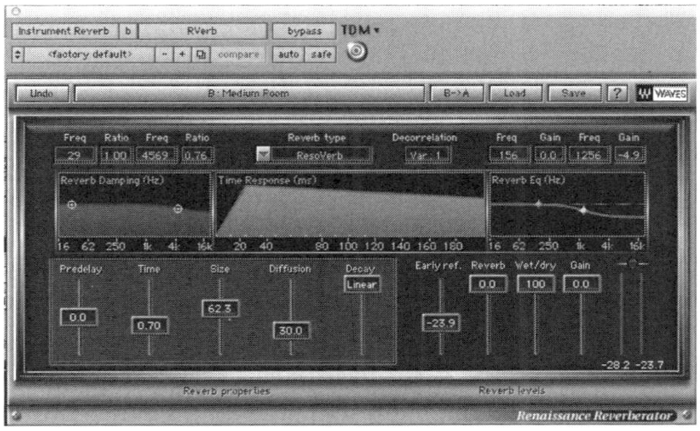

Fig. 10.29. Instrument Reverb

Waves Renaissance Instrument Reverb Settings	
parameter	**setting**
REVERB DAMPING	
frequency 1	29
ratio 1	1.00
frequency 2	4,569
ratio 2	0.76
reverb type	Resoverb
decorrelation	var:1
REVERB EQ	
frequency 1	156
gain 1	0
frequency 2	1,256
gain 2	–4.9 dB
predelay	0.0
time	0.70
size	62.3
diffusion	30
decay	linear
early reflection level	–23.9 dB
reverb	0.0 dB
wet/dry	100%
gain	0

The vocal reverb used for this mix was a Waves TrueVerb, which was set to a Nice Plate preset; the output level of the reverb was set to unity gain, or 0 dB.

Fig. 10.30. Vocal Reverb

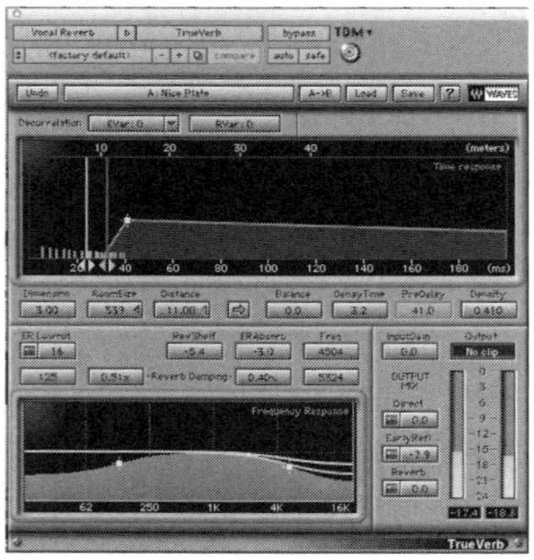

Waves TrueVerb Vocal Reverb Settings	
parameter	**setting**
dimension	3.00
room size	539
distance	11.08
balance	0.0
decay time	3.2
predelay	41.0
density	0.410
EARLY REFLECTION (ER)	
low cut	16
reverb damping frequency low	125
damping	0.51 x
reverb damping frequency high	5,324
damping	0.40 x
reverb shelf	–5.4
ER absorb	–3.0
ER absorb Freq	4,504
input gain	0.0
direct output	0.0
early reflection output	–7.9
reverb output	0.0

The long reverb was a Waves TrueVerb set to a Large Concert preset; the output level of the reverb was set to unity gain, or 0 dB.

Fig. 10.31. Long Reverb

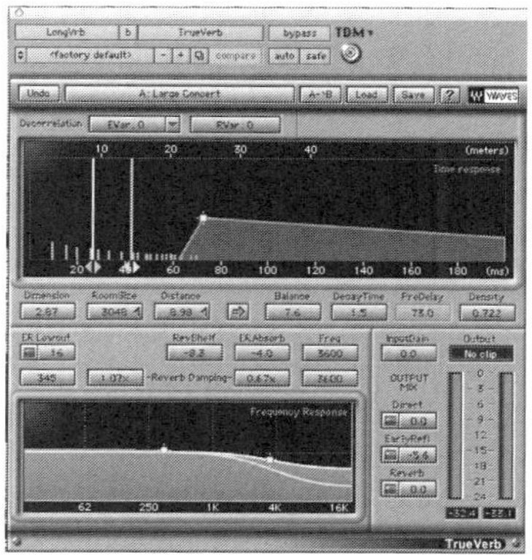

Waves TrueVerb Long Reverb Settings	
parameter	**setting**
dimension	2.87
room size	3,048
distance	8.98
balance	9.4
decay time	2.8
predelay	73.0
density	0.722
EARLY REFLECTION (ER)	
low cut	16
reverb damping frequency low	345
damping	1.07x
reverb damping frequency high	3,600
damping	0.67x
reverb shelf	–8.3
ER Absorb	–4.0
ER Absorb Freq	3,600
input gain	0.0
direct output	0.0
early reflection output	–5.6
reverb output	0

MASTER OUTPUT

The plug-ins on the master output are a Renaissance Compressor, a 6-band Waves Renaissance EQ, a Waves L3 Ultramaximizer and a Pow-R Dither plug-in.

The Renaissance Compressor's threshold is set to –3 dB, the attack time is 4 ms, and the release time is 119 ms. The compression ratio is 2.51:1 and the maximum amount of gain reduction is 4 dB.

The Renaissance EQ has a 0.3 dB boost at 39 Hz, a 0.4 dB boost at 2.9 kHz, and a 4.5 dB boost at 17.5 kHz. The L3 Ultramaximizer's threshold is set to –3.0 dB, and the out ceiling is set at –0.3 dB.

Fig. 10.32. Buss Compressor

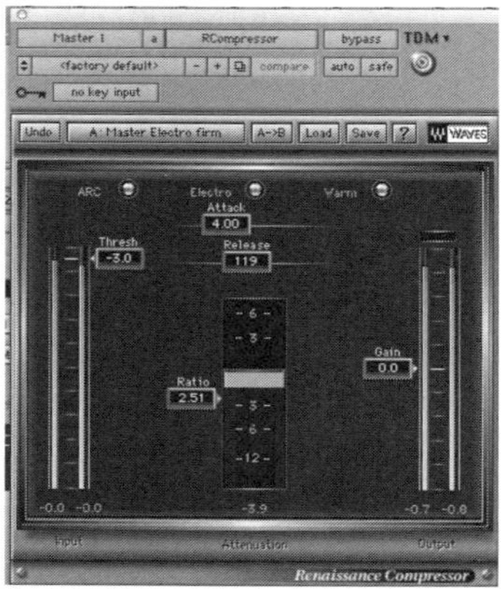

Waves Renaissance Compressor Master Output Settings				
threshold	**attack**	**release**	**ratio**	**gain**
–3.0 dB	4.00	119	2.51:1	0 dB

Fig. 10.33. Buss EQ

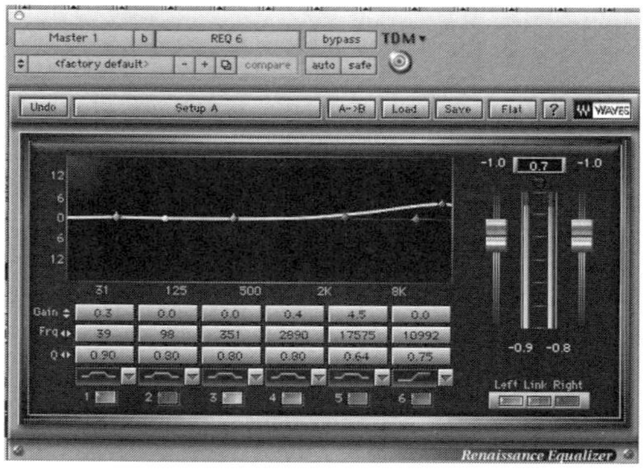

Waves Renaissance REQ-6 Master Output Settings						
parameter	**band 1**	**band 2**	**band 3**	**band 4**	**band 5**	**band 6**
gain	+0.3 dB	0 dB	0 dB	+0.4 dB	+4.5 dB	0 dB
frequency	39 Hz	98 Hz	351 Hz	2,890 Hz	17.5 Hz	11 kHz
Q	0.90	0.80	0.80	0.80	0.64	0.75
shape	bell	bell	bell	bell	bell	shelving

Fig. 10.34. Buss Limiter

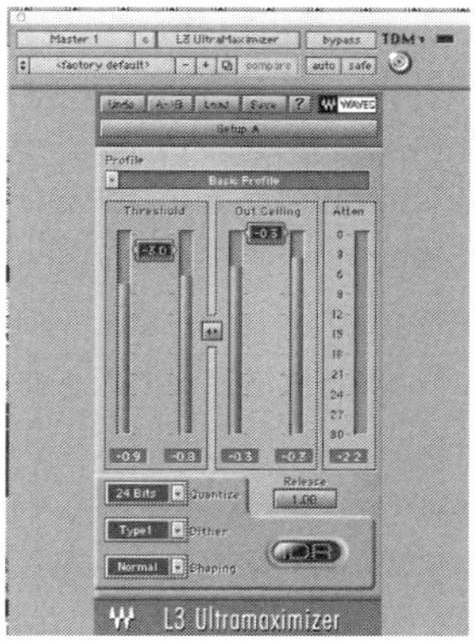

Waves L2

Threshold:–3.0 dB

Out Ceiling: –0.3 dB

Release: 1.00

Fig. 10.35. Dither

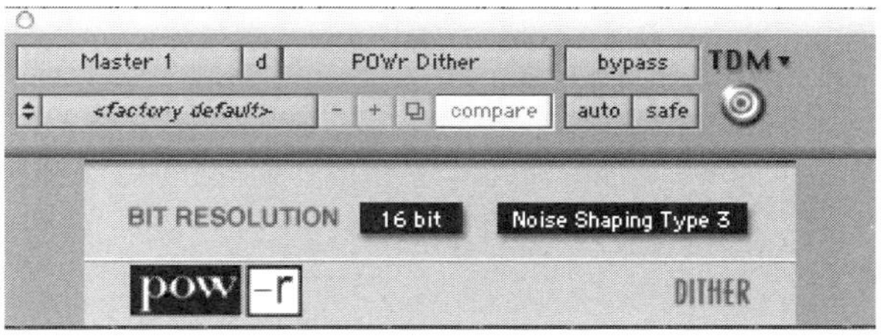

Pow-R Dither

16 bit

Noise Shaping Type 3

AUTOMATION

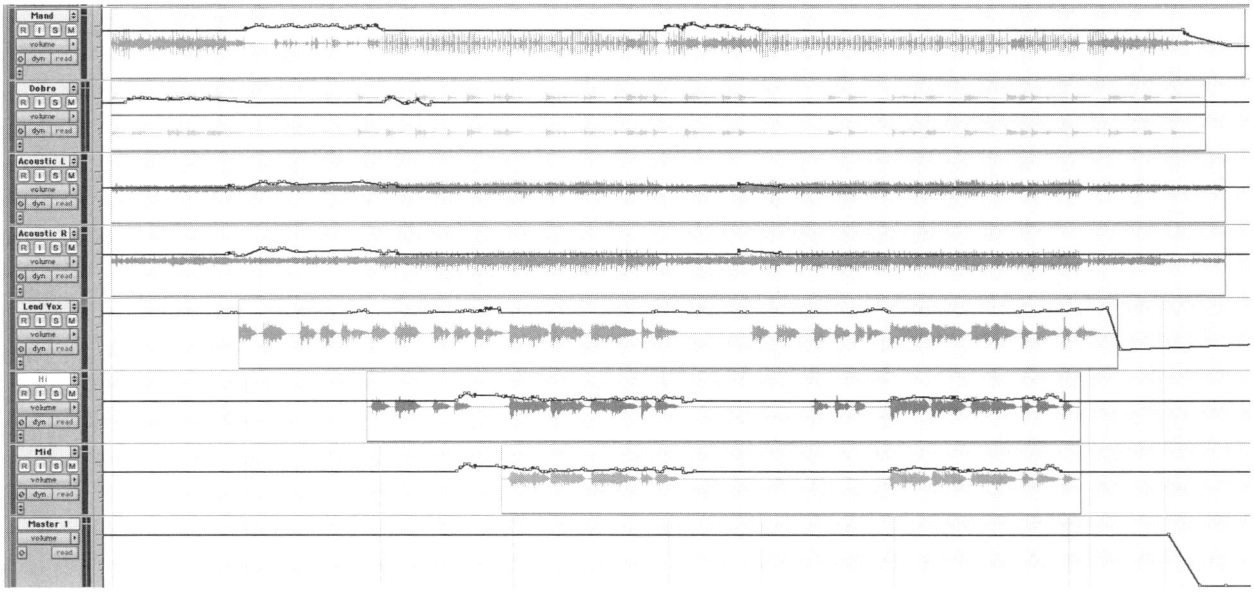

Fig. 10.36. Automation

Volume automation has been written for a number of the individual tracks on "Would You Go With Me." The mandolin's level was adjusted during the first verse and the solo, and the dobro tracks were automated during the intro and the second verse. The acoustic guitar volume was raised for the first verse and the first couple of measures of the third verse.

The lead vocal track was automated as well—mostly to support the low notes the singer had to hit. The BGVs were also automated, and since the two tracks were grouped together, the automation was written to both background vocal tracks. (As an aside, the automation could just as easily have been written with the BGV buss fader; the result would have been almost the same.) Finally, the fade-out at the end of the song was written on the master fader.

EDITS

Few changes were made to the audio tracks at the mixing stage of "Would You Go With Me." As with many of the other songs included in this volume, each of the tracks were trimmed up to the point that the audio started on that track. For example, the lead vocal was trimmed to the beginning of the first verse and was cleared until the first chorus where it entered. Many of the tracks were also trimmed at the end of the song. But all of this is simply for visual clarity—the only actual edit that was made to any track was the banjo track. At approximately 1:08, some sort of digital glitch appeared on the banjo track. To fix it, a piece of the track from a couple of measures later was copied and then pasted in. This covered the glitch just fine.

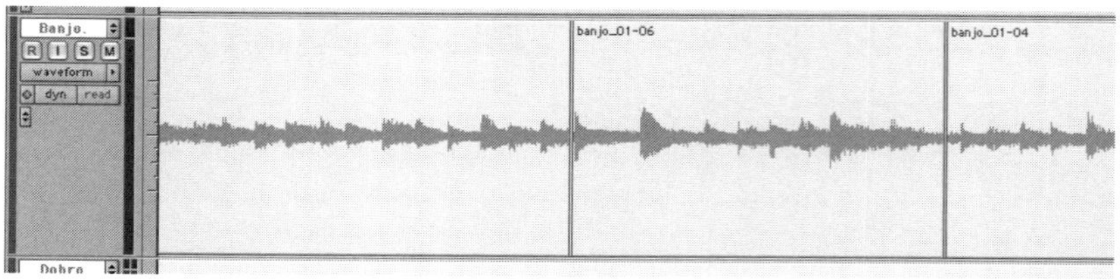

Fig. 10.37. Banjo Edit

PRINTING MIXES

When printing the mix of each of the songs in this volume, a consistent approach was used: a track was used to set the final length of the song. The start and end times for the printed mix of "Would You Go With Me" was set by selecting the overhead track, though any of the drum tracks would have served the purpose. In Pro Tools, selecting this trimmed track will cause the program to play from the beginning to the end of that track with no excess audio or time at the beginning or end. In those situations where multiple mixes of a song must be done—for example, if a producer wants vocal up or vocal down versions, TV mixes, instrumental mixes—all of the versions are the same length, and can be easily lined up for editing.

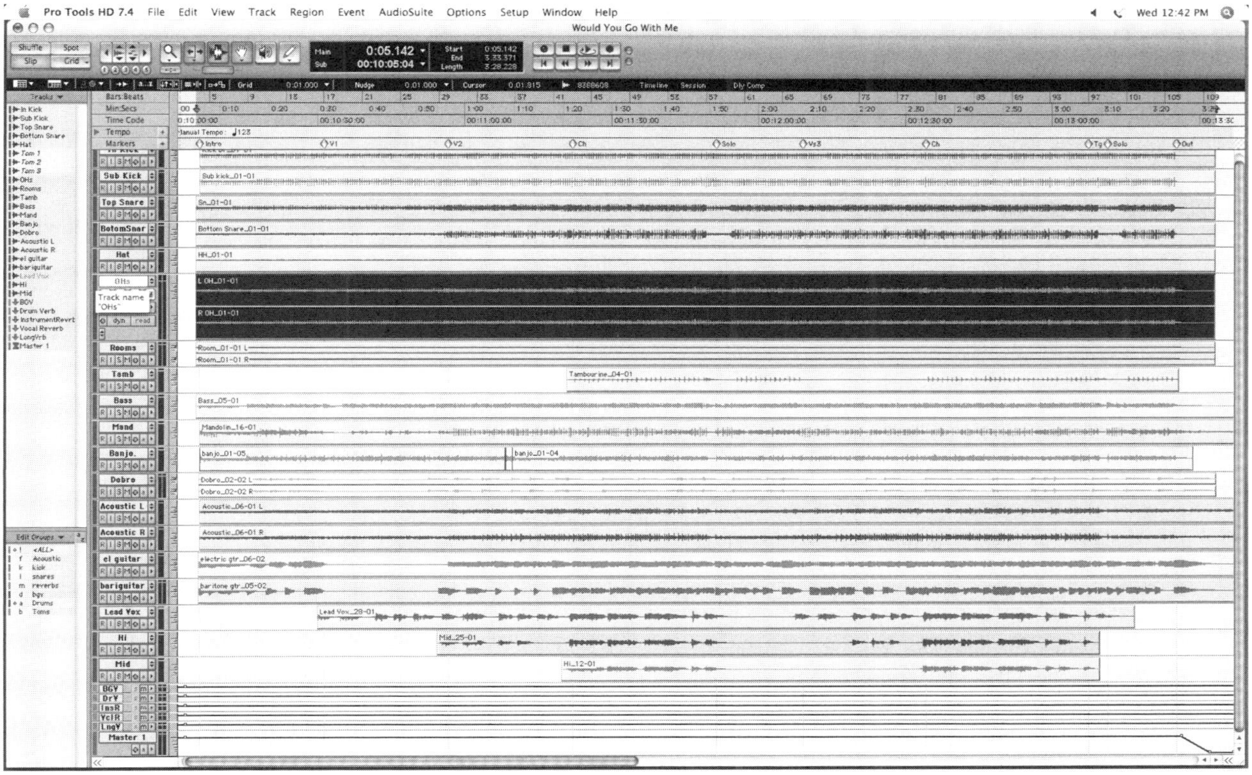

Fig. 10.38. Print Mix

APPENDIX A

Recording Tools and Concepts

TEMPLATES AND PRESETS

Though they have not been explicitly discussed during the main part of the book, session templates are the primary tools for any engineer who regularly mixes partly or totally in the box. For that matter, they are also one of the primary tools (though in a different form) for every engineer who mixes through a console.

Templates

At its most basic, a template is a layout that shows how tracks should be arranged for the convenience of the engineer. As they become more complete, templates can be built that include routing, auxiliary sends, effects, and even specific plug-ins set up with presets. For example, one of the templates used to mix the songs in this book used a number of aux busses; that template bussed all of the drum tracks to a drum buss, the various keyboard tracks to a keyboard buss, the acoustic guitar tracks to their own buss, and so on, while another of the templates did not use a drum buss as part of the setup. Another of the templates used for mixing the songs in this book used specific reverb setups that were common to several of the songs. In total, all or parts of four different templates were used to mix the songs that make up *Mixing the Hits of Country*, though they were generally altered from song to song—not merely to meet the needs of the specific songs (though that was part of it), but also to give the reader an idea of the choices that can be made when mixing in the box. Admittedly, a wider range of effects, processing plug-ins, and routing could have been chosen, but most working engineers work from one or two templates that change very little from song to song.

Presets

The only presets that were explicitly mentioned in the book are those that are part of the various reverbs; it must be pointed out that in those cases where a given preset was used (for instance, the Large Concert preset that was used as a Long Reverb), the factory presets are generally most useful as a starting point for finding the appropriate reverb sound. Since a modified preset can be saved, (as the Nice Plate TrueVerb preset was) over a period of time, the presets that an engineer uses can be far different from a factory preset under the same name. It's certainly true that most engineers have a few favorite reverb sounds, and there's no reason that the number of favorites should change because the reverbs are coming from inside a computer and not from a rack-mounted device.

In addition to the reverb presets, a number of other plug-ins have presets as well. Those from Waves and MacDSP come to mind as plug-ins that have a full range of presets. These are enormously useful, but only as a starting point and as a learning tool. For example, the Waves V-EQ3 plug-ins that were used on Martina McBride's "Anyway" were modified presets. These presets are definitely useful, but only if the parameters on those presets are studied, listened to, changed if necessary, and listened to again. When you find a sound that you like (for a certain instrument or application), save it so that it can be called up again in a different session.

If, as you read through the book and look at the screen shots, you feel that you've seen some of this before, you probably have—but that's because those things that you've seen before have proven themselves to work through the course of creating thousands of mixes over a long period of time.

MIXING TOOLS

The primary audio tools used for manipulating audio signals are dynamic processors, equalization, and ambience. A short discussion of each of these tools follows:

Dynamic Processors

A number of items fall under the general heading of dynamics processors (compressors, limiters, and de-essers), which are used to control the volume of a signal. Compressors and limiters are generally used to make loud signals closer to the volume of quieter signals, while expanders are designed to make loud parts louder and quiet parts quieter. De-Essers (and other frequency-conscious dynamic processors) work to control specific bands of the audio spectrum. Noise gates will also be discussed as dynamic processors.

Compressors and Limiters

The basic function of a compressor and a limiter is to control the volume or dynamics of a signal by controlling the volume of louder signals while not affecting quieter signals. This process shrinks the dynamic range of a signal; by making the loudest parts of the signal less loud, the track (as a whole) can usually be turned up. This allows the quieter passages to be heard while keeping the louder sections under a modicum of control.

While not all compressors and limiters offer access to all of the parameters below, the list includes:

Threshold. The point at which the onset of compression begins.

Compression Ratio. Refers to the amount of compression applied to the signal when crossing the threshold. Ratio is typically a division of the signal above the threshold; for example, a 2:1 ratio will reduce signals over the threshold by one half. For each 2 dB the signal rises above the threshold, the output of the compressor will rise 1dB. With a ratio of 4:1, if the signal goes 4 dB over the threshold, the output will rise 1 dB, and if the signal is 8 dB over the threshold, the output will rise 2 dB.

Slope. Slope is another way to describe ratio, since when depicted on a graph, the ratio of input to output looks like a slope.

Attack Time. The attack time is how quickly after a signal goes above the compressor threshold that the compression circuitry begins to act on the signal.

Release Time. The release time is the amount of time it takes the output of the compressor to return to a given percentage of its uncompressed level.

Makeup Gain. Makeup gain is the amount of gain added to the output of the compressor, either to compensate for gain reduction from the compression circuitry or simply to add gain to the signal.

Knee. With a hard knee compressor, the compressor circuit reacts immediately when a signal crosses the threshold and it begins working at the preset ratio. With a soft knee compressor, things happen a bit differently right around the onset of compression. As the signal approaches the threshold, the compressor begins to compress at a milder ratio than is set, and doesn't begin compressing at the preset ratio until the signal is slightly above the threshold of compression.

Limiter

Although compressing and limiting are often discussed as though they are completely different processes, that's not exactly true; the difference between a compressor and a limiter is simply the compression ratio. When ratios greater than 10:1 are used, the result is considered to be limiting, while ratios less than that signify compressing. In the digital world, however, there are some other items that should be addressed.

While detection circuits on modern equipment (and modern software) are quite fast, it's not possible to stop every transient peak without some help. Those transients are so fast (and often of such short duration) that the fastest detection circuitry would often produce unacceptable levels of distortion. So when Waves introduced the L1 limiter (since superseded by the L2 and L3), it used look-ahead technology. This means that the audio signal is delayed by a couple of milliseconds so that the detection software can see what's about to happen with the audio. That allows the limiter to act so that the audio signal is reduced for the bare minimum possible time—without the distortion levels that had previously accompanied super-fast analog limiters. With software having the ability to catch even small peaks and reduce the signal level accordingly, the average signal level can be increased several dB's with no apparent degradation of the sound. It also makes possible brick-wall limiters, which prevent *ANY* signal over a preset level to pass.

De-Esser

A de-esser is a frequency dependent compressor. In the analog world, engineers discovered that they could create a de-esser by inserting an EQ into the sidechain of a compressor and boosting the EQ at the offending frequency. This causes the compressor circuitry to become sensitive to that frequency, which essentially transforms the unit into an automatic gain control that turns the signal down whenever that frequency occurs.

While de-essers are typically used to control sibilance in a vocal track, they also can be used to control high frequency information in overhead microphones as well. Typically, sibilance is somewhere in the 5 to 8 kHz range, though the exact frequency is, to a certain extent, gender specific. An even more flexible approach to de-essing is a multi-band compressor.

Multi-Band Compression

Where a compressor is a full-range, single-band unit that affects the entire audio spectrum, a multi-band compressor is made up of a set of filters that splits the audio signal into two or more frequency bands, much like the crossover on a two-way speaker cabinet operates. After being split, each band is fed into its own compressor, and then recombined. The biggest advantage of multi-band compressors is that a loud signal in one band will not cause gain reduction in the rest of the audio frequency. For example, a loud kick drum wouldn't have any effect on the high frequency signals.

Expansion

Compression ratios—that is, compression ratios greater than 1:1—dictate the way a compressor reduces the gain of signals that exceed a threshold (where the onset of compression occurs). A 4:1 compression ratio means that for every 4 dB that the signal exceeds the threshold, the output of the compressor will only increase by one decibel. An 8:1 compression ratio means that a signal that is 8 decibels over the threshold will increase by 1 dB. The higher the ratio, the greater the amount of signal reduction.

When the compression ratio is less than 1:1, the inverse happens; at a ratio of 0.5:1, for every half of a decibel of the signal over the threshold, the output of the compressor increases by 1 dB. For example, at the 0.5:1 ratio, a signal that exceeded the threshold by 2 dB would be increased by 4 decibels at the output of the compressor. Expansion is not used as often as compression, but it's a powerful tool for re-gaining dynamics.

Gates

Noise Gates are electronic devices (and software plug-ins) that allow signals that are over a given threshold to pass while not allowing signals under that threshold to pass. All gates share a number of parameters, though some offer controls that can make them more useable for a given application. The basic parameters for a simple gate are: Floor, Gate Open, Gate Close, Attack, Release and Hold.

Floor. The floor setting of a gate is the level of the signal that is allowed to pass through the unit when the gate is closed. The lower the number, the less signal is allowed through. An infinite level simply means that nothing at all is passed through the gate when it's closed, while 0.0, or unity, means that all of the signal may pass through the gate unchanged—the gate has no effect, whether it's open or closed.

Gate Open. This parameter determines the threshold at which the gate opens. For example, if the Gate Open setting is at −12.0 dB, the gate opens only when the signal exceeds −12.0 dB. Once the gate is open, a number of other settings will determine when the gate closes again.

Gate Close. The first of these is the Gate Close parameter; all other things being equal, when the signal strength drops below the level of the Gate Close setting, the gate would close again, and wouldn't open until the signal level once again exceeds the Gate Open threshold. But things aren't quite equal in this regard; both the Gate Open and Gate Close settings can be modified by other parameters.

Attack. The Attack setting controls how fast, once the signal strength exceeds the Gate Open threshold, the gate actually opens. The attack time can vary from a couple of microseconds (very fast) to a number of milliseconds (pretty slow). There are applications where either fast or slower attacks are more appropriate. With drums, the faster attack times are usually chosen.

Release. As a signal falls below the Gate Close setting, the Release rate determines how fast the gate closes again. Fast release settings would be the sonic equivalent of slamming a door closed while slower settings are gentler, more akin to quietly easing the door closed behind you when sneaking into the house late at night.

Hold. Once the gate opens (when the signal strength passes the Gate Open threshold), the Hold parameter comes into force. The Hold setting determines the minimum time that the gate remains open—whether or not the signal strength falls below the Gate Close threshold during that time. As an example, if the Hold setting is at 1 second, then even if a signal peak opens the gate but immediately falls back below the threshold that would cause the gate to close, it will remain open for the 1 second determined by the Hold parameter.

Some gates offer a sidechain function that will allow frequency-conscious gating. Others may offer an external key function where the gate will function on one signal while being triggered by another signal, and still others are capable of a broad range of gating, ducking, de-essing, compressing, and filtering.

Equalization

An equalizer (EQ) allows for manipulation of the frequency response of a signal by cutting or boosting specific frequencies. A number of different types of EQ's have been developed over the years; quite often one type of EQ might be more suited to a given task than another.

The Basics

All equalizers are at their simplest, filters. The simplest version of a filter is passive—that is, it is not used to boost the signal, but only to attenuate it. Passive filters are generally one of four types—high pass, low pass, band pass, and notch. High pass filters remove frequencies below a specified cutoff point, allowing the frequencies above that to pass through unchanged. Low pass filters do the opposite—they remove frequencies above the specified cutoff point, and allow everything below that cutoff to pass through. A band pass filter removes the frequencies above and below a given frequency range while leaving the rest unchanged, while a notch filter does the opposite—it removes frequencies in a given range (usually quite narrow) while leaving everything above and below the notch unchanged.

Active filters—that is, those that can boost a given frequency as well as cut it, come in two basic varieties: shelving and bell. Shelving filters are the active version of high and low pass filters; a high shelving EQ can raise or lower all of the frequencies above a certain point, while a low shelving EQ boosts or cuts the frequencies below a given point. And while band pass filters typically have cutoff frequencies, bell filters boost or cut frequencies around a given center point of the bell curve.

With both active and passive filters, the amount of attenuation at the cutoff points is measured in dB-per-octave increments, with 6 dB-per-octave a pretty mild slope and 24 dB-per-octave being a quite aggressive slope. If you were to send a full-range signal (pink noise, for example) into a high pass filter set at a cutoff point of 400 Hz with a 6 dB-per-octave slope, then at 200 Hz, the signal would be 6 dB quieter than it was at 400 Hz, and at 100 Hz, it would be 12 dB quieter than at 400 Hz (or 6 dB quieter than the 200 Hz level). But with a 24 dB-per-octave slope, the signal at 100 Hz would be 48 dB quieter than the signal at 400 Hz.

The above is a theoretical discussion of single-band equalizers; in the world of plug-ins, EQ's are usually multi-band; a 4-band EQ has 4 filters that are available at the same time. Many of today's popular plug-ins are emulations of vintage analog designs; in the original versions, many of the variables—slope, frequency, and the width of the bell—were fixed in the design and not variable. Those fixed variables, along with other properties of the circuits are responsible for the signature sounds of units like Pultec's EQP-1A, API's 550 EQs, and even Rupert Neve's 1073 EQ. Circuit design is the art of compromise: it's been said that all analog EQ designs are at least in part attempts by the designer to overcome the effects of the real world on what should have been a clean and transparent circuit.

In any event, a really smart guy named George Massenburg wrote a paper that discussed the possibility of building an equalizer circuit that was completely variable—and more important, he actually designed and built several. In his 1972 AES paper, Massenburg used the phrase "parametric equalizer" to describe this circuit, which offered control of frequency and amplitude and coherent control of Q, or shape. The parametric EQ remains one of the most often-emulated software plug-ins in the world of DAWs. Each band of a parametric EQ has three controls. One selects the center frequency of the band to be affected, one controls the amplitude (how much that band will be boosted or cut), and the third controls the bandwidth, or the width of the range around the center frequency that will be affected by that particular band. Bandwidth is measured in Q: the higher the Q, the narrower the bandwidth.

Most styles of equalizers—at least in the analog world—are simply implementations of the filters discussed above; a simple EQ with bass and treble controls is usually a pair of shelving EQ's (many consoles were built with 3-band EQs that simply added a midrange bell filter to the high and low shelving filters). A graphic EQ is comprised of a number of bell filters with center frequencies that divide the audio spectrum into even frequency bands that can be adjusted in amplitude. They're referred to as graphic equalizers because, as the front-panel sliders are adjusted, their positions give an approximate display of the resultant frequency response. Quite a number of plug-ins emulate a switchable frequency, variable amplitude circuit like those in vintage Neve and Trident EQs, while still others are modeled on the "quasi-parametric" sweepable frequency, fixed Q designs that became popular as a lower cost alternative to the full parametric.

Ambience

The development of artificial reverbs was discussed earlier, but the goal with delay and reverb is usually (though not always) to create a sense of space around the performers or their instruments. There are also times where delays or reverbs are used simply as another texture in the sonic palette, or to add rhythmic interest, or just because they sound good.

Delay

A delay is a simulated echo, a very powerful effect, but simple in concept. The echo's duration (the delay time) can be anywhere from a few tens of milliseconds to many seconds; the number of repeats can also be adjusted from a simple slapback to a cascade of echoes. In addition, chorusing and flanging effects can be created with a delay.

Delay Parameters

Delay Time. The interval between the original signal and the first repeat of that signal.

Feedback. By feeding the output of the delay back into the input, more repeats are audible. A feedback setting of 50% means that each of the repeats after the first would be half as loud as the preceding one, and the repeat after that would be at a quarter of the original volume. Raising the feedback setting allows more repeats to be heard.

Modulation. A low-frequency oscillator changes the delay time based on the settings of the oscillator. This section makes the delay time modulate to a different time from the original delay time. The modulation section is typically used to create chorus and flange effects using the depth and rate controls.

Depth. The depth controls sets how far the modulated delay moves from the preset delay time.

Rate. The rate adjustment controls how fast the delay time will modulate from the extremes of the depth setting and back to the original delay settings.

Waveform. The waveform setting changes the algorithm for the modulation. The most common setting is a sine wave, which will modulate smoothly.

Reverb

Though artificial reverb processors are primarily used to simulate the sounds of real acoustic spaces, plate reverbs and, occasionally, spring reverbs (the last two were also developed to emulate acoustic spaces, though the state of the art in the 1950s and early 1960s precluded real spatial accuracy), also can be used in creative ways that do not imply any sort of real space. In the digital world, there are two main tools for creating reverb—algorithm-based processors and convolution reverbs.

Algorithm-based reverbs synthesize the sound of an acoustic space through mathematical calculations of delay times, while convolution reverbs are essentially samples of actual spaces that are captured through a series of impulse responses. (Methods used to record impulse responses for use in convolution reverbs are discussed at the end of the section.) These impulse responses are manipulated to make them suitable for use with the software and then saved as presets. When a dry signal is fed into the convolution software, the dry signal and the impulse response are subjected to an algorithm that essentially combines—or convolves—the reverberant characteristics of the impulse response with the dry signal.

Each approach has advantages and disadvantages; algorithm-based reverbs can offer a great deal of control over the parameters used to create the sound of a room (or the sound of non-existent rooms). Although convolution reverbs typically have fewer adjustable parameters than algorithm-based reverbs, they have the advantage of realism—convolution reverbs can successfully sound like actual spaces because they are based on recordings done in actual spaces.

Reverb Parameters

Reverb Time. Reverb time is generally accepted as the amount of time it takes for a level of the reverb tail to decay by 60 dB (often referred to as RT60). RT60 is a measurement of sound level—it doesn't necessarily correspond to the size of a given room (small room with hard surfaces can have RT60s longer than a larger room which is covered by sound-absorbing surfaces).

Pre-Delay. Pre-delay is the time between the initial signal and the onset of reverberation. For example, if you were to stand in a room and clap your hands, the sound of the clapping hands must travel (at 1,130 feet per second) to the floor of the room, the ceiling, the nearest walls, and back (these initial echoes are called "early reflections," and become "reverb" when the individual echoes become so dense that single echoes can no longer be noticed). In general, the larger the room, the longer the pre-delay.

Early Reflections. Early reflections are the direct echoes one hears in an acoustic space before the later reverb (made up of indirect echoes that have reflected off of multiple surfaces) becomes prominent. Much like pre-delay, early reflections offer the most apparent sonic information about the size of a space.

Diffusion. Diffusion is a term used primarily to describe indirect reflections—reverb density is determined by the amount of diffusion; a greater number of indirect reflections correlate to more diffusion.

Room Size. Most software reverbs link a number of parameters to emulate a given room size—a smaller room, for example, would have a shorter pre-delay, faster (and louder) early reflections, and a lower density than a large room.

Sampling Rate

Sampling rate and bit depth are related to the frequency response and the dynamic range, respectively, of the file. The science behind sample rates goes back to the 1940s, with the development of the Nyquist–Shannon theorem. This theorem states that perfect reconstruction of a signal is possible when the sampling frequency is greater than twice the maximum frequency of the signal being sampled. Another way to put it is that if the Nyquist frequency (half the sample rate) exceeds the highest frequency of the signal being sampled, the original analog signal can be reconstructed. If lower sampling rates are used, the original signal's information may not be completely recoverable from the sampled signal.

With a sampling frequency of 44.1 kHz, the highest frequencies that can be captured and stored are a bit less than half of the sampling frequency, or around 22 kHz (remember that the accepted standard for the human hearing range is from 20 Hz to 20,000 Hz or 20 kHz, though in reality, most of the readers of this book do not hear frequencies that high). Raising the sampling rate to 48 kHz raises the cutoff frequency to a bit less that 24 kHz, and recording at 96 kHz moves the cutoff frequency to a bit less that 48 kHz—far beyond range of audibility.

Bit Depth, Dither, and Noise Shaping

The theoretical dynamic range of a 16-bit signal is 96 dB—and a 24-bit signal has a theoretical dynamic range of around 144 dB—far more than is actually usable (or practical). With 0 dB being the softest sound that an average human can hear, normal conversation being from 60 to 70 dB, and sustained exposure to 95 dB being capable of causing permanent hearing damage, it's easy to see that the average recording will need nowhere near 96 dB of dynamic range. But there's more to it than that, and here's why: every time a mathematical function is performed on a digital audio signal, (and every thing you do with a digital audio track is a mathematical function—from changing the level to adding a compressor plug-in), the bit depth of that track increases. A number of different approaches to dealing with this increased bit-depth have been implemented by software manufacturers; some will use floating point processing, some use fixed point processing with intermediate bit depths up to 56 bits. In any case, at the end of the process, the file needs to be reduced back to the original 16- or 24-bit depth.

The three options for this are truncating, rounding, and dithering. Truncating simply chops off those bits that are longer than needed. This can add undesirable artifacts in the form of distortion to the signal. Rounding effectively performs a mathematical function to the last usable bit—for example, when converting a 24-bit file to a 16-bit file, the 16th bit will be rounded up or down in a consistent manner. While this is generally less obtrusive than truncating, it can also add artifacts, because of the consistent manner of the rounding. Dither, at its most basic, simply adds a small amount of noise to make the processing more random, and therefore, less noticeable.

There are a number of ways that dither can be created; since the point of dithering a digital signal is to add a random quality to how the program handles the last useable bit, these approaches are essentially ways to generate the random numbers used in the dithering process. Among these approaches are:

RPDF. An acronym for "Rectangular Probability Density Function," RPDF is equivalent to rolling a die, and using the number that appears in the dithering algorithm. Any number has the same random probability of surfacing.

TPDF. TPDF stands for "Triangular Probability Density Function," equivalent to rolling a pair of dice (the sum of two independent samples of RPDF) and using that sum with the algorithm.

Gaussian PDF. This is more or less the same idea, but rather than rolling one or two dice, it's like rolling a large number of dice. The relationship of probabilities of results follows a bell-shaped, or Gaussian curve.

Colored Dither. This is dither that has been filtered to be different from white noise (the more common approach to dither). Some dither algorithms use noise that has more energy in the higher frequencies so as to lower the energy in the audio band, making the noise less noticeable.

Noise Shaping. Though not actually dither, noise shaping is a feedback process that includes dither within the process. It is used for the same purposes, though it's a different approach.

While the discussion above is pertinent to all of the audio tracks within a mix, most of this is invisible to the user—it isn't generally possible to change the way that a given plug-in reduces the results of its processing. However, when reducing a mixed track from a 24-bit original depth to the 16-bit depth that is required for a standard audio CD, the user generally does have some choices to make in the process. Most DAW software offers not only a choice of whether or not to dither a mixed track, but also choices in the type of dither available. For example, the Pow-R Dither plug-in used on all the songs in this volume provides three types of noise shaping, each with its own characteristics:

Type 1. This type has the flattest frequency spectrum in the audible range of frequencies, modulating and accumulating the dither noise just below the Nyquist frequency. Type 1 is recommended for less stereophonically complex material such as solo instrument recordings.

Type 2. Type 2 has a psychoacoustically optimized low-order noise-shaping curve, and is recommended for material of greater stereophonic complexity.

Type 3. This type has a psychoacoustically optimized high-order noise-shaping curve, and is recommended for full-spectrum, wide-stereo field material.

Routing possibilities

Much like an analog console, a DAW allows any given signal to be routed to a number of different areas; aux sends can go to effects, or signals can be bussed together for processing. (This book uses the term "processing" for those plug-ins—equalization and compression are the primary processors used— that change the actual signal, while "effects" will be used for such things as reverb and delay—sounds that are added to the original signal.)

Recording consoles have been at the heart of the control room for most of the history of recording; in the beginning, they were very simple switching devices designed to allow broadcast engineers to choose which microphone was going out over the airwaves. Soon, though, radio stations needed to do more than simply switch between two or more devices. They needed to be able to combine multiple microphone signals into one and to switch between microphones and line-level devices (or blend the two together). They needed to be able to send the various signals to multiple destinations at once, and these signals needed various forms of processing. Ultimately, the console was changed, expanded, or otherwise modified to perform functions that grew ever more complex, culminating in the modern recording console.

You might be asking yourself why any of this stuff matters—after all, you're mixing in a computer, not on a console. The answer lies in the way that all of those functions of a console are duplicated in the mixing environment of a work station—in fact, there's even a resonance back to the early days of custom console design. If you need to have an EQ on a certain channel, you may insert one; if you don't need it, you don't have to add it.

In any case, the mixes on the accompanying DVD were typically routed in fairly consistent ways; drums, keyboards, acoustic guitars, electric guitars and background vocals are routed to their own stereo busses. The outputs from these busses are themselves routed to another buss, the submaster, which is finally sent to the main L-R output from the workstation. These busses are used as a way to easily add plug-ins across a group of tracks or adjust the volumes of multiple tracks at one time when "roughing in" a mix. Grouping allows a number of tracks to be linked: in Pro Tools, not only can the volume of grouped tracks be adjusted together, but also other functions from editing to resizing can be done to a group of tracks rather than to each track individually.

Why do I use a submaster buss instead of sending all the tracks (and effects returns) directly to the master output fader? The reason is that inserts (where you add plug-ins or aux sends) are pre-fader on aux returns but post-fader on the master output. When automating such things as fades, if a plug-in like Waves L3 or Digidesign's Maxim (both are hard limiters), is inserted after the fader then the effect that the limiter has on the signal changes as the fade progresses—and this can change the tone of the overall mix. So all of these sessions have the final buss processing on the submaster while only a dither plug-in is inserted on the master output.

The other main console-style features that need to be duplicated in the mixing session are auxiliary sends and returns; the function of the aux sends is to provide a convenient method of adding effects to the mix. As a general rule, I'll begin by setting up three aux sends for reverbs (and if the song calls for it, another that can be used as a delay line). As mentioned earlier, one of the aux sends will be used for drum reverb, another will be used for instrument reverb, and the third will be used for the vocals. While Pro Tools allows reverbs to be inserted on individual tracks, each reverb plug-in requires a fairly substantial amount of processing; to minimize the amount of processing power required, aux sends are quite useful. More auxes can be created as needed, either to accommodate more effects or to route signals to a place where they might be needed. Any other routing possibilities that arise with a particular song have been discussed within the context of that song.

APPENDIX B

Recording the Songs in This Book

RECORDING BASICS

Until the late 1950s, all recording was done live; that is, all of the singers and musicians on a record were present and performing together. The technology of the time required it. Even with the development of multitrack recording—and all the way to the present day—Nashville recording sessions are still typically done in this manner. Those of us who regularly record full rhythm sections feel that while there are some undeniable issues that must be dealt with, the advantages of full band recording—including the feel that musicians create playing together and the simple ability to know what the track actually sounds like as you record it—far outweigh the potential issues involving an instrument like drums bleeding into the other instruments' tracks.

The individual songs contained in the accompanying DVD were not necessarily recorded with the whole rhythm section playing together; the preceding paragraph was intended to suggest that music would be better all around if we all played together more. But as this book is concerned with mixing songs rather than recording them, let's look briefly at the recording methods used to create these tracks.

DRUMS

The drums used on these recordings were made by Pearl. The kit included a 22-inch kick drum, 10-inch and 12-inch mounted toms, and a 16-inch floor tom. Paiste cymbals were used for all of the drum tracks. The specific cymbals used were (from the drummer's left to right): a 12-inch Sound Formula splash and 14-inch Sound Formula medium heavy hi-hats. The left crash cymbal is a 2002 19-inch crash while the ride is a Paiste Signature 19-inch Dry Ride. The right side crash is a 2002 18-inch crash with a 2002 18-inch Novo China cymbal on the far right of the drummer. A number of different snare drums were used; the choice of snare drum is song specific.

The drum tracks were recorded during two different sessions in a single day. In an effort to add a bit of variety to the processing used on a given mix, many extra microphones were set up. The kick drum alone had a total of four different microphones—a Shure Beta 52 and an Electro-Voice RE20 inside the drum, and a Yamaha Subkick and a CAD Trion 6000 condenser mic placed outside the drum. The snare drum had both a Shure SM57 and a Neumann KM 84 i positioned above the drum and another KM 84 set up underneath it. Two different pairs of overhead microphones were used as well—a pair of Telefunken M16s and a pair of Telefunken 251s (with vintage capsules). All of the toms were recorded using Sennheiser 421s, while an AKG 460 was used on the hi-hat.

Three room mics were set up—a Telefunken U 47 was used as a mono microphone, and a pair of Neumann TLM 103s was used for the stereo room mic tracks.

All of these microphones were recorded to a Pro Tools HD3 workstation, and specific combinations were chosen for each track.

GUITARS

Electric guitars

The electric guitars were recorded through a Mesa Boogie Triaxis, and then recorded thought the DI input on a Great River NV preamp with no compression or EQ.

Acoustic guitars

The acoustic guitars were recorded with either a pair of Shure KSM44s or a pair of Neumann KM 84 microphones, plugged into Manley 40 dB preamps and a Manley ELOP compressor. It happened that the acoustic guitarist was available to play with the drummer on some of the tracks; the others were recorded after the drummer was finished recording (curious listeners will be able to discern which is which by soloing the acoustic tracks; there's a bit of drum bleed into those tracks).

KEYBOARDS

Piano

The piano, a Yamaha C7 grand, was recorded with a pair of AKG 480B mics in an XY pattern or as a spaced pair placed a bit behind the hammers. Some tracks were recorded with either a pair of Telefunken AK47s or with a pair of Telefunken 251 microphones with one microphone positioned over the bass strings and one over the high strings. Again, in an effort to provide a variety of possible sound sources and mixing approaches, a few of the piano tracks were not recorded with a real piano, but with a Kurzweil K2500RM sampler.

Organ

The sound of the 1957 Hammond C3 and modified 21H Leslie was captured with a pair of AEA R84s placed at the corners of the Leslie on the upper rotor and an EV RE20 on the lower rotor. Vac-Rac preamps were used for all three mics; these three channels were bussed to a stereo track through the console and then to the recorder. The Leslie cabinet was set up in an iso booth.

Wurlitzer Electric Piano

The Wurly has a long and storied career in pop music—from Ray Charles' "What'd I Say" to The Doors' "Riders on the Storm." Though the Fender Rhodes electric piano challenged the Wurly's primacy in the mid to late 1970s, the Wurlitzer's tone seems to blend with electric guitars much better than the Rhodes. The Model 200 used on these tracks was recorded direct, with an A Designs REDDI DI into a Phoenix DRD-2 preamp. There are two 1/4" jacks on the bottom of the Wurlitzer electric piano on the left side of the instrument; the one closest to the keyboard is a headphone jack, while the other is an unbalanced output. A 1/4" adapter is plugged partway into the headphone jack, which mutes the speakers on the Wurly. (At Java Jive, electric pianos are turned all the way up; the sound through the speakers is pretty distorted, so muting those speakers works best for the players.)

Synths

All other keyboard sounds, from strings to bells, were recorded direct through the console to Pro Tools with the DI Active from Desk Doctor.

OTHER INSTRUMENTS

Fiddle

All of the fiddles were recorded using a Neumann/Gefell M 582 with an M91 capsule; the M 582 is a small-diaphragm tube microphone made in East Germany in the 1960s. Its western counterpart would likely be Neumann's KM 54. The preamp used was a Vintech X73 plugged into a Tube-Tech CL1B compressor, but only lightly compressed.

Steel

The steel guitar tracks were recorded with the steel player's XLR output from his rack plugged into a Vac-Rac preamp and Vac-Rac compressor.

Mandolin and bouzouki

The mandolin (and the bouzouki) were recorded with a THE microphone and a Vintech X73 preamp, routed through a Tube-Tech CL1B that was set to a minimal (less than 3 dB) amount of compression.

Banjo

The banjo tracks were recorded with an M 582 with an M62 capsule, plugged into a Great River Preamp and a Tube-Tech CL1B. The typical placement of this mic is about four inches away from the instrument, pointed at a spot a bit below and behind the bridge.

Dobro

The dobro tracks were recorded with a two-microphone setup, though only one of the two microphones was used on any one song. A Telefunken 251 was placed above the point where the neck meets the body of the instrument, while a Crowley and Tripps Naked Eye was placed above the resonator. Both microphones were approximately a foot above the instrument.

Vocals

A number of different microphones were used to record the vocals for this DVD; the specific microphone used depended on the singer and the song. Neumann and Telefunken U47s, Telefunken 251s and M12s were the primary mics. These mics would be plugged into a Vintech X73 preamp and a Tube-Tech CL-1B compressor.

Background Vocals

In most cases, the singer who sang the lead vocal also sang all the backgrounds, so the signal path remains the same as the lead vocal. Those songs with multiple singers ("Redneck Woman," for example) also used the same mic as the lead vocal track.

Charts

Though not strictly within the purview of this book, it must be pointed out that all of the musicians worked from charts written using the Nashville Number System. Here's how it works:

In the 1960s, the members of the Jordanaires, one of Nashville's busiest vocal groups on recording sessions, developed a system of writing numbers instead of letters to represent notes; if, for example, a song was in the key of C, the tonic note C would be 1, with the other notes in the scale designated by their place in the scale: D is 2, E is 3—all the way to B, the 7th note in the scale. The group could write the appropriate number over each word on a lyric sheet (or even each syllable if necessary), and have a good representation of the melody. This would give them a starting point for creating their harmony parts. (Numbers started being used instead of letters for the simple reason that it wasn't uncommon for the key of a song to be changed during the session; if the melody notes to a song were written as letters, then changing the key would mean that those notes were worthless. As numbers that represented the notes in a scale were used, the numbers were independent of the actual key.) It quickly became apparent that this same method would work for the rhythm section, too.

Using the above example, in the key of C, a C chord would be 1, the F chord would be a 4, and the G chord would be 5. There were a few differences, of course, between what the Jordanaires developed and what the session musicians started to use—rather than designating the notes in the melody, the rhythm section needs to know where the chords change. The most logical way to do this is to write a chord for each measure of the song—whether or not the chord actually changes. This meant that if a song in the key of C had two measures of C, two measures of F, and two measures of G, it would be written as 11 44 55. Of course, not all chords are major, so common symbols were to designate whether a chord was minor, augmented or diminished; also, conventions were developed to designate two or more chords in one measure, accents, and many other items that the session musicians needed to know.

The above description is not intended to teach the number system, but merely to serve as a basis for understanding the charts written for these songs.

Permissions

The following songs are referred to in this book and were recorded for the purpose of creating digital audio files on the accompanying DVDs by permission of the following authors and publishers.

"Anyway"
Brad Warren, Brett Warren, and Martina McBride
StyleSonic Music, LLC, Bucky And Clyde Music, and Delemmava Music Publishing

"Before He Cheats"
Josh Kear and Chris Tompkins
Sony/ATV Tunes LLC, Mighty Underdog Music and Big Loud Songs

"Bless The Broken Road"
Marcus Hummon, Bobby Boyd, and Jeff Hanna
Universal Music–Careers, Floyd's Dream Music, and Jeff Diggs Music

"It Just Comes Natural"
Jim Collins and Marv Green
Hope-N-Cal Music, Sexy Tractor Music, Warner-Tamerlane Publishing Corp., and Sycamore Canyon Music

"My Give a Damn's Busted"
Tom Shapiro, Tony Martin, and Joe Diffie
Sony/ATV Songs LLC, Wenonga Music, Music of Stage Three, and Difftunes

"Play Something Country"
Ronnie Dunn and Terry McBride
Sony/ATV Songs LLC, Showbilly Music, and Still Working for the Man Music, Inc.

"Redneck Woman"
Gretchen Wilson and John Rich
Sony/ATV Tunes LLC, Hoosiermama Music, and WB Music Corp.

"Stealing Kisses"
Lori McKenna
Melanie Howard Music, Inc.

"Summertime"
Steve McEwan and Craig Wiseman
EMI Blackwood Music Inc., Birds with Ears Music, and Big Loud Shirt

Would You Go With Me
John Scott Sherrill and Shawn Camp
Sony/ATV Songs LLC, All Mighty Dog Music, City Wolf Music, and Travelin' Arkansawyer Music

Index